A Suggestive Inquiry into the Hermetic Mystery and Alchemy

with a dissertation on the more celebrated of the Alchemical Philosophers being an attempt towards the recovery of the ancient experiment of Nature

Mary Anne Atwood

Alicia Editions

Iterum ad hominem rationemque redeamus, ex quo divino dono homo animal dictum est rationale, minus enim miranda, etsi miranda sunt, quae de homine sunt dicta ; sed omnium mirabilium vincit admirationem, quod homo Divinam potuit invenire Naturam, eamque efficere.

— MERCURII TRISMEGISTI, ASCLEPIUS, CAP. XIII.

Contents

Part One
An exoteric view of the Progress and Theory of Alchemy

CHAPTER 1. A PRELIMINARY ACCOUNT OF THE HERMETIC PHILOSOPHY, WITH THE MORE SALIENT POINTS OF ITS PUBLIC HISTORY   13
gathered from the best extant Authorities, with notices of the works of various writers, ancient and modern, in succession, on the subject of Alchemy — their evidence in support of the art of gold-making and transmutation.

CHAPTER 2. OF THE THEORY OF TRANSMUTATION IN GENERAL, AND OF THE FIRST MATTER   64
showing the true basis on which the rational possibility of Transmutation rests; with Definitions from Albertus Magnus, Aquinas, Friar Bacon, Raymond Lully, Arnold Di-Villa-Nova, Synesius and others, descriptive of the Hermetic Material — with some suggestions additional concerning the Ethereal Nature and analogous phenomena of Light.

CHAPTER 3. THE GOLDEN TREATISE OF HERMES TRISMEGISTUS, CONCERNING THE PHYSICAL SECRET OF THE PHILOSOPHER'S STONE.   88
In Seven Sections — esteemed one of the best and oldest pieces of Alchemical Philosophy extant; comprising, in epitome, the whole Art and secret method of the confection — to which some elucidatory annotations are added from the Scholium and elsewhere.

Section First   88
Section Second   90
Section Third   93
Section Fourth   94
Section Fifth   96
Section Sixth   96
Section Seventh   97

Part Two
A More Esoteric Consideration of the Hermetic Art and its Mysteries

CHAPTER 1. OF THE TRUE SUBJECT OF THE HERMETIC ART, AND ITS CONCEALED ROOT   115
opening, by way of evidence, the Alchemical Laboratory and only vessel which the Adepts employed to sublime the universal Spirit of Nature and concentrate her Light — how, when, and where the Spirit may be arrested, introverted in the circulation, and brought forth from immanifest being into power and act, leading on from thence towards an outline of the Hermetic Art.

CHAPTER 2. OF THE MYSTERIES   144
beginning from the early initiations, to show the imperfection of the natural life and understanding — the artificial means and media employed by the ancients to rectify these — connecting together Alchemy and Mesmerism, also, with those preliminary Rites.

CHAPTER 1. OF THE EXPERIMENTAL METHOD AND FERMENTATION OF THE PHILOSOPHIC SUBJECT, ACCORDING TO THE PARACELSIAN ALCHEMISTS AND SOME OTHERS   160
which indicate the greater ordeals and disciplines which the vital Spirit is made to pass through in the progress of a physical regeneration by art, from out the sensual dominion of the Selfhood, through a temporary death and annihilation to a new life and consciousness.

CHAPTER 4. THE MYSTERIES (CONCLUDED)   184
with a view of the ultimate object of these initiations to prove the perfection, purity, and integral efficiency to which the human spirit may arrive by divine assimilation coming in vital contact with its Source.

Part Three
Concerning The Laws and Vital Conditions of the Hermetic Experiment

CHAPTER 1. OF THE EXPERIMENTAL METHOD AND FERMENTATION OF THE PHILOSOPHIC SUBJECT, ACCORDING TO THE PARACELSIAN ALCHEMISTS AND SOME OTHERS   215
whereby the Principles of the Art are yet more intimately unfolded, and the methodical order in which the experiment was conducted to discover that hidden Light which is the specific Form of Gold — how to educate this and multiply it by the ethereal conception until it is made concrete and substantially brought forth.

CHAPTER 2. A FURTHER ANALYSIS OF THE INITIAL PRINCIPLE, AND ITS EDUCTION INTO LIGHT   260
comprising the Metaphysics of the Matter; gathered more particularly from the Greek Ontologists and Cabalists, to show the progress of the consciousness through the various stages of purification and dissolution until the rectified ferment, overwhelming, becomes established in life.

CHAPTER 3. OF THE MANIFESTATION OF THE FIRST MATTER, AND ITS INFORMATION BY LIGHT   295
exhibiting how, when, and where the invisible Spirit of Nature is by Art made visible and brought through a vital distillation into substantive effect — with power and will to transfuse its luminous aurific virtue and draw the universal life of Nature to its homogeneal accord.

CHAPTER 4. OF THE MENTAL REQUISITES AND IMPEDIMENTS INCIDENTAL TO INDIVIDUALS EITHER AS MASTERS OR STUDENTS IN THE HERMETIC ART   332
to which are added various practical instructions concerning the means and instruments that have to be arranged and called together in furtherance of this undertaking, the qualifications of external circumstances and accordances of fitting seasons and places for operation.

Part Four
The Hermetic Practice

CHAPTER 1. OF THE VITAL PURIFICATION, COMMONLY CALLED THE GROSS WORK   365
which developes the actual mode of operation practised by the Ancients, and mechanic means employed to dissolve the vital compound and eradicate the inbred evil of life — the mode of rational investigation likewise by which the Spirit is induced to yield up her light and hidden virtue to increase it.

CHAPTER 2. OF THE PHILOSOPHIC OR SUBTLE WORK   387
which affords by a theoretic conduct suggestions amply leading to a practical understanding of the most abstruse secret of the Hermetic philosophy, showing the Trinitarian method of operation which Reason follows recreatively for the verification of her light to discover, magnify, and know the Causal Nature transitively in being and in imaged manifestation.

CHAPTER 3. THE SIX KEYS OF EUDOXUS, OPENING INTO THE MOST SECRET PHILOSOPHY   404
leading into the most secret Philosophy of the Multiplication and Projection, Rewards and Potencies, Nature, Properties, Analogies, and Appliances of the Philosopher's Stone.

THE FIRST KEY   404
THE SECOND KEY   405
THE THIRD KEY   406
THE FOURTH KEY   410
THE FIFTH KEY   411
THE SIXTH KEY   412

CHAPTER 4. THE CONCLUSION   435
in summary of the whole, comparing this Philosophy, its method, relations, and ultimate promise, with those of more modern acceptation and repute.

Part One
An exoteric view of the Progress and Theory of Alchemy

Chapter 1. A Preliminary Account of the Hermetic Philosophy, with the more Salient Points of its Public History

gathered from the best extant Authorities, with notices of the works of various writers, ancient and modern, in succession, on the subject of Alchemy — their evidence in support of the art of gold-making and transmutation.

The Hermetic tradition opens early with the morning dawn in the eastern world. All pertaining thereto is romantic and mystical. Its monuments, emblems, and numerous written records, alike dark and enigmatical, form one of the most remarkable episodes in the history of the human mind. A hard task were it indeed and almost infinite to discuss every particular that has been presented by individuals concerning the art of Alchemy; and as difficult to fix with certainty the origin of a science which has been successively attributed to Adam, Noah and his son Cham, to Solomon, Zoroaster, and the Egyptian Hermes. Nor, fortunately, does this obscurity concern us much in an inquiry which rather relates to the means and principles of occult science than to the period and place of their reputed discovery. Nothing, perhaps, is less worthy or more calculated to distract the mind from points of real importance than this very question of temporal origin, which, when we have taken all pains to satisfy and remember, leaves us no wiser in reality than we were before. What signifies it, for instance, that we attribute letters to Cadmus, or trace oracles to Zoroaster, or the Cabbal to Moses, the Eleusian mysteries to Orpheus, or Freemasonry to Noah; whilst we are profoundly ignorant of the nature and true beginning of any one of these things, and observe not how truth, being everywhere eternal, does not there always originate where it is understood?

We do not delay, therefore, to ascertain, even were it possible, whether the Hermetic Science was indeed preserved to mankind on the Syriadic pillars after the flood, or whether Egypt or Palestine may lay equal claims to the same; or, whether in truth that Smagardine table, whose singular inscription has been transmitted to this day, is attributable to Hermes or to any other name. It may suffice the present need to accept the general assertion of its advocates, and consider Alchemy as an antique arifice coeval, for aught we know to the contrary, with the universe itself. For although attempts have been made, as by Herman Conringius[1], to slight it as a recent invention, and it is also true that by a singularly envious fate, nearly all Egyptian record of the art has perished; yet we find the original evidence contained in the works of A. Kircher[2], the learned Dane Olaus Borrichius[3], and Robert Vallensis in the first volume of the *Theatrum Chemicum*[4], more than sufficient to balance every objection of this kind, besides ample collateral probability bequeathed in the best Greek Authors, historical and philosophic.

In order to show that the propositions we may hereafter have occasion to offer are not gratuitous as also with better effect to introduce a stranger subject, it will be requisite to run through a brief account of the Alchemical philosophers, with the literature and public evidence of their science; the more so, as no one of the many histories of philosophy compiled or translated into our language advert to it in such a manner as, considering the powerful and widespread influence this branch formerly exercised on the human mind, it certainly appears to deserve.

This once famous Art, then, has been represented both as giving titles and receiving them from its mother land, Cham; for so, during a long period, according to Plutarch, was Egypt denominated, or Chemia, on account of the extreme blackness of her soil:—or, as others say, because it was there that the art of Vulcan was first practiced by Cham, one of the sons of the Patriarch, from whom they thus derive the name and art together. But by the word Chemia, says Plutarch, the seeing pupil of the human eye was also designated, and other black matters, whence in part perhaps Alchemy, so obscurely descended, has been likewise stigmatized as a Black Art[5].

Etymological research has doubtless proved useful in leading on and corroborating truths once suggested, but it is not a way of first discovery; derivations may be too easily conformed to any bias, and words do not convey true ideas unless their proper leader be previously entertained. Without being able now, therefore, to determine whether the art gave or received a title from Cham, the Persian prince Alchimin, as others have contended, or that dark Egyptian earth; to take a point of time, we may begin the Hermetic story from Hermes, by the Greeks called Trismegistus, Egypt's great and far-reputed adeptest king, who, according to Suidas, lived before the time of the Pharoahs, about 400 years previous to Moses, or, as others compute, about 1900 before the Christian era[6].

This prince, like Solomon, is highly celebrated by antiquity for his wisdom and skill in the secret operations of nature, and for his reputed discovery of the quintessential perfectibility of the three kingdoms in their homogeneal unity; whence he is called the Thrice Great Hermes, having the spiritual intelligence of all things in their universal law[7].

It is to be lamented that no one of the many books attributed to him, and which are named in detail by Clemens Alexandrinus, escaped the destroying hand of Dioclesian; more particularly if we judge them, as Jamblicus assures us we may, by those Asclepian Dialogues and the Divine Poimander, which yet pass current under the name of Hermes[8]. Both are preserved in the Latin of Ficinus, and have been well translated into our language by Dr Everard. The latter, though a small work, surpasses most that are extant for sublimity of doctrine and expression; its verses flow forth eloquent, as it were, from the fountain of nature, instinct with intelligence; such as might be more efficacious to move the rational skeptic off from his negative ground into the happier regions of intelligible reality, than many theological discourses which, of a lower grade of comprehension, are unable to make this highly affirmative yet intellectual stand. But the subjects treated of in the books of the Poemander and Asclepias are theosophic and ultimate, and denote rather our divine capabilities and promise of regeneration than the physical ground of either; this, with the practical method of alchemy being further given in the Tractatus Aureus, or Golden Treatise, an admirable relic, consisting of seven chapters, attributed to the same author[9]. The Smaragdine Table, which, in its few enigmatical but remarkable lines, is said to comprehend the working principle and total subject of the art, we here subjoin: from the original Arabic and Greek copies, it has been rendered into Latin by Kircher as follows: —

Tabula Smaragdina Hermetis / The Smaragdine Table of Hermes

"True, without error, certain and most true; that which is above is as that which is below, and that which is below is as that which is above, for performing the miracles of the One Thing; and as all things were from one, by the mediation of one, so all things arose from this one thing by adaptation; the father of it is the Sun, the mother of it is the Moon; the wind carries it in its belly; the nurse thereof is the Earth. This is the father of all perfection, or consummation of the whole world. The power of it is Integral, if it be turned into earth. Thou shalt separate the earth from the fire, the subtle from the gross, gently with much sagacity; it ascends from earth to heaven, and again descends to earth: and receives the strength of the superiors and of the inferiors—so thou hast the glory of the whole world; therefore let all obscurity flee before thee. This is the strong fortitude of all fortitudes, overcoming every subtle and penetrating every solid thing. So the world was created. Hence were all wonderful adaptations of which this is the manner. Therefore I am I called Thrice Great Hermes, having the Three Parts of the philosophy of the whole world. That which I have written is consummated concerning the operation of the Sun".

This Emerald Table, unique and authentic as it may be regarded, is all that remains to us from Egypt of her Sacred Art. A few riddles and fables, all more or less imperfect, that were preserved by the

Greeks, and some inscrutable hieroglyphics are still to be found quoted in certain of the alchemical records: but the originals are entirely swept away. And, duly considering all that is related by the chroniclers of that ancient dynasty, her amazing reputation for power, wealth, wisdom, and magic skill;—and, even when all these had faded, when Herodotus visited the city, after the priestly government of the Pharoahs had been overthrown by Cambyses, and that savage conqueror had burned the temples and almost annihilated the sacerdotal order,—after the influx of strangers had been permitted, and civil war had raged almost to the fulfillment of the Asclepian prophecy,—the wonders then recorded by the historian of her remaining splendor and magnificence;—what shall we now conclude, when, after the lapse of many more destroying ages, we review the yet mightily surviving witnesses of so much glory, surpassing and gigantic even in the last stage of their decay? Shall we suppose the ancient accounts fallacious because they are too wonderful to be conceived; or have we not now present before our eyes the plain evidence of lost science and the vestiges of an intelligence superior to our own? For what did the nations flock to Memphis? For what did Pythagoras, Thales, Democritus, and Plato become immured there for several solitary years, but to be initiated in the wisdom and learning of those Egyptians? For what else, but for the knowledge of that mighty Art with which she arose, governed, and dazzled the whole contemporary world; holding in strong abeyance the ignorant, profane, vulgar, until the evil day of desolation came with self-abuse, when, neglecting to obey the law, by which she governed, all fell, as was foretold, and sinking gradually deeper in crime and presumption, was at last annihilated, and every sacred institution violated by barbarians, and despoiled? "Oh, Egypt! Egypt! Fables alone shall remain of thy religion, and these such as will be incredible to posterity, and words alone shall be left engraved in stones narrating thy pious deeds. The Scythian also, or Indian, or some other similar nation, shall inhabit Egypt. For divinity shall return to heaven, all its inhabitants shall die, and thus Egypt bereft both of God and man shall be deserted. Why do you weep, O Asclepias? Egypt shall experience yet more ample evils; she was once holy, and the greatest lover of the gods on earth, by the desert of her religion. And she, who was alone the reductor of sanctity and the mistress of piety, will be an example of the greatest cruelty. And darkness shall be preferred to light, and death shall be judged to be more useful than life. No one shall look up to heaven. The religious man shall be counted insane; the irreligious shall be thought wise; the furious, brave; and the worst of men shall be considered good.

For the soul, and all things about it, by which it is either naturally immortal, or conceives it shall attain to immortality, conformable to what I have explained to you, shall not only be the subjects of laughter, but shall be considered as vanity. Believe me, likewise, that a capital punishment shall be appointed for him who applies himself to the Religion of Intellect. New statutes and new laws shall be established, and nothing religious, or which is worthy of heaven or celestial concerns, shall be heard or believed in the mind. Every divine voice shall, by a necessary silence, be dumb: the fruits of the earth shall be corrupted; and the air itself shall languish with a sorrowful stupor. These events, and such an old age of the world as this, shall take place—such irreligion, inordination, and unseasonableness of all good" [10].

Such is the substance of a prediction which, as it was supposed to have reference to the Christian era, has been abused and reputed a forgery by the faithless learned of modern times. It is, however, difficult to conceive why it should have been considered so obnoxious, for the early history of Christianity certainly does not fulfill it; it was a falling off from Divinity that was predicted, and not such a revival as took place upon the teachings of Jesus Christ and his apostles. At that period philosophy too flourished, and the Spirit of the Word was potent in faith to heal and save. If the prediction had been a forgery of Apuleius, or other contemporary opponent of Christianity, the early fathers must have known it, which they did not as is plain from Lactantius, and St Augustine mentioning, without expressing any doubt about its authenticity; and though the latter (then adopting probably the popular notion) esteemed it instinctu fallacies spiritus[11], he might subsequently perhaps have thought otherwise, had he lived so long. Christianity was yet in his time glowing, bright, efficacious, from the Divine Fountain; faith was then grounded in reality and living operation, and the mystery of human regeneration, so zealously proclaimed, was also rationally understood. The fulfillment, with respect to Egypt, appears to have taken place in part long previously, and in part to have been reserved to later times, when sacred mysteries, too openly exposed to the multitude, became perverted and vilified by their abuse.

But this prophecy carries us out of all order of time: it will be necessary, in tracing the progress of our science, to pass again to Egypt. The period of her true greatness is, as is well known, shrouded in oblivion; but, during the long succession of the Ptolemies, the influx of strangers, so long before successfully prohibited, became excessive: her internal peace was destroyed, but her Art and Wisdom spread abroad with her renown: foreigners obtained initiation into the mysteries of Isis; and India, Arabia, China and Persia vied with her and with each other in magian skill and prowess.

Pliny informs us that it was Ostanes, the Persian sage accompanying the army of Xerxes, who first inoculated Greece with the portentous spirit of his nation[12]. Subsequently the Greek Philosophers, both young and old, despising the minor religion of their own country, became anxious to visit the eastern temples, and that of Memphis above all, in order to obtain a verification of those hopes to which a previous spirit of inquiry and this new excitement had abundantly given rise.

Amongst the earliest mentioned of these, after Thales, Pythagoras, and a few others, whose writings are lost, is Democritus of Abdera, who has been frequently styles the father of experimental philosophy, and who, in his book of *Sacred Physics*, treats especially of the Hermetic art, and that occult discovery on which the systems of ancient philosophy appear to have been very uniformly based[13]. Of this valuable piece there are said to be several extant editions, and Synesius has added to it the light of a commentary[14]. Nicholas Flammel also, of more recent notoriety, has given extracts from the same at the conclusion of a very instructive work[15]. That its authenticity should have been disputed by the ignorant is not wonderful; but the ancients are nowhere found to doubt about it. Pliny bears witness to the experimental fame of Democritus, and his skill in the occult sciences and practice of them, both in his native city of Abdera and afterwards at Athens, when Socrates was teaching there. *"Plenum miraculi et hoc pariter utrasque artes effloruisse, medicinam dico, magiciemque eadem aetate, illam Hippocrate hanc Democrito illustrantibus"*, &c[16]. Seneca also mentions his artificial confection of precious stones[17]; and it is said that he spent all his leisure, after his return home, in these and such-like hyperphysical researches.[18]

During the sojourn of Democritus at Memphis, he is said to have become associated in his studies with a Hebrew woman named Maria, remarkable at that period for the advances she had made in Philosophy, and particularly in the department of the Hermetic Art. A treatise entitled *Sapientisima Maria de Lapide Philosophica Praescripta* is extant; also *Maria Practica*, a singularly excellent and esteemed fragment, which is preserved in the alchemical collections[19].

But amongst the Greeks, next Democritus, Anaxagorus is celebrated as an alchemist. The remains of his writing are unfortunately scanty, and even those to be found in manuscript only, with exception of some fragments which have been accidentally translated. From these, however, we are led to infer favorably of the general character of his expositions, which Norton, our countryman also, in the Proheme to his quaint *Ordinal of Alchemy*, lauds, thus holding him up in excellent comparison with the envious writers of his age.

> *"All masters that write of this solemn werke,*
> *Have made their bokes to manie men full derke,*
> *In poysies, parables, and in metaphors alsoe,*
> *Which to schollors causeth peine and woe;*
> *Forin their practice wen they would assaye*
> *They leefe their costs, as men see alle daye.*
> *Hermes, Rasis, Geber, and Avicen,*
> *Merlin, Hortolan, Democrit and Morien,*

> *Bacon and Raymond with many moe*
> *Wrote under coverts and Aristotle alsoe.*
> *For what hereof they wrote clear with their pen,*
> *Their clouded clauses dulled; from manie men*
> *Fro laymen, fro clerks, and soe fro every man*
> *They hid this art that noe man find it can.*
> *By their bokes thei do shew reasons faire,*
> *Whereby much people are brought to despaire:*
> *Yet Anaxagoras wrote plainest of them all*
> *In his boke of Conversions Naturall;*
> *Of the old Fathers that ever I founde,*
> *He most discloses of this science the grounde;*
> *Whereof Aristotle had great envy,*
> *And him rebuked unrightlfully,*
> *In manie places, as I can well report,*
> *Intending that men should not to him resort,*
> *For he was large of his cunnying and love,*
> *God have his soul in bliss above;*
> *And such as sowed envious seede*
> *God forgive them for their mis-deede"*[20].

Aristotle is much blamed by Adepts in general for the manner in which he has not only veiled the knowledge which he secretly possessed, but also for having willfully, as they complain, led mankind astray from the path of true experiment. We hesitate to judge this question, since, however much the barrenness of his philosophy may be deplored, it appears improbable that any philosopher, much less one who took such pains as Aristotle, should designedly labor to deceive mankind. His idea was peculiar and appears itself unjust. He blames his predecessors for the various and contradictory positions they had made in philosophizing; *i.e.,* apparently contradictory, as respects their language when taken in a literal sense; for he never quarrels with their true meaning, and carefully avoids disputing their general ground. His metaphysics indeed, which are the natural touchstone of his whole system, differ in no one fundamental aspect or particular that is essential from those of Anaxagoras, Plato and Heraclitus. Certain epistles to Alexander the Great on the Philosophers' stone, attributed to Aristotle, are preserved in the fifth volume of the Theatrum Chemicum; and the Secretum Secretissima is generally acknowledged to be authentic. In the book of Meteors also a clearer intelligence of intrinsic causes is evinced than may be apparent to the common eye[21].

But the whole philosophy of Plato is hyperphysical; the Phaedrus, Philebus, and seventh book of Laws, the beautiful and sublime Parmenides, the Phaedo, Banquet, and Timaeus have long been admired by the studious without being understood; a mystic semblance pervades the whole, and recondite allusions baffle the pursuit of sense and ordinary imagination. Yet the philosopher speaks more familiarly in his Epistles;—and if the correspondence with Dionysius of Syracuse had concerned moral philosophy only and the abstract relations of mind, why such dread as is there expressed about setting the truth to paper? But the science which drew the tyrant to the philosopher was more probably practical and profitably interesting than abstracts would appear to be to such a mind. "Indeed, O son of Dionysius and Doris, this your inquiry concerning the cause of all beautiful things is endued with a certain quality, or rather it is a parturition respecting this ingenerated in the soul, from which he who is not liberated will never in reality acquire truth"[22]. Wisdom must be sought for her own sake, neither for gold or silver or any intermediate benefit, lest these all should be denied together without the discovery of their source. There is a treatise on the philosophers' stone in the fifth volume of the *Theatrum Chemicum* attributed to Plato, but the authenticity is doubtful; and since the principal Greek records of the art were afterwards destroyed with the remnant of Egyptian literature at Alexandria, we are not desirous to enroll either of these names without more extant evidence to prove their claim to the title of Hermetic philosophers. They are mentioned here in their series, because we hope to make it probable, as the nature of the subject comes to be developed, that the most famous schools of theosophy have in all ages been based on a similar experimental ground and profound science of truth in their leaders.

It was about the year 284 of the Christian era when, as Suidas relates, the facility with which the Egyptians were able to make gold and silver, and in consequence to levy troops against Rome, excited the envy and displeasure of the Emperor to such an extent, that he issued an edict, by which every chemical book was to be seized and burned together in the public market-place; vainly hoping, as the historian adds, by this shameful act, to deprive them of the means of annoying him any more. Thus Suidas also endeavors to account for the silence of antiquity with respect to the Egyptian Art[23]. Yet, notwithstanding all this sacrilege, the art appears to have been continually revived in Egypt throughout the whole period of her decline; and, though the records are scanty, we have the memorable story of Cleopatra, the last monarch, dissolving her earring in such a sharp vinegar as is only known to philosophers on the ground of nature. Mystical tales, too, there are related to her pursuits with Mark Antony, and certain chemical treatises attributed to this princess are yet extant[24].

It will be unnecessary to delay our enquiry long at Rome; a city so pre-eminently famous for luxury and arms was not likely to arrive at much perfection in the subtler sciences of nature. Some failing attempts of Caligula there are recounted by Pliny[25] and Virgil, Ovid, Horace, Vitruvius, and other men noted of the Augustan Age, have been gravely accused of sorcery and dabbling in the black art. But the perpetual lamps best prove, and without offence, that the Romans understood something of chemistry and the occult laws of light; several of these are described by Pancirollus; and St. Augustin mentions one consecrated to Venus in his day, that was inextinguishable. But the most remarkable were those found in Tullia's (Cicero's daughter's) tomb;—and that one near Alestes in the year 1500, by a rustic who, digging deeper than usual, discovered an earthen vessel or urn containing another urn, in which last was a lamp placed between two cylindrical vessels, one of gold the other of silver, and each of which was full of a very pure liquor, by whose virtue it is probable these lamps had continued to shine for upwards of fifteen hundred years; and, but for the recklessness of barbarian curiosity, might have continued their wonderful illumination to this time. By the inscription found upon these vessels, it appears they were the work of one Maximus Olybius, who certainly evinced thereby some superior skill in adjusting the gaseous elements, or other ethereal adaptations than is known at this day. The verses graven on the urn are as follows: —

> Platoni sacrum munus ne attingite fures:
> Ignotum est vobis hac quod in urna latet.
> Namque elementa gravi clausit digesta labore
> Vase sub hoc modico Maximus Olybius
> Adsit fecundo custos sibi copia cornu,
> Ne pretium tanti depereat laticis.

Which have been translated thus :

> *Plunderers, forbear this gift to touch*

> *'Tis awful Pluto's own ;*
> *A secret rare the world conceals*
> *To such as you unknown.*
> *Olybius, in this slender vase,*
> *The elements has chained.*
> *Digested With laborious art,*
> *From secret science gained.*
> *With guardian care, two copious urn.*
> *The costly juice confine, -*
> *Lest through the ruins of decay,*
> *The lamp should cease to shine.*

On the lesser urn were these :

> Abite hinc pessimi fures!
> Vos quid voltis vestris cum oculis emissititiis?
> Abite hinc vestro cum Mercurio petasato caduceatoque!
> Maximus maximo donum Plutoni hos sacrum facili.

> *Plunderers, with prying eyes, Away!*
> *What mean you by this curious stay?*
> *Hence with your cunning patron god,*
> *With bonnet winged and magic rod!*

Sacred alone to Pluto's name This mighty art of endless fame![26]

Hermolaus Barbaras, in his corollary to Dioscorus, or some other, where he is treating of the element of water in general, alludes to a particular kind that is distinct from every other water or liquor, saying, — There is a celestial, or rather a divine water of the chemists, with which both Democritus and Trismegistus were acquainted, calling it divine water, Scythian latex, &c., which is a spirit of the nature of the ether and quintessence of things; whence potable gold, and the stone of philosophers, takes its beginning: The ancient author of the Apocalypse of the Secret Spirit of Nature is also cited by H. Kuhnrath, concerning this water; and he devoutly affirms, that the ether in this praeter-perfect aqueous body will burn perpetually, without diminution or consumption of itself, if the external air only be restrained[27]. There are also, besides those mentioned by Poncirollus, modern accounts of lamps found burning in monuments and antique caves of Greece and Germany. But the Bononian Enigma, long famous, without a solution, should not be omitted here, since this relic has puzzled many learned antiquaries; and the adepts claim it as having exclusive reference to the occult material of their art.

AELIA LAELIA CRISPIS

Nec vir, nec mulier, nec androgyna,
Nec puella, nec juvenis, nec anus,
Nec casta, nec meretrix, nec pudica,
Sed omnia!
Sublata neque fame, neque ferro, neque
Veneno, sed omnibus!
Nec coola, nec terris, nec aquis,
Sed ubique jacet!

LUCIUS AGATHO PRISCUS

Nec maritus, nec amator, nec necessarius,
Neque moerens, neque gaudens, neque flens,
Hanc
Neque molem, neque pyramidem. neque sepulcrum.
Sed omnia,
Scit et nescit cui posuerit,
Hoc est sepulcrum certe. cadaver Non habens, sed cadaver idem,
Est et sepulcrum![28]

The following excellent translations appeared amongst some original contributions in the early number of a literary periodical, a few years since[29]:

AELIA LAELIA CRISPIS

Nor male, nor female, nor hermaphrodite,
Nor virgin, woman, young or old,
Nor chaste, nor harlot, modest hight,
But all of them you're told —
Not killed by poison, famine, sword,
But each one had its share,

Mary Anne Atwood

Not in heaven, earth, or water broad
It lies, but everywhere!

LUCIUS AGATHO PRISCUS

No husband, lover, kinsman, friend,
Rejoicing, sorrowing at life's end,
Knows or knows not, for whom is placed
This—what?
This pyramid, so raised and graced,
This grave, this sepulcher?
'Tis neither,
'Tis neither—but 'tis all and each together.
Without a body I aver,
This is in truth a sepulchre;
But notwithstanding, I proclaim
Both corpse and sepulcher the same!

All these contradictory claims are said by the alchemists to relate to the properties of their universal subject, as we shall hereafter endeavor to explain. Michael Mayer has detailed the whole allusion in his *Symbola*[30]. And N. Barnaud, in the *Theatrum Chemicum*, has a commentary on the same[31].

But to proceed; transferring our regards from Rome to Alexandria, we find many Christian Platonists and divines studying and discussing the Occult Art in their writings. St John, the Evangelist Apostle, is cited as having practiced it for the good of the poor; not only in healing the sick, but also confecting gold, silver and precious stones for their benefit. St Victor relates the particulars in a commentary, and the Greek Catholics were accustomed to sing the following verses in a hymn appointed for the mass on St John's day.

Cum gemmarum partes fractas
Solidasset, has distractas
Tribuit pauperibus.
Inexhaustum fert thesaurum
Qui de virgis fecit aurum
Gemmas de lapidibus[32].

Looking to the general testimony of the Fathers, we observe that the early Church Catholic did not neglect to avail herself of the powers which sanctify of life and a well-grounded faith had gotten her. There is no doubt either that the Apostles, when they instituted and left behind them certain ordinances and elementary types, as of water, oil, salt and light, signified some real and notable efficacies. But our Reformers, mistaking these things for superstitions, and since they had ceased to have any meaning, turned them all out of doors; retaining, indeed, little more of the mystery of regeneration than a traditional faith. The Papists, on the other hand, equally oblivious, evinced only to what a length of human credulity and ignorance may be carried, by placing inherent holiness in those material signs, apart from the spirit and only thing signified; adding, moreover, to the original ordinations many follies of their own, they fell into a very slavish and stupid kind of idolatry. And since one of the most fertile sources of dissension that have arisen in the Christian Church has been about these very shadows and types of doctrines, it is to be hoped that, if ever again they should come to be generally reintroduced, it will not be on the ground of ecclesiastical persuasion, or any mere written authority, which, however high and well supported, has never yet been found sufficient to produce unanimity; but from a true understanding and cooperation of that original virtue, apart from which they do but mimic an efficacy, and gather unwholesome fruits. There is a curious story of an early Christian mission to China, related by Thomas Vaughan, in his *Magia Adamica*, showing how the faith became originally established there and elsewhere by its open efficacy, and the power of works, in healing and purifying the lives of men.

But we are at Alexandria, and during that grand revival which took place and continued there some centuries subsequent to the Christian epoch, Plotinus, Philo-Judaeus, Proclus, Porphyry, Jamblicus, Julien, and Apuleius, each professing a genuine knowledge of the Theurgic art, and experimental physics on the Hermetic ground. We shall have frequent occasion to quote their evidence hereafter; Heliodorus, Olympiodorus, Synesius, Athenagoras, Zosimus, and Archelaus, have each left treatises which are extant on the philosophers' stone[33] The excellent Hypatia, also, should be mentioned amongst these, so celebrated for her acquirements and untimely end; it was from this lady that Synesius learned the occult truths of that philosophy, to which he ever afterwards devoted his mind, and which he never abandoned, pursuing it still more zealously when, converted to Christianity, he became a bishop of the Alexandrian Church.

He was careful, however, to protect the mysteries of his religion from vulgar abuse, and refused to expound in public the philosophy of Plato; he and his brethren having unanimously bound themselves by oath to initiate none but such as had been worthily prepared and duly approved by the whole conclave[34]. Of Synesius, we have the remaining Alchemical commentary on Democritus before mentioned, with an admirable piece commonly found appended to other treatises, those of Artefius and Flammel's *Hieroglyphics*, for example, and translated into English, with Basil Valentine's *Chariot of Antimony* and the useful commentaries of the adept Kirchringius[35].

Heliodorus was a familiar friend of Synesius, and brother adept; besides the writings already named, the mystical romance of Theagenes and Chariclea being attributed to him as an offence, rather than disavow it, as was required, he relinquished his bishopric of Tricca, in Thessaly, and went to pursue his studies in poverty and retirement.

Zosimus was an Egyptian, and reputed a great practitioner. The name of Athenagoras is familiar in Church history; his tract, which has been translated into French, and entitled Du Parfait Amour, shows him to have been practically conversant with the art he allegorizes.

The taking of Alexandria by the Arabs, in the year 640, dispersed the choice remnant of mind yet centered there; and it was not long afterwards that the Calif Omar, mad in his Mohamedan zeal, condemned her noble and unique library to heat the public baths of the city, which it is said to have done for a space of six miserable months. A wild religious fanaticism now prevailed; Christians and Mahomedans struggling for temporal supremacy:—and here we may observe something similar to a fulfillment of the Asclepian prophecy, but the evil was more profusely spread even than was predicted; for religion had everywhere fallen off from her vital foundation; tradition and secular delirium had taken place of intellectual enthusiasm, and idle dreams were set up as oracles in the place of Divine inspiration. The priests, above all blameworthy, having forsaken the law of conscience, attempted to wield without it the rod of magic power. Confusion and licentiousness followed; and from gradual sufferance grew, and came to prevail, in the worst imaginable forms. Necessity, at length, compelled an abandonment of the Mysteries; Theurgic rites, no longer holy, were proscribed; and a punishment, no less than death, was menaced against him who dared to pursue the "Religion of Intellect". In the interim, those few who had withstood the torrent of ambitious temptation, indignant at the multiform folly, and observing by the aid of their remaining wisdom, that the ingression of evil was not yet fulfilled, hastened rather than delayed the crisis; and by burying themselves with their saving science in profound obscurity, have left the world to oblivion, and the deceit of outer darkness, with rare individual exceptions, to this day.

It is a peculiarity of the Hermetic science that men of every religion, time and country and occupation, have been found professing it; and Arabia, though she was guilty of so great a sacrilege at Alexandria, has herself produced many wise kings and renowned philosophers. It is not known exactly when Prince Geber lived; but since his name has become notorious, and is cited by the oldest authors, whereas he himself quotes none, he merits, at all events, an early consideration. Besides, he is generally esteemed by adepts as the greatest, after Hermes, of all who have philosophized through this art.

Of the five hundred treatises, said to have been composed by him, three only remain to posterity: *The Investigation of Perfect*, *The Sum of the Perfect Magistery*, and his *Testament*[36]; and the light estimation in which these are held by more modern chemists, forms a striking contrast to the unfeigned reverence and admiration with which they were formerly reviewed and cited by the adepts, Albertus Magnus, Lully, and many more of the brightest luminaries of their age.

"If we look back to the seventh century (we quote from the address given at the opening meeting of the Faraday Society, 1846), the alchemist is presented brooding over his crucibles and alembics that are to place within his reach the philosophers' stone, the transmutation of metals, the alkahest, and the elixir of life. With these we associate the name of Geber, the first authentic writer on the subject; from whose peculiar and mysterious style of writing we derive the word geber or gibberish".

Yet, notwithstanding this and much more that they descant upon, if our modern illuminati were but half as experienced in nature as they might be—had they one ray even of the antique intellect they deride, how different a scene would not that remote age present to them? Instead of imagining greedy dotards brooding over their crucibles and uncouth alembics, in vain hope of discovering the elixir and stone of the philosophers, they would observe the philosophers themselves, by a kindred light made visible, on their own ground; experimenting, indeed, but how and with what? Not with our gross elements, our mercuries, sulfurs, and our lifeless salts; but in a far different nature, with stranger arts, and with laboratories too, how different from those now in use:—of common fittings, yet not inferior either; but most complete with vessels, fuel, furnaces, and every material requisite, well adapted together and compact in one. Right skillfully has old Geber veiled a fair discovery, by his own art alone to be unmasked: his gibberish is not of the present day's commonplace, tame and tolerable; but such ultra-foolishness in literality are his receipts, as folly is never found to venture or common sense invent. For they are a part of wisdom's envelope, to guard her universal magistery from an incapable and dreaming world; calculated they are, nevertheless, though closely sealed, to awaken rational curiosity, and lend a helping hand to those who have already entered on the right road; but to deceive in practice only the most credulous and inept. They who have really understood Geber, his adept compeers, declare with one accord that he has spoken the truth, though disguisedly, with great acuteness and precision: others, therefore, who do not profess to understand, and to whom those writings are a mere unintelligible jargon, may take warning hence, lest they exhibit to posterity a twofold ignorance and vanity of thought.

Rhasis, another Arabian alchemist, was even more publicly famous than Geber, on account of the practical displays he made of his transmuting skill. Excellent extracts from his writing, which are said to exist principally in manuscript, often occur in the works of Roger Bacon.

The story of Morienus, how in early life he left his family and native city (for he was a Roman), to seek the sage Adfar, a solitary adept, whose fame had reached him from Alexandria; the finding him, gaining his confidence, and becoming at length his devoted disciple;—is related by his biographer in a natural and very interesting manner; also his subsequent sojournings, after the death of his patron, his intercourse with King Calid, with the initiation and final conversion of that prince to Christianity. But the details are given at much too great length for extract in this place. A very attractive and esteemed work, purporting to be a dialogue between himself and Calid, is extant under the name of Morien, and copied into many of the collections[37]. Calid also wrote some treatises: his *Liber Secretorum*, or Secret of Secrets, as it has been styled, is translated into English, French, and Latin[38].

Prince Averroes, and the notorious Avicenna, next demand notice. The latter became known to the world somewhere between the ninth and tenth centuries. His strong but ill-directed genius, so similar to that of Paracelsus, was the occasion of much suffering and self-desolation; but his name was illustrious over Asia, and his authority continued pre-eminent in the European schools of medicine until after the Reformation. He is said to have carried on the practice of transmutation, with the magical arts in general, to a great extent; but his Alchemical remains are neither lucid nor numerous, not those at least which are well authenticated[39].

Artefius was a Jew who, by the use of the elixir, is reported to have lived throughout the period of a thousand years, with what truth or credibility opinions may vary; he himself affirms it, and Paracelsus, Pontanus, and Roger Bacon appear to give credence to the tale[40], which forms part of his celebrated treatise on the philosophers' stone, and runs as follows: —I, Artefius, having learnt all the art in the books of the true Hermes, was once, as others, envious; but having lived one thousand years, or thereabouts (which thousand years have already passed since my nativity, by the grace of God alone, and the use of this admirable quintessence), as I have seen, through this long space of time, that men have been unable to perfect the same magistery on account of the obscurity of the words of the philosophers, moved by pity and a good conscience, I have resolved, in these my last days, to publish it all sincerely and truly; so that men may have nothing more to desire concerning this work. I except one thing only, which it is not lawful that I should write, because it can be revealed truly only by God, or by a master. Nevertheless, this likewise may be learned from this book, provided one be not stiffnecked, and have a little experience[41].

This Artefius forms a sort of link in the history of Alchemy, carried as it was in the course of time from Asia into Europe, about the period of the first crusades, when a general communication of the mind of different nations was effected by their being united under a common cause. Sciences, arts, and civilization, which had heretofore flourished in the East only, were gradually transplanted into Europe; and towards the end of the twelfth century, or thereabouts, our Phoenix too bestirred herself, and passed into the West.

Roger Bacon was amongst the first to fill his lamp from her reviviscent spirit; and with this ascending and descending experimentally, he is said to have discovered the secret ligature of natures, and their magical dissolution; he was moreover acquainted with theology in its profoundest principles; medicine, likewise physics and metaphysics on their intimate ground; and, having proved the miraculous multiplicability of light by the universal spirit of nature, he worked the knowledge to such effect, that in the mineral kingdom he produced gold[42]. What marvel, persecuted as he was for the natural discoveries which he gave to the world, without patent or profit to himself, if he should appropriate these final fruits of labor and long interior study? Yet it does not appear that he was selfishly prompted even in this particular reservation; it was conscience, as he declares, that warned him to withhold a gift somewhat over rashly and dangerously obtained. His acutely penetrative and experimental mind, not content even with enough led him by a fatal curiosity, as it is suggested, into forbidden realms of self-sufficiency and unlawful peace of mind, and finally induced him to abandon altogether those researches, in order to retrieve and expiate in solitude the wrongs he had committed. We know that the imputation of magic has seemed ridiculous, and every report of the kind has been referred to the friar's extraordinary skill in the natural sciences. The rejection of his books at Oxford has often been cited as an instance of the exceeding bigotry of those times, as indeed it was; and yet are we not nearly as far off perhaps from the truth in our liberality as were our forefathers in their superstition? An accusation of magic has not occurred of late, nor would be likely to molest seriously any philosopher of the present age; but then it did occur often during the dark ages, and who can tell whether it may not again at some future day, when men are even more enlightened and intimate with nature than they are now?

There are still remaining two or three works of Roger Bacon, in which the roots of the Hermetic science are fairly stated; but the practice most carefully concealed, agreeably to that maxim, which in his later years he penned, *that truth ought not to be shown to every ribald, for then that would become most vile, which, in the hands of a philosopher, is the most precious of all things*[43].

Many great lights shone through the darkness of those middle ages; Magians, who were drawn about the fire of nature, as it were, into communication with her central source. Albertus Magnus, his friend and disciple the acute Aquinas, Scotus Erigina the subtle doctor, Arnold di Villa Nova, and Raymond Lully, all confessed adepts. John Reuchlin, Ficinus the Platonist, Picus di Mirandola, blending alchemy and therapeutics with neoplatonism and the cabalistic art. Spinoza also was a profound metaphysician and speculator on the same experimental ground. Alain de l'Isle the celebrated French philosopher, Merlin (St Ambrose), the abbot John Trithemius, Cornelius Agrippa his enterprising pupil, and many more subsequent to these, great, resolute, and philosophic spirits, who were not alone content to rend asunder the veil of ignorance from before their own minds, but held it still partially open for others, disclosing the interior lights of science to such as were able to aspire, and willing to follow their great example, laboring in the way. Medium minds set limits to nature, halting continually, and returning, before barriers which those others over-leaped almost without perceiving them. Faith was the beacon light that led them on to conviction, by a free perspicuity of thought beyond things seen, to believe and hope truthfully, which is the distinguishing prerogative of great minds. But it will be necessary to regard this extraordinary epoch of Occult Science more in detail, with the testimony of its heroes, whose reputation, together with that of alchemy, has suffered from the faithlessness of biographers, compilers, commentators, and such like interference.

Most of the alchemical works of Albert, for instance, have been excluded from the great editions of his works, and the authenticity of all has been disputed, but without lasting effect; for in that long and laborious treatise, *De Mineralibus*, unquestionably his own, even if the rest were proved spurious, there is sufficient evidence of his belief and practice to admit all. Therein he describes the first matter of the adepts with the characteristic minuteness of personal observation, and recommends alchemy as the best and most easy means of rational investigation. *"De transmutatione horum corporum metallicorum et mutatione unius in aliud non estphysici determinare, sed artis quae est Alchimica. Est autem optimum genus hujus inquisitionis et certissimum, quia tunc per causam unius cujusque rei propriam, res cognoscitur, et de accidentibus ejus mimime dubitatur, nec est difficile cognoscere"*[44].

This passage is one amongst many that might be adduced from his own pen to prove that Albert was an alchemist; but Aquinas' disclosures are ample, removing all doubt, even if he himself had left room for any. Besides the treatise of minerals already mentioned, there is the *Libellus de Alchemia*, published with his other works[45]; also, the *Concordanditia Philosophorum de Lapide*, the *Secreta Secretorum*, and *Breve Compendium* in the *Theatrum Chemicum*, all treating of the same subject. Albert's authority is the more to be respected in that he gave up every temporal advantage, riches, fame, and ecclesiastical power, to study philosophy in a cloister remote from the world during the greater portion of a long life. An opinion has commonly obtained that the philosophers' stone was sought after from selfish motives and a blind love of gain; and that such has been frequently the case there is no doubt; but then such searchers never found it. The conditions of success are peculiar, as will be shown. Avarice is of all motives the least likely to be gratified by the discovery of wisdom. It is philosophers only that she teaches to make gold.

> "Querant Alchimiam, falsi quoque recti;
> Falsi sine numero, sed hi sunt rejecti;
> Et cupiditatibus, heu, tot sunt infecti
> Quod inter mille millia, vix subt tres electi Istam as scientiam"[46].

The true adepts have been rare exceptions in the world, despite of all calumny, famous, and favored above their kind. Let any one but with an unprejudiced eye regard the writings of those who may be believed on their own high authority to have succeeded in this art, and he will perceive that the motives actuating them were of the purest possible kind; truthful, moral, always pious and intelligent, as those of the pseudo-alchemists, on the other hand, were reckless and despicable. But more of this hereafter. Albertus died, *"magnus in magiâ, major inphilosophia, maximus in theologia"*[47]; and his learning and fame descended fully on him who had already shared it, his disciple, the subtle and sainted Aquinas.

The truth was not likely to die in such hands; Aquinas wrote largely and expressly on the doctrine of transmutation, and in his *Thesaurus Alchimiae*, addressed to his friend, the Abbot Reginald, he alludes openly to the practical successes of Albert and himself in the Secret Art[48]. Vain, therefore, are attempts of his false panegyrists, who, anxious it would seem rather for the intellectual than the moral fame of their hero, have ventured to slur over his assertions as dubious. Aquinas is much too far committed in his writings for their quibbling exceptions to tell in proof against his own direct and positive affirmation. *"Metalla transmutari possunt unum in aliud",* says he, "cum *naturalia sint et ipsorum material eadem"*. Metals can be transmuted one into another, since they are of one and the same matter"[49]. Declarations more or less plain to the same effect are frequent, and his treatise, *De Esse et Essentia*, is eminently instructive. It is true he slurs over points and sophisticates also occasionally in order to screen the doctrine from superficial detection; for Aquinas was above all anxious to direct inquirers to the higher purposes and application of the Divine Art, and universal theosophy, rather than to rest its capabilities of quickening and perfection in the mineral kingdom, as at that period many were wont to do, sacrificing their whole life's hope to the multiplication of gold. *"Fac sicut te ore tenens docui, ut scis quod tibi non scribo, quoniam peccatum esset hoc secretum virissecularibus revelare, qui magis hanc scientiam propter vanitatem quam propter debitum finem et Dei honorem quaerunt".* And again, "ne *sis garrulous sedpone ori tuo custodiam; et it filiam sapientum margaritam ante porcas non projicies. Noli te, charissime, cum majori opere occupare, quia propter salutis et Christi praedictionis officium;et lucrandi tempus magni debes attendere divitiis spiritialibus, quam lucris temporibus inhiare"*[50].

The pretensions of Arnold di Villa Nova have not been contested, nor are his writings the only evidence of his skill in the Great Art. Contemporary scholars bear him witness, and instances are related of the wonderful projections he made with the transmuting powder. The Jurisconsult, John Andre, mentions him, and testifies to the genuine conversions of some iron bars into pure gold at Rome. Oldradus also and the Abbot Panorimitanus of about the same period, praise the Hermetic Art as beneficial and rational, and the wisdom of the alchemist Arnold di Villa Nova.[51] The works of this philosopher are very numerous. The *Rosarium Philosophicum*, esteemed amongst the best, is published in the *Theatrum Chemicum*, and at the end of the folio edition of his works. The *Speculum*, a luminous treatise; the *Carmina, Questiones ad Bonifacium*, the *Testamentum*, and some others are given entire in the *Theatrum Chemicum*, but have not been translated.

About this time and towards the close of the 14th century, an excitement began to be perceptible in the public mind. So many men of acknowledged science and piety, one after another, agreeing about the reality of transmutation, and giving tangible proofs of their own skill, could not fail to produce an effect; the art became in high request, and its professors were invited from all quarters, and held in high honor by the world. Lesser geniuses caught the scattered doctrines and set to work, some with sufficient understanding and with various success.

Alain de l'Isle is said to have obtained the Elixir, but his chief testimony has been excluded by the editors of his other works; soften and unscrupulously has private prejudice interfered to defraud the public judgment of its rights and true data. The rejected treatise, however, was printed separately, and may be found in the third volume of the *Theatrum Chemicum*[52]. This philosopher also wrote a commentary on the *Prophecies of Merlin*, which are reported to have sole reference to the arcane of the Hermetic Art[53].

Raymond Lully is supposed to have become acquainted with Arnold, and the Universal Science, late in life; but when the fame of his Christian zeal and talents had already become known and acknowledged abroad, his declarations in favor of alchemy had the greater weight. Unlike his cloistered predecessors, secluded and known as they were by name only to the world, Raymond had traveled over Europe, and a great part of Africa and Asia; and with his former fame was at length mingled the discovery of alchemy and the philosophers' stone. John Cremer, Abbot of Westminster, had worked for 30 years, it is related, assiduously with the hope of obtaining the secret. The enigmas of the old adepts had sadly perplexed and led him astray; but he had discovered enough to convince him of the reality, and to encourage him to proceed with the investigation; when, Lully's fame having reached him, he determined to seek that philosopher, then resident in Italy; was fortunate in meeting with him and gaining his confidence, and not a little edified by the pious and charitable life Lully led there, and recommended to others. Desirous of becoming still more intimately enlightened than was convenient in that place, Cremer invited and brought over with him Raymond Lully to England, where he was presented to the king, then Edward II, who had also before invited him from Vienna, being much interested in the talents and reputed skill of the stranger, and now more than ever by the promise of abundant riches which the sight of Cremer's gold held out to him. Lully, still as ever zealous for the promulgation of the Christian religion, promised to produce for the king all monies requisite, if he felt disposed to engage in the crusades anew. Edward did not hesitate, but complied with every condition respecting the appliance of the gold, provided only Lully would supply it. The artist accordingly set to work, soothe story runs, in a chamber set apart for him in the Tower, and produced 50,000 pounds weight of pure gold. His own words relative to the extraordinary fact in his testament, are these;—"*Converti una vice in aurum et millia pondo argenti vivi, plumbi, et stannic.* I converted", says he, "at one time 50,000 pounds weight of quicksilver, lead and tin, into gold"[54].

The king no sooner received this, than breaking faith with Lully, in order to obtain more, the artist was made a prisoner in his own laboratory, and without regard at all for the stipulation, before engaged in, ordered to commence on his productive labors anew. This base conduct on the part of the king was much lamented by Cremer, who expresses indignation thereat openly in his *Testament*[55]; and the whole story has been repeatedly recorded in the detailed chronicles of those times. But to be short, our hero fortunately escaped from his imprisonment, and a coinage of the gold was struck in pieces weighing about 10 ducats each, called *Nobles of the Rose*. Those who have examined these coins pronounce them to be of the finest metal, and the inscription round the margin distinguishes them from all others in the Museums, and denotes their miraculous origin. They are described in Camden's Antiquities, and for the truth of the whole story, we have, besides Cremer's evidence and the declarations of Lully, a great deal of curious allusion to be found in the books of Olaus Borrichius, R. Constantius, l'Englet Dufresnoy, and Dickenson. The last relates that some time after the escape of Lully, there was found in the cell he occupied at Westminster with Cremer, whilst it was undergoing some repairs, a certain quantity of the powder of transmutation, by means of which the workmen and architects became enriched[56].

Lully's writings on Alchemy are, as the rest, obscure; and have only been understood with great pains and application even by those who have been so fortunate as to possess the key of his cabalistic mind. Whether his equivocal and contradictory language was so contrived to baffle the sordid chemists; or whether, as before said, he learned the art late in life, and was convinced at last only by Arnold exhibiting the transmutation in his presence; it would require scrupulous examination to judge at this day: certain it is there are passages in his writings which leave room for controversy, though none, we think, virtually denying the art, whilst his essays in favor of it are acknowledged excellent and numerous; as many as 200 are given in the catalogue of Dufresnoy treating exclusively on this subject[57].

Those were singular times when few any longer doubted the possibility of gold-making, and individuals of the highest repute devoted their lives to the subtle investigation. We have adduced this notable instance of Lully's prowess in England, as one only amongst many others, quite as well authenticated, which are told by the authors before cited and in the alchemical collections. Public curiosity was stimulated to the highest pitch; experiments were made reckless of consequences, and the spirit of avarice, bursting forth expectant, absolutely raged. Whether the incaution of adepts, in making their art too publicly profitable, had given rise to the frenzy, or whether it was spontaneously kindled, or from whatever cause, the fact is lamentably certain; the Stone was no longer sought after by philosophers alone; not only have we Lully, Cremer, Rupicessa, De Meun, Flammel, John Pontanus, Basil Valentine, Ripley, and the host of contemporary worthies, successively entering the lists; but with these a spurious brood of idlers living on the public credulity, and which the practical evidence of these others continued to ferment; men of all ranks, persuasions and degrees of intelligence, of every variety of calling, motive and imagination, were, as monomaniacs, searching after the stone.

> "As Popes with Cardinals of dignity,
> Archbyshops with Byshops of high degree
> With Abbots and Priors of religion,
> With Friars, Hermites, and Preests manie one,
> And Kings with Princes and Lords great of bloode,
> For everie estate desireth after goode;
> And the Merchaunts alsoe, which dwelle in fiere
> Of brenning covetise, have thereto desire;
> And common workmen will not be out-lafte
> For as well as Lords they love this noble crafte.
> As Gouldsmithes, whome we shall leaste repreuve
> For sights in their craft meveth them to believe;
> But wonder it is that Brewers deale with such werkes,
> Free Masons, and Tanners, with poore parish clerkes;
> Ailors and Glaziers woll not therefore cease,
> And eke sely Tinkers will put them in prease
> With great presumption; yet some collour there was
> For all such men as give tincture to glasse;
> But manie Artificers have byn over swifte,
> With hastie credence to sume away their thrift;
> Yet ever in hope continued their hearte;
> Trusting some tyme to speede right well,
> Of manie such truly I can tell;
> Which in such hope continued all their lyfe,
> Whereby they were made poore and made to unthrive:
> It had byne good forthem to have left off
> In seaon, for noughte they founde except a scoffe,
> For trewly he that is not a great clerke,
> Is nice and lewd to medle with this werke;
> Ye may trust me it is no small inginn,
> To know alle secrets pertaining to this myne.
> For it is most profounde philosophye
> This subtill science of holy Alkimy"[58].

Many usurped the title of the adepts, who had no knowledge even of the preliminaries of the Art; sometimes deceiving, at others, being themselves deceived; and it has been principally from the fraudulent pretensions of those dabblers that the world has learned to despise alchemy, confounding the genuine doctrine with their sophistical and vile productions; and a difficulty yet remains to distinguish them, and segregate, from so great an interspersion of darkness, the true light. For a multitude of books were put forth with the merest purpose of deception, and to ensnare the unwary; some indeed affirming, that the truth was to be found in salts, or niters, or boraxes; but others, in all vegetable bodies indiscriminately, committing a multifarious imagination to posterity. Not did these alone content the evil spirit of that day, but it must introduce mutilated editions of the old masters, filled with inconsistencies, and the wicked inventions of designing fraud; and thus, as the adept observes, they have blasphemed the Sacred Science, and by their errors have brought contempt on men philosophizing.

> "As of that Monke which a boke did write
> Of a thousand receipts in malice for despighte,
> Which he copied in manie a place,
> Whereby hath byn made manie a pale face
> And manie gowndes have been made bare of hewe,
> And men made fals which beforetimes were trewe"[59].

Nor has the literature alone suffered from such knavish interpolation; but the social consequences are described, at the time, as deplorable; rich merchants, and others, greedy of gain, were induced to trust quantities of gold, silver, and even precious stones, which they lost, in vain hope of getting them multiplied ; and these rogueries became so frequent and notorious, that at last acts of Parliament were passed in England, and Pope's Bull's issued over Christendom, forbidding transmutation, on pain of death, and the pursuit of alchemy[60]. But this, whilst giving an external check, did not smother the desire of riches, or that morbid desire of them, so long fostered in the expectation; experiments continued to be carried on in secret with no less ardour than before, both by knaves and philosophers. Pope John XXII who interdicted it, is said to have practiced the art himself extensively, and to have wonderfully enriched the public treasury through its means. But to bring forward each extraordinary tradition and character of the various artists who flourished during the fourteenth and fifteenth centuries, would trespass too far on our pages; and for the present purpose, it may be needful only to detail the more remarkable.

Amongst them, the story of Nicholas Flammel, and his wife Pernette, has been thought interesting. Their humble origin, their charitable distribution of it, and the eminent piety and mystery of their lives, attracted great attention in their own country, and a widespread fame has descended and connects their name honorably with the history of the Hermetic art. The relation given simply by the author concerning himself as follows:—"I, Nicholas Flammel, Scrivener, living in Paris, in the year of our Lord, 1399, in the Notary street, near St James, of the Boucherie, though I learned not much Latin, Because of the poverty of my parents, who, notwithstanding were, even by those who envy me most, accounted honest and good people; yet, by the blessing of God, I have not wanted an understanding of the books of the philosophers, but learned them, and attained to a certain kind of knowledge, even of their hidden secrets. For which cause's sake, there shall not be any moment of my life pass wherein, remembering this so vast good, I will not render thanks to this my good and gracious God. After the death of my parents, I Nicholas Flammel, got my living by the art of writing, ingrossing, and the like; and in the course of time, there fell by chance into my hands a gilded book, very old and large, which cost me only 2 florins. It was not made of paper or parchment, as other books are, but of admirable rinds, as it seemed to me, of young trees; the cover of it was brass, well bound, and graven all over with a strange kind of letters, which I took to be Greek characters, or some such like. This I know, that I could not read them; but as to the matter which was written within, it was engraven, as I suppose, with an iron pencil, or graver, upon the said bark leaves; done admirably well, and in fair neat Latin letters, and curiously colored. It contained thrice seven leaves, for so they were numbered on the top of each folio, and every seventh leaf was without writing; but in place thereof were several images and figures painted".

Further, going on to describe the book and these hieroglyphics minutely, Flammel relates how, at length, after much study and fruitless toil, their meaning was explained to him by a Jew stranger , whom he met with in his travels; and how on his return home, he set to work and succeeded in the discovery, is thus familiarly declared: "He that would see the manner of my arrival home, and the joy of Pernette, let him look upon us two in the city of Paris, upon the door of the chapel of James, in the boucherie, close by one side of my house, where we are both painted, kneeling, and giving thanks to God: for through the grace of God it was, that I attained the perfect knowledge of all that I desired. I had now the *prima material*, the first principles, yet not their *preparation*, which is a thing most difficult above all things in the world; but in the end I had that also, after a long aberration and wandering in the labyrinth of errors, for the space of three years. During which time, I did nothing but study and search and labor, so as you see me depicted without this arch, where I have shown my process, praying also continuously unto God, and reading attentively in my book, pondering the words of the philosophers, and then trying and proving the various operations which I thought they might mean by their words. At length, I found that which I desired; which I also soon knew, by the scent and odor thereof. Having this, I easily accomplished the magistery. For knowing the *preparations of the prime agents*, and then literally following the directions in my book, I could not then miss the work if I would. Having attained this, I came now to the Projection; and the first time I made projection, was upon mercury; a pound and a half whereof, or thereabouts, I turned into pure silver, better than that of the mine; as I proved by assaying it myself, and also causing others to assay it for me, several times. This was done in the year A.D. 1382, January 17, about noon, in my own house, Pernette alone being present with me. Again following the same direction in my book, word by word, I made projection of the Red Stone, on a like quantity of mercury, Pernette only being present, and in the same house; which was done in the same year, April 25, at five in the afternoon. This mercury I truly transmuted into almost as much gold, much better indeed than common gold, more soft also, and more pliable. I speak in all truthfully. I have made three times with the help of Pernette, who understands it as well as myself; and without doubt, if she would have done it alone, she would have brought the work to the same, or full as great perfection as I had done. I had truly enough, when I had once done it; but I found exceeding great pleasure and delight in seeing and contemplating the admirable works of nature, *within the vessels*. And to show you that I had then done it three times, I caused to be depicted under the same arch, three furnaces, like to those which serve the operations of the work. I was much concerned for a long time, lest Pernette, by reason of extreme joy, should not hide her felicity, which I measured by my own; and lest she should let fall some words among her relations, concerning the great treasure which we possessed. But the goodness of the great God, had not only given and filled me with this blessing, in giving me a sober chaste wife; but she was also a wise prudent woman, not only capable of reason, but also to do what was reasonable; and made it her business, as I did, to think of God, and to give ourselves to the works of charity and mercy. Before the time wherein I wrote this discourse, which was at the latter end of the year 1413, after the death of my beloved companion; she and I had already founded and endowed with revenues fourteen hospitals, three chapels, and seven churches, in the city of Paris; all which we had built from the ground, and were able to enrich with gifts and revenues. We have also done at Bologne about the same as at Paris, besides our private charities, which it would be unbecoming to particularize. Building, therefore, these hospitals, churches, etc, in the aforesaid cities, I caused to be depicted under the said fourth arch, the most true and essential marks and signs of this art, yet under veils and types and hieroglyphical characters, demonstrating to the wise and men of understanding, the direct and perfect way of operation and *lineary work* of the philosophers' stone; *which being perfected by anyone, takes away from him the root of all sin and evil*; changing his evil into good, and making him liberal, courteous, religious, fearing God, however wicked he was before, provided only he carries through the work to its legitimate end. For from thenceforward he is continually ravished with the goodness of God, and with his grace and mercy, which he has obtained from the foundation of eternal goodness; with the profundity from the fountain of eternal goodness; with the profundity of his Divine and adorable power, and with the contemplation of his admirable works".

Part of this relation is given of himself by the author in his *Hieroglyphics*, and part is taken from his *Testament*; and chronicle recount as late as the year 1740, that the evidence of his charitable deeds remained and the symbols of the art in the cemetery of the Holy Innocents at the church of St James, on the Marivaux door, at the portal of St Genevieve", &c.[61], Amongst the writings of Flammel, besides those already quoted from, we have *Le Sommaire Philosophique*, in French verse, which is also translated in the *Theatrum Chemicum*, an esteemed work, with important annotations at the end; *Le Désir desiré*, and *Le Grand Eclaircissement*, which are more rarely to be met with.

The Isaacs, father and son, Dutch adepts, are said to have worked successfully, and are much lauded by Boorhaave, who appears not either to have been a stranger to their pursuit or to the principles of occult science[62].

But Basil Valentine is the star of the 15 the century; he is generally reported to have been a Benedictine hermit; but a mystery hangs about his individuality which has never been satisfactorily cleared up, though careful researches have been made, and his numerous works written in all languages, called forth much curiosity on their appearance and have been held in high esteem by students in the Hermetic Art. He ranks high amongst his brethren for having, as they say, discovered a new method of working the Red Elixir, and facilitated the process materially, which had been hitherto laborious and a rare effect, as appears from those lines of Norton.

> *"How that manie men patient and wise,*
> *Found our White Stone with exercise;*
> *After that they were trewly taught,*
> *With great labor, that stone they caught,*
> *But few (saith he) or scarcely one;*
> *In fifteen kingdoms hath our Red Stone.*
> *Wheom to seeke it availeth right noughte,*
> *Till the white medicine be fully wrought;*
> *Neither Albertus Magnus, the Black Freere,*
> *Neither Freer Bacon his compeere,*
> *Had not of our Res Stone consideration*
> *Him to increase in multiplication"*, &c[63].

The Hamburg edition of Basil Valentine's works may be considered the most perfect[64]. The English translations are rambling and incomplete: with the single exception of that one which is taken from the Latin of Kirchringius, with his admirable commentary on the *Triumphal Chariot of Antimony and Stone of Fire*. *The Twelve keys* are rendered in the *Bibliothèque des Philosophes Chimiques*, second edition.

A valuable collection of English Alchemy in verse was published by Elias Ashmole, himself a lover of occult science, and the great patron, in his day, of those who made it their study. Neither was he ignorant of the subject, if we may judge by the preface and curious notes appended to his *Theatrum*, wherein he exposes certain principles of magic, and alludes to the manual artifice without much disguise. I must profess, says he, I know enough to hold my tongue, but not enough to speak; and the no less real than miraculous fruits I have found, in my diligent inquiry in these arcane, lead me on to such degrees of admiration, they command silence, and force me to lose my tongue, lest, being not wholly experiences, as he goes on the say, I should ass to the many injuries the world has already suffered, by delivering the bare medley of my apprehensions without the confident attestations of practice; and by justly esteemed as indiscrete as those whom Ripley mentions, that prate,

> "Wyth wondreng,
> Of Robin Hood, and of his Bow,
> Whych never shot therin I trowe"[65].

Norton's *Ordinal*, dated 1477, with which this Hermetic *Theatre* opens, is a praiseworthy performance, and with the exception of the Subject Matter and certain preliminaries, which are constantly concealed, the process is presented in a candid, orderly, and attractive manner. So much cannot be said for the Canon Ripley of Bridlington, whose private misfortunes would seem to have made him envious. His composition is disorderly, and those *Twelve Gates* have, we conceive, little edified any without the Lodge. Added also to his own willful misguidance, the verses are said to have suffered spoliation and displacement from the order in which they were originally written, according to the mischievous cabalistic method in vogue at that time. Ripley, therefore, is universally complained of, though reputed a good adept. The commentary published by the celebrated anonymous Eireneus Philalethes, under the title of *Ripley Revived*, though it explains a great deal practically and may serve to lead on the initiated, yet will appear infamously sophistical and inevitably disgust a beginner[66].

All Ashmole's collection is valuable, even were it only as a specimen of early mystic literature. The Fragment from Pierce, the Black Monke, Bloomfield's *Blossoms, and Philosophy and Experience*, are among the most instructive. Ashmole's intention of collecting the English prose writings on Alchemy was not accomplished; only a few scattered portions were edited and those not of the best.

Ficinus, an Italian of highly cultivated genius, well known as the Latin translator of Plato, and savior of other valuable remnants of antique literature, was also an amateur in the Hermetic art. He collected and translated the works imputed to Hermes, before mentioned, from Greek into Latin, and took pains elsewhere theoretically to explain the art[67]. Picus, prince di Mirandola, was his contemporary, and wrote a treatise, in which he connects Alchemy with the most profound metaphysical science[68].

Then we have the remarkable instance of Cornelius Agrippa, a man of powerful and penetrating genius who, having possessed himself of the means and principles of the Occult Science from his friend, the wary and learned Abbot Trithemius, set to work something it would seem after the example of Friar Bacon, proving them in a self-sufficient order. His three books *Of Occult Philosophy*, especially the first two, illustrate the practical bias and enterprising nature of his mind; but as he declares, he had not, when he wrote them, arrived at a full experience, nor was he able to make the philosophers' stone. But it was this discovery, made later in life, which caused him to be discontented with his former revelation, and to publish that book on the *Vanity of the Sciences*, which has been considered as a recantation of his former philosophy; but which is in fact no recantation at all, but a consummation rather and conclusion in general of his works. Any one taking the pains to read may perceive that Agrippa wrote it neither in ignorance nor in despair of human knowledge. It was by searching and proving the magnitude of the Mystery that he arrived at that final and convictive faith, which is as much above ordinary science as the vulgar credulity of mankind is below it. It is not the part of a mind, sane and philosophic to fall back content in ignorance, or to retrograde passively in despair of its object. The vanity of particular and temporal sciences is discovered by comparison only in the broad day light of universal truth; and there stood the magician at last when, as it were from the top of Celsus' ladder, looking down upon the steps by which he had climbed, and whereon he had successively rested, he observed their inferiority and the small prospect they afforded in comparison with that which he now, at their clear summit, enjoyed. Let any one read from the *Vanity of the Sciences* the chapter on *Alchemy*, and judge whether the author contradicts, as the report has said, or contemns merely the experience of his early youth; and where, after showing the folly of pretenders, speaking of the genuine Hermetic art, he says,—"I could tell many tings of this art, if I had not sworn to keep silence, and this silence is so constantly and religiously observed of the ancient philosophers, that there is bound no faithful writer of approved authority that hath openly described this art: which thing has induced many to believe that all books of this art were but of late years invented, etc. Finally of the one blessed stone alone, besides which there is no other thing, the subject of the most holy stone of the philosophers, to speak rashly, would be a sacrilege and I should be foresworn"[69]. Looking to the final chapters of the same work also, we observe the ground of the whole Hermetic philosophy laid out, and the relative vanity of worldly science to that, which is universal, rational, and divine. The capabilities of the subject are great; and had it been treated in the usual and masterly style of a scholar of Nettesheim, it would have remained a work of lasting value; but he was fettered by oaths and had been somewhat conscience stricken; and the monks, whom he had formerly censured, eagerly promulgated the whole as a recantation of former errors, holding it in this light and as an acknowledgment of the sufficiency of their own doctrine and of the common faith for salvation.

In the beginning of his extraordinary career, Theophrastus Paracelsus proposed openly to discover the hidden secret of philosophy; but the world scoffed at his pretensions, abused and persecuted him; and all the revenge he indulged in was to leave it unenlightened. The writings he put forth are, with few exceptions, filled with subtle malice, as it were, so many sarcasms upon mankind and leading them far away, through alluring sophisms, from the straight way of truth. Surely, as Ashmole remarks, incredulity appears to have been given to the world as a punishment; yet neither in its belief did it speed better, but has still plodded on in error for want of thought, and through all ages men have suffered in ignorance, on account mainly of the indefiniteness and selfishness of their desires. Of the numerous books attributed to Paracelsus, and given together as his works, the three *Addresses to the Athenians*, and the *Aurora*, are amongst the best. Those to the Athenians have been translated into English, and published with *The Philosophy* of J. Crollius, a disciple, and the *Aurora* also is to be met with, though more rarely, in company with the *Water Stone of the Wise Men*, by J. Grasseus. With respect to the private history and character of this extraordinary man, accounts differ, and opinions accordingly; but his fame, and the authority of his doctrine, lasted down through a long period of time. His early death has been adduced as an argument against the probability of his being possessed of the elixir he boasts; and by others as a proof of his having been poisoned: but the poison of intemperance and irregular living has also been considered as especially likely to be fatal to one who was in the habit of taking a potent spiritual medicine, which would heighten the spiritual consequences of depravity and habitual excess, and accelerate dissolution in the conflict of opposite principles[70]. Paracelsus, notwithstanding the world's neglect, had numerous disciples, increasing also after his decease: some intelligent and worthy the name of philosophers, as Van Helmont, Crollius, Fludd, Helvetius, Faber, and many more anonymous, but there were others, mountebank pretenders, more in number still, who, pursuing the baser line of their master's example, whilst they enviously suppressed the little truth they knew, wrote and practiced for lucre, leading mankind into error and the commitment even of egregious crimes by their receipts. And the world which would not be drawn by the true light, gave easy way to their false stimulants, and encouraged the enemies growth in literature, until the tares possessed the field; nor could it be well otherwise, as a modern adept has observed on the occasion, for this bushel being placed over the light, the darkness of it invited ignorance abroad.

The burlesque of Erasmus, which, towards the close of the 16th century, were turned upon the follies then continually going on amongst the credulous chemists and their dupes, show that it was the prevailing mania of the age; when rich men and potentates fell easily into the snares of the lowest vagabonds, who had acquired the tact only to write and talk mysteriously. Chaucer, in the tale of the *Chanon's Yeoman*, gives an example of this kind of the boastings, bereavements, and surpassing beliefs of ignorance; as Ripley also, in his *Erroneous Experiments*, tells how he

> "Made solucyons full many a one,
> Of spyrytts, ferments, salts, yerne and steele;
> Wenying so tomake the philosophers; stone;
> But finally I lost eche dele,
> After my bokes yet wrought I well;
> Which evermore untrew I provyd,
> That made me oft full sore agrevyd.
>
> Waters corrosive and water ardent,
> With which I wrought in divers wyse,
> Many one I made but all was shent;
> Egg shells I calcenyd twyse or thryse,
> Oylys fro calcys I made up ryse;
> And every element fro other I did twye
> But profytt found I right none therein.
>
> Also I wrought in sulphur and in vitriall,
> Which folys doe call the Grene Lyon,
> In arsenicke, in orpemint, fowle mot them fall;
> In delibi principio was myne inception:
> Therefore was frawde in fine the conclusion:
> And I blew my thrift at the cole,
> My clothes were bawdy, my stomache was never hole.

I proved uryns, eggs, here, and blod,
The scalys of yern which smthys do off smyte.
Oes, ust, and crokefer which dyd me never good:
The sowle of Saturn and also marchisyte,
Lythage and antimony not worth a mite:
Of which gey tinctures I made to shew,
Both red and white which were untrew.

Oyle of Lune and water with labor great,
I made calcynyng yt with salt precipitate,
And by hytself with vyolent heatt
Grindyng with vinegar tyll I was fatygate:
And also with a quantitye if syces acuate;
Upon a marble which stode me oft in cost
And oyles with corrosives I made; but all was lost.

Thus I rostyd and boyled as one of Geber's cooks,
And oft times I was dysceivyd with many falce books
Whereby untrue, thus truly I wrought:
But all such experiments avaylyd me nought;
But brought me in danger and cumbraunce,
By loss of goods and other grievaunce", &c[71].

The tide so long encroaching, however, began at last to fluctuate; and as mistrust, gathering from disappointment, ripened, a change somewhat suddenly took place in the public mind, and turned finally into an absolute odium of the deluding alchemists and the art. Then it was that several were obliged to retire into exile; and even the true adepts—for the public knew not to distinguish—suffered equal cruelty and abundant inconvenience. They who before had been courted and lauded in hopes of obtaining gold, or the means of making it, were arrested and tortured, in order to extort confession; accordingly we find mixed up with their philosophy, bitter complaints of injury, thefts, murders, and unjust imprisonments. Alexander Seton was hunted through Europe in disguise, not daring to remain in any town, for fear of detection.—"I am suffering", says this author, in his *Open Entrance*, "a continual banishment: deprived of the society of friends and family, and, as if driven by the Furies, am compelled constantly to fly from place to place and from kingdom to kingdom, without delaying anywhere. And thus, though I possess all things, I have no rest or enjoyment of any, except in the truth, which is my whole satisfaction. They who have not a knowledge of this art imagine, if they had, they would do many things: I also thought the same, but am grown circumspect by experience of many dangers and the peril of life. I have seen so much corruption in the world, and those even who pass for good people are so ruled by the love of gain, that I am constrained even from the works of mercy, for fear of suspicion and arrest. I have experienced this in foreign countries, where, having ventured to administer the medicine to sufferers given over by physicians, the instant the cures became known, a report was spread about of the Elixir, and I have been obliged to disguise myself, shave my head, and change my name, to avoid falling into the hands of wicked persons, who would try to wrest the secret from me, in hopes of making gold. I could relate many incidents of this kind which have happened to me. Would to God that gold and silver were as common as the street mud; we should not then be obliged to fly and hide ourselves, as if we were accursed like Cain"[72]. Michael Sendivogius was imprisoned by his prince; even the pious Kuhnrath is moved to bitterness, when speaking of the treatment he had experienced: George Von Welling, Fichtuld, Muller, Harprecht, also; for the good and innocent now suffered more and more than ever cautious to conceal their names, with the evidence of Alchemy, from the world. And as the mind of the day became gradually engaged in puritanical discussions, and the interests of political leaders, indifference to the art again succeeded, and a skepticism, as blind and nearly pernicious as the former credulity settled upon the minds of men. But philosophers were content to have it so; observing the incapability of the common herd, and how little they cared for the truth, or the witness of nature's greatest miracles, in comparison with their own selfish emolument. Some gathered themselves together for better protection, and carrying on their work into the Rosicrucian Fraternity, a widely celebrated, though secret association, established, as the report is, by a German adeptest who had traveled into the East, and in Arabia was initiated into many arcane mysteries of nature. Their *Fame and Confession*, with the story of their first institution, has been rendered into English with an excellent preface by Thomas Vaughan, and an appendix showing the true nature of their philosophy, place of abode, and other particulars connected with their magian prowess and renown.

But we must not omit to notice the names of Dee and Kelly, two notorious magicians of Queen Elizabeth's time; for though the latte was somewhat of a knave, and a little over-presumptuous, yet there is reason to believe that he practiced transmutation, and became possessed of the Red Powder by some secret kind of information, if not of the means of perfecting it by his own art. Thus it was generally reported of Dr Dee and Kelly, that they were so strangely fortunate as to discover a large quantity of the Powder of Projection in a niche amongst the ruins of Glastonbury Abbey, and which was so rich in virtue (being 1 upon 272,330) that they lost a great portion in trial before they found out the true height of the medicine. With this treasure they went abroad, fixed their abode at Trebona, and transmuted occasionally. In Dee's diary we have the account of Kelly making projection with one small grain (in proportion no larger than the least grain of sand) upon an ounce and a quarter of common mercury, which produced almost an ounce of pure gold[73]. Then there is the story of the warming-pan, related by Ashmole, from no very distant testimony, of a piece of metal being cut out and, without Kelly touching or handling it, or melting the copper even, only warming it in the fire, the elixir being projected thereon, it was transmuted into pure silver. The pan, he goes on to relate, was sent to the Queen Elizabeth by her ambassador, who then lay at Prague; that by fitting the piece into the place whence it was cut out, it might exactly prove to be once a part of that pan. Bloomfield had likewise seen in the hands of one Master Tyre and Scroope, rings of Sir Edward Kelly's gold, the fashion of which was only gold wire twisted thrice about the finger; of which fashioned rings he gave away to the value of 4000 l. at the marriage of one of his servants. This was highly generous; but to say the truth, he was openly profuse beyond the modest limits, as Ashmole observes, of a sober philosopher. This kind of profusion has been frequently exhibited by such as are reported to have come by the treasure casually, never by those who have themselves confected it.

During the abode at Trebona, Dee and Kelly appear to have tried many experiments, and their conversations with their spiritual informants are ludicrously mundane and abortive[74]. Whether or not they finally succeeded in the object of their research remains uncertain; the story runs that they did not, but that the secret of making of the Powder was confided to Kelly some years afterwards by a dying monk. In Dee's *Diary*, towards the latter end, there certainly are expressions of joy and gratitutde, as if he had suddenly attained to some great and important discovery;—*Haec est dies quam fecit Dominus, omne quod vivit laudet Dominum*; and upon the thirtieth day of the month following, he writes,—Master E. Kelly did open the great secret to me, God be thanked.

Things were not carried on so privately abroad, but the Queen had notice of the proceedings of her subjects; and she sent letters and messages summoning them to return home: Dee obeyed, but Kelly remained behind, was taken prisoner by Emperor Rudolph, who had long set a watch on their movements. It was during this detention that he wrote that little book, *De Lapide Philosophorum*, which is commonly to be met with, but it is of little more value than repute. The death of Kelly is involved in mystery, and Dee is said to have expired in poverty in Mortlake.

The writings of Jacob Böhme, the profound theosophist of Prague, and those of the Pordage and Lead school. May not be undervalued, since these enthusiasts were all on the same original track; and the first would seem to have attained something better even than a view of the Promised Land. Moreover, Böhme has discovered such a ground of experience and principles of the Divine Art in his writings, as may help the student to conceive profoundly and lead him to the means of understanding the enigmas of the old adepts. For this author is, of all who have hitherto entered experimentally into the mystery, the plainest, simplest, and most confidential exponent. The *Aurora,* or *Day Spring*; *The Discourse of the Three Principles*; *The Mysterium Magnum*; *The Tree of Life*; *The Turned Eye,* or *Forty Questions Concerning the Life of Man*, and his *Epistles*, are full of explicit indications concerning the physical basis of magic and occult material of the philosophers' stone[75]. So that the following eulogy, copied from a manuscript found in a volume of his works, may not be considered misplaced, or altogether extravagant:—

> "Whateer the Eastern Magi sought,
> Or Orpheus sung, or Hermes taught,
> Whatever Confucius would inspire,
> Or Zoroaster's mystic fire;
> The symbols that Pythagoras drew,
> The wisdom godlike Plato knew,
> What Socrates debating proved,
> Or Epictetus lived and loved;
> The sacred fire of saint and sage,
> Thro' every clime in every age,
> In Böhme's wondrous page we view,

Mary Anne Atwood

Discoverd and revealed anew", etc.

Revealed anew, it will be observed, theosophically, but not intellectually. Nothing, since the Greeks, has been found to approach their doctrine of Wisdom in perspicuity, grace of utterance, and scientific explication of the divine source. Of all the successors on the same road, none have exceeded their authority, and very few have attained to the perfect veracity and ideality of their ground; but of this hereafter. Numerous works on Alchemy have issued from the German press, detailing the experience of excellent and learned adepts; amongst those of later years may be mentioned Ambrose and Phillip Mueller[76]; Herman Fichtuld[77]; and his friend George Von Welling[78]; J. Crollius[79]; the Van Helmonts, father and son[80]; Grasseus, the reputed author of the *Water Stone*[81], a personal friend of Böhme's; Henry Kuhnrath, a pious and learned adeptest[82]; Andrew Libavius[83]; J.J. Beccher[84]; and J. Tollius, a Dutchman and an elegant classical expositor on the same ground[85]. Faber also[86]; but of all those who have connected ancient fable with philosophy, and explained them by the Hermetic key, Michael Mayer ranks first; and his works are more esteemed and sought after even in the present day, than is easily accountable, since he is profoundly guarded in his revelations[87]. Highly curious engravings and woodcuts adorn the works of these authors, and even the title pages of many of them convey more idea and food for reflection than other modern tomes, oftentimes throughout the whole of their development.

The *Novum Lumen Chemicum*, which passes under the name of Michael Sendivogius, the Polish adept, is one of the best known and popular of modern works on the subject. It has been translated into English by John French, also a practitioner[88]; whose introductory preface is bold and striking, and was published in London under the title of *The New Light of Alchemy*, with the nine books of Paracelsus, *De Natura Rerum*, in 1650. This New Light, professedly drawn from the fountain of nature, and grounded in manual experience, is cleverly handled, and of an attractive character; though in consequence of the willful disorder and perplexity of the composition, repeated perusal and a certain knowledge are requisite, in order to gather its recondite drift; and so much the more, as its theory and asserted facts are at variance with our common conceptions and experience of the possibility of nature. The French edition of this work, also, has been translated by Digby, and contains, besides the *Treatise on Salt* omitted in the above, other curious additions, with a concluding Dialogue, which is instructive[89].

There is a multitude of little English books on alchemy afloat on the book-stalls; amongst them some original, well-written, and worthy of perusal; for although Britain has not been so fertile in adepts as France and Germany, yet her scarce ones have been great; the profundity and comparative candor of their writings, being very generally acknowledged by their foreign compeers to which Dufresnoy, though himself a skeptic, in his *Histoire Hermétique* bears this characteristic witness:—"*D'ailleurs on ne sauroit disconvenir que les Anglois n'écrivent sur la science hermétique avec beaucoup de lumière et de profondeur. Ils y font paroitre leur jugement et leur esprit de relexion. Il seroit à souhaiter qu'ils portassent la même attention et la même maturité à tout ce qu'ils entreprennent, on seroit beaucoup plus content d'eux et ils ne s'exposerait pas à perdre l'estime des autres nations comme ils s'y risquent tous les jours*"[90].

This piece of flattering French testimony refers, we suppose, to the writings of our early adepts; otherwise, of all that have flourished in latter times, the most celebrated and *facile princeps*, is that Anonymous who styles himself Eireneus Philalethes: the many works that have appeared under this signature indicate so excellent and perfect an artist, that his brethren, always speaking with admiration, unanimously award him the garland. Yet of himself, his name, and habits of life nothing is known; no cotemporary mentions him; Starky, indeed, professes to have been his servant once for a time in America, and to have assisted him in the art; and describes him as an English gentleman of an ancient and honorable family then living on his own estate and rarely learned.—"I saw", says he, "in my master's possession the White and Red elixir in very large quantity; he gave me upwards of two ounces of the White medicine of sufficient virtue to convert 120,000 times its weight into the purest silver: with this treasure I went to work ignorantly and was caught in the trap of my own covetousness, for I expended or wasted nearly all of this tincture, and did not know its value until it was nearly gone. However, I made projection of a part, and have tinged many hundreds of ounces by it into the best silver: of a pound of mercury I have made within less than a scruple of a pound of silver", etc[91]. It is also reported that Eiraneus was intimate with the chemist Boyle; but the rumors are all uncertain, and, as if to increase the mystery, he has been confounded with other English adepts, as Harprecht and Thomas Vaughan, and his writings also with those of Sendivogius, who has been identified with him under the name of Alexander Seton and others. He himself informs us that he was born in England, somewhere towards the beginning of the 17th century, that he possessed the secret at a very early age, and was the victim of unremitting persecution. His principal works are, *An Open Entrance to the Shut Palace of the King, Ripley Revived, The Marrow of Alchemy,* in verse; *Metallorum Metamorphoses, Brevis Manuductio as Rubinum Coelestum, Fons Chemicae Veritatis,* and a few others in the *Museum Hermeticum* and in Manget's collection.

Thomas Vaughan, whose pseudonyme of Eugenius Philalethes has, notwithstanding the very obvious distinction of his mind and style, caused him to be confounded with the foregoing Eireneus, was the author of several luminous little treatises, bearing on the higher grounds of this mystic science, full of ideas and the recondite spirit of antiquity. In these Vaughan makes casual reference to the gold-making possibility, but is at little pains to attract in this direction, or indicate, as is usual, any sophistic order of practical operation; and thus repelling impertinent inquiry, he leads at once to the true and only valuable speculation of the subject. Moreover, unless we be mistaken, the one Art and medium of vital perfectibility is more clearly shown in his writings than in those of any other English author.

They are as follows: *Magia Adamica,* or *the Antiquity of Magic*; whereto is added, *A Discovery of the Coelum Terrae,* or *Magician's Heavenly Chaos*; *Anthroposophia Theomagica,* a discourse on the nature of man grounded on the protochemistry of Hermes, and verified by a practical examination of principles; *Anima Magia Abscondita,* a discourse of the universal spirit of nature, with its strange, abstruse, and miraculous ascent and descent; *Euphrates,* or Waters of the East, a practical discourse of that secret fountain whose water flows from fire; *Lumen de Lumine,* a new magical light discovered and consummated, with an allegorical display of the first matter, and other valuable magnetical introductions and guides. This author's death is reported to have befallen extraordinarily, something after the manner of Virgil's, and from an overdose of the elixir; nor should it appear wonderful, as the narrative runs, that the subtle light of life should in these instances have been swallowed up in the superior attraction of a greater flame. Agrippa gives a similar account of the death of Alexander the Great, saying that he died suddenly by the hand of his preceptor, *administering the venom of the waters of the Styx,* to whom the youthful monarch had previously intrusted his life, body and soul without reservation[92].

The Authors we have brought forth as distinguished and genuine, are but few in comparison with the whole number; some reckon as many as four thousand[93]; but there are enough without forcing any into the ranks. Borricius, from standing testimony, counts as many as two thousand five hundreds[94]. L'Englet Dufresnoy has reduced the number still more, but then he was ignorant of the subject and excludes according to titles, rather that the matter, of several books covertly treating of the Hermetic art[95]. The Bodlerian library contains many hundred volumes by separate authors. The Royal Library of France was reputed still richer in 1742, especially in manuscripts; and the Vatican and Escurial have large and valuable collections in the same branch.

And it is in these archives alone that the ancient Art is now preserved, in which we hoard the memory of long bygone hopes. To declare a man an Alchemist in the present day would be to brand him as insane, and the Hermetic ground is as far out of the road of common thought as if it were tabooed; not indeed that anyone regards it as sacred, but devilish rather, or delirious, or ridiculous, as the bias may be. Meanwhile, therefore, to reconcile this science or the teachers of it to the world, we should feel to be a task above our ability, were it very far greater than it is; the prejudice having grown so old and strong that neither reason nor authority is longer able to balance it. But in whatever light we be disposed to regard Alchemy, whether as the acme of human folly, or contrariwise, as the recondite perfection of wisdom and causal science, it appears almost equally remarkable: considered in the former way we have before us a huge amount of avarice, mad credulity, and fraud accumulating on continually from immemorial time, with the deplorable conclusion, that the greater part of those to whom the world has been taught to look up as philosophical authorities were in fact dupes and worse deceivers; on the other hand, if we hesitate in thus denouncing all the many well-approved and religious professors of this art, and suppose them, even in this particular, to have been sincere, what then ought we to conclude? That they were deluded? It is true their assertions are startling, but then the means of realization proposed are actual; the transmutation of metallic bodies was a proof addressed to the senses and so uniformly stated as to preclude subterfuge or any medium fulfillment.—"I have seen the Stone and handled it", says Van Helmont, "and projected the fourth part of one grain, wrapped in paper, upon eight ounces of quicksilver boiling in a crucible, and the quicksilver, with a small voice, presently stood in its flux, and was congealed like to yellow wax; after a flux by blast we found eight ounces all but eleven grains which were wanting of the purest gold;

therefore one grain of this powder would transmute 19,186 parts of quicksilver into the best gold. I am constrained to believe, for I have made projections divers times of one grain of the philosophers' gold upon some thousands of grains of boiling quicksilver, to the admiration and tickling of a great multitude. He who gave me that powder" (the stranger Butler, whom he first found in prison) "had so much as would transmute two hundred thousand pounds' worth of gold"[96]. "Our tincture of gold", says Paracelsus, "has within it an astral fire which conquers all things and changes them into a nature like itself; it is a most fixed substance and immutable in the multiplication; it is a powder having the reddest color, almost like saffron, yet the whole corporeal substance is liquid like resin, transparent like crystal, frangible like glass. It is of a ruby color of the greatest weight; and this is a true sign of the tincture of the philosophers, that by its transmuting force all imperfect metals are changed, and this gold is better than the gold of the mines; and out of it may be prepared better medicines and arcane"[97]. So likewise Friar Bacon says, and Lully, and Arnold in his *Speculum*, that he had seen and touched, after much labor and industry, the perfect thing transmuting[98]. And Geber in these words—"The things are manifest in which the verity of the work is nigh, and we have considered the things perfecting this work is nigh, and we have considered the things perfecting this work by a true investigation, with certain experience, whereby we are assured that all the words are true which are by us written in our volumes, according as we found them by experiment and reason"[99]. And again,—"By the goodness of God's instigation and by our own incessant labor, we have searched out and found, and have seen with our eyes and handled with our hands the completement of matters sought after in our magistery"[100]. And Pico di Mirandola, in his book *De Auro:*—"I come now", says the prince, "to relate what my eyes have seen plainly without veil or obscurity; one of my friends, who is now living, has made gold and silver several times in my presence, and I have seen it and done it myself"[101].

We do not adduce these testimonials in proof either of the truth or plausibility of the Hermetic art; but to lead on inquiry, without which it would be equally vain to believe as to deny; and further, to show the pretension was not ambiguous, but absolutely provable, if at all, we have the story of the transmutation before Gustavus Adolphus in the year 1620, the gold of which was coined into medals bearing the king's effigy with the reverse, Mercury and Venus; and that other at Berlin, before the king of Prussia, widely celebrated in 1710[102]. The story related by Kircher in his *Mundus Subterraneus* also is explicit, and that of Helvetius; but the foregoing, taken casually, may be sufficient to indicate that the evidence of Alchemy was neither abstract nor hidden, nor

> "*vaguely opinable,*
> *But clean, experimental and determinable* »:—

And that if there was deception at all, it must have been willful and not the offspring of self-delusion on the part of the adepts. And then what should induce men to invent, age after age, and to reiterate and confirm a shameful and unpopular falsehood?—Pious hermits and ecclesiastics, physicians and metaphysicians, men of high rank and reputation, far above and out of the way of sordid allurements, most of whom had in fact relinquished station, power, wealth, and worldly benefices for the science, sake and the cause of true religion? What interest should have moved them, even supposing minds so degraded as to deceive so far and frequently their fellow men? Or shall we conclude that Ripley wither was so mad and simple a knave as to write the offer to his king to show him the actual working of the Stone, if he had possessed nothing? But he even promises to unfold the whole confection conditionally. Would he so far have ventured, or what motive had he to deceive?

> "*Never trewly for merke nor for pounde*
> *Make yt I common; but to you conditionedly*
> *That to yourself ye shall keep yt secretly;*
> *And only yt use, as may be God's pleasure,*
> *Els in tyme comynge of God I shoulde abye*
> *For my discoveringe of hys secret treasurye*"[103].

And if the notion of willful deceit is improbable, then, their problem being one of tangible facts, it is still less likely that they were themselves deceived.—"I write not fables", says H. Kuhnrath in his *Ampitheater*; "with thine own hands thou shalt handle and with thine own eyes thou shalt see Azoth, viz., the Universal Mercury, which alone with its internal and external fire is sufficient for thee; which transforms itself into what it will by the fire". And again,—"I have traveled much and visited those esteemed to know what by experience and not in vain, amongst whom, I call God to witness, I got of one the universal tincture, and the blood of the Lion, which is the gold of the philosophers. I have seen it, touched it, tasted it, smelt it, and used it efficaciously towards my poor neighbors in most desperate cases. Oh, how wonderful is God in his works!"[104].

The liberal mind naturally experiences a difficulty in disbelieving where, a possibility being granted, the testimony in support of a matter is fair and honorable. And though sensible evidence and more than this sometimes is required to silence negative assertion; yet reason, supported by her witnesses, may enervate it, and induce that strict investigation and thought which should always precede experiment, but which the multitude have never yet been found willing to undertake; and are consequently led astray in progress, and learn as it were by chance. It is said that Lord bacon instituted certain experiments with a view to the discovery of the philosophers' stone, and in the *Advancement of Learning* he faithfully recognizes the possibility, as does also Sir Isaac Newton in his works: nor did either of these great men, though they were practically unsuccessful themselves, condemn the ancient tradition or deny its validity. Yet it would seem to be more ordinarily natural to the human mind to reject these things, which it has neither been early imbued in the belief of, nor instructed to understand; besides individual research into mere possibilities, and because facts only are alleged, is too hopeless and arduous for this short life, which requires a definite assurance of success, and fruit even from the smallest labor. And this is the world's palliation for despising Alchemy, and many things which the ancients have asserted in like manner, without the requisite means of realization. For they would not, not have they anywhere openly declared, even the common Subject of their Art; but left mankind to imagine, as they did, all that was erroneous concerning it, as of their salts, sulfurs, mercuries, magic elements, and occult confections. What a chaos of metaphor and monstrous allusion does not the literature of Alchemy present at first view! With what fantastic images and inconclusive positions is it not replete—sings, symbolisms, and subtle enigmas innumerable, as if to try the ingenuity at every point? Contrary to the usual endeavor of writers to enlighten, by rendering their ideas intelligible, the adepts appear to have a directly contrary aim, at least so it would occur to anyone from a cursory survey; now leading along by some ingenious allegory, full of deep and exciting suggestions, yet withal enveloped in a mystery so obscure that without more light it were impossible to penetrate it; then, further to seduce, adding, it may be, another gleam of argument, tantalizing the hope and wearying the understanding with unequal assertions, until all passes away again, with all possibility of discernment, behind some clouded metaphor or word of warning that the secret of the ages may not be profaned. A variety of artifices according to the cabalistic method, moreover, have been employed, and the Hermetic discourses are not infrequently found introverted in their order, and dispersed with repetitions, to prevent the truth from becoming openly obvious, even to those who had already become possessed of the true key; but only of the vestibule and entrance rights;

> *"If you consider how the partes of the werkes*
> *Be out of order set by the old clerkes,*
> *As I said before, the master of this arte,*
> *Every and each of them disclosed but a parte;*
> *Wherefore tho' ye perceived themas ye woulde,*
> *Yet ye cannot order or joine them as ye shoulde"*[105].

"For is not our art cabalistic", asks Artefius, "and full of mysteries? And you, fool, believe we teach the secret of secrets openly, and understand our words according to the letter; be assured, we are not envious, but he that takes the philosophers' saying according to the outward sense and signification has already lost the clue to Ariadne, and wanders up and down the labyrinth, and it would be of the same benefit to him as if he had thrown his money into the sea"[106]. And Sendivogius, to the same effect in the Preface of the *Twelve Treatises*,—"I would", says he, "have the candid reader be admonished that he understand my writings, not so much from the outside of my words as from the possibility of nature; let him consider that this Art is for the wise, not for the ignorant; and that the sense of the philosophers is of another nature than to be understood by vaporizing Thrasoes, or the letter learned scoffers, or vicious, against their own consciences; or ignorant montebanks, who, most unworthily defaming the most commendable art of Alchemy, have with their Whites and Reds deceived almost the whole world"[107]. And agin, in the Epilogue, —"All things indeed", says the adept, "might have been comprehended in a few lines; but we are willing to guide into the knowledge of nature indirectly, by reasons and examples: that thou may knowest what the thing truly is thou shouldst seek after, also that thou might have nature, her light and shadow, discovered to thee. Be not displeased if thou meetest sometimes with contradictions in my treatises, it being the custom of philosophers to use them; thou hast need of them: if thou understandest them, thou shalt not find a rose without prickles"[108].

"Each artist striving yt how to conceal
Lest wretched caitiffs shulde the treasure steal.
Nor villains shulde their vyllanyes maintain
By this rare art; which danger they to heal
In horrid metaphors veiled are an art most plain,
Lest each fool knowing yt shulde yt when known disdayne"[109].

And Roger Bacon advises, therefore, to leave off experiments until the ground of wisdom is properly conceived.—"And though I say, take this, and this, believe me not but operate according to the blood; *i.e.*, according to the understanding, and so of all; leave off experiments, apprehend my meaning, and you will find, believe me, being a lighted candle"[110]. And Basil Valentine and Eiraneus, and most adepts in short, warn their readers against running into the practice upon vague premises, and before they have attained to a full understanding of the matter to be taken in hand; yet, notwithstanding all their injunctions, many seekers, and faithful ones too, have been led astray: Geber's receipts and Basil's, though at variance with all common-sense probability, have been the means of surrounding many a literal soul with stills, coals, and furnaces, in hope by such lifeless instruments to sublime the Spirit of Nature; or by salt, sulfur and mercury, or the three combined with antimony, to extract the Form of gold. But they who have thus fallen to practice, without the true Light or heeding their injunctions, had no right to charge their error on the adepts, the disappointment and misery of those fanatical chemists having been attributable to their own misunderstanding bias, and more frequently owing to the deceit of sophists than to the genuine tradition of Hermetic science.

Since difficulties however are apparent, and the pretenders to the Art were in latter times far more numerous than the true adepts, and the literature has suffered in consequence grievous disgrace and spoliation, it is not surprising that the public, having been so long and grossly deluded, should at length have shut out Alchemy from amongst its credenda. If there was no desire to search deeper, it was wisely done, and checked the raging of a sore distemper. But that many have fallen into error and suffered, or others proved deceivers, or that the world has chosen to disbelieve, are no proofs in philosophy, even if it were without so many witnesses, that the Hermetic mystery is groundless. The world is fully as ignorant of the genuine doctrine and Art of Wisdom as were the imposters whom it repudiated, and their judgment concerning it is of as little value. The words of the philosophers remain, though modern science is not able to confirm them, or present anything analogous to the powers they professed, not in the advancement of the mineral kingdom only, but over all nature. And since they unanimously recommend a studious examination, in order to conceive rightly of the promises held out, before attempting to judge them or the pretensions of their Art, we propose to investigate preliminarily the theoretic ground and matter on which the physical possibility of transmutation rests.

---

1. De Hermetica Aegyptior, vetere et Paracelsior. Nova Medicina.
2. Oedipus Aegyptiacus. Idem, de Lapide Philos. Dissert.
3. De Ortu et Progressu Chemiae. Idem. AEgyptior et Chemicor. Sapentia, ab H Conringü Animad. Vindic.
4. De Veritate et Antiquitate Artis Chemiae.
5. See Plutarch de Iside et Osiride, and Bryant's Analysis of Ancient Mythology, vol ii.
6. See Suidas de Verbo Chemiae, Credo Mercurio Trismegistum, sapientem AEgyptium, floruisse ante Pharanoem, etc.
7. See Terullianus de Anima, cap ii, adverts Valentinanus cap xv. Hermetem vocat Physicorum Magistrum.
8. See Jamblichus de Mysteriis, sect viii, cap. iv, etc.
9. Hermetis Trismegisti Tractatus Aureus de Lapidis physici secreto.
10. From the Asclepian Dialogue of Hermes, by Ficinus, as rendered by T. Taylor.
11. See Taylor's notes to the Prophecy, in Plotinus' Select Works, at the end, p. 57, etc.
12. De Ostane Magno, vide Plinium, Hostor. Nat. lib. xxx, cap. I.
13. Democriti Abderitae de Arte Sacra, sive de rebus naturalibus et mysticis libellus, ex venerandae Graecae vetustatis de Arte Chimica reliquiis erutus.
14. Synesius in Democritum Abderitam de Arte Sacra.
15. Flamelli Summario Philosophico.
16. Hist. Nat. lib . xxx, cap. I.
17. Epistola, xci.
18. Petronius Arbiter in Satyrico.
19. Syncellus, Chronographia, p. 248
20. See Norton's Ordinal in Ashmole's Theatrum Chemicaum Britannicum.
21. See lib. Iii, cap. 15... See also Aristotleis de Lapide ad Alexandrum Magnum; Theat. Chem., vol.
22. Epistle II. Platos' Works, by Taylor, vol. v.
23. Suidas in Verbo Chemeia.
24. Cleopatra Regini Egypti Ars auri faciendi, etc., in the catalogue of the Royal Library at Paris, 1742. See Dufresnoy, Hist. Herm., vol. iii.
25. Invitaverat spec Caium Caligulam Principem avidissumum auri; quam ob rem jussit ex coqui auri pigmenti pondus ; et plane fecit aurum excellens, sed ita parvi ponderis ut detrimentum sentiret, etc. (Hist. Nat., lib. xxxiii, cap. iv).
26. See Theat. Chem., vol 1 p.24 ; Ex petri Apiani Antq. Desumpta; also, Taylor's notes to his Pausanias, vol iii.
27. Ampitheatrum Sapientae Eternae, circa medium.
28. Theat. Chem., vol. v, p. 744. Kircheri Oedipus Aegyptiacus, vol. i.
29. The Critic, new series, No. 13, 1845, p. 352.
30. Symbola Auriae Mensae, p. 170, etc.

31. Commentariolum in Enigmaticum quoddam Epitaphium Bononiae studiorum, ante multa secula marmoreo lapidi insculptum. Theat, Chem., vol v.
32. See Alexander Beauvais in Speculo Naturalis.
33. Heliodurus Phil. Christ. De Arte Sacra Chimicor ad Theod. Idem versus Graec circa Chimiam... See Dufresnoy, Hist. De l'Art Hermétique, vol. iii, Cat. Gr. Mss.
34. Synesius, Epistola 36, 142.
35. Troics, Traités de la Philosophie, etc. (Paris 1612), The Triumphal Chariot of Antimony, from Kirchringius'ed, and The True Book of Synesius, on the Philosophers' Stone.
36. Gebri Arabum Summa Perfectionis Magisterii in sua Naturâ, Idem de Investigatione Perfectionis Metallorum. Idem Testamentum.
37. Morienus Eremita Hierosol. De Transfiguratione Metallorum seu Dialogus Morieni cum Calide rege, de Lapide Philos.
38. See That. Chem. Vol v. ; Salmon's Pratical Physics ; and La Bibliothèque des Philosophes Chimiques.
39. The following have been attributed to him:—Avicenna de Tinctura Metallorum, Idem, Porta Elementa. Idem, de Mineralibus— printed with the Dantzic edition of Geber and a few others.
40. See Theophrastus Paracelsus in Libro de Vita longa, Pontanus, Epistola, etc. R, Bacon in Libro de Mirab. Natur. Operib.
41. Artefii Antiquissimi Philosophi de Arte Occulta atque Lapide Philosophorum Liber secretus.
42. See Speculum Alchimiae Rogerii Bachonis, Theat. Chem., vol. ii. De Mirabilibus Potestatibus Artis et Naturae, etc.
43. See Speculum Alchimiae, in fine. Fr. Bachonis Anglici libellus cum influenctiis Coeli, relates to the same mystical subject.
44. Lib. iii de Mineralibus, cap. i.
45. Tom. 21 in fol. Lugduni, 1653, and in Theat. Chem., vol. ii.
46. Norton's Ordinal of Alchemy, Preface, in Ashmole's Theat. Chem. Brit.
47. See Chronicon Magnum Belgicum.
48. Tractatus D. Thomae Aquino datus fratri D. Reinaldo de Arte Alchimiae.
49. Meteorum Initio, lib. iv; and again, Praecipuus Alchimistarum scopus est transmutare metalla scilicet imperfecta secundum veritatem et non sophistice.
50. Thesaurus Alchimiae, cap. 1 and 8. Tractatus datus Fratri Reinaldo. This with the Secreta Alchimiae and another are given in the Theatrum Chemicum, and other collections of the Art.
51. Nostris diebus habuimus magnum... (J. Andraeas in addit. ad Speculum Rub de crim. Falsi.)... Haec ille Andaeas... (R. Vallensis de Veritate, etc., in Theat. Chem., vol. 1). Alchimia est ars perspicaci... (D. Fabianus de Monte, S. Severin in Tractatu de Emptione et Venditione, Quest 5. Oldranus, lib. Concilio, Quest 74.)
52. Alani Philosophi, Dicta de Lapide.
53. Prophetia Anglicana Merlini, una cum Septem Libris Explicationum in eandem Prophetiam etc., Alani de Insulis, Francf. 1608.
54. Ultimum Testamentum R. Lullii.
55. Cremeri Testamentum.
56. Aureas illas nobiles Anglorum primum profectas memorat (ex Raymundi) Camdemus. Idem hodieque asseverantissime confirmant Anglorum curiosi... See Olaus Borrichius de Ortu et Progressu Chemiae, 4 to., p. 242; and E. Dickenson, de Quintessentia.
57. Histoire Hermétique, vol iii. His Theoriea et Practica, given in the third volume of the Theat. Chem., appears to us one of the very best pieces of Alchemical philosophy extant.
58. Norton's Ordinall in Ashmole's Theat. Chem. Brit. p.7.
59. Norton's Ordinall, cap. i.
60. See Dufresnoy, Hist. Herm. vol. ii, p. 11, etc.

61. See Histoire Hermétique, vol. i. p. 206 ; lives of the Adepts, p. 38; Les Hiéroglyphiques de N. Flammel.
62. Joan Issac Hollandus de Lapide Philosophico, Francf. 1669. Issac Hollandus Opera Universalia, sive de Lapide Philm, etc.
63. Norton's Ordinall, chap. v.
64. Chimische Schriften, Fr. Basilii Valentinii, in 12 mo., 1717.
65. Ashmole's Theatrum Chemicum Britanicum, London 1652.
66. Ripley Revived being an Exposition of Sir George Ripley's Gates and his Epistle to King Edward, by Eireneus Philalethes, London 1678.
67. Marsilii Ficini Florent. Liber de Arte Chemica.
68. J.F. Picus, de Auro in Theat. Chem., vol ii ; also J.F.P. Mirandolae Domini, Concordieque, Opus Aureum de Auro. Idem, Libri tres de Auro tum conficiendo, etc.
69. See De Vanitate Scientiarum, Alch., etc.
70. See Lives of the Alchemists, p. 52.
71. An Admonition of Erroneous Experiments, Theat. Chem. Brit., p. 189.
72. See Introitus Apertus ad Occlusum Regum Palatio, cap. xiii.
73. Dee's Diary, Spet. 1586.
74. See : A True and Faithful Relation of what passed for many Years between Dr. John Dee and some Spirits, The book is comparatively rare: London, 1659.
75. See Böhme's Works, edited by Law and others, 4 vols.
76. Philippi Mulleri Miracula et Mysteria Medico-Chemica, Wirtemburg 1656. Amb. Muller's Paradeis-Spiegel, Launenberg, 1704.
77. Probier Stein, Frankfurt 1740.
78. Opus mago-Cabbalist, etc., Frankf. 1760.
79. Crollius, Philosophy Reformed, etc., trans. By Pinnel, London 1657.
80. Van Helmont de Ortu Medicinae has been translated under the titles of Oreastrike, or Physic Reformed. J. B. V. Helmont, Paradoxes.
81. Das Wasser-Stein des Weissens, is translated into English in the Musaeum Hermeticum; Arca Arcano, Lillium inter Spinas, etc., by the same author are in the collection of Manget.
82. Ampitheat. Sapientiae Eternae, in fol. 1608. Magnesia Catholica, etc.
83. And. Libavius, Opera Omnia Medica, in fol. 2 vol. A ponderous compilation.
84. Physica Subterranea, Lips. 8 vol. Idem, Oedipus Chemicus Aperius Mysteria, etc., Francf. 1664. Idem, Laboratorium Chemicum, Francf. 1680.
85. Tollii Fortuita, Amsterdam 1687. Manudcutio ad Coelum Chemicum, 1688. Sapientia Insanies, sive Promissa Chemica.
86. Opera Medico-Chimica, 2 vols., Francf. 1652.
87. Symbola Aurea Mensae.Idem, Ulysees.Idem, Septimana Philosophica,rare,... etc.
88. See French's Art of Distillation.
89. Sendivogius' New Light of Alchemy, by John Digby, London 1722.
90. Vol. i, p. 446.
91. See Starky's Pyrotechny Asserted.
92. Vanity of the Sciences, c. 54.
93. Petri Norelli, Bibliot. Chem. Paris, 1656.
94. De Ortu et Progressu Chimiae.
95. Histoire Hermétique, tom. iii, accompagné d'un Catalogue Raisonné des Ecrivains de cette Science, Paris, 1762.
96. Book of Eternal Life, Ortus Med., fol. P. 590, etc.
97. Signatura Rerum, fol. page. 358.
98. Speculum Alchimiae, sub initio, Theat. Chem., vol. iv. p. 515.
99. Epilogue to the Investigation of Verity, Russel's Geber, p. 20
100. Idem., book I, p. 215.
101. Picus Mirandolae, de Auro, lib iii, cap. 2.

102. See Borrichius, de Ortu et Progressu; and Dufresnoy, hist. Herm., vol. ii.
103. Sir George Ripley's Epistle to King Edward IV, v. 5.
104. Ampitheatrum Sapientae Eternae.
105. Norton's Ordinal, cap. ii.
106. Phil. Antiquis. Tract. Secret.
107. See New Light of Alchemy, preface.
108. Epilogue to the Twelve Treatises.
109. Ripley's Fifth Gate.
110. De Arte Alchemica, p. 345, etc.

Chapter 2. Of the Theory of Transmutation in General, and of the First Matter

showing the true basis on which the rational possibility of Transmutation rests; with Definitions from Albertus Magnus, Aquinas, Friar Bacon, Raymond Lully, Arnold Di-Villa-Nova, Synesius and others, descriptive of the Hermetic Material — with some suggestions additional concerning the Ethereal Nature and analogous phenomena of Light.

Est in Mercurio quicquid quaerunt Sapientes

— Turba Ecercit. 1.

The theory of Alchemy, though arcane, is very simple; its basis indeed may be comprehended in that only statement of Arnold di Villanova, in his *Speculum,—That there abides in nature a certain pure matter, which, being discovered and brought by art to perfection, converts to itself proportionally all imperfect bodies that it touches.*

And this would seem to be the true ground of metalline transmutation, and of every other; namely, the homogeneity of the radical substance of things; and on the alleged fact that metals, minerals, and all diversified natures, being of the same created first principles, may be reduced into their common basis or mercurial first matter, the whole Hermetic doctrine appears to hinge and proceed.

The multiform body of the world lies open, but the source everywhere is occult; nor does ordinary analysis at all discover this Universal Matter of the adepts. It has been accordingly objected, that natural species cannot be transmutable, because the transmutation of different species one into another necessarily implies mixtion and a spurious offspring: thus, that if it were even admitted possible by any means to infuse gold into lead or other inferior form, it would still remain imperfect, and the better species be defiled by the vile admixture; that the result would not in fact be gold at all, but of a middle nature, according to the proportionate virtue of the metals conjoining, golden or leaden, or as the case might be. Since species are indestructible, therefore, the transmutation of metals has been regarded as a sophistical proposition and not a true art.

And this argument the alchemists also admitting, have sometimes seemed to contradict themselves and their science; but such is not really the case and only from want of understanding them has it been supposed so. It is not species that they profess to transmute; nor do they ever teach in theory that lead as lead, or mercury as mercury specificate, can be changed into gold, any more than a dog into a horse; a tulip into a daisy, or vice versa, in this way, anything of unlike kind; but it is the subject-matter of these metals, the radical moisture of which they are uniformly composed, that they say may be withdrawn by art and transported from inferior Forms, being set free by the force of a superior ferment or attraction.

Species, says Friar Bacon, are not transmuted, but their subject-matter rather, *Species non transmutantur, sed subjecta specierum optime et propriisime*: —therefore the first work is to reduce the body into water, that is, into mercury, and this is called Solution, which is the foundation of the whole art[1]. And the first preparation and foundation of the Hermetic art, says the author of the *Rosarium*, is Solution and a reduction of the body into water, which is argent vive: for it is well known to artists that species cannot, as themselves, be transmuted, since they are not liable to sensible action and corruption; but the Subjects of species rather, since they are corruptible and may be changed; yet neither can the Subjects of species be transmuted, unless they are reduced first into their first matter, and made free to pass from one into another form. But this is not contrary to reason, because one form being expelled, another may be introduced, as is evident in rustic operations—as in the making of glass from flints, stones and ashes: much more then should the experienced philosopher be able to corrupt the Subject-matter of natures and to introduce a new Form[2]. Arnold, also admitting that species are indestructible, advises therefore that the Subject be freed by an artificial reduction. Species non transmutari sed individual specierum³. And Avicenna⁴, and Aristotle⁵, who is also quoted from by Ripley.

> *As the Philosopher who in the Book of Meteors did wryte,*
> *That the likeness of bodyes metallyne be not transmutable.*
> *But afterwards he added theis words of more delyte,*
> *Without they be reduced to their beginning materiable;*
> *Wherefore such bodies as in nature be liquable*
> *Mineral and metalline may be mercurizate,*
> *Conceive ye may theis science is not opinable,*
> *But very true by Raymond and others determinate⁶.*

When therefore Lully, speaking of the Art, declares that species are absolute and cannot be changed one into another,—*Elementiva habent vera conditiones et una species se non transmutet in alium*⁷,—We shall not understand him as denying the art by any means, but a false position of it only; the fundamental possibility and principle of transmutation being not of species, but of their Universal Subject or first matter.

And this Universal Subject is the alleged foundation of the whole Hermetic experiment; not only the thing transmutable in natures, as is above the thing transmutable in natures, as is above shown, but the thing transmuting also, when set free and segregated in its proper essentiality, the fermented Spirit assimilates the Light throughout.—Trust not, says the adept, those imposters who tell you of a *sulphur* tingens, and I know not what fables; who pin also the narrow name of *Chemia* on a science ancient and infinite. It is the Light only that can be truly multiplied, for this ascends and descends from the first fountain of multiplication and generation. This Light (discovered and perfected by art) applied to any body, exalts and perfects it in its own kind: if to animals, it exalts animals; if to vegetables, vegetables; if to minerals, it refines minerals, and translates them from the worst to the best condition; where, note by the way, that every body hath passive principles in itself for this Light to work upon, and therefore needs not to borrow any from gold or silver⁸.

This last advice is given to correct a common error, that the alchemists extracted from the Form out of these metals to transmute and increase with. Gross misconception of their initial principle has indeed caused their positions frequently to appear ridiculous; as of the common talk, for instance, of weighing and proportioning the elements so exactly as to constitute them into lasting accord; of consolidating the metalline vapor by heat artificially introduced, or by the rays of the sun and moon drawn to simultaneous cooperation, and several such-like literally imputed follies, far from their minds, who protested against such misunderstanding, having assumed to themselves another principle and another method of generating metals, by which they were enabled to follow nature independently, and help her to exceed the ordinary limits of her law: not by the condensation of imaginary vapors in the mines, or by the assistance of the great luminary or lunar light, but by working, as it is said, the only universal living and occult nature by and through itself, scientifically, which contains within itself the original of all these, even of the whole manifested existence. Thus, we read, in the *Lucerna Solis*,

> *A certain thing is found in the world*
> *Which is also in every thing and in every place.*
> *It is not earth, nor fire, nor air, nor water,*
> *Albeit it wants neither of these things,*
> *Nay it can become to be fire, air, water, and earth;*
> *For it contains all nature in itself purely and sincerely;*
> *It becomes white and red, is hot and cold,*
> *It is moist and dry and is diversifiable every way.*
> *The band of Sages only have known it,*
> *And they call it their salt.*
> *It is extracted from their earth:*
> *And has been the ruin of many a fool;*
> *For the common earth is worth nothing here,*
> *Nor the vulgar salt in any manner,*
> *But rather the salt of the world,*
> *Which contains in itself all Life:*
> *Of it is made that medicine which will preserve you from all*
>   *maladies*[9].

The Stone is one, says the monk in his Rosary; the medicine is one, in which the whole mystery consists, to which we add nothing nor take away anything, only in the preparation, removing superfluities[10]. All is made of Mercury, says Geber; for when Sol is reduced to his first original, *i.e.*, the mercury, then nature embraceth nature, and by open and manifest proof we have concluded that our Stone is no other than a foetant spirit and living water, which we have named dry water, by natural proportion cleansed and united with such union, that they can never more be absent each from other[11]. And Aquinas says,—It is Mercury alone which perfects in our work, and we find in it all we have need of; nothing different must be added. Some, mistaking, believe that the work cannot be perfected with mercury alone without his sister (*i.e.*, as agent and patient) that thou addest nothing different from mercury; and know also that gold and silver are not unlike in kind to this our Mercury; for it is their root: if thou workest therefore with Mercury alone, without foreign intervention, thou obtainest thy desire. The White and Red proceed from one root, for it dissolves and coagulates itself; whitens, rubifies, and makes itself to be both yellow and black; it unites with itself, conceives itself, and brings itself forth, to the full perfecting of its intention[12].

It is only in her manifold changes that nature is known and made apparent in ordinary life; but, since these alchemists profess to have enjoyed another experience, and through their Art to have discovered her in her simple essentiality, to be that total which works all conditionedly throughout existence, it will therefore be requisite to consider their whole doctrine with reference to this presumed unity, and by no means be led aside by their metaphoric language into a common misconstruction of its meaning; but since, according to the old maxim, *All is in Mercury which the wise men seek*, let us seek therefore if we may be able at all to identify this mercury, and whether the same ancient material be yet on earth.

It is well known, that the Greeks and eastern sages derived all things in common from a certain pure and hidden fire; Stoics, Pythagoreans, Platonists, and Peripatetics view with each other in celebrating the occult virtues of the Ether; its all-pervading essence and perfective power: in it they place the providential regulation of nature; it was the very life and substance of their theosophy, in which from the highest to the lowest confines of existence, from Jove to the last link in the infernal monarchy, all were inhabiting the ethereal world; for, as Virgil says, it lights and nourishes the innermost earth as well as the air and starry heavens.

Principio coelum, ac terras, composque liquentes,
Lucentemque globum Lunae, Titaniaque astra,
Spiritus intus alit; totamque infusaper artus
Mens agitat molem, et magno se corpore miscet[13].

And the assertions of the Ethnics, about the Anima Mundi, differ very little or nothing in substance from the Hebrew doctrine, but in words only; neither are their opinions so heinous or ridiculous as the zealous policy of ignorance, under a Christian guise, has too often caused them to appear. That there is a fluid or vitalizing principle invisibly permeating all things, and resident in the air we breathe, common experience indicates, for life cannot subsist without air, not in all kinds of air; but there is some one quality or ingredient in the atmosphere which is a secret food of life, and on which it immediately depends; what this aliment is, though many names have been invented, the moderns in default of knowledge are not agreed; and seeing it escapes the test of their closest vessels and analyses, and that it can be neither seen, heard, felt, nor naturally understood, the ancient theory of the One Element has been very much derided. The chemist, Homberg, indeed, with Boerhaave, Boyle, and others eminent of that period, hold with the alchemists, that there is a distinct substance universally diffused, though sensible only in its mixed forms and powerful effects; that it is the alone pure and active source of all things, and most firm bond of the natural elements, giving life to all bodies, penetrating and sustaining all things, and enlivening all; that this mighty Ether moreover is always at hand, ready to break forth into action on predisposed subjects; fermenting, producing, destroying, and governing the total course of nature. Bishop Berkeley, too, in his *Siris*, contends learnedly in favor of the same universal material, which he likewise calls ether, and a pure invisible fire—the most subtle and elastic of all bodies pervading all, and considers that it is from thence, and not from any mingled property, that the air has its power of sustenance and vitalization.

These then, with a few others, in recent times have so far concurred with the ancients in distinguishing the fontal Spirit of nature, apart from its manifestation, and as distinct from that elementary ignition with which we are sensibly familiar; for they do not allow that to be fire indeed, but an excitation only or effect of the antecedent potency which they describe. But then they could adduce no tangible proof of their doctrine. The worked could not see their invisible fire. It has therefore been regarded as a mere speculative chimera (which in part it was perhaps, in their minds, without experience), and, accordingly, disbelieved. For philosophy, at length, laudably anxious to prove all things, yet too idle to theorize, will suppose nothing that is not openly shown; how then should she recognize that recondite fire?

Neither are we desirous absolutely to assume it here, for though experiments of recent date seem to supply concurrent evidence, and the phenomena of Mesmerism have helped to force again on the minds of the more observing portion of mankind the supposition of a *New Imponderable*, or *Od-ic Force*, yet, few believe; and we pass it now to continue our research concerning that elder Quintessence of the magi which they introduce, not as a being of speculation merely, but of experimental science; not perceptible only in mingled forms, in the common air or elementary water, but as an essence compact and tangible without heterogeneity; in which pure estate, the Cabalists, also describing, call it, *Lumen Vestimenti*, the Vehicle of Light; and the Greeks, the Free Ether, that is to say, freed from the prison of gross matter, and able to work of itself intimately by the virtue of its own included light. Thus Zeno defines it,—*Ignem esse artificiosum, ad gignendum progredientem via;*—as a plastic fire, ever generating by rule. And Cicero, as that *coelestis alstissima aethereaque natura, id est ignea aquae per se omnia gignat,*—that most heavenly high ethereal igneous nature, which spontaneously begets all things[14].

> *That light of life; the vital draught*
> *That forms the food of every living thing,*
> *And e'en the high, enthroned, all-sparkling eye*
> *Of ever-mounting fire; th' immense expanse,*
> *The viewless Ether in his genial arms*
> *Clasping the earth; Him call thou Lord and Jove*[15].

It is requisite, however, to distinguish airs here, lest we speak profanely, calling that Jove which is not Jove; and mistaking Olympus, embrace some cloud whilst the life-giving Juno is far away above all our idea and sight. For the goddess is subtilely mingled in nature commonly observable in her action only, as adepts say, and to the world unknown, as we, as we may observe Lully, amongst others telling us, she is of another birth, and cannot be brought to knowledge without sagacious handling and human help.—*Imo argentums vivum nostrum est aqua alterius naturae, quae reperiri non potest supra terram, cum in actionem venire non posit per naturam, absque adjutorio ingenii et humanarum manuum operationibus*[16].

> *Haec vere nulibi est quod quaerimus.*

Nowhere; for the ethereal spirit does not subsist of itself, separate or tangibly on earth; but, giving subsistence to other beings, is occultated even in their life, and defiled. It is moreover, an especial doctrine of adepts, that nature operates her ordinary manifestation in direct contrariety to her perfect law; that, as darkness and imperfection are now apparent, the true Light is made occult; and that neither sanity nor beauty can permanently supervene in bodies, unless the contrary be operated in them; so that that which is fixed becoming volatile and the volatile nature fixed, the adventitious or externally generated image may be constricted utterly, and the central form contrariwise developed into life and act.

> *Si fixum solvas faciasqu volare solutum*
> *Et volucrem figas, facient te vivere tutum:*
> *Solve, Coagula, Fige.*

Thus, it is said that by a real experimental inversion, the Hermetic Art has proved imperfections to be accidental to nature, and introduced to her from without; that as water, spread abroad upon a many-colored surface of earth, salts, or spices takes the hue and flavor of the spot on which it rests, so it is with the prolific source of things; specie subsist in it adventitiously, as it were, by sufferance, and may be expelled, and ought to be for the attainment of perfection.—Whoever desires to attain this end, says Arnold, let him understand the conversion of the elements, to make light things heavy, and to make spirits no spirits, then he shall not work in a strange thing. *Converte elementa et quod quaeris invenies*[17].

And if any skillful minister of nature shall apply force to nature; and, by design, torture and vex it in order to its annihilation, says the philosopher; it, on the contrary, being brought to this necessity, changes and transforms itself into a strange variety of shapes and appearances; for nothing but the power of the Creator can annihilate it or truly destroy; so that, at length, running through the whole circle of transformations, and completing its period, it in some degree restores itself, if the force be continued. And that method of torturing or detaining will prove the most effectual and expeditious which makes use of manacles and fetters; *i.e.*, lays hold and works upon matter in the extremist degree[18].

So much does Lord Bacon assume upon the declaration of Democritus; our philosopher had in him the bright light of genius, which enabled in him independently of experience to conceive well and grapple with the possibility of nature. His mind glanced intuitively through and beyond the darkness which time had cast before the Wisdom of antiquity, and he discerned her yet beaming afar off with venerable splendor in her old domain. Though chained to the superficies, observing and collecting facts, he honored those sages who long before him had experimented into the center, and proved there a firm and immutable foundation of truth; but thither he was not himself able to pass, for he knew nothing of their Great Art, or of its subject even, and naturally mistook their hidden ground. Had the smallest glimpse only been revealed to him, he would have imagined all differently, or even proposed that the dissolution of nature should be attempted mechanically, or by help of such "particular digesters applied to the fire", as in the *Sylva Sylvarum* he seriously designs for this end[19].

Such instruments do, in fact, expel the very nature which the ancients prized; leaving us without all recompense in the dead ashes of her consuming vesture; whereas, the proposal of Democritus is not only to reduce the matter, with her false forms, to the verge of annihilation, but to entrap the bare spirit and help her on from thence to operate her own intrinsical freed will, which according to this testimony she possesses, and is able to manifest, wrapping herself spontaneously about it, even to a recreation. But if she is suffered to depart invisibly without pursuit or amendment, which is the common catastrophe, then she is caught up by other external compellents, and becoming defiled, is imprisoned by them and no better than she was before. The contrariation proposed by the proposed by the alchemists, indeed, is not the power of ordinary art, any more than of nature herself; but she passes through death from one form into another, as in the chemic vessels, without self-discovery, being instigated by a most forcible excentric will, which she has no power but to obey: yet, as the passage runs,—If any skillful minister shall apply another force, and by design torture and vex the spirit in order to its annihilation, it, being brought under this necessity, transforms and presently restores itself, the force being continued.

And that magic, says Paracelsus, is the most singular secret that directed such an entrance into nature; which, if it were divinely done by God alone, it would be to no purpose to study for it. But the Deity doth not make himself especially operative herein: if that magic then were natural, certainly it was most wonderful, very excellent for quickness of separation, the like whereof nature can neither give nor express. For whilst that is at work, beyond all things fall apart into their elements, breaking forth into their act and simple essence. The greatest miracle of all in philosophy is separation: *separation* was the principle and beginning of all generation. And as it was in the great mystery, so it is in the lesser. The *truphat*, or matter of the metals, brings everything into its due form[20].

—Convert the elements, says Arnold, and you will find what you seek; for our operation is nothing else than a mutation of natures, and the method of conversion in our Argent vive is the reduction of natures to their first root[21].—The elements of Mercury being separated, says Ripley, and again commixed by equal weight or proportion, make the elixir complete[22].

Now as we are taught from the beginning, that the whole of the Hermetic theory and practice proceeds upon the assumption of a certain Universal Being in nature, which is occult, and since the whole Art therefore has respect to this, we may be careful to observe that in speaking of elements, our authors do not allude to the common elements—as of fire, air and water—with which we are familiarly conversant, or to those subtler gases, so called simples of modern Chemistry, all of which are impure and equally irrelevant to this philosophy but the elements they speak of, as being introverted and transformed are the elements of the Mercury, properties of the universal spirit; in which, and by which alone, they profess to have operated the perfective miracle of their Stone. We must not limit, says Paracelsus, an element to a bodily substance or quality. That which we see is only the receptacle; the true element is a spirit of life, and grows in all things, as the soul in the body of man. This is the First Matter of the elements, which can neither be seen nor felt, and yet is in all things; and the first matter of the elements of the elements is nothing else but that life which the creatures have; and it is these magical elements which are of such an excellent and quick activity that nothing besides can be found or imagined like them[23].

Concerning the same, Hermes also advises men to understand that the knowledge of the four elements of the ancient philosophers, was not corporally or without wisdom sought after, but they are through patience only to be obtained, according to their kind, which through their own operation are everywhere in nature hidden and obscured[24].

We do not know whether we have set the position clearly, that the order of natural procedure ought to be introverted for a true and perfect manifestation; the point is subtle, and as it may be more easily apprehended hereafter on more intimate ground, we leave it for the present to consider especially what that nature was, which the alchemists profess to have revolutionized, in order that gathering their definitions of the whole, we may be better able afterwards to conceive the particulars. —*Quis Proteum non novit, adeum Pana.*

Fortis subtilis Pan, integer et generalis;

> *Et totus ignis, aura, terra, sive aqua,*
> *Qui resides solio cum tempore semper eodem*
> *Medio, supreme et infimo regno tuo.*
> *Concipiens, generans, producens, omnia servans,*
> *Exordium rerumque finis omnium*[25].

Yet not in his elementary immanifest diffusion let us invoke the most Ancient Nature, but as he was discovered by the Hermetic masters; whole, and singularly, and before any alteration had been induced in his uniform substance by their art. Thus Albertus Magnus defines the mercury of the wise to be a watery element, cold and moist, a permanent water, an unctuous vapor, and the spirit of body; and again,—the first material of the metals is an unctuous subtle humidity, forcibly incorporated with a subtle terrestreity[26]. Artefius describes it as a white fume, in substance like to pure silver, resolving bodies into their original whiteness; and as a vegetable life making all things to grow, multiply and resuscitate[27]. Which Lully, not dissimilarly viewing, calls Hyle, saying, that it is a clear compounded water, most like in substance to argent vive, that it is found flowing upon earth, and is generated in every compound out of the substance of the air, therefore the moisture is extremely heavy[28]. Seek our Argent vive, says Arnold, and you will have all you desire from it; it is a stone and no stone, in which the whole Art consists, spirit, soul and body; which if thou coagulatest, it will be coagulated; an if thou makest it fly, it will fly; for it is volatile, and clear as a tear. And afterwards, it is made citrine, then saltish, but without crystals; and no man may touch it with his tongue, for it is a deadly poison. Behold, I have described it to thee; but I have not named it, lest it should become common in the hands of all; nevertheless, I will in a manner name it, and tell thee that if thou say it is water, thou dost say truth; and if thou sayest it is not water, thou dost lie. Be not therefore deceived with manifold descriptions and operations, for it is One Thing to which nothing extraneous is added[29]. There is another found speaking after the same sense—Belus, in the classic synod of Aristaeus; and this, he says, amongst all great philosophers is magisterial, that our stone is no stone; though with the ignorant this is ridiculous; for who will believe that water can be made a stone, or a stone water; noting is more different than these two? Yet, in very truth, it is so; for this very permanent water is the stone, but whilst it is water it is no stone[30]. Again:

It is a stone and no stone,
In which the whole art consists;
Nature has made it such,
But has not yet brought it to perfection.
You will not find it on earth, since there it has no growth;
It grows only in the caverns of the mountains.
The whole art depends on it;
For he who has the vapor of this thing,
Has the gilded splendor of the Red Lyon,
The pure and clear Mercury.
And he who knows the red Sulfur which it contains,
Has within his power the whole foundation[31].

Basil Valentine, more intimately defining the nature of the First Matter, declares it to be comparable to no manifested particular whatever, and that all description fails in respect of it, without the light of true experience. And Rupecissa says the same: and Ripley, that is not like any common water or earthy material, but a middle substance,—*Aquosa substantia sicca reperta,*—partaking of extremes celestial and terrestrial; and though it may seem contradictory so to speak of a fist matter, as of a middle, or third; yet this is done in respect to its generation by active and passive relations of the Universal Spirit, whence it proceeds as a third, yet homogeneal from its radix; Lully also calls it *tertium*, and compounded in this sense; and Basil Valentine, —

> *Corpus anima spiritus in duobus existit,*
> *Ex quibus tota res procedit:*
> *Procedit ex uno et est res una,*
> *Volatile et fixum simul colliga,*
> *Sunt duo et tria et saltem unum*
> *Si non intelliges, nihil obtines*[32].

And Vaughan, for example of a modern authority, say that the First Matter is indeed the union of masculine and feminine spirits; the quintessence of four, the ternary of three, and the tetract of one; and that these are his generations, physical and metaphysical. The thing itself, continues he, is a world without form, a divine animated mass of complexion like silver, neither mere power nor perfect action, but a weak virgin substance, a certain soft prolific Venus, the very love and seed of nature, the mixture and moisture of heaven and earth[33]. As Sendivogius likewise declares,—Our water is heavenly, not wetting the hands, not of the vulgar, but almost rain water[34]; and by such familiar analogies as tears, rain, dew, milk, wine, and oil, the fermental principle of the spirit and her distilled quintessence are very ordinarily denoted. We conclude these verbal instructions with the following summary passage from the ancient book of Synesius, and the *New Light*—It is, says this esteemed author, speaking of the same Matter, a clear Light, which fills with true virtue every mind that has once perceived it; it is the nucleus and bond of all the elements which are contained in it, and the spirit which nourishes all things, and by means of which nature operates universally; it is the virtue, true beginning, and end of the whole world; in plain terms, *the quintessence is no other than our viscous celestial and glorious soul drawn from its minera by our magistery*. But nature alone engenders it; it is not possible to make it by art; for to create is proper to God alone; but to make things that are not perceived, but which lie in the shadow to appear, and to take from them their veil, is granted to an intelligent philosopher by God, through nature. And this Latex is the sharp vinegar which makes gold a pure spirit, seeing she is even that blessed water which engenders al things, Our subject is presented to the eyes of the whole world, and it is not known! O our heaven, O our water, O our mercury, O our slat nitre, abiding in the sea of the world! O our vegetable; O our sulfur, fixed and volatile; O our caput mortuum, or dead head, or foeces of our sea! Our water, that wets not the hands; without which nothing grows or is generated in the whole world! And these are the Epithetes of Hermes, his Bird, which is never at rest. It is of small account, yet no body can be without it, and so thou hast discovered to thee a ting more precious than the whole world; which I plainly tell thee is nothing else than our sea water, which is congealed in gold and silver, and extracted by the help of our chalybs, or steel, by the art of philosophers, in a wonderful manner by a prudent son of science[35].

Thus obscure, after all, is the true Matter of the Alchemists; and if we presume to add here, that it is the simple generated substance of life and light, immanifestly flowing throughout nature, and define it as that without which nothing that exists is able to be, we are not for this yet wiser how to obtain or work it apart; nor are words sufficient to convey a just notion where there is no ground of apprehension; and whether a thing be most like water, earth, fire, quicksilver, azote, or ether, is indifferent to the mind, needing actual experience to fix its idea. This the art promises to a patient and true philosopher, but as a reward of individual labor and perseverance only. We may content ourselves thus early, therefore, with the exclusive assurance that it is no one of the many things with which sense brings us acquainted; that it is neither water, nor earth, nor air, nor fire, though it contains in principle the nature of all these; neither gold, nor silver, nor mercury, nor antimony, nor any alkali, or gas, or vitriol of the vulgar; though these titles are found interspersed abundantly with others, equally deceptive, in the pages of the adepts. Neither is it animal absolutely, or vegetable, or mineral, or any natural particular whatever: but the alone *Laelia Aelia* latent in and about all, which the Enigma celebrates as comprehending all; but which the Alchemists alone teach experimentally to expound.

The ordinary phenomena of light, however, may occur, as not dissimilar from those which they describe; only that they are shadowy and mingled, compared with the alleged virtue and perfective properties of the Philosophic Subject. Yet as colors—blue, red, yellow and purple—are blended in the one uniform solar light, and are shown apart simply by a prismatic parting of the rays, or particles of their essence; and again, when the disposition is exchanged, relapsing, they exhibit the uniform whiteness whence they came; so is it said to be with the Alchemical Pan, who, being but one himself, is in his offspring multitudinous, and manifold in every diversity of form, hue, and complexion.

> *The ever varying substance of the whole*
> *Etherial, watery, earthy general soul, Immortal Fire!*
> *Even all the world is thine*
> *And pars of thee, O Proteus, power divine;*
> *Since all things nature first to thee consigned,*
> *And in thy essence omniform combined.*

Then, again, as light and heat mingle with bodies entering their composition, hardening some, softening others, destroying or cherishing, changing their aspect continually, and modifying their qualities; so is the Mercurial quintessence said to produce all various effects, but within itself consummately without external reference, or elementary confusion. Hitherto we have had account of the Matter only as it first appears, pure, as they say, and white, out of the philosophical contrition; and so far, we find the testimony sufficiently congruous:—but when the wise artist has brought all into this annihilate condition, and pressed out the waters of her extreme life; nature re-acting, as it is said, exhibits from out her unity three great magnetic principles of being—the Salt, Sulfur, and Mercury of adepts, in relation to each other of agent, patient, and offspring universal,—perpetually flowing forth to multitudinous manifestation. For Pan contains Proteus, as we have seen before from Democritus, and exhibits himself through this god; evolving every particular property and form of beings, out of his central will, of necessity, as the Orphic oracles declares; also of Mercury, with like allusion.

> "Hear me, O Mercury, and Son of Maia; the bright expositor of things!".

This Proteus, then, or Mercury, or quintessence of philosophers, is warily concealed by them under an infinity of names, all more or less applicable, yet delusive; for though every epithet is admissible, inasmuch as nothing can be said amiss of a Universal Subject, yet the right conception is hard to gather from their books. In its artificial fermentation and progress towards perfection, the changes it undergoes are manifold; and as the common life of nature, it becomes any and every conceivable thing in turn that it wills to be; now it is mineral, now vegetable, now animal; by predominance of either principle, it is fire, spirit, body, air, earth, and water; a stone, a vapor, or an aqua sicca; an essential oil of life, and a most sharp vinegar, a phoenix, a salamander, a poisonous devouring dragon, and a chameleon; every color, every thought is included in its circulations; nourishing, destroying, living, dying, corrupting, purifying, it is all things; and, anon, it is nothing,—but a potential chaos and egg of philosophers; a precedential, nameless principle, always in mutation, becoming to be,—first, last, greatest, least, the servant of art and queen of nature. Proceeding homogeneal through each omniform variety, and returning into herself manifestly the life and all phenomena which she as constantly supplies, the great Identity is as herself unchanged;

> *Et, quanto illa magis formas se vertet in omnis,*
> *Tanto, nate, magis tenacia vincla*[36].

Adepts have taken advantage of the mutable nature of their subject, to baffle the blind searcher, as well to confound false premises as to led the intelligent to a discovery of the simple truth; and where we find them speaking confusedly of elements, colors, and operations, it is very requisite to bear in mind the idiosyncracy of their ground, and that it is to the qualities and changes which take place during the preparation, and multiplying the Mercury by its proper Light, they allude, and not to any superficial phenomena or those elements which the moderns have so triumphantly decomposed. The three principles, the Salt, Sulfur, and Mercury, are merely different as modes of being of the same thing, and the many names arising out of the action and passion of these, do but indicate the stages of progress and development, as of a tree, which with its leaves, trunk, flowers, buds, fruit and branches, all differing, is nevertheless one individual, of one original, and of one root.

In the common estate, as the Spirit is in nature, said to be everywhere, it is called a thing vile and cheap; in its perfectly prepared form, a medicine the most potent and precious in the whole world; and the intermediate stages partake of the predominance of either extreme; being sublimed at first, it is called a serpent, dragon, or green lion, on account of its strength and crude vitality, which putrefying, becomes a stronger poison, and their venomous toad; which afterwards appearing calcined by its proper fire, is called magnesia and lead of the wise; which again dissolving, becomes their vitriolic solvent and most sharp acetum; and this afterwards is changed into an oil, which, whitening, is called milk, dew, quintessence, and by may other names; until raised to the final perfection, it is henceforth a phoenix, salamander, their royal essence and Red Stone.

> *Our great Elixir most high of price,*
> *Our Azot, our Basiliske, and our Adrop, our Cockatrice.*
> *Some call it also a substance exuberate,*
> *Some call it Mercury of metalline essence,*
> *Some limus derti from his body evacuate,*
> *Some the Eagle flying fro' the northwith violence,*
> *Some call it a Toade for his great vehemence,*
> *But few or none at all doe name it in its kinde,*
> *It is a privy quintessence; keepe it well in minde*[37].

Some speaking of it thus in metaphor, others in abstract terms, and all ambiguously; one regarding only certain properties, which another as entirely passes by, now describing in the natural state, then in its purified condition, or otherwise in any one of the intermediate stages through which it passes, without note of order in the art; altogether it passes, without note of order in the art; altogether it is by no means wonderful that so many erroneous conclusions have arisen respecting it, ingenuity having been rather directed to obscure than reveal the truth, which indeed can hardly be well conceived, without an insight into the experimental ground. And there are other difficulties which beset an exoteric theory of occult science, and inconsistencies will continually appear betwixt the sound of alchemical writings and their true sense, until the initial ground is understood. Practice in the beginning is required, therefore, to interrogate and discern, from amongst so many shadowy representatives, the true light. Constantly holding in mind the simplicity of the Substance, whence these images are all derived, we may nevertheless be enabled to thread in comparative security this Hermetic labyrinth of birds and wild beasts: and when Geber says, that the thing which perfects in minerals, is the substance of argent vive and sulfur, proportionally commixt in the bowels of clean inspissate earth[38]; or Sendivogius, that the matter of the metals is twofold[39];or Lully, or Ripley, or Basil, calls it a third thing; we shall not understand them, or any others so speaking, as of a variety of things, of sulfur, mercury, or earth in a commonsense interpretation, but of the magnetic relation, action, and passion of the Ethereal being in itself.

And from the foregoing we may also judge that when Hermes says that the separation of the ancient philosophers is made upon Water, dividing into four substances[40], that it is not the common elementated water to which he alludes; any more than did Thales when he said that all things were generated from thence, or Moses when he taught that the Spirit of God moved creatively upon the face of the same. This water they speak of is not the fluid with which in this life we are conversant, either as dew, or of clouds, or air condensed in caverns of the earth, or artificially distilled in a receiver out of sea fountains, either of pits, or rivers, as the empirical chemists formerly imagined—but it is the ethereal body of life and light which they profess to have discovered,—a certain tortured water, having suffered alteration by art and becomes corporified. O how wonderful, exclaims the Arabian, is that thing which has in itself all things which we seek, to which we add nothing different or extract, only in the separation removing superfluities![41]

The sense of all these philosophers is the same and from their gathered evidence we may infer that their stone is nothing more or less than the pure Ethereality of nature, separated by artificial means, purified and made concrete by constriction and scientific multiplication of its proper Light—the preparation, generation, birth, specification—all proceeding, arte mirabili, on the hidden basis of its primal eduction. Earliest and easiest it attains to the perfection of the mineral kingdom; and the seed of gold, says the adept, is a fiery form of Light inspissate, and this is the Stone of Fire;—*Lapis noster, hic est ignis, ex igne creatus, et in ignem veritur, et anima ejus in igna moratur*[42]. Thus nature, by the help of art, is said to transcend herself, and Light is the true fermentative principle which perfects the Ether in its proper kind.

> *Nor can one be so stupid as to think*
> *That water of its own accord should cause*
> *Within itself so great a change, and link*
> *Sulphur and mercury with so firm laws,*
> *Its own dimensions to penetrate*
> *So many times a metal to create.*
>
> *No, there must be an inward agent granted,*
> *Else would a thing unchanged still remain;*
> *This agent is the form that matter wanted,*
> *While it its proper nature did retain;*
> *This Form is Light, the source of central heat,*
> *Which clothed with matter doth a seed beget.*
>
> *The seed no sooner is produced, but soon*
> *Essays to bring the matter to a change,*
> *On it it stamps its character, which done,*
> *The Matter lives, and that which may seem strange,*
> *Co-worketh with the Form t'attain the end*
> *To which the seed implanted doth intend...*[43].

This of the mineral kingdom, where the Formal Light, by multiplication in its Ether, is said to produce gold; through superior skill and coction in the vegetal life, the elixir of the wise; and more rarely yet in the animal kingdom, and most of all in man; wherein all these are include, and a mystery of Universal being, profound and difficult to govern and no less arduous than glorious to sustain. For though the material is one throughout, forms are diverse, and in him it assumes an Image that is Divine and more potent than all the rest: which is in this life yet an embryo, but when unfolded through a new birth in universal intelligence, transcends the limits of this nether sphere, and passes into communion with the highest life, power, science, and most perfect felicity.

Of the phenomena of light, electricity, magnetism, etc., great account is taken at the present day; both to exhibit them, and to apply their various potencies to the affairs of life: but of the real source of these potencies, or of the true efficient in any case, nothing is known. The beam has been tried and tortured, through prismatic glasses and crystals, every chemical agent has been exhausted upon it, and electrical machines have been instituted to trap the fluid, but in vain. The learned are free to admit that, though they have discovered much of the mysterious influences of light, the more is discovered the more miraculous do they appear.—It has passed through every test without revealing its secrets, and even the effects which it produces in its path are unexplained problems still to tax the intellects of men[44]. These phenomena are effects then of a Cause unknown, and that very unknown Cause it was the alleged object of the Hermetic experiment to prove. Shall we no therefore revert to the inquiry, and search earnestly, if a glance of faith be granted only, to ascertain whether, recovering the ancient method of philosophizing, we may advance by it to the same end?

Truth is no where manifested upon the earth, because her forms or sulfurs are perplexed, and the passive spirit of nature is included and impure. She is moreover specified elsewhere, and does not consequently, as a true passive, reflect without truly to itself. But by the Hermetic dissolution the right recipient is said to be obtained, the pure is separated from the impure, the subtle from the gross, and the agent and the patient are one identity, as in the Emerald Table it is graven,—That which is below is as that which is above, and that which is below is as that which is above, for the performing of the miracles of the One Thing whence all the rest proceed by adaptation.—And on this unitary basis of production the metamorphosis of species is not so ridiculous. Have we not example in the common process of fermentation, the wild juice of grapes converted into wine, and milk into butte and cheese and whey; and these each proceeding out of one thing without requiring the addition of anything different: but only by operation of their own ferment they become changed into different specific natures? Just so is the Vital Spirit said to be, by the art of Alchemy, promoted from one form of being into another by its won prepared must or leaven; and as such, in turn, it reacts convertively on the elements of its original extraction; having previously passed on, through many stages, from imperfection to perfection.

Analogy of this, likewise, we have in the animal kingdom; caterpillars changing their neuter forms quiescently, and becoming winged moths. There remains the great difference, however, that whereas, in these familiar examples, imprisoned nature rests necessarily within the limiting law of her species; the will of the philosophic Proteus is free to be drawn without hindrance to form itself about the universal magnet of its own infinite self-multiplicative Light; which being transmuted, transmutes; and multiplying, multiplies its proper substance freely, in proportion to the virtue which it has acquired in the fermentation. And hence it may be better conceived, perhaps, how this fermented Spirit or Stone, (as in the crystalline perfectness of its essence it has been called,) when brought into contact with the crude life of nature whence it sprung, transmutes, *i.e.*, attracts the same away from other forms into intimate coalescence with its own assimilative light. And notwithstanding metals and all things in the world, as the adepts say, derive their origin from the same Spirit, yet nothing is reputed so nearly allied to it as gold; for in all other metals there is some impurity, and therefore a certain weight is lost in transmuting from them; but in gold there is none, but the Formal Light is wholly swallowed up in it without residue, dissolving intimately, gently, and naturally, as they compare it to ice in warm water; an excellent simile, by the way, inasmuch as the commingling natures differ in state only and were originally one. And I say to you, adds Sendivogius, that you must seek for that hidden thing, out of which is made, after a wonderful manner, such a moisture or humidity which doth dissolve gold without violence or noise, but sweetly and naturally; if you find this out you have that thing out of which gold is produced by nature. And although all metals have their origin from thence, yet nothing is so friendly to it as gold; it is even like a mother to it; and so finally I conclude[45].

And the method of working to this discovery, and to supply the deficiency of Form to the purified body of the Spirit, is described as the same in each of the three kingdoms of nature: the preparation only being diversified according to the variety of things indigent or intended to be changed. And if the Art has been more frequently proved in the mineral kingdom than in the other two, we learn that this has happened, not because the power is limited here, or because adepts have desired gold above every other good, but because the metalline radix first presents itself in the experimental process, and is most easily apportioned; and because the responsibility involved is less vital and consequential, it has been more freely exhibited and worked at large. In metals, says Geber, is lesser perfection than in animals; and the perfection of them consists more in proportion and composition than in anything else. Therefore, seeing in them less perfection than the other, we can more freely perfect these. For the Most High hath so distinguished perfections from each other in many forms; and those things in which the natural composition were weakest (*i.e.*, where life predominates over corporeal consistency), are by God endued with greater and more ignoble perfection, viz., that which is from the way of proportionate mixtion of the matter[46]. But metals, notwithstanding their inferiority of proportion, are said to be produced originally, as all other things are produced, from metalline seeds out of the Universal Spirit or Mercury, by which also they may be exalted and multiplies, and by no other thing; for that without this spirit growth is impossible, or transmutation or increase, and by it all natures are generated externally in their proper kinds. And the reason that is given why metals which thus include the prolific principle do not naturally increase, is a deficiency of heat, the Spirit being overcome in the gross, preponderating elements of their hard composition, so that they cannot fructify, unless they be first purged from their terrestreity and their tincture set free in the subtle Origin of all life. Vulgar gold Sendivogius compares to a herb without seed, which when it is ripe bears seed; and as trees from southern climates cease to blossom and bear fruit when transplanted into colder soils, so it is with the metals hindered by the crud earth f which they are composed. But, he adds, if at any time nature be sweetly and wittily helped, then art may perfect that which nature could not: gold may yield fruit and seed in which it multiplies itself by the industry of a skillful artificer, who knows how to exalt nature, and this by no other medium than fire or heat; but seeing this cannot be done, since in a congealed metallic body there appear no spirits, it is necessary that the body be loosened and dissolved, and the pores thereof opened, whereof nature may work[47]. And thus, continues another, when the mineral spirit is pure, it will, by its especial forms, do more than generate their forms to produce something like themselves, for it will work such an alteration in things of like nature with themselves, that they shall equalize the Philosophical Elixir, whose divine virtues wise men so much admire, and fools condemn because their blinded eyes cannot penetrate within to the center of the mystery[48].

We do not presume to suppose that such a view of nature will be immediately acceptable, or that the Hermetic theory presents itself even in a plausible aspect as yet; the Laws on this ground are directly inverse to our ordinary notions of natural procedure and to our acquired conception of simplicity and specific variation. But we are not investigating for those who make their mere individual experience a negative measure of belief, and who understand the possibilities of nature and art so far as to limit them; but for such who, more observing, see reason for hope beyond their present vision, and are able to imagine at least those surpassing realities which the ancients assert convectively as having apprehended in intellect and experimentally known. We have hitherto brought their testimony so far only as to the existence of a Homogeneal Subject in nature, showing that the same was the material basis of their philosophy, and the only principle of transmutation, life, increase, and perfection. We have endeavored also to explain (as well as the fence without which we placed ourselves for the preliminary discussion would admit), that the reduction of bodies to their original matter, by introversion of the generated life, is requisite to a true manifestation and permanence in any form, as by the ordinary process of unassisted nature, as is evident; indeed, she never withstands or alters for an instant her mode of being or vital perpetuity. It is vain, therefore, to seek for that in nature which is an effect beyond her strength; she must be helped, that she may exceed herself, or all will be useless. For the Mercury of the philosophers is not found of itself on earth, nor can be detained or perfected without this occult and needful Art assisting her. And these are the grand desiderate, to know what the true matter is, where and how it may be taken, and to find an artist able and fitted to perfect it: —without the former we are advised to attempt nothing; and without the latter the former can be practically of no avail.

Having premised thus much concerning the matter with the ground of the hermetic theory, so far only, however, as may enable us to guard against gross misapprehension; we propose, previous to entering on a more intimate discussion, to set the whole fairly before the reader's judgment, in the following translation of the *Tractatus Aureus, or Golden Treatise of Hermes, concerning the Physical Secret of the Philosopher's Stone*, which has been considered to be one of the most ancient and complete pieces of alchemical writing extant; and may be regarded as an exposition in epitome of the whole Art. Mystical and disorderly as this relic is, and must especially appear at first to any one unaccustomed to the antique style, we trust that the short pains may not be grudged that it will cost in passing on with us to the discovery of its idea. The treatise has been held in high esteem by the alchemists, and the Scholia given in part may assist in the perusal. Whoever the author may have been (for, though it bears the name of Hermes, the true origin is doubtful), it wears the impress of very great antiquity, and claims better than to be frivolously judged of by those who are uninitiated in science and ignorant of the kind of wisdom it unfolds. Prudence, patience, and penetration, the author owns, are required to understand him, and more than these for the discovery of his Great Art. Books were not written in those days for the information of the illiterate, as though any vulgar distiller or mechanic might carry away the golden fleece; or in such a guise that the covetous, who made gold their only idol, should readily, without research or the due Herculean labor, gather the apples of the Hesperides: not yet that any, though learned, as the adept adds, should by once or twice overly and slightly reading, as the dogs lap the waters of Nilus, straightway be made a philosopher. No, the magistery of this science forbids so great a sacrilege: our books are made for those who have been or intend to become conversant about the search of nature[49]. For this is the first step towards the recovery of truth, to be diligent in the investigation; other requirements there are and reasons for the extraordinary caution that has been used to keep the Art concealed, which may in the sequel be appreciated when it is intimately understood.

> *And ye may trust me 'tis no small inginn,*
> *To know all the secrets pertaining to this myne,*
> *For it is most profound philosophy,*
> *This subtill science of holy Alkimy...*[50].

---

1. See Roger Bacon, Radix Mundi et Speculum *Alchemiae*
2. See Tract ii. De Lapide in Thet. Chem., vol iii
3. See in Rosario, lib. I. Cap. ix.
4. See Lib. ii, Tractat. i, Cap. iv, De Operat.Med. Sing.
5. See Metoer lib. iii cap. iv
6. Epistle to King Edward, stanza 10.
7. De Arte Magna, part ix.
8. See Vaughan's Anima Magia Abscondita, p. 30.
9. Lucerna Salis, from the Latin verse, p. 150.
10. Rosar., Abbrev. Tract. iii and v.
11. Invest. of Perf., cap. xi.
12. Rosar. Abbrev. Tract. iii and v.
13. Aenid, lib. vi 724.
14. De Nat. Deor., lib. ii.
15. Euripides. See Blackwells's Letters on Mythology
16. Lullii Theorica et Practica in Theat. Chem., vol. iv.
17. Arnoldi Speculum, Octava Dispositio, etc.

18. See Bacon, De Sapientia Veterum, Fable of Proteus.
19. See the Sylva Sylvarum, in two places; and the History of Rarity and Density.
20. To the Athenians, book i, text 9.
21. Speculum Alchimiae, Octava Dispositio.
22. Medulla Alchimiae, cap. i.
23. To the Athenians, book ii, text 2 and 5.
24. Tractatus Aureus, cap. I., prop. 4. See also Lulli Theoria et Pratica, c. iii.
25. Orpheus Hymni—1.
26. See De Mineralibus, cap. ii et Breve Compendium in That. Chem. vol. ii.
27. See Liber Secretissimus Artefii.
28. See R. Lullii Theorica et Practica, cap. iii. De Forma Minori.
29. See Speculum Alchimiae, Octava Disp.
30. See Turba Philosophoru, Sermo Vigesima.
31. Lucerna Salis Phil. p. 33. From the Latin verse, Est quidam lapis et non lapis... See Digby's Trans. p.277.
32. B. Valentinii, De Prima Materia, in Museo Hermetico, Lullii Theor. Et Pract., cap. iii.
33. Lumen de Lumine, p.46, etc.
34. New Light of Alchemy, Tract 10, Of the Supernatural Generation.
35. See at the end of Kirchringius Valentine, in English, the Treatrise of Synesius, p.166, and Sendivogius, New Light of Alchemy, page 44.
36. Georgics, lib. iv, 411.
37. Bloomfield's Camp of Philosophy, book i, in Ashmole.
38. Investig. Of Perfection, cap. i.
39. New Light, Tract. 3.
40. Tract. Aur., cap. i, prop. v.
41. Rosarium, Aristotele Arabus.
42. Rosarium, Democritus Phil. Artis. Auriferae, vol. ii.
43. Eiraneus, Marrow of Alchemy, book i, 45.
44. See Hunt's Poetry of Science.
45. New Light of Alchemy, Preface to the Phil. Enigma.
46. Invest. Of Perf., Russell's Geber, p.44.
47. New Light of Alchemy, Tract 10; also Augurellus Chrysopaea, lib. i.
48. Nuysement, Sal, Lumen et Spiritus Mundi, Phil. ed. Combachius.
49. See Eireneus, Ripley Revived.
50. Norton's Ordinal.

Chapter 3. The Golden Treatise of Hermes Trismegistus, concerning the physical secret of the Philosopher's Stone.

In seven sections — esteemed one of the best and oldest pieces of Alchemical Philosophy extant; comprising, in epitome, the whole Art and secret method of the confection — to which some elucidatory annotations are added from the Scholium and elsewhere.

Section First

Even thus saith Hermes: Through long years I have not ceased to experiment, neither have I have spared any labour of mind; and this science and art I have obtained by the inspiration of the living God alone, who judged fit to open them to me His servant[1]. To those enabled by reason to judge of the truth He has given power to arbitrate, but to none occasion of delinquency[2].

For myself, I had never discovered this matter to anyone had it not been from fear of the day of judgment, and the perdition of my soul, if I concealed it. It is a debt which I am desirous to discharge to the faithful, as the Father of the faith did design to bestow it upon me[3].

Understand ye then, 0 sons of Wisdom, that the knowledge of the four elements of the ancient philosophers was not corporally or imprudently sought after, which are through patience to be discovered according to their causes and their occult operation. For their operation is occult, since nothing is done except it be compounded, and because it is not perfected unless the colours be thoroughly passed and accomplished[4].

Know then, that the division that was made upon the Water, by the ancient philosophers, separates it into four substances; one to two, and three to one; the one third part of which is colour, that is to say—a coagulating moisture; but the two third waters are the Weights of the Wise[5].

Take of the humidity an ounce and a half, and of the Meridian Redness, that is the soul of gold, a fourth part, that is to say, half an ounce; of the citrine Seyre, in like manner, half-an-ounce; of the Auripigment, half—which are eight—that is three ounces; and know ye that the vine of the wise is drawn forth in three, and the wine thereof is perfected in thirty[6].

Understand the operation, therefore, Decoction lessens the matter, but the tincture augments it; because Luna after fifteen days is diminished; and in the third, she is augmented. This is the beginning and the end[7].

Behold, I have declared that which has been concealed, since the work is both with you and about you; taking what is within and fixed, thou canst have it either in earth or sea[8].

Keep, therefore, thy Argent vive, which is prepared in the innermost chamber in which it is coagulated; for that is Mercury which is spoken of concerning the residual earth[9].

He therefore, who now hears my words, let him search into them; I have discovered all things that were before hidden concerning this knowledge, and disclosed the greatest of all secrets[10].

Know ye, therefore, Enquirers into the rumor, and Children of Wisdom, that the vulture standing upon the mountain crieth out with a loud voice, I am the White of the Black, and the Red of the White, and the Citrine of the Red, and I speak the very truth[11].

And know that the chief principle of the art is the Crow, which in the blackness of the night and clearness of the day, flies without wings. From the bitterness existing in the throat, the tincture is taken; the red goes forth from his body, and from his back is taken a pure water[12].

Understand, therefore, and accept this gift of God. In the caverns of the metals there is hidden the stone that is venerable, splendid in colour, a mind sublime, and an open sea. Behold, I have declared it unto thee; give thanks to God, who hath taught you this knowledge; for He loves the grateful[13].

Put the matter into a moist fire, therefore, and cause it to boil in order that its heat may be augmented, which destroys the siccity of the incombustible nature, until the radix shall appear; then extract the redness and the light part, till the third part remains[14].

Sons of the Sages! For this reason are philosophers said to be envious; not that they grudged the truth to religious or just men, or to the wise; but to the ignorant and vicious, who are without self-control and benevolence, lest they should be made powerful in evil for the perpetuation of sinful things; and in consequence philosophers are made accountable to God. Evil men are unworthy of this wisdom[15].

Know that this matter I call the Stone; but it is also named the feminine of magnesia, or the hen, or the white spittle, or the volatile milk, the incombustible ash in order that it may be hidden from the inept and ignorant, who are deficient in goodness and self-control; which I have nevertheless signified to the wise by one only epithet, viz., the Philosopher's Stone. Include, therefore, and conserve in this sea, the fire, and the heavenly Flyer, to the latest moment of his exit. But I abjure you all, Sons of philosophy, by our Benefactor who gives to you the ornament of His grace, that to no fatuous, ignorant, or inept person ye open this Stone[16].

I have received nothing from any, to whom I have not returned that which had been given me, nor have I failed to honour and highly respect Him[17].

This, O son, is the concealed Stone of many colours; which is born in one colour; know this and conceal it. By this, the Almighty favouring, the greatest diseases are escaped, and every sorrow, distress, and evil and hurtful thing is made to depart. It leads from darkness into light, from this desert wilderness to a secure habitation, and from poverty and straights, to a free and ample fortune[18].

SECTION SECOND

My Son, before all things I admonish thee to fear God, in whom is the strength of thy undertaking; and the bond of each separated element. My son, whatsoever thou hearest, consider it rationally. For I hold thee not to be a fool. Lay hold, therefore, of my instructions and meditate upon them, and so let thy heart be fitted, as if thou wast thyself the author of that which I now teach. If thou appliest cold to any nature that is hot, it will hurt it: in like manner, he who is rational shuts himself within from the threshold of ignorance; lest supinely he should be deceived[19].

Take the flying volatile and drown it flying and divide and separate it from its rust, which yet holds it in death; draw it forth, and repel it from itself, that it may live and answer thee, not by flying away into the regions above, but by truly forbearing to fly. For if thou shalt deliver it out of its strainess, after this imprisonment, and in the days known to thee shalt by reason have ruled it, then will it become a suitable companion unto thee, and by it thou wilt become to be an conquering lord, with it adorned[20].

Extract from the ray its shadow and impurity by which the clouds hang over it, defile and keep away the light; since by means of its constriction and fiery redness, it is burned. Take, my Son, this redness, corrupted with the water, which is as a live coal holding the fire, which if thou shalt withdraw so often until the redness is made pure, then it will associate with thee, by whom it was cherished, and in whom it rests[21].

Return, then, O my son, the extinct coal to the water for thirty days, as I shall note to thee; and, henceforth, thou art a crowned king, resting over the fountain as known to thee, and drawing from thence the *Auripigment* dry, without moisture. And now I have made glad the heart of the hearers, and the eyes looking unto thee in hope of that which thou possessest[22].

Observe, then, that the water was first in the air, then in the earth; restore thou it also, to the superiors by its proper windings, and altering skillfully before collecting; then to its former red spirit let it be carefully conjoined[23].

Know, my Son, that the fatness of our earth is sulphur, the auripigment, siretz, and colcothar, which are also sulphur, of which auripigments, sulphur, and such like, some are more vile than others, in which there is a diversity, of which kind also is the fat of glewy matters, such as are hair, nails, hoofs, and sulphur itself, and of the brain, which too is auripigment; of the like kind also are the lions' and cats' claws, which is siretz; the fat of white bodies, and the fat of the two oriental quicksilvers, which hunt the sulphurs and contain the bodies[24].

I say, moreover, that this sulphur doth tinge and fix, and is the connection of the tinctures; oils also tinge, they fly away, which in the body are contained, which is a conjunction of fugitives with sulphurs and albumninous bodies, which hold also and detain the fugitive Ens[25].

The disposition sought after by the philosophers, O son, is but one in our egg; but this in the hen's egg can, by no means be found. But lest so much of the Divine Wisdom as is in a hen's egg should be extinguished, its composition is from the four elements adapted and composed[26].

Know, My son, that in the hen's egg is the greatest proximity and relationship in nature; for in it there is a spirituality and conjunction of elements, and an earth which is golden in its tincture[27].

But the Son, enquiring of Hermes, saith—The sulphurs which are fit for our work, whether are they celestial or terrestrial? And he answers, certain of them are heavenly, and some are terrestrial[28].

The Son—Father, I imagine the heart in the superiors to be heaven, and in the inferiors earth. But saith Hermes—It is not so; the masculine truly is the heaven of the feminine, and the feminine is the earth of the masculine[29].

The Son—Father, which of these is more worthy than the other, to be the heaven or the earth? He replies—Each needs the other; for the precepts demand a medium. As if thou should say that a wise man governs all mankind, because every nature delights in Society of its own kind, and so we find it to be in the Life of Wisdom where Equals are conjoined. But what, rejoins the Son, is the mean betwixt them? To whom Hermes replies—In every nature there are three from two, first the needful water, then the oily tincture, and lastly, the faeces or earth which remains below[30].

But a Dragon inhabits all these, and are his habitation; and the blackness is in them, and by it he ascends into the air. But, whilst the fume remains in them. But, whilst the fume remains in them, they are not immortal. Take away therefore the vapour from the water, and the blackness from the oily tincture, and death from the faeces: and by dissolution thou shalt achieve a triumphant reward, even that in and by which the possessors live[31].

Know then, my Son, that the temperate unguent, which is fire, is the medium between the faeces and the water and is the Perscrutinator of the water. For the unguents are called sulphurs, because between fire and oil and the sulphurs there is a very close propinquity, even as so the fire burns, so does the sulphur also[32].

All the wisdoms of the world, O son, are comprehended in this my hidden Wisdom; and the learning of the Arts consists in discovering these wonderful hidden elements beneath which it hides completed. It behooves him, therefore, who would be introduced to this hidden Wisdom, to free himself from the vice of arrogance; and to be just and good, and of a profound reason, ready at hand to help mankind, of a serene countenance, diligent to save, and be himself a guardian of the secrets of philosophy open to him[33].

And this know, that except one understandeth how to mortify and induce generation, to vivify the Spirit, to cleanse and introduce Light, until they fight with each other and grow white and freed from their defilements, as blackness and darkness, he knoweth nothing, nor canst perform anything; but if thou knoweth this, he will be of a great dignity, so that the kings shall reverence him. These secrets, son, it behooves us to guard and conceal from the wicked and foolish world[34].

Understand, also, that our Stone is from many things and of various colours, and composed from four elements, which we ought to divide and dissever in pieces, and segregate in the limbs; and mortifying the same by its proper nature, which is also in it, to preserve the water and fire dwelling therein, which is from the four elements and in their waters, to contain its water: this, however, is not water in its true form, but fire, containing in a pure vessel the ascending waters, lest the spirits should fly away from the bodies; for, by this means they are made tinging and fixed[35].

O, blessed watery pontic form, that dissolvest the elements: Now it behooves us, with this watery soul, in order to possess ourselves of the sulphurous Form, to mingle the same with our Acetum. For when, by the power of the water, the composition is dissolved, it is the key of the restoration; then darkness and death fly away from them, and Wisdom proceeds[36].

Section Third

Know, my son, that the philosophers bind up their matter with a strong chain, that it may contend with the Fire; because the spirits in the washed bodies desire to dwell therein and rejoice in them. And when these spirits are united to them, they vivify them and inhabit them, and the bodies hold them, nor are they separated any more from them[37].

Then the dead elements are revived, the composed bodies tinge and are altered, and operate wonderful works which are permanent, as saith the philosopher[38].

O, permanent watery Form, creatrix of the regal elements! who, having united to thy brethren and by a moderate regimen obtained the tincture, findest rest[39].

Our most precious stone cast forth upon the dunghill, being most dear is made altogether vile. Therefore, it behooves us to mortify two Argent vives together, and to venerate the Argent vive of Auripigment, and the oriental Argent vive of Magnesia[40].

O, Nature, the most potent creatrix of Nature, which containest and separatest natures in a middle principle. The Stone comes with light, and with light it is generated, and then it generates and brings forth the black clouds or darkness, which is the mother of all things[41].

But when we marry the crowned king to our red daughter, and in a gentle fire, not hurtful, she doth conceive a son, conjoined and superior, in it, and he lives by our fire. But when thou shalt send forth fire upon the foliated sulphur, the boundary of hearts doth enter in above it, let it be washed from the same, and the refined matter thereof be extracted. Then is he transformed, and his tincture by help of the fire remains red, as flesh. But our son, king-born, takes his tincture from the fire, and death even and darkness, and the waters flee away[42].

The Dragon, who watches the crevices, shuns the sunbeams, and our dead son will lives king comes forth from the fire and rejoices in the espousal; the occult treasures will be laid open, and the virgin's milk is whitened. The Son, already vivified, is become a warrior in the fire and over the tincture super-eminent. For this son is himself the treasury, even himself bearing the Philosophic Matter[43].

Approach, ye sons of Wisdom, and rejoice; let us now rejoice together, for the reign of death is finished, and the son doth rule, and now he is invested with the red garment, and the purple is put on[44].

SECTION FOURTH

Understand, ye Sons of Wisdom, the Stone declares; Protect me, and I will protect thee; give me my own, that I may help thee! My Sol and my beams are most inward and secretly in me. My own Luna, also, is my light, exceeding every other light; and my good things are better than all other good things; I give freely, and reward the intelligent with joy and gladness, glory, riches, and delights; and what they ask about it I make to know and understand and to possess divine things.

Behold, that which the philosophers has concealed is written with seven letters; for Alpha follows, viz.: Yda and Liber; and Sol, in like manner, follows: nevertheless, if desirous to have dominion to guard the Art, join the son to Buba, which is Jupiter and a hidden secret[45].

Hearers, understand: then let us use our judgment; for what I have written I have with most subtle contemplation and investigation demonstrated to you; the whole matter I know to be one only thing. But who is he that understands the true investigation and inquires rationally into this matter? There is not from man anything but what is like him; nor from the ox and bullock; and if any creature conjoins with one of another species, that which is brought forth is like neither[46].

Now saith Venus: I beget light, nor is the darkness of my nature, and if my metal were not dry all bodies would desire me, for I liquefy them and wipe away their rust, and I extract their substance. Nothing, therefore, is better or more venerable than I and my brother being conjoined[47].

But the King, the ruler, his brethren attesting, saith: I am crowned, and I am adorned with a diadem: I am clothed with the royal garment, and I bring joy and gladness of heart; for, being chained to the arms and breast of my mother, and to her substance, I cause my substance to keep together; and I compose the invisible from the visible, making the occult matter to appear. And everything which the philosophers have hidden will be generated from us[48].

Hear then these words, and understand them; keep them, and meditate thereon, and seek for nothing more: Man is generated from the principle of Nature whose inward substance is fleshy, and not from anything else. Meditate on this letter, and reject superfluities[49].

Thus saith the philosopher: Botri is made from the Citrine, which is extracted out of the Red, and from nothing else; and if it be citrine and nothing else know it will be thy Wisdom. Be not concerned if thou art not anxious to make extract from the Red. Behold, I have written to the point, and if ye understand I have all but opened the thing[50]. Ye Sons of Wisdom! Burn then the Brazen Body with an exceeding great fire; and it will imbue you with the grace which you seek. And make that which is volatile so that it cannot fly from that which flies not. And that which rests upon the fire though itself a fiery flame, and that which in the heat of the boiling fire is corrupted is Cambar[51].

And know ye that the Art of this permanent water is our brass, and the colourings of its tincture and blackness is then changed into the true red[52].

I declare before God, I have spoken nothing but the truth. The destroyers are the renovators, and hence the corruption is made manifest in the matter to be renewed, and hence the melioration will appear and each side is a signal of Art[53].

Section Fifth

My Son, that which is born of the crow is the beginning of this Art. Behold, I have obscured matter treated of, by circumlocution, depriving it of light. I have termed this dissolved, and this joined, this nearest I have termed furthest off[54]. Roast those things, therefore, and boil them in that which comes from the horse's belly for seven, fourteen, or twenty-one days. Then it becomes the Dragon eating his own wings and destroying himself; this being done, let it be put into a furnace, which lute diligently, and observe that none of the spirit may escape. And know that the periods of the earth are in the water which is bound until you put the bath upon it[55].

The matter being thus melted and burned, take the brain thereof and triturate it in most sharp vinegar till it becomes obscured. This done, it lives in the putrefaction; the dark clouds which were in it before it died in its own body will be changed. This process being repeated, as I have described; it dies again as I said, thence it lives[56]. In the life and death thereof we work with the spirits, for as it dies by the taking away of the spirit, so it lives in the return and is revived and rejoices in them. Being arrived then at this, that which thou hast been searching for is made apparent. I have even related to thee the joyful signs, that which doth fix its own body. But these things, and how they attained to the knowledge of this secret, are given by our ancestors in figures and types: I have opened the riddle, and the book of knowledge is revealed; the hidden things I have uncovered and have brought together the scattered truths within their boundary, and have conjoined many various forms, even I have associated the Spirit. Take it as a gift of God[57].

Section Sixth

It behooves us to give thanks to God, who bestows liberally to the wise, who delivers us from misery and poverty. Along with the fullness of his substance and his provable wonders I am about to try and humbly pray God that whilst we live we may come to him.[58]

Remove thence, O sons of Science, the unguents which we extracted from fats, hair, verdigrease, tragacanth, and bones, which are written in the books of our fathers[59].

But concerning the ointments which contain the tincture coagulate the tincture, coagulate the fugitive and adorn the sulphurs, it behooves us to explain their disposition more at large. It is the Form of all other unguents in which is the occult and buried unguent, and of which there appears to be no preparation. It dwells in his own body, as fire in trees and stones, which by most subtle art and ingenuity it behooves us to extract without burning[60].

And know that the Heaven is to be joined mediately with the Earth; but the middle nature, which is the Water, is a form along with the Heaven and the Earth. But the water holds of all the first place which goes forth from this Stone; the second is gold; and the third is our almost or medial gold which is more noble than the water with the faeces[61].

But in these are the smoke, the blackness, and the death. It behooves us, therefore, to drive away the vapour from the water, the blackness from the unguent, and death from the feces, and this by dissolution. Which being done we have the sovereign philosophy and secret of all hidden things[62].

Section Seventh

Know ye then, O sons of Science, there are seven bodies—of which gold is the first, the most perfect, the king of them, and their head—which neither the earth can corrupt nor the fire devastate, nor the water change; for its complexion is equalised, and its nature regulated with respect to heat, cold, and moisture; nor is there anything in it which is superfluous, therefore the philosophers have preferred and magnified it, saying that this gold, in relation of other bodies, is as the sun amongst the stars, more splendid by his light; and as, by the will of God, every vegetable and all the fruits of the earth are perfected through it, so gold, which is the ferment Ixir, vivifies and contains every metallic body[63].

For as dough, without a ferment, cannot be fermented, so when thou hast sublimed the body and purified it, separating the uncleanness from the faeces, thou wilt then conjoin and mix them together, and put in them the ferment confecting the earth with the water until the Ixir ferment even as dough ferments. Think of this, meditate and see how the ferment in this case doth change the former natures to another thing; observe, also, that there is no ferment otherwise than from the dough itself[64].

Observe, moreover, that the ferment whitens the confection and hinders it from combustion, and holds the tincture lest it should fly, and rejoices the bodies, and makes them intimately to be joined and to enter one into another, and this is the Key of the philosophers and the end of their works; and by this science bodies are meliorated, and the operation of them, God assisting, is consummate[65].

But, through negligence and a false opinion of the matter, the operation is perverted, as bad leaven on the dough, or curds for cheese, and musk among aromatics[66]. The colour of the golden matter points to redness, and the nature thereof, is not sweetness; therefore we make of them Sericum, *i.e.*, Ixir; and of them we make the encaustic of which we have written, and with the king's seal we tinge the clay, and in that have set the colour of heaven which augments the sight of them that see it[67].

The Stone, therefore, is the most precious gold without spots—evenly tempered, which neither fire nor air, nor water, nor earth is able to corrupt; the Universal Ferment rectifying all things by its composition, which is of the yellow or true citrine colour[68].

The gold of the wise, concocted and well digested, with a fiery water, makes Ixir; for the gold of the wise is more heavy than lead, which, in a temperate composition is the ferment Ixir, and contrariwise, becomes distempered by an equal composition.

For the work begins from the vegetable, next from the animal, as in the egg of a hen, in which is great support; and our earth is gold, of all which we make seriacum, which is the ferment Ixir[69].

---

1. There are three things said to be necessary for the attainment of the Hermetic science: viz., study, experience, and the divine benediction; and these depend upon each other: study is required for the theory, and this for entering into the central experience which, in the Universal Spirit, is not found without God.
2. Without theoretic knowledge and a right principle to begin with, many have wearied themselves in experimenting, even with the right subject in vain ; but the true intention once discovered, the whole truth opens, as practice succeeds to theory, alternating in the philosophic work. You must know, says Geber, that he who in *himself* knows not natural principes is very remote from our art; because he has not a true *root* whereon to found his intention; but he who knows the principles and the way of generation, which consists according to the intention of nature, is but a very short way from the completement. (Sum. Of Perf., book 1). See also Norton's Ordinal Proheme, and chapters I and iv. ; and the Introitus Apertus ad Occlusum Regem Palatio., cap. viii., etc.
3. Our author hereby declares that it was conscience which moved him to disclose his dearly-acquired knowledge, but in such terms only to the world that the studious might understand and follow in is steps. He nowhere, therefore, addresses the ignorant, lest his instruction should be abused, but the predestined sons of wisdom, to guide them, already initiated, further into the practice of his high Art.
4. Here we have a premonitory opening of the philosophic work which Hermes calls a knowledge of the elements; which elements, however, are not commonly to be understood; *non corporaliter*, as the Scholiast explains, *sed spiritualiter et sapienter*,—not corporally but spiritually and wisely; for the properties of the Universal Spirit are abstrusely included in all existence, and to be understood only by its own intimate analysis and

introverted light. But nothing is done except that the matter be decompounded; for there are many heterogeneous images and superfluities adhering to this subject in its natural state, which render it unfit for progress; these therefore must be entirely discharged; which, say the adepts, is impossible without the theory of their arcanum, in which they show the medium by which the radical element is discovered and set free to the accomplishment of its inclusive law. See The Scholium—Paracelsus 1 st book to the Athenians. R. Lulli Heoria at Practica, cap. iii. Norton's Ordinal, cap. v. Ripley's Third Gate, cap. 3, Norton's Ordinal, cap. v., Ripley's Third Gate, etc. Introitus Apertus ad Occlusum Regem Palatio, cap.viii.

5. The philosophic water then, being divided into four parts or hypostatic relations, they are called elements. First, the one part, being divided, produces two, which are as agent and patient in the ethereal world; further afterwards, from their conjunction, three are said to be made manifest as body, soul, and spirit, which cooperating together in the unity of the same spirit, beget all things, giving birth to the whole substratal nature. The differences of the colors, observes the Scholiast, Hermes divides into two threes, i.e., into three red spirits and three white, which have their growth all from the same identical water, and are resolved into the same again. By considering, therefore, that this water or mercury of the adepts has, within itself, its own good sulfur, or vital flame, thou mayest perfect all things out of mercury; but if thou shalt know to add *thy weights* to the weights of nature, to *double* mercury and triple sulfur, it will quickly be terminated in good, then in better, until into best of all. See the Scholium; Sendivogius' New Light of Alchemy, p. 117; Arnoldi Speculum, Disp. viii.

6. The proportional working of the philosophic mater upon its parts is indicated by adepts under variously perplexed forms and measures. Those distinctions which Hermes makes of the humidity, the southern redness, soul of gold, seyre, citrine, auripigment, the cine of the philosophers and their wine, have no other signification, says the Scholiast, but that the spirit should be seven times distilled, which after the eighth distillation is converted by force of the fire into ashes, or a most subtle poser which, by reason of its purity and perfection, resists the fire. Neither wonder, he adds, that eight parts and three ounces are equivalent; for by the former section the one part is divided into two, to each of which there are added three parts, which are the true philosophic proportions called also by Hermes the Weights of the Wise. See the Scholium; Ripley's Epistle; Introit. Apert., cap. vii; Norton's Ordinal, cap. v.

7. Understand here the diminution and increase of that ethereal light, which is the passive luminary in the Philosophic Heaven, whose changes and manifest operations are descried as wonderfully parallel with those of the familiar satellite, by which the philosopher is pleased covertly to indicate her. Some divide the operation of the philosopher's stone into two parts; the former Hermes calls decoction, which dissolving the matter discharges also its impurities by a proper rule; until, being at length on the verge of annihilation; i.e., freed from every exteriorly attracting form, it prepares, as Democritus in the fable of Proteus alludes, to restore itself through a powerful inbred revolutionary force. Then follows what is called the Second Work, which is only, in continuation of the First, to perfect the newly informed embryo and multiply its vivific light. In such few words, Hermes professes to comprehend the whole of the artificial process of working the Spirit.

8. Herein is the work commended and suggested to true enquirers, that they may forsake the beaten road of experiment, and seek to know intrinsical within themselves the substance of that Universal Nature in which they, with all beings in common, as it were, unconsciously live; which, in the natural order of generation, is made occult, abiding throughout invisibly. And as was explained in the theory concerning other gross elementary bodies, that the true original cannot be made manifest except they be reduced into it; so with respect to man, that which is sown (viz., the catholic germ of his existence which comprehends all things, according to the Hermetic tradition, and mystery of the

whole causal nature, with the faith and assurance of a better life), is not quickened except it die. That which is within, viz., the causal light, must be drawn forth by art and fixed; and that which is without, viz., the sensual spirit of life must be made flexible and occultated before reason can become into that Identity by which the powers of the Universal Nature are made manifest and intrinsically understood. But intending to enlarge inquiry on this head, we defer our comments.

9. Our Mercury, says the wise Scholiast, is philosophic, fiery, vital, running, which may be mixed with all other metals and again separated from them. It is prepared in the innermost chamber of life, and there it is coagulated, and where metals grow there they may be found, even in the ultimate axle of each created life. If you have found this argent vive, then, which is the residuum of the philosophic earth after the separation, keep it safely, for it is worthy. If you have brought your mercurial spirit to ashes or burnt it by its own fire, you have, continues our informant, an incomparable treasure, a thing more precious than gold; for this is that which generates the Stone, and is born of it, and it is the whole secret which converts all other metalline bodies into silver and gold, making both hard and soft, agent and patient, putting tincture and fixity upon them. See the Scholium, Maria Practica, circa finem; Introit. Apert. Cap. iv. and v.; Kuhnrath, Amph. Isag. in fig.

10. Give not that which is holy unto the dogs, neither cast ye your pearls before swine, says the Divine Teacher; and some men the Scriptures have compared to dogs, yea greedy dos, wolves and foxes; these are unfit to be admitted to the Causal Knowledge, lest, handling the powerful machine of nature recklessly or unjustly for selfish ends, they subvert the order of final causes, and, rifling her treasury, turn again and rend her. Hermes leaves the Mystery thus, therefore, to unfold itself through study and faithful experiment, that the mind by searching and patient investigation may be prepared and able to appreciate the truth when found. We, also, intending to explore the Intellectual Ground more fully hereafter, follow in its own willful order the Hermetic mind.

11. The vulture, according to our Scholiast, is the new born quintessential spirit or Proteus; the mountain upon which the vulture stands is a fit vessel placed in a well-built philosophic furnace encompassed with a wall of fire. In him all the multifarious virtues of nature are declared to be held in capacity, as in rapid evolution he passes about his axis, making the light manifest without refraction in every variety of its coloring and creative imagination.

12. The vulture and the crow are interpreted to be one and the same thing, only differing somewhat in estate. Whilst the Spirit of life appears active and devouring in the process, it has been called the vulture, and when it lies in a more obscured and passive condition, the crow. The vulture is the first sublimed quintessence not yet perfected by art; the crow is also in the infancy of that work wherein the revivified spirit is united with its solar ferment, The blackness of the night is the putrefaction of the same, and the clearness of the day signifies its resurrection to a state of comparative purity. IT flies without wings, being borne and carried by the fixed spirit; and the bitterness existing in the throat occultly indicates the death of the first life, whence the soul is educed; which is also the red and living tincture taken from the body; and the thin water is the viscous humidity made by the dissolution which radically dissolves all metals, and reduces them into their first ens, or water.

Montis in excelso consistit vertice vultur,
Assidue clamans, Albus ego atque niger,
Citrinus, rubeusque feror nil mentior: idem est Corvus, qui pennies absque volare solet Nocte tenebrosa emediaque in luce diei Namque ortis caput est ille vel iste tuae
— See The Scholium—Atalanta Fugiens Emblema, xliii.

13. Our author here, repeating his exception of the unintelligent, at the same time eloquently identifies the philosophic matter, calling it mens sublimes et mare patens. It is hidden in the caverns of the metals; that is to say, in the central motion of the mineral life, where the spirit is first coagulated and conceives itself into a concrete form. It is

called a stone, say the adepts, and it a true mineral petrification: therefore Alphidus writes—Si lapis proprium nomen haberet lapis esset nomen ejus; and Arnold—Ii is a stone and no stone, spirit, soul, and body, which if thou dissolvest, it will be dissolved; and if thou coagulatest, it will be coagulated; and if thou dost make it fly, it will fly, for it is volatile and clear as a tear, etc. See Arnoldi Speculum—Kuhnrath Amph. Isag. in fig. Cap. iii.

14. Many ways are mentioned by adepts of acting with their matter as by sublimation, calcinations, inceration, fixation, etc; which may all however be comprehended under the first term rightly understood; for the Hermetic sublimation, repeatedly operated over and over again, is the occasion of many changes in the matter and effects, which, though differently designated, are in their source the same. This sublimation is not, therefore, exactly to be conceived by analogy with the ordinary chemical process, which is a mere elevation of the subject to the top of the vessel; but the Hermetic sublimation is said to change the matte, qualifying and meliorating each time that it succeeds; urging on life, as it were, to the utmost exercise of vivacity, to save itself from death and a total disseveration. Concerning the peculiar nature, origin, and artificial excitation of the philosophic fire, we may more effectively inquire hereafter.—See Ripley Revived; Lumen de Lumine; Introit. Apert., cap. iii.

15. The monitions to secrecy are no less stringent than frequent in the writings of adepts, modern as well as ancient. Thus, Raymond Lully, in his Thesaurus, gives the following charge:—Juro tibi supra animam meam quod si ea reveles, damnatus es : nam a Deo omne procedit bonum et ei soli debetur. Quare servabis et secretum tenebis illud quod ei debetur revelandum, etc. And Norton writes—

>So this science must ever secret be,
>The cause whereof is this, as ye may see:
>If one evil man had hereof his will,
>All Christian peace he might easily spill;
>And with his pride he might pul down
>Rightful Kings and Princes of renown.
>Wherefore the sentence of peril and jeopardy
>Upon the teacher reseth dreadfully.

See Lullii Testam.; Aquinas Thasau. Alchim.; Norton;s Ordinal, cap. i. ; R. Bacon, Speculum.

16. The philosophic matte has indeed received many perplexing appellations, some more, some less significative of its real origin and essence; but in the concrete form, and for reasons before given in part, it has been properly called the Stone. In this same universal matter of the Stone also Hermes includes all its multinominal ingredients. In its flowing, humid state it is called the sea of the wise, passive to all impression and influences of the light. By the fire and heavenly bird are dignified, says the scholiast, the external and internal agents in the Hermetic work, by either of which it is conserved and nourished to the end.

17. In friendship, gratitude, and reciprocity of benefaction, say the adepts, consists the chief art of operating with their matter; and no man, for reasons hereafter explicable, can operate the Hermetic artifice alone.

>So saith Arnolde of the New Towne,
>As his Rosary maketh mencione;
>He sayeth right thus withouten any lye
>There may noe man Mercury mortify,
>But it be with his brother's knowledging.
>Lo, now he which first declared this thing
>Of philosophers' father was, Hermes the King.

See Chaucer's Tale of the Chanon's Yeoman; Theat. Chem. Brit., p. 254; Arnoldi Rosarium, circa finem.

18. The consummate union of the purified spirit with its course is thus covertly indicated by Hermes as the true cornerstone of his philosophy; and that tincture of many dyes which, being dissolved renews itself, and dying survives itself, until its final cause is fully manifest and accomplished. This is the elixir of Light from the central essence, so set free, that it is said to prolong life, and cure disease and moral indulgence and physical defects, mingling with the common breath of nature the efficacy of an exalted life and love.
19. Further suggestions are now given concerning the true subject and operation of the Hermetic work. Having previously shown that the way to the attainment of the magistery is by communion with the ruling Spirit of nature; entering yet deeper as the work progresses toward the Causal discovery, Hermes admonishes the student earnestly to fear and obey its Law; lest, being transgressed in any part, man should work evil instead of good through its means.—The fear of God is the beginning of wisdom, and the knowledge of the Holy is understanding;—and this, in the most profound sense, is said to be proved in Alchemy, and that they only who have become conversant by experience in the Fontal Nature have truly and properly understood what it is, and why God is to be feared. Ingrafted in that root, writes our scholiast, the true understanding will grow up in thee, and fill thee, even as the body is filled, with life. Thou must enter with thy whole spirit into the center of nature, and there behold how all things are begun, continued, and perfected. But thou must first enter into that Spirit which is the Framer of all things, which pierces through and dwells in that central root; and by entering into that, it will, as a vehicle, carry thee into the same root where all things are hidden, and reveal to thee the most recondite mysteries, and show thee, as in a glass, the whole work and laboratory of the most secret nature. Hermes, therefore, recommends him who is rational, and desires the further instruction of his reason, to shut himself within, away from the distractions of sense and this life's ignorance, and learn to open to himself the door of a higher consciousness, lest in the outward acceptation of words or things he should be deceived. Having premised thus much, he proceeds to detail the process by which the spirit is carried on from each succeeding dissolution into a more perfect form of being.
20. These images, indicating the mode of rational operation with the freed spirit and its soul, will appear inevitably obscure. The entire process is repeated many times before perfection is arrived at; and instructions for each, according to the arising phenomena, are given by the scholiast at full length.
21. A shadowy darkness passes always along with the philosophic body, moving in its own light until it is thoroughly purified from sensual defilements. Now that the clearness may be manifest throughout without obscurity, says the scholiast, the body must be repeatedly opened and made thin after its fixation and dissolved and putrefied, and as the grain of wheat sown in the earth putrefies before it springs up into a new growth or vegetation, so our Magnesia, continues he, being sown in the Philosophic Earth, dies and corrupts, that it may conceive itself anew. It is purifies by separation, and is dissolved, digested, and coagulated, sublimed, incerated, and fixed by the reciprocated action of its own proper Identity, as agent and patient, alternating to improve. The water spoken of by Hermes is the passive spirit, the redness is its soul, and the earth begot betwixt them is the substance or body of both—the spirit thereafter penetrates the body, and the body fixes the spirit—the soul being conjoined, tinges the whole of its proper color, whether white or red. This process is given in the following enigma, by the excellent author of the Aquarium Sapientum, or Water Stone: —

>Spiritus ipse datur pro tempore corpori, at ille
>Exhilarans Animam Spiritus arte cluet.
>Spiritus ille Animan subito si contrahit ad se,
>Nullum se abjungit segregat aque suo.
>Tunc tria consistent et in una sede morantur,
>Donec solvatur, nobile corpus, opus.
>Putrescat nec non moriature, separate istis:

Temporeat elapso Spiritus atque Anima
Aestu convenient extremo sive calore,
Quisque suam sedem cim gravitate tenet.
Integritas praesto est, nulla et perfectio desit
Amplis laetitiis glorificatur opus.
See the Scholium, and Aquarium Sapientum, Musaeum Hermeticum, p.95.

22. Here again the allusions will appear willfully obscure to the uninitiated, for the master presupposes not only a knowledge of the Matter, but of the Vessel also in which it is scientifically concocted; but we must pass on. The life of the coal is fire, which being extinct, becomes a dead body; nor of coal alone, but of other things light is the life, and it is heat that conserves it. But the essence of life, says the scholiast, is nothing else than a pure, naked, unmingled Fire; not that indeed which is corrupting and elementary, but that which is subtle, celestial, and generating all things. The same is of metals their first matter containing the three principals, the Salt, Sulfur, and Mercury, of which so much has been spoken and ignorantly misapplied. By the crowned king, Hermes signifies the first manifested resplendence of the vital tincture; the well is, as the catholic spirit of life, inexhaustible; at the bottom, or center rather, of which subsists the occult Causality of all; even from this, the true efficient wheel, is drawn, according to tradition, that auripigment of philosophers which is the multiplicative virtue of their stone. When thou shalt see thy exaltations to return, teaches the adept, and by continuance of them on they body, light shall begin to appear with such admirable colors as never were seen by the eye of man in so little a room before; then rejoice, for now our king hath triumphed over the miseries of death, and behold him returning in the East, with clouds, in power and great glory. Here thou mayest rest and wait, and enjoy the glory of thy white elixir; now is the time at hand in which that of the poet is fulfilled.

Ne te poeniteat faciem fuligine pingi
Adferet haec Phoebi nigra favilla jubar.

See Eiraneus, Ripley Revived; Vaughan, Lumen de Lumine p.58, etc.; Anthrop. Theomag. p.22 , and the Scholium.

23. Convert the elements, says Arnold, and you shall have what you desire; that is to say, separate the matter into its essential relationships, and join them again together in harmonious proportion.—See Arnoldi Speculu sub initio, Basil Valentine's Stone of Fire, Smagardine Tablet, etc.

24. Hermes alludes here in part to the various manifestations of the spirit in this natural life, and the vegetable growth of it in animal bodies. The occult luminous principle of vitalization he calls sulfur, auripigment, etc., hiding it also under a variety of other covertures.

25. A distinction is here made by our author of the different estates and uses of the philosophic sulfur, or Light, as it becomes developed in the Hermetic work.

26. Hermes divides the matter into four parts, as was before seen, comparing also its vital composition to that of a hen's egg, which answers in all respects, excepting the catholicity, to the compound simple of this art.

Est avis in mundo sublimior omnibus, ovum
Cujus ut inquiras, cura sit una tibi.
Albumen luteum cicumdat molle vitellum,
Ignito (ceu mos) cautus id ense petas:
Vulcano Mars adat opem: pullaster et inde
Exortus, ferri victor et ignis erit.
See Atalanta Fugiens p.41. ; Epigramma viii. and the Scholium.

27. The Alchemists uniformly recommend us to observe nature, that from analogy we may be better able to imagine and judge of the proper method of experimenting, and learn to cooperate with her Spirit effectually to regenerate it. For particulars of the Hermetic similitude, see the Scholium.

28. A short dialogue hereupon ensues between Hermes and his son; the father explaining that the distinctions of lights or sulfurs in the process ought not to be indifferently understood, as if they were all of one quality or idea. For the spirit, though one is essence, is extremely diversified, in its conception, as also according to the degree and order of its rectification by art.
29. The purified sulfur, fixed and incombustible, is the generating seed of the universal nature, according to the adepts; but the mercury (which is the recreated body of the spirit, passive and pure) is sometimes called the earth of the wise, conceiving into itself the same seed by which it is also nourished, digested, perfected, and brought to birth— that is, to a visible manifestation of its intrinsical virtue and light. But the son's allusion is intimate to the art, and particular. See the Scholium.
30. When, by their strong attracting law, the active and passive relations are conjoined in the Spirit, they become equalized in their progeny; and as the mystical problem of the Trinity includes three in one and one in three—agent, patient and offspring universal and co-equal; so these three are found to be in all created things imitatively, the paternal, maternal, and proceeding ens of life. And there are the Salt, Sulfur, and Mercury of the Adepts, without which, they say truly, nothing ever is or can be vitally substantialized. And thou hast in these three principles, says Sendivogius, a body, a spirit, and an occult soul; which three (being of one only substance in a triple relationship), if thou shalt join them together, *having been previously separated and well purified*, will without fail, by imitating nature, yield most pure fruits, etc. When the adept speaks therefore of a natural triplicity, he speaks, reiterates Vaughan, not of kitchen-stuff, those three pot-principles of water, oil, and earth—or, as some call them, salt, sulfur, and mercury; but he speaks of hidden intrinsical natures, known only to absolute magicians, whose eyes are in the center and not on the circumference, and in this light, every element is threefold.—See Anthrop.Theomag., p. 22; Digby's Ed., p. 3; and the Scholium.
31. The dragon is the self-willed spirit, which is externally derived into nature, by the fall into generation. And by it, says the scholiast, Hermes especially signifies the blackness of the matter on its first ascension, which is operated with difficulty on account of its thick glutinous body, which has to be resolved, by force of the philosophic art, into an aerial and vaprous substance; and during this process, we are informed, the powers of the Philosophic Heaven are wonderfully shaken and defiled, insomuch, that like a poisonous dragon it destroys all that it touches, and hence it is said to have its houses in darkness, and to possess blackness and mortality and death; for the root of this science is a deadly poison. Therefore, says Hermes, takes away the vapor from the water, and the blackness from the oily tincture, and death from the faeces, that the component principles may be pure, and by dissolution thou shalt possess a triumphant reward, even that in and by which the possessors live.

Thus, the evil of the original sin is said to be discovered by a radical dissolution of the spirit, and without this discovery and the arising evil, it cannot return to its pristine purity and the immortality of its first source. Cause, therefore, adds a no less subtle than experienced adept, such an operation in our earth, that the central heat may change the water into air, that it may go forth into the plains of the world and scatter the residue through the pores of the earth; and then, contrariwise, the air will be turned into water, far more subtle than the first water was. And this is done thus: if thou give our old man fold or silver to swallow, that he may consume them, and then he also dying may be burned, and his ashes scattered into the water, and thou shalt boil that water until it be enough, thou shalt have a medicine to cure the leprosy (of life). See the Scholium; Sendi- vogius, New Light; Maria Practica.
32. The knowledge of this secret sulfur, says the Scholiast, and how to prepare it and use it in this work includes the whole art of perfection. It is the stirrer-up of the whole power and efficacy and purifier of the matter; hence Hermes calls it the Perscrutinator,

eminently distinguishing the Rational Ferment, concerning which it will be our purpose to inquire hereafter.

33. The whole paragraph will speak plainly for itself when it is understood, which we leave for the present therefore unexplained.

34. The principles of the art of working the matter are here repeated. The two contrary natures of light and darkness must contend together, as it were, in mortal strife, and the war must be waged unceasingly for the destruction of the foreign life until it succumbs, grows white, as Hermes says, in order that the internal agent may return to vivify the whole, and yield the abundant tincture of its light.

35. The catholic nature is multifarious in its conception, and passes in the art through a strange variety of forms and appearances; but she operates her proper progress necessitously under the threefold law of life; the ingress, egress, and alternating action of which, under dominance of either of its principles, constitutes the whole phenomena of the Hermetic process.

36. Great is the reputed virtue of this Aqua Philosophica, which distills itself finally to manifestation by the Art of Life; for, as common water washes and cleanses things outwardly, so this inwardly effects the same, even itself purifying itself from its inbred defilements, so that no vestige of evil remains. And, being conjoined in consciousness with the central Efficient, it becomes all-powerful, and the key of every magic art. The preparation of it is not known to many, says the Scholiast, and a very few have obtained it; because the well is deep out of which it is drawn; not do the vulgar chemists understand it. Nor can this secret be truly learned either from a master at all, but practice reveals it by the instinct of nature. See the Scholium and Lumen de Lumine p.67.

37. This may again remind the reader of the passage from Democritus, where, describing the universal experiment, he says that that method of working with nature is the most effectual that makes use of manacles and fetters, laying hold on her in the extremest degree. And this constriction, according to the scholiast's teaching, is not made by chance, but by means of the affinity which is between the body and its spirit, as Mayer also alludes, in his Emblems—Naturam natura docet, debellat ut ignem; for they both proceed form one fountain, though, of the two, the agent, because it vivifies and holds the particles of the matter together, is repesentatively superior in operation, to compel the Protean Hypostasis of Nature to enter into his true Form.

Nam sine vi non ulla dabit praecepta, nequw illum
Orando flectes: vim duram et vincula capto
Tende. Doli circum haec demum frangentur inanes.

See the Georgics,lib. iv., 397; Maieri Atalanta Fugiens Emblema, xx; Democritus in the Fable of Proteus; Aquarium Sapientum Enigma; and the Scholiast on Hermes.

38. The bodies of the metals, explains our Scholiast, are the domiciles of their spirits, which when they are received by the bodies, their terrestrial substance is by degrees made thin, extended, and purified, and by their vivifying power, the life and fire hitherto lying dormant is excited and made to appear. *For the life which dwells in the metals is laid, as it were, asleep* (in sense), nor can it exert its powers, or show itself, unless the bodies (i.e., the sensible and vegetable media of life) be first dissolved and turned into their radical source; being brought to this degree, at length, by the abundance of their internal light, they communicate their tinging property to other imperfect bodies, transmuting them into a fixed and permanent substantive. And this, he adds further, is the property of our medicine, into which the previous bodies (of the spirit) are reduced; that, at first, one part thereof will tinge ten parts of an imperfect body, then one hundred, then a thousand, and so infinitely on. By which the efficacy of the creative word is wonderfully evidenced, Crescite et multiplicamini. And by how much the oftener the medicine is dissolved, by so much more it increases in virtue, which otherwise, without any more solution, would remain in its single or simple state of perfection. Here there is a celestial and divine fountain set open, which no man is able to

draw dry, nor can it be exhausted should the world endure through an eternity of generations.—See the Scholium; Introit. Apert. Cap. viii. ; Trevisanus Opusculum circa finem.

39. The fixed watery Form of the philosophic matter, which Hermes here apostrophies, is the same as was before celebrated only more mature; this is the fountain which Berhard Trevisan mentions, of such marvelous virtue above all other fountains in the world, shining like silver and of caerulean clearness. It is the Framer of the royal elements, says Hermes, i.e., it draws to itself the rubified light of its internal agent permeating the same throughout the whole essentiality. Separate, says Eiraneaus, the light from the darkness seven times, and the creation of the philosophic mercury will be complete, and this seventh day will be for thee a Sabbath of repose; from which period, until the end of the annual revolution, thou mayest expect the generation of the supernatural son of Sun, who comes about the last age into the world to purify his brethren from their original sin.—See the Scholium, Trevisanus, end of his Opusculum; New Light of Sendivogius, 10th Treatise; and the Introit. Apert., cap. iii., etc.

40. The same catholic nature, which in its preternatural exaltation appears so very precious in the eyes of the philosopher, is in the common world defiled; abiding everywhere in putrefactions and the vilest forms of life. It is likewise despised by mankind, who are, for the most part, unconscious even of its subsistence, much ore are they not ignorant of the method of exculpating it and handling their life to good effect? Hermes, indeed, gives instruction, as did Moses also, but under a veil, which it may be hardly expedient to look through at this stage of our investigation. We have signified from the testimony of the adepts already, though without particularizing, that light or sulfur, as they call it, is the true form or seed of gold, and the concentering virtue of their philosophic stone. Thus far, then, the theory of the Hermetic process may be supposed to run by the analogy of nature; grain, being cast into the common earth, grows and fructifies and brings forth its increase, and his eduction is in its middle principle, that is to say, in the specificative form by which it is intrinsically generated and made to be that particular kind of grain and no other. Thus, the aurific seed, if truly such can be found to be specific seed of gold, needs only to be planted in its proper ethereal vehicle, well prepared and fallow to bring forth its virtue in manifold increase. But the Alchemical art has been continually compared to agriculture; and the analogy, indeed, appears to bear throughout so intimately as to suggest and, almost without deviation, point out the method of its application. The body is gold, says the author of the New Light, which yields seed, our lune or silver, not common silver, is that which receives the seed of the gold, afterwards it is governed by our continual fire for seven months (philosophical), and sometimes ten, until our water consume three and leave one; and that in duplo or a double. Then it is nourished with the milk of the earth, or the fatness thereof, which is bred in the bowels of the earth and is governed and preserved from putrefaction by the salt of nature: and thus the infant of the second generation is produced; and when the seed of that which is now brought forth is put again into its own matrix, it purifies it, ad makes it a thousand time more fit and apt to bring forth the best and most excellent fruits. But, before the metallic light is brought to this ultimate perfection, it must many times, therefore, suffer itself to be eclipsed, and die and corrupt, as the adepts teach, according to the similitude of nature; yet, with this difference, that whereas the produce of common husbandry exhausts and deteriorates rapidly the earth whence it springs, and is always terminated in its kind without progression, the ethereal seed, on the other hand, tends always to improve its generation, fertilizing by the return of each successive growth, and enriching its maternal soil; and this process , according to Hermes, is repeated seven times before the final resurrection of the Quintessence into a permanent form of life.—See the Scholium; Maieri Atalanta Fugiens, Epigram 6; Sendivogius, New Light, Treatise 9 and 10.

41. The new-born Quintessences are here shown to be reunited for fructification and to be further promoted, and, as the fable relates to Isis, that she brought forth Horus, even feeding him with fire; so it happens in the Hermetic work. And this is wonderful, observes the scholiast, that the parents, who were before the nurses and feeders again by the law of the same spirit, are to be nursed and fed. It is nourished with a gentle heat, not in the vulgar way of decocting, but conformable to the heavenly fire. But when we say, adds the adept, that our stone is generated by fire, men neither see nor do they believe there is any other fire but the common fire, nor any other sulfur or mercury—thus they are deceived by their own opinions, saying that we are the cause of their errors; but it is not so. The philosophers uniformly distinguish their own special fire as magical, creative, vital; whereas the common element is without sagacity or discrimination. Our fire is a most subtle fire, inhabiting in himself an infernal secret fire, and in its kind extremely volatile. Some call it the miracle of the world, the nucleus of the superior and inferior forces of nature, etc. See the Scholium, Lumen de Lumine.

42. O happy gate of blackness, cries the sage, which art the passage to this so glorious a change. Study, therefore, whosoever appliest thyself to this Art, only to know this secret, for to know this is to know all, but to be ignorant of this is to be ignorant of all. For putrefaction precedes the generation of every new form into existence, It is the business of the philosophic fire not only to vivify, but also to depurate and segregate the heterogeneity of its vehiculum, which being done there appears at length in the faeces, a most pure and rubicund tincture of the color of flesh and blood. And as flesh is nothing but blood coagulated, abounding with a full and vigorous spirit, so, adds the adept, likewise our tincture is of blood coagulated, which blood is the boundary or satisfaction of hearts, as Hermes alludes, the object sought for, and which satisfies when attained.—See Scholium, and Ripley Revived, 5th Gate.

43. The nature and origin of this Dragon was before discussed, which becomes so occultated in the rising of the internal light to manifestation.

   Si fixum, solvas faciasque volare solutum,
   Et volucrem figas, facient te vivere tutum Solve, Coagula, Fige.

   O Nature, cries the experimental adeptist, how dost thou interchange thy being, casting down the high and mighty and again exalting that which was base and lowly? O death how art thou vanquished, even when they prisoners are taken from thee and carried into an estate and place of immortality? The son, says Hermes, has gotten the Tincture, for is he not in truth the whole quintessential nature concentrated, as it were personified, bearing in hand the golden light of life to perpetualize it universally.—See the Philosophical Epitaph of W.C., title page, and Ripley Revived.

44. The internal light, once made manifest to sense, so far is ready for the perscrutination of another life into which it must be induced to enter, to suffer again, and die in order to transmute the foul material into itself. Hermes proceeds, in the next chapter, to describe the work, which, in principle, differs nothing from the foregoing but in the images and delineation of phenomena only.

45. The seven letters are taken to signify the necessary phases which the philosophic material passes in order of color and qualitative virtue; some call them planets, others metals (for the radical life of the spirit is indeed mineral); and the rest of Hermes' allusion is to the conjunction of active and passive principles for the reproduction of light out of the whole.

46. The profound significance of the first monition to use our reason may be better appreciated on inquiry; for Hermes has chosen to conceal the philosophic vessel. I say to you, writes Maria, laconically, that this science may be found in all bodies; but philosophers have thought fit to say little of it, because of the shortness of life and the length of this art. They found it most easily in that matter which most evidently contains the four philosophic elements. It is prepared in the innermost chamber of life, says the wise Scho-

liast, and there it is coagulated; and where metals grow, there they may be found.—See Maria Practica, and the Scholium.

47. All here is to be understood ethereally, according to the principles before laid down. Venus personifies the central light of nature, which is occultated in her generations, and in metalline bodies is more especially bound on account of their terrestreity, and therefore they gladly adhere to this moist spirit, that it may vivify them. And when she appears, writes a no less experienced adept, the artist is rejoiced, and thinks perhaps his work is finished, and that he has the treasure of the world in hand; but it is not so; for if he tries it, the light still be found imperfect, alone, and transient, without the masculine tincture to fix it in manifestation. Hence the fable of Mars and Venus taken together by Vulcan, as will be hereafter explained, in the last extremity of life.—See the Scholium; Freher's Analogy; and Democritus, in Flammelli Summula.

48. By the king, the Rational Efficient is signified; by the brethren, the inferior degrees of illumination in the spirit, which are finally gathered up into accord with her first source. This same reason, being artificially constrained, lest it should escape the fiery ordeal, returns, fastening, as Hermes says, upon the wheel of its proper life, as it were, introverting the natural channel and order of generation, whereby a door is marvelously opened into the most intimate recess of life.—See the Scholium; Introitus Apertus, cap. viii.

49. With what force and earnestness does the master here speak, as if the whole ground of the mystery lay in these words. And truly not in vain, observes the Scholiast, does he bid to understand them, and meditate upon them, and to inquire after nothing else, Man, it is said, was created of the dust of the earth; that is, interprets the adept, of the arising quintessence of the universal nature; but the understanding has never reached us, who, without self-investigation, are unable to perceive the reality of those things which are spoken out of an experimental knowledge of Life.

50. By the term Botri is here signified the Philosopher's Stone. The red root is the Terra Adamica, called sometimes Magnesia by the wise, and Salt after the purification. It is not gotten by art, but of nature spontaneously, when the conditions are supplied and a pure receptacle to give it evidence.

51. The self-willed hypostasis of nature must die, as we before explained, in order to evolve her universal being and this also must suffer and die necessarily in order to multiply the perfection of its first form. Thus, in his own operative language, as it were pyrographically, does Democritus exemplify the Hermetic process at this juncture, when the innate evil being made manifest, the will proceeds to operate its proper solution in life.— Drawing the Fixed Brass out bodily, writes our Abderite, thou shalt compose a certain oblong tongue, and placing it upon the coals, stir Vulcan into it: now irradiating with the Fossil Salt, now with the incessant Attic Ochre, adorning now the shoulder and the breast of Paphia, till she shall appear more manifestly beautiful, and throwing the glaucus veil aside, she shall appear entirely golden. Perchance, it was when Paris gazed on such a Venus, he did prefer her both to Juno and Minerva.—But when the artist seeth, adds a more modern experimentalist, the masculine tincture rise from death, and come forth out of the black tincture from death, and come forth out of the black darkness together in union with the white virginal spirit, he will then know that he hath the great Arcanum of the world, and such a treasure as is inestimable.—See the Scholium; Democritus in Flammelli Summula; and Freher's Analogy.

52. By a conjunction with its own permanent prepared spirit, the albified water is made red. Adonis ab apro occuditur, cui Venus occurens tinxit rosas sanquine.—See the Scholium; Atalanta Fugiens, Emb. xli.

53. Thus, even as the hermetic material is one the art is one; and the stone is also one mineral spirit, exalted by fermentation intrinsically in its proper kind; and as leaven makes leaven, and every ferment begets its own exaltation; as vinegar makes vinegar, says the Scholiast, so this art beginning in our Mercury, likewise finishes in the same. It

is a kind of Proteus, indeed, which, while creeping upon earth, assumes the nature of a serpent, but being emersed in water, it represents itself as a fish; and presently being in air, and taking to itself wings, it flies as a bird; yet is, not withstanding, One throughout the multiformity of nature. With this the artist works, and with it he transacts all the necessary operations of our Stone.

54. The philosophic work is not considered to begin until after the dissolution; the preliminary preparation of the matter being very generally termed the gross work. The manner of obscuring the truth, by repetitions and circumlocutions, has been everywhere adopted by the Alchemists; the nature of the process gives room for this, and our author set an example, imitating the devious instinct of the spirit in his illustrations.

55. The process of the dissolution is here gone over again, with certain practical instructions, which the Scholiast explains under another veil. The matter, he says, is to be decocted in the philosophic furnace called Athanor, with a continual fire. And the vessel which holds the matter must be exactly sealed, lest the penetrative mineral vapor should expire and leave the dead body. And this maybe done with the lutum Sapientiae, or Hermetic seal, about which he gives particular instructions, and how the orifices and junctures of the philosophic vessel must be encircled, so that no breath may go forth.

56. The cerebral, or superior life of the Spirit, is obscured during the purification, and for the revealment of its true mineral radix or source

57. In a scientific association of the Spirit the Hermetic Art has been said summarily to consist—

Ut ventus qui fiat est ille qui dat.—Qui capit ille sapit.

58. He who shall have received so much grace from the Father of Lights, as to obtain in this life the inestimable gift of the philosopher's stone; who carries about with them, as the Scholiast expresses it, even in his own breast, the treasury of universal nature; has need not only to be grateful but to be watchful of every temptation, lest he should be drawn, even unwittingly, to abuse it; for he is then proven indeed, and taught how, in the midst of so much abundance of power, wealth and happiness, he should humble himself and sink away from every appetite of self love into the single adoration of the divine goodness; for in this humble state, God only is to be met with, as the law of reason proves in its ordinary development, much more so in the awakening of its objective light.

59. The fixed sulfur of adepts, according to our Scholiast, is the true balsam of nature, which the dead bodies of the metals imbibe, and are as it were thoroughly moistened with, to preserve them perpetually from distemper and rust. The more anything abounds with this balsam, the longer it lives and is preserved from perishing. From things, therefore, abounding with a balsam of this kind, the universal medicine is concreted, which is most effectual to preserve human bodies in a state of health, and to root out diseases, whether accidental or hereditary, by propagation, restoring the sick to health and integrity.—See the Scholium and Lucerna Salis towards the end.

60. Here again we are reminded of the simplicity of the matter worked with, and its formal light. But if, in the natural world, the spirit is invested with multitudinous and various forms externally introduced, it behooves the artist to extract these, therefore, and to dissolve without destroying the continental life.

61. The two invisible poles of the Spirit are here especially signalized by Hermes, and that consummate medium which brings them forth into manifestation. The water alluded to is the mercurial quintessence, as it is first born in a humid and vaprous consistency; which being successively informed by the central light becomes golden and aurific, communicating its tincture; and as fire by means of fuel increases continually, and a small seed drawing strength and sustenance from the earth and air grow to be a large and prolific tree; so this wonderful being, essentialized in its proper vehicle or understanding substance, is said to increase, transmuting the catholic nature into itself Our gold is not common gold, says the adept, but a depurated substance, in the highest degree perfected and brought to an astral or heavenly complexion. This is the Elixir, Ixir, or true

Ferment tinging and fixing, and without which bodies cannot be made pure.—See the Scholium, Laucerna Salis, etc.

62. By an artificial dissolution of the vital bond, by means of Alchemy, the Causal principle of nature is said to be developed into reminiscence and to arise in the experience of the recreated life. Modern philosophy is far removed from such investigation, nor is it easy, perhaps, without habitual study, to conceive the possibility of an experiment that would lead into such a science of nature as the ancients propose.

63. The gold of the philosophers, or living gold, as they sometimes call their luminous concrete, is here alluded to throughout; for though the dead metal also is eminently endued above other metals with the color of its formative virtue, yet this does not fructify, being imprisoned, or meliorate anything beyond itself. But as the solar luminary is the medium that perfects all sublunary nature, subliming by his beams of light and heat, so does our soul of gold, writes the Scholiast, which is the true aurific principle, even as a medium, perfect all the other seven bodies; i.e., to signify here, according to Hermes, the inferior spheres of vitality in which it moves. For though the virtues of the philosopher's gold are manifold, when applied to external nature, restoring her energies, and converting her circumferential manifestations into their central whole conditionedly, yet these things are not so much denoted of the paragraph which refers to the spontaneous operations in the divine Law in life.

64. This is a very favorite analogy with the alchemists, and eminently suggestive; Hermes, therefore, advises us to meditate here, that we may imbibe the principle of perfecting in our understanding and observe that except the past of flour be leavened, or the liquor receive the ferment of its own advanced virtue, it will not be exalted; but die and corrupt in the inferior elements of its nature. See the Scholium and Basil Valentine's Chariot of Antimony throughout, and the Stone of Fire.

65. In saying that the ferment whitens the confection, our author may be thought to contradict what has been before stated; but he only confounds the order of his instruction, retrograding at the latter end, for the fermentive light is indeed white before the multiplication of its internal form has rubified it, and the silvery spirit is made manifest before the solar ray. Take the white, clear, and dignified herb, says Maria, which grows upon the little mountains, grind it fresh when it is arrived at its determined hour, for in it is the genuine body which evaporates not, neither does it at all flee from the fire. But, after this, it is necessary to rectify Kibric and Zibeth (the soul and spirit) upon this body; i.e., the two fumes which comprise and embrace each other in the two luminaries, and to put them upon that which softens them, which is the accomplishment of the tinctures and spirits, the true weights of the wise; then, having ground the whole, put it to the fire; admirable things will then be seen. There is nothing further required but to maintain a moderate fire; after which it is wonderful to see how, in less than an hour, the composition will pass from one color to another, till it comes to the perfect red or white; when it does, then abate the fire and open the vessel, and when it is cold, there will appear in it a body clear, shining like a pearl or the color of wild poppy mingled with white. It is then incerating, melting, penetrative, and one weight of this body cast upon 12,000 of the imperfect metal, will convert it into gold. Behold, the concealed secret and these two fumes are the root of the Hermetic science; which, being of one root, are separated, dissolved, and reunited so often until their fermentive virtue survives the utmost efforts of art or nature any more to decompose.—See the Scholium and Maria Practica and Freher's Analogy, etc.

66. An unskillful artist may doubtless make errors in this art as in any other, either in chemistry or in housewifery, without understanding the proper method and matter of fermentation. The remark of the master, therefore, needs not further illustrating.

67. The apparition of the new light to the outward qualifications of the spirit is not welcome or sweet at first, but causes a terrification of the whole circumferential life. The wrathfulness is mightily exasperated by this appearance of love, says the theosophist, and pres-

seth violently to swallow it up in death; which actually it doth: but perceiving that no death can be therein, the love sinketh only down, yielding up itself unto those murderous properties for awhile and displaying among them its own loving essentiality. Thus is found, at last, a poison to death and a pestilence to hell; for the wrathful properties are terrified at this entering of love into them, which is contrary to their quality, and renders them weak and impotent, so that they lose at length their own will, strength and predominance. See Freher's Analogy at the end. By the King's seal, Hermes signifies the great Law of Light or universal reason, which is finally impressed upon the regenerated vitality of nature.

68. This most precious Stone, are we at length to conclude then, is Light essentialized in its proper substance, and exalted by fermentation into an immutable magnet, able to draw and convert the radical homogeneity of nature into its own assimilative accord? Yet this is an ultimate promise only, and the reward of ardent and continual toil; the art offers many intermediate benefits by the way, alluring health, science and riches, of her mineral stores. Our stone, says the adept, drives away and cures all sorts of maladies whatever, and preserves any one in good health to the last term of his life; it tinges and can change all metals into silver and gold, even better than those which nature is accustomed to produce; and, by its means, crystals may be transformed into precious gems. But, if the intention be to change metals into gold, it is requisite they should be first fermented with the most pure gold; for otherwise the imperfect metals would not be able to support its too great and supreme subtility; but there would ensue loss and damage in the projection. The imperfect metals, also, ought to be purified, if any one will draw profit therefrom. One drachm of gold is sufficient for the fermentation in the Red, and one of silver for the fermentation in the White; and the artist need not be at the trouble of buying gold and silver for this fermentation, because, with one single very small part, the tincture may be afterwards augmented more and more; for if this medicine be multiplied and be again dissolved and coagulated by the water of its mercury, white or red, of which it was prepared, then the tinging virtue will be augmented each time by ten degrees perfection which may be reiterated at will.—See Lucerna Salis, Kuhnrath Amphitheat., circa finem.

69. The seven chapters of the Golden Treatise are here concluded; which are a fair example of the Alchemical writings in general, and less sophistical than many, which may be considered perhaps as a small recommendation of the rest. For, although the discourse is sententious, and analogies are dispersed throughout with philosophic tact and plausibility, yet the whole is covered with an obnoxious veil; for neither the does Hermes discover the true Art, either whence, when or how the Matter is to be taken; but the philosophic vessel, with the whole apparatus for working the Spirit to perfection, is wrapped up under an ambiguous disguise. It is impossible almost to convey an adequate idea of the extent to which the mystification has been carried: the literature of Alchemy has not its parallel in the entire range, but is the problem of contradictions by excellence, as it were, framed after the pattern of the cruel Sphinx herself; so that the very abundant evidence which, under other circumstances, would be advantageous, becomes burdensome in this inquiry, occasioning a difficulty of discretion where to believe and vindicate the true light. In these easy reading days, too, when the fruits of science are laid open and books are made suitable for the instruction of the meanest capacities, few are disposed to study for anything—even the most lucrative gain—still fewer will there be found of a mind ready to exert itself about the traditionary report of bygone wisdom. We had not ourselves, thus singly without modern precedent, ventured within the confines of this magic wild, but for the theoretic promise of possibility held out; having observed also much of the doctrines and tangled enigmas to unfold and arrange themselves slowly, yet in peculiar order, by the leading of a certain experimental clue. By this we hope to point out, as we discern them, the disjecta membra long since mangled and concealed there, and to discover the abode, at least, of that queenly Isis who is alone able to gather them together into the beauty and perfection of their original form.

Part Two
A more esoteric consideration of the Hermetic Art and its Mysteries

Chapter 1. Of the True Subject of the Hermetic Art, and its Concealed Root

opening, by way of evidence, the Alchemical Laboratory and only vessel which the Adepts employed to sublime the universal Spirit of Nature and concentrate her Light — how, when, and where the Spirit may be arrested, introverted in the circulation, and brought forth from immanifest being into power and act, leading on from thence towards an outline of the Hermetic Art.

Opus vobuscum et apud est, quod intus arripens et permanens in terra vel in mare habere potes.

— Tractatus Aureus, cap. 1

Hitherto we have regarded this mystic labyrinth of Alchemy from without, considering the superficial scheme only; before we enter, it may be well to offer the consenting reader our clue, lest, observing merely our indirect and sudden outset, he suppose the way mistaken, and losing faith accordingly, should decline to pass with us further to the end.

For the paths through which we would conduct him are dark, intricate, lonely, and in a measure fearful; far receding, and out of reach of this outer daylight, with all its corporeal witnesses and scenes. Nor has the way become smoother from beings so long a while untrodden. We shall have to thread many windings, to pass round and through thick tangles of doubt and overgrown prejudice, which time has accumulated and thrown up together at the gates; before we can hope to enter the sanctuary of Minerva, much less behold the sacred light which burns there before her pure presence for ever, refulgent and still.

No modern art or chemistry, notwithstanding all its surreptitious claims, has any thing in common to do with Alchemy, beyond the borrowed terms, which were made use of in continuance chiefly to veil the latter; not from any real relation, either of matter, method, or practical result. For though aqua fortis and aqua regia seem to dissolve metals, and many salts be found useful in analysis, and fire for the tearing in pieces of bodies; yet nothing vitally alternative is achieved, unless the vital force be present and in action. But modern art drives out, in fact, the very nature which the ancients prized; distilling and dissecting superficies, harassing forever, without the more evolving any true cause, just because their notion of experience and method of experimenting are superficial and essentially atheistic.

The pseudo-Alchemists dreamed of gold, and impossible transformations, and worked with sulfur, mercury, and salt of the mines, torturing all species, dead and living, in vain, without rightly divining the true Identity of nature; the means they employed were from literal readings of receipts; they had no theory whereby to direct their research, and making trial of nature; as if she were a thing of chance, by chance, found nothing. Some few, of superior imagination to these, who had glimpses of the Universal Subject, endeavored to draw light into focus of their vessels, to compress and entice the ether by mangetical disposition and attractions of various kinds; but their hopes were too vaguely based, there was no wisdom in their magistery, being ignorant of that internal fire and vessel of the adepts, so essential to the accomplishment of the Hermetic work. For how hardly should they divine without instruction, or interpret the dark hieroglyphic seal?

It is declared, in the ancient book of Tobit, to be honorable to reveal the works of the Lord; but good t keep close the secret of a king; and old adepts, as if emulous of the sacred ordinance, whilst they display all the grandeur and abundant riches of his monarchy, make little or no mention of the king at all. And whilst the light has remained so long under the bushel of ignorance, with the Divine Wisdom under the bark of the Law, it is deplorable to think how many worthy and truth-loving intellects have languished and perished for lack of knowledge; knowledge too that is attainable, since it has been attained. For their few sakes, we now write therefore, and feel emboldened to hazard evidence of the forbidden truth; and without, we trust, transgressing the spirit of the prophet's advice, it may be allowed to lay open the regalia so far as we shall induce inquiry, and a more respectful consideration than heretofore.

The inquiries hitherto made by us, concerning the physical basis of the Hermetic Science, have helped to identify it with a matter now, at best, hypothetically conceived of only, since the means of proving it are unknown, and the obscure instructions of the ancients concerning the nature of their conceptive vehicle, has caused incalculable error and confusion; and though the says of gross credulity have passed away, and a more widespread education has helped to awaken the common sense of mankind to a perception of the improbable and ridiculous in most things, yet other obstacles supervene, as great, if not more obnoxious to the pursuit of causal science. The human mind, indeed, has been so long unaccustomed truly to know anything, or even think of, much less investigate, its own intrinsical phenomena, that to speak of them at the present time may subject us to every imputation of error and presumption. And why a barren period has supervened; and man has no longer any experience in the life of wisdom, nor yet surmises the virtue that is in him, to prove and magnify the Universal Source. Yet that was the foundation of the whole Hermetic magistery, whence it is said, that if the wise had not found a proper vessel in which to concoct it, the ethereal corner stone would never have been brought to light. This Hali declares and Morien, and Albert, saying, that the place is the principle also of the supernatural generation; and Hermes, vas philosophorum est aqua eorum; but they do not openly reveal either, as Maria concludes in her admonition,— Philosophers have spoken sufficiently of all that is necessary concerning the work, with exception of the vessel; which is a divine secret, hidden from idolators, and without this knowledge no one can attain to the magistery[1].

Thus, it appears to have been a religious principle with the ancients, to withhold the means of proving their philosophy from an incapable and reckless world; and if by hazard, less prudent or envious than the rest, alluded openly in his writings wither to the concealed vessel or art of vital administration, his revealment was instantly annulled by false or weakening commentaries, or as quickly as possible withdrawn by means not less sure, because hidden from the world. Of the former expedient we have a notable example in Sendivogius, who, towards the conclusion of his treatises, referring to the honest Hermit Morien's advice to King Calid,—Haec denim re ex te extrahitur—This matter, O king, is extracted from thee—endeavors to draw attention off from it, by inveigling the reader into a doubt artfully raised about some gold found sticking between a dead man's teeth[2]. Such instances are not rare, and it has been found easy by such similar equivocations, without absolute denial, to protect from foolish and profane intrusion that living temple wherein alone the wise of all ages have been securely able to raise their rejected Corner Stone and Ens of Light.

When, however, the writings of Jacob Böhme appeared in Germany, some century and a half ago, the Alchemists who lived at that period, write as if they supposed their art could little longer remain a secret; a similar alarm had previously arisen amongst certain Rosicrucians about the books of Agrippa and Paracelsus' disciples, and in both instances because those great theosophists spoke openly, applying the practice of Alchemy to human life; suggesting also, as did the latter, the method and medium of attraction. For, notwithstanding these, in common with the rest, teach that the Mercurial Spirit is everywhere, and to be found in all things according to the nature of each, yet they do not so much profess to have sought for it in many things, or that it may with equal advantage be drawn forth from all; since it is neither apt to become universal of its own accord, or in every Form of virtue sufficient for the Hermetic work. Therefore, they say, the best and noblest ought to be chosen to operate with, unless the searcher proposes to waste labor and ingenuity without obtaining his desired end. Besides, to search out the identity through all creatures and minerals, by way of experiment, would seem to be a matter of no small difficulty if we must need investigate each; but if one subject should be presented which contains all, and the comprehension of each subordinate form in a superior essence, then this one needs only to be investigated for the discovery of all. But the universal orb of the earth, adds the Moorish philosopher, contains not so great mysteries and excellences as Man *reformed* by God into his image; and he that desires the primacy amongst the students of nature, will nowhere find a greater or better reserve to obtain his desire than in himself, who is able to draw to himself the Central Salt of nature in abundance, and in his regenerate Wisdom possesseth all things, and with this light can unlock the most hidden and recluse mysteries of nature[3]. As Agrippa, moreover, testifies, that the soul of man, being estranged from the corporeal senses, adheres to a divine nature, from which it receives those things which it cannot search into by it sown power; for when the mind is free, the reins of the body being loosed and going forth, as out of a close prison, it transcends the bonds of the members, and nothing hindering, being stirred up in its proper *essence,* comprehends all things. And therefore man was said to be the express Image of God, seeing he contains the *Universal Reason* within himself, and has a corporeal similitude also with all, operation with all, and conversation with all. But he symbolizes with matter in a proper subject; with the elements in a fourfold body; with plants in a vegetable virtue; with animals in a sensitive faculty; with the heavens in an ethereal spirit and influx of the superior parts upon the inferior; with the angelical sphere in understanding and wisdom, and with God in all. He is preserved with God and the intelligences by faith and wisdom; with celestial things by reason and discourse; with all inferior things by sense and dominion; and acts with all, and has power on all, even on God Himself, continues the magician, by knowing and loving Him. And as God knoweth all things, seeing he has for an adequate object Being in general, or, as some say, Truth itself: neither is there anything found in man, nor any disposition in which something of divinity may not shine forth, as out of a close prison, it transcends the bonds of the members, and, nothing hindering, being stirred up in its proper essence, comprehends all things. And therefore man was said to be the express Image of God, seeing he contains the Universal Reason within himself, and has a corporeal similitude also with all, operation with all, and conversation with all. But he symbolizes with matter in a proper subject; with the elements in a fourfold body; with plants in a vegetable virtue; with animals in a sensitive faculty; with the heavens in an ethereal spirit and influx of the superior parts upon the inferior; with the angelical sphere in understanding and wisdom, and with God in all. He is preserved with God and the intelligences by faith and wisdom; with all celestial things by reason and discourse; with all inferior things by sense and dominion; and acts with all, and has power on all, even on God Himself, continues the magician, by knoweth all things, so man, knowing Him, also can know all things, so man, knowing Him, also can know all things, seeing he has for an adequate object Being in general, or, as some say, Truth itself: neither is there anything found in man, not any disposition in which something of divinity may not shine forth; neither is there anything in God which may not also be represented in man. Whosoever, therefore, shall know himself, shall know all things in *himself*; but especially he shall know God, according to whose image he was made; he shall known the world, the resemblance of which he beareth; he shall know all creatures with which in essence he symboliseth, and what comfort he can have and obtain from stones, plants, animals, elements; form spirits, angels, and everything; and how all things may be fitted for all things, in their time, place, order, measure, proportion, and harmony; even how he can draw and bring them to himself as a loadstone, iron[4].

And this the adept, Sendivogius, moreover declares: That nature, having her proper light, is by the shadowy body of sense, hidden from our eyes; but if, says he, the light of nature doth enlighten any one, presently the cloud is taken away from before his eyes, and without any let, he can behold the point of our lodestone, answering to each center of the beams (viz. of the sun and moon philosophical) for so far doth the light of nature penetrate and discover inward things; the body of man is a shadow of the seed of nature; and as man's body is covered with a garment, so is man's nature covered with the body. Man was created of the earth, and lives by virtue of the air; for there is in the air a secret food of life, whose invisible congealed spirit is better than the whole world. Oh, holy and wonderful nature! Which knowest how to produce wonderful fruits by water, out of the earth and from the air to give them life! The eyes of the wise look upon nature otherwise than the eyes of common men. The most high Creator, having been willing to manifest all natural things to man, hath even showed us that celestial things themselves were naturally made; by which his absolute power and wisdom might be so much the better known; all which things the philosophers in the light of nature, as in a looking-glass, have a clear sight of; for which cause they esteemed this art of Alchemy, viz., not so much out of covetousness for gold or silver, but for the knowledge's sake; not only of all natural things, but also of the power of the Creator. But they are willing to speak of these things sparingly only, and figuratively, lest those divine mysteries, by which nature is illustrated, should be discovered to the unworthy; which *thou, if thou knowest how to know thyself, and art not of a stiff neck*, mayest easily comprehend, who art created after the likeness of the great world, yea after the image of God. Thou hast in thy body the anatomy of the whole world, and all thy members answer to some celestials; let, therefore, the searcher of this Sacred Science know that the soul in man, the lesser world or microcosm, substituting the place of its center, is the king, and is placed in the vital spirit in the purest blood.

That governs the mind, and the mind the body; but this same sol, by which man differs from other animals and which operates in the body, governing all its motions, hath a far greater operation out of the body, because out of the body it absolutely reigns; and in this respect, it differs from the life of other creatures which have only spirit and not the soul of Deity[5].

Such are the distinctive assertions of one esteemed an adept by his contemporaries, and who professes to ground them also on his own manual experience in the proto-chemistry of Hermes. And, whether they be entirely credited or not, these may help to elucidate the words of Trismegistus, where, in the first chapter of the *Golden Treatise*, he says,—that the work is both in us and about us; and that the whole mystery is comprehended in the hidden elements of his Wisdom[6]. And Geber, in the same sense, where he declares that he who in himself knows no natural principles, is very remote from this sacred science, because he has not the true root in him whereon to base his labor and intention[7]. Observe, therefore, and take heed, says Basil, that all metals and minerals have one root from whence their descent is; he that knows that rightly needs not destroy metals in order to extract the spirit from one, the sulfur from another, or salt from another; for there is a nearer place yet in which these three, viz., the mercury, slat and sulfur—spirit, body and soul—lie hid together in one thing, well known, and whence they may with great praise be gotten. He that knows exactly this *golden seed or magnet*, and searcheth thoroughly into its properties, he hath the true root of life, and may attain to that which his heart longs for; wherefore I intreat, continues the monk, all true lovers of mineral science, and sons of art, diligently to inquire after this metallic seed, or root, and be assured that it is not an idle chimera or dream, but a real and certain truth[8].

It was from such an internal intimacy, and central searching of the mystery, that the Paracelsian Crollius tells us he came to know that the same light and mineral vapor, which produces gold within the bowels of the earth is also in man, and that the same is the generating spirit of all creatures[9]. And Albertus Magnus, in his book of Minerals, after asserting that gold may be found everywhere, in the final analysis of every natural thing, concludes by showing that the highest mineral virtue nevertheless resides in man; for fire, which is the true aurific principle in the life of all, burns more than all glorious in him erect.—Our Mercury is philosophic, fiery, vital—which may be mixed with all metals and again be separated from them; it is prepared in the innermost chamber of life, and there it is coagulated, as the Hermetic phrase runs, and where metals grow where they may be found[10].

> *Remember how man, ys most noble creature*
> *In Erth's composycion that ever God wrought,*
> *In whom are the fowre elements proportioned by nature,*
> *A naturall mercuryalyte which cost right nought,*
> *Out of hy myner by arte yt most be brought;*
> *For our mettalls be nought ells but miners too,*
> *Of our Soon and Moone, wyse Reymond seyd so*[11].

And though the philosophers have chosen to say little about it, on account of the shortness of this work, as Maria says, yet they themselves found out these hidden elements, and themselves increased them. And thou, oh, Man, cries the Arabian Aliphili, even thou art he who through the breath and power of the water and earth in thyself, conjoinest the elements and makest them one; and thyself not knowing what a treasure thou hast hidden in thee, from the coagulation and consent of these powers, producest an essence, called, by us, the expert, the great and miraculous mystery of the world; that is the true fiery water.—*Eschva mayim, Erascha mayim,* yea, it surmounts in its power, the fire, air, earth and water; for it dissolves radically, incrudates even the mature, constant, and very fixed, fiery and abiding mass and matter of gold, and reducing it into a fit black earth, like to black spittle; wherein we find a water and the true salt destitute of all odor, vehemency, and corrosive nature of the fire: there is nothing in the whole world besides to be found which can do this; to which nothing is shut; and though it is a precious thing, more precious than everything, yet the poor as well as the rich may have it in the same equal plenty. The wise men have sought this thing, and the wise men have found it[12].

And it behooves him, therefore, who would be introduced to this hidden Wisdom, says Hermes, to quit himself from the usurpations of vice, to be good and just and of a profound reason, ready at hand to help mankind; for these subtle chemical secrets may never be handled by the idle or vicious unbelievers of these matters in which they are only ignorant, who, being destitute of light, defile by an evil imagination the very Spirit that ought to be refined.—*Omne Aurum est aes, sed non omne aes est aurum:*—and the true physician, according to Crollius (whom Paracelsus called a natural divine) is true, sincere, intelligent, faithful: and being well exercised in the vital analysis of bodies, knows that there is no constant quality of any body which is not to be found in the salt, mercury, and sulfur thereof[13]. And these three principles of attraction, repulsion, and circulation, the universal accord of life, are everywhere and in all.

> *Blood containeth the three things I have told,*
> *And in his tincture hath nature of gold:*
> *Without gold, no metal may shine bright;*
> *Without blood no body hath light:*
> *So doth the greater and less world still*
> *Hold the circle according to God's will.*
> *Blood hath true proportion of th' elements foure.*
> *And of the three parts spoke of before;*
> *For blood is the principle matter of each thing,*
> *Which hath any manner of increasing.*
> *The true blood to find without labour or cost,*
> *Thou knowest where to have it, worthy wits be lost;*
> *See out the noblest, as I said before,*
> *And now of the Matter, I dare say no more*[14].

Or, what more shall I say? (asks Morien, emphatically, discoursing with the Arabian monarch about the confection of the Stone, and after showing the distinctive supremacy of man in nature). The thing, O king, is extracted from thee, in the which mineral thou dost even exist; with thee it is found; by thee it is received; and when thou shalt have proved all by the love and delight in thee, it will increase; and thou wilt know that I have spoken an enduring truth[15].

Although few write so clearly to the purpose as those we have selected, yet the more modern class of adepts have in general left hints and suggestions to the same effect; they describe the life of man, as by their Art revealed, to be a pure, naked, and unmingled fire of infinite capability, differing from that of the prone creatures in form, educability, and capacity for melioration in itself. And though it might be supposed, according to the alleged diffusion of the Matter, that, if the Art of separating it were known, it might be taken anywhere (which in part also is true) yet we may consider the object was not simply to obtain the Matter or prove it only, but to improve, perfect, and bring the Causal light to manifestation. And in what our human circulatory system differs and occultly approximates, so that it can be made to comprehend all inferior existences, and supersede nature in her course, may be gathered from this philosophy; and may reasons are given why the most noble subject was chosen, and this only vessel for its elaboration. The foregoing evidence, however, without more defense at present, may help to lead on the inquiry to a more explicit ground.

Attraction is the first principle of motion in nature; this is generally admitted, but the origin of this universal attraction is occult and incomprehensible to the ordinary human understanding. Repulsion is the second principle, and a necessary consequence of the first by reaction. Circulation is the third principle, proceeding from the conflict of the former two.

All motion is derived from this threefold source in its reciprocal relations, which are diversified according to its qualifications with the matter. The attraction, repulsion and circulation in the sun and stars move the planets in their orbits; the same principle in each globe performs the rotation on its axis, and the satellites partake the same motion from their primaries. Every quantity of matter, solid, fluid, or gaseous, when separated from the rest by its quality or discontinuity, is possessed individually by the same principles, however infinite the variety of substances, natural or artificial, great or small; vegetable and animal forms and motions are no less evidences of these three principles than the heavenly and earthly bodies. Hence chemical affinity, called Elective Attraction, is ruled by the same laws; and it is found that when two matters unite, one is attractive and the other repulsive; when either attraction or repulsion predominates in a matter, the circulation is in ellipse; but when they are in equilibrium, a circle is produced. Repulsion, being produced in its origin by attraction, equals it, as reaction equals action: but *in nature one principle is everywhere more latent or inert, or weaker than another;* and there are degrees accordingly, in which either predominates in external manifestation; hence the different degrees of natural affinity for union. There are also degrees of strength, from harshness to mildness, and in the operation of the Three Principles, from the compactness of a hard rock to the loose adherence of the particles of a globule of mercury or dew, from explosion to expansion, and from a violent whirling motion to a gentle evolution. But the medium is always in the circulation produced from the action and reaction of centrifugal and centripetal forces, and the equality of these forms a circle, as was before observed, and which labors to harmonize the conflict of these two, and will succeed if the matter be duly qualified for it.

But, according to the Alchemists, there is but One Matter truly qualifiable or capable of qualifying matter to be harmonized in this way, since nature has fallen off from her original balance, and the wheel of human life turns forth, deviating from its axis, into a line which terminated finally in dissolution; which nothing but their Antimonial Spirit rectified by Art, being in bright lines of equal attraction and repulsion, as it were a perfect magnet in a star-like circle of irradiated circulation, can contrariate or withstand[16].

And the agent in the preparation of this spirit, continues Bohme, is the Invisible Mercury, and no process can finally fail where the invisible Universal Mercury, or spiritual air of Antimony, is present, condensed in its proper vehicle in any of the degrees of permanency; *and the Principle of its operation consists in the power of harmonizing the three discordant principles ofAttraction, Repulsion, and Circulation*[17]. And this is the vital spirit of the arterial blood, where the universal principles are in their natural generation unequally composed: the repulsive force so far predominating over the interior attraction, that the total circulatory life is expulsive, and drawn without to a debilitated consciousness away from its First Cause. Which inverse order of relationship and vital ignorance it is the object of the Hermetic art to remedy, and, by occultation of the opposive principle, to restore the true rector to his original rule. *Sanquinem urinamque pariter dat nobis natura, et ab horum natura salem dat Pyrotechnia, quem circulat ares in salem Paracelsi. Hoc addam: sanguinis salem per urinaceum fermentum sic transmutari debere, ut ultiman vitam amittat, mediamque servet, salsedinemque retineat*[18].

> *Si fixum solvas faciasque volare solutum*
> *Et volucrem figas, faciunt tutum*
> *Sove, Coagula, Fige.*

This know, therefore, says Hermes, that except thou understandeth how to mortify and induce generation, to vivify the spirit, to cleanse and introduce light, until they fight and contend with each other, and grow white and freed form their defilements, rising, as it were, from blackness and darkness, thou knowest nothing, nor canst perform anything; but if thou knowest this, thou shalt be of a great dignity[19]. All which our modern exponent, further illustrating the Hermetic process, confirms. For, in three months circulation, says he, by digestion, the powder becomes black, the opposition of attraction and repulsion ceases (in the vital spirit), and the attraction of the fixed which produced the repulsion of the volatile, is slain by the circulation which also dies itself, and all three enter into rest. Then there is no more compression or expansion, ascent or descent, but the action and reaction have, by the equilibriate radiation of forces and the subtlety of the spirit, formed a circulation which has consumed all discordant opposites, and sunk down black and motionless. And thus the head of Hermes' crow is said to be in the beginning of this work; that which at first was fixed, viz., the sentient medium, is dissolved, and by the same process more profoundly operating, the original evil is made manifest in the matter to be renewed, and hence the principle of amendment and rectification also will appear, and on either side it is a signal of Art.

The same Three Principles gradually assume a new life, continues Böhme, infinitely more powerful in virtue, but without any violent contest, and in three months farther, mild action of the principles in harmony have produced a brilliant whiteness in the matter, which in three months more become a brilliant yellow, red, or purpling tincture:— Approach, ye sons of Wisdom, and rejoice; let us now rejoice together, for the reign of sin is finished, and the king doth rule, and now he is invested wit the red garment, and now the scarlet color is put on[20].

That was the process of working with the Vital Spirit, so often reiterated by Hermes, Democritus, and the rest before cited, which also is many times passed through for the practical accomplishment. But every other matter labors for this perfection in vain; it can only attain to combustion, heat, and temporary light, and the consumption of the common elements in their analysis is a separation into gas and ashes; but this mystical nature revives, fortified from every successive dissolution, renewing its Whole resolutely from either extreme by union. This Spirit is so full of life, says the adept, that if the process fails in any stage, an addition of the same will renew it. The white or red powder is increased tenfold in strength and quantity by each digestion of it with fresh i, wet with *gas water, or oil of this antimony*, and each digestion is made in tenfold shorter time than the preceding from a week to a few hours. For this gold is endued with a magnetical virtue, which by the inspirate fulgor of its tincture, draws the divine increase after it; in which nature expends all her forces, but leaves the victory to Art, which by graduation to the full height, adds to the natural effulgence a supernatural light; for what else but light should multiply? Whence it has been called likewise the terrestrial or Microcosmic Sun, the triumphal Chariot of Antimony turned swift upon the current wheel of life; and this is the Stone of Fire seen in bright lines, of equal attraction and repulsion, when made manifest, as it were, an armed magnet included and circulating in a perpetual heaven[21]. Know, therefore, and consider, says Basil Valentine, that this true tincture of Antimony, which is the medicine of men and metals, is not made of crude melted antimony, such as the apothecaries and merchants sell, but is extracted from the *true mineral*, as it is taken from the *mountains*; and *how* that extraction should be made, is a principal secret in which the whole art of Alchemy consists. Health, riches, and honor attend him who rightly attains it.—*Lapis noster inter duos monticulos nascitur; in te et in me at in nostri similibus latet*[22]. And when the mechanical part of the Three Principles passes into the hands of its proper manufacturers equally and generally in all countries, concludes Böhme, then will the school of adepts come out from this captivity, and will find their proper level as true physicians for the body and soul, dispensing the leaves of life for the healing of the nations. But now the Seal of God lieth before it, to conceal the true ground, unless a man knew for certain that it would not be misused; for there is no power to obtain, no art or skill availeth, *unless one intrust another with somewhat* (as Hermes and Arnold bear witness); yet the Work is easy and simple, but the wisdom therein is great and the greatest mystery[23].

The greatest mystery of all is in Existence, and the only mystery; and as fire and light are one and everywhere perceived after the same manner, so is life in every particular the same inscrutable Identity through all. Or does a vast and filled creation hang before our eyes, and we think it to be without a foundation? Do we ourselves exist and consciously breathe, denying a mystery; or rather, admitting this, does any doubt that it is discoverable? Does not everything imply a necessary cause, and is not each sustained still living in the same? And is it not absurd to suppose that we are entirely depending on externals, or that being in part self-dependent, we are so far depending on nothing? If, therefore, we contain within us a proper principle of being, why should not this, thus proximate, be known? Behold, says the apostle, He is not far off from every one of us; for in Him we live, and move, and have our being,—And again, to those forgetful Athenians,—God made man to the end that he should seek the Lord, if haply he might feel after him he should seek the Lord, if haply he might feel after him and find him[24]. And is not this a promise worth the certifying, an end worthy to be sought out, to feel and know God? Seek and ye shall find, knock and it shall be opened unto you; yet it remains hidden still: and that Philalethean Welshman, Vaughan, indeed advises that we give ourselves no trouble about these mysteries, or attempt to dabble in the subtle philosophy of Wisdom, until we have a knowledge of the Protochemic Artifice; for that by means of this, and this only, the true foundation is discoverable, and without it nothing can be intrinsically understood. It were a foolish presumption, he observes, if a lapidary should undertake to state the value or luster of a jewel that is shut up, before he opens the cabinet; yet men will presume to judge of invisible celestial things, which are shut up within the closet of matter, and all the while perusing the outside which is the crust of nature. But advise them to use their hands and not their fancies, and to change their abstractions into extractions; for verily as long as they lick the shell after their fashion, and pierce not experimentally into the center of things, they can do no otherwise than they have done; they cannot know things intrinsically, but only describe them by their outward effects and motions, which are subject and obvious to every common eye. Let them consider, therefore, that there is in nature a certain Spirit which applies himself to the matter, and actuates in every generation; that there is also a passive intrinsical principle where he is more immediately resident than in the rest, and by mediation of which he communicates with the more gross material parts. For there is in nature a certain chain or subordinate propinquity of complexions between visibles and invisibles, and this is it by which the superior spiritual essences descend and converse here below with the matter. But, he continues, have a care lest you misconceive me. I speak not in this place of the divine spirit, but *I speak of a certain Art by which a Particular Spirit may be united to the Universal; and nature by consequence be strongly exalted and multiplied*[25]. And Agrippa speaks yet more specifically to this point, where, in the third book of his *Occult Philosophy*, he declares (calling Apuleius also to witness) that by a certain mysterious recreation and appeasing, the human mind, especially that which is simple and pure, may be converted and laid asleep from its present life so utterly as to be brought into its divine nature, and become enlightened with the divine light, and withal receive the virtue of some wonderful effects[26].

Both these passages are in allusion to the art of Alchemy; and this, persists Agrippa, is that which I would have you know; because in us is the Operator of all wonderful effects; who know how to discern and to effect, and that without any sin or offense to God, whatsoever the monstrous mathematicians, the prodigious magicians, the envious alchemists, and bewitching necromancers can do by spirits, in us, I say, is the Operator of miracles.

> *Not the bright stars of the skie, nor flames of hell,*
> *But the Spirit begetting all doth in us dwell*[27].

How many earnest and curious books there have been written relative to the powers of magic and transformations by spells, talismans, and circumstantial conjurations of all sorts, which, taken according to the letter, are ridiculous without the key. But the records of Alchemy are, above all, calculated to mislead those who have gone abroad thoughtlessly seeking for that perfection which was to be found only by experimentally seeking at home within themselves.

> *Quid mirum noscere mundum*
> *Si possunt hominess, quibus est et mundus in ipsis*
> *Exemplumque Dei quisque est in imagine parva?*[28].

Man then, shall we conclude at length, is the true laboratory of the Hermetic art; his life the subject, the grand distillatory, the thing distilling and the thing distilled, and Self-Knowledge to be at the root of all Alchemical tradition? Or, is any one disappointed at such a conclusion, imagining difficulties, or that the science is impracticable because it is humanly based?—Or some may possibly think the pursuit dangerous, or inexpedient, or unprofitable, scientific investigation having been so long and successfully carried on in every adverse direction? Behold we invite not the unwilling, nor will these studies be found to reward the sordid seeker after riches or gold only; such may find better employ and better emolument from the abundant offering of the precious metal upon the earth, nor do we anticipate that many will in the present day be attracted to our goal.

Yet, notwithstanding so much skepticism and the slur which ignorance has cast now for centuries upon the every early creed and philosophy, modern discoveries tend evermore to reprove the same; identifying light, as the common vital sustenant, to be in motive accord throughout the human circulatory system with the planetary spheres and harmonious dispositions of the occult medium in space; and as human physiology advances with the other sciences in unison, the notion of out natural correspondency enlarges, proving things more and more minutely congruous, until at length, the conscious relationship would seem to be almost only wanting to confirm the ancient tradition and lead into its full faith. Yet on no ground with which we are now actually acquainted could it be proved that man is a perfect microcosm, wherein, as it was said, the great world and all its creatures might be summarily discerned: we have no evidence of any such thing; our affinities with external nature are bounded in sense, and our knowledge of her integral operations is proportionately defective. All that we do know is learned by observation, and we should be hardly induced, from anything we are commonly conversant with, to conclude that Self-Knowledge would be a way to the knowledge of the Universal Nature. Yet this was taught and believed formerly, not either as it were an arbitrary conceit, but as a truth understood and proved beyond speculation.

It may be well to observe, however, and lest misunderstanding should at all arise in this respect, that it is not so much with reference to physical particulars, either to the perfection of his bodily constitution, or because he is composed of the four elements, that man was formerly distinguished; for these other animals and vegetables even partake, and often in a superior degree: but it was rather on account of a Divine Reason, on occult principle of Causal Efficience, said to be originally resident in his life, that man was made to rank so high in the cabalistic scriptures and schools of antique experience. And here we remark that the outer body, mentioned indeed, yet as amongst the last of things accordant; nevertheless we remark the outer body, mentioned indeed, yet as amongst the last of things accordant; nevertheless it is nearly all we are now able to observe; as, of the rest, the Universal Reason so magnified and its ethereal vehicle, very meager evidence is afforded to the senses or this life. Yet man, say they, is demonstrated to be a compendium of the whole created nature, and was generated to become wise and have a dominion over the whole of things; having within him, besides those faculties which he exerts ordinarily and by which he judges and contemplates sensible phenomena, with the germ of a higher faculty or Wisdom, which, when revealed and set alone, all the forms of things and hidden springs of nature become intuitively known and are implied essentially. This Being, moreover, or Faculty of Wisdom, is reputed so to subsist with reference to nature as her substratal source, that it works magically withal, discovering latent properties as a principle, governing and supplying all dependent existence; and of this they speak magisterially, as if in alliance they had known the Omniscient

Nature and, in their own illumined understanding, the structure of the universe.

Now if it be true that such an experience was ever granted to man on earth, it is now either wholly departed or the conditions are estranged. We can but with difficulty imagine, much less are we able to believe, ourselves capable of enjoying that free perspicacity of thought in universal consciousness which is cognizant by support with essential being. Man from his birth employs sense prior to reflection, and all our knowledge begins in this life with sensible observation; most persons pass on well contented with such evidence as legitimate, or, indeed, possible objects of knowledge. But some few there have been in all ages, exceptions to the multitude, intellects in whom the standard of reality has been too far unfolded to suffer them to yield implicitly to the conclusions of sense. It is not those who have studied the philosophy of the ancients that have denounced it as chimerical; our metaphysicians, without exception amongst those deserving the appellation, and who aspired after the same convictive truth, have lamented the inadequacy of natural reason, at the same time that they recognized the supremacy of its Law as measuring and determining sensible particulars; but they have not been able to redeem it from dependency on these; for every attempt of the unassisted reason terminates negatively, as the Subject Identity slides evermore behind the retardant mind; it is only able at best, therefore, to maintain a counter ground, whereby to prove the shifting evidence of its own and other earthly phenomena.

But although satisfaction is thus denied to modern inquiry, and philosophers have disputed about the conditions and difficulty of the Absolute ground, yet are there none found, even in latter times, so presumptuous as to deny the possibility, seeing it thus doubly implied, no less in the testimony of the highest reason than of tradition: and so they have honored the ancients afar off either in despair or admiration of their Wisdom, unable themselves to break the enchantment which isolates the reflective faculty, and disables it in the inquiry after that Fontal Nature which, by a necessary criterion, it craves.

For we may observe, that the evidence of reason, even in common life, is irresistible, or, more exactly to speak, intuition is the evidence and end of every rational proof. We believe in the phenomenon of existence spontaneously, but in a power of antecedents to produce their effects necessarily; in the idea of time, eternity is implied; with bound, infinity; as the unit is included in each dependent of a numerical series, and the mathematics have their evidence in intellectual assent; nor do we ever question the validity of the Law, which thus abstractedly concludes within us, though our inferences from external facts are for ever varying, and perpetually at fault.

Locke, discoursing upon the intrinsic superiority of the Intellectual Law in his Essay, observes that Intuitive faith is certain beyond all doubt, and needs no proof beyond itself, nor can have any, this being the highest of all human certainty. And it is this very truth, that a no less eminent French philosopher, Victor Cousin, has successfully employed within these few years, to shake the sensual system of Locke and Condillac to its foundation[29]. And this subsistence of Universals in the human mind deserves to be profoundly considered by all who are interested in the pursuit of truth; for it includes a promise far beyond itself and stable proof of another subsistence however consciously unknown. Thus, if ordinary conviction is not attained by an assurance of reason to itself, and if, in the discovery of and assent to reason to itself, and if, in the discovery of and assent to universal propositions, there is no use of the discursive faculty or of external facts to witness; if, in short, we really know anything of self-evident intellectual necessity, independent of sensible persuasion, then does it not follow, there is a higher evidence of truth than the senses afford, and a superstantial nature of things implied which, though now latent and succeeding in order of time, is first in thought absolutely, and in the circular progression of nature may be so practically manifested at last? Aristotle compares the subsistence of Universals in the natural understanding to colors, since these require the splendor of the sun to discover their beauty, as do those the inspiring afflux of their frontal illumination: therefore, too, he denominates human reason, *intellect in capacity*, both on account of its subordination to essential intellect, and because it is from a new awakening, a divine recreation, as it were, that it conceives the full perfection of a life in accordance with its won intelligible beauty, goodness, and truth.

Thus strictly regarding the Intellectual Law, as it proves and orders inquiry in common life, we have an image, as it were, an embryo conception have and image, as it were, an embryo conception of that Archetypal Wisdom which the ancients celebrated as the occult essence of that Law. And here we remark the grand divergence between modern and ancient metaphysics: that same Law which the former recognizes but as an abstract boundary of thought only, having its object in sensibles, the latter proclaims absolutely to be the catholic subject of the great efficient force of nature, as known also, and proved in the human conscience, when this is purified and passed back into contacting experience with its source. And this was Wisdom, Intellect, Divination; and the true man, according to Plato and Aristotelians, is this Intellect; for the essence of everything is the summit of its nature. And as man is the summit of this sublunary creation, and reason is the highest faculty with which he is here endowed, should not this probably be the next in progress to make manifest the alleged divinity of his first source?

Lest doubt should still lurk, however, about such a divinity, and whether the notion is rightly conceived according to the teaching of the best philosophers, it may be well to bring them forward here, speaking for themselves.

Thus Aristotle, for first example, since he will not be rated altogether as an enthusiast, in the beginning of his *Metaphysics*, declares Wisdom to the highest science; adding that a wise man possesses a science of all things in intellect; not indeed derived from sensible particulars, but according to that which is universal and absolute in himself[30]. In the *Nichomachean Ethics*, too, after showing Intellect to be that power of the soul by which we know and prove things demonstratively, he further distinguishes Wisdom as the true being of that Intellect; the science and intellection of things most honorable by nature; that though this par this small in bulk, yet it abounds in energy, and as much exceeds the composite nature of man in power as in this energy, which is the most delectable of all energies[31]. And throughout the *Metaphysics*, but more especially in the Twelfth Book, he demonstrates the necessary subsistence of incorporeal (*i.e.*, essential) being, and its efficacy in operation when by the help of certain mystical exercises and preparations, the human Understanding Medium is made to pass into contact with its Antecedent Cause; that then it becomes to be a life in energy, and enjoys the most exalted and excellent faculty of discernment, which was before occult, and the knowledge of which is inexpressibly blessed, and not to be conceived of by such as are not duly initiated and capable of this deification.—True Intellect, he says, is that which is essentially the most essential of that which is most essential; and it becomes intelligible by contact and intellection; and that Intellect is the same with the intelligible, the understanding recipient of the intelligible essence[32]. Which essence, too, is Wisdom, and the faculty we are discussing. But Plato yet more plainly declares that to know oneself is Wisdom and the highest virtue of the soul; for the soul rightly entering into herself will behold all other things, and Deity itself; as verging to her own union and to the center of all life, laying aside multitude and the variety of all manifold powers which she contains, she ascends to the highest watchtower of beings[33]. According to Socrates, also, in the *Republic*, we read that Wisdom is generative of truth and intellect; and in the *Theaetus* Wisdom is defined to be that which gives perfection to things imperfect, and calls forth the latent Intellections of the soul—and again, by Diotima, in the *Banquet*, that mind which is become wise needs not to investigate any further (since it possesses the true Intelligible); that is to say, the proper object of intellectual inquiry in itself; and hence the doctrine of Wisdom according to Plato may be sufficiently obvious.

But Wisdom, says the Pythagorean Archytas, as much excels all the other faculties as sight does the other corporeal senses, or the sun the stars: and man was constituted to the end that he might contemplate the Reason of the whole nature, in order that, being himself the work of Wisdom, he might survey the Wisdom of all things, which exist. Wisdom is not conversant with a certain definite existing thing but simply with all things; and so subsists with reference to all that it is the province of it to know and contemplate the universal accidents of things and discover the Principles of all Being. Whoever therefore is able to analyze all the genera which are contained under one and the same principle and again to compose and connumerate them, he appears to be wise and to possess the most perfect veracity. Further still he will have discovered a beautiful place of survey, from which it will be possible to behold Divinity and all things that are in coordination with and successive to Him, subsisting separately and distinct from each other, Having likewise entered this most ample road, being impelled in a right direction by Intellect, and having arrived at the end of his course, he will have conjoined ends with beginnings, and will know that God who is the principle, middle, and end of all things which are accomplished according to justice and right reason[34].

Here again we have a faculty discussed which is far above ordinary reason, since this verges to sensibles and is dependent on them; but Wisdom implies the whole of life, being returned into its principle, and coming into the consciousness of a vision at once powerful and sublime. Thus Crito, of the same school: God so fashioned man as to comprehend the Good according to right reason, and gave him a sight called Intellect, which is capable of beholding God. For it is not possible without God to discern that which is best or most beautiful; nor without Intellect to see

God. And *every mortal nature is established (in this life) with a kindred privation of Intellect; this however is not deprived by God but by the essence of generation.*

The term Intellect, as it is here taken in its highest sense, is synonymous with Wisdom, and bears the same relation to our Intellectual Law as does this to the reasoning faculty, being the self-evident antecedent and end of its inquiry, which, according to these philosophers, is God. Pythagoras himself defined Wisdom as the science of truth which is in all beings[35]; and Jamblicus in his life of this Samian, speaking of Wisdom, says that it is truly a science which is conversant with the first and most beautiful objects (*i.e.*, the Divine Exemplars), and these undecaying, possessing invariable sameness of subsistence; but the participation of which other things also may be called beautiful[36]. Proclus, Porphyry, the graceful Plotinus, and others of the Neoplatonists, too numerous to mention, dilate on the same asserted ground; and there is, according to all these philosophers, a Principle of Universal Science latent in human life, real and efficacious though cognizable only under certain conditions which they specify, and wherein reason becomes also into the substantive experience of her Law.

This is that which the Egyptians, industrious searchers of Nature, proclaimed upon their temple's front, that *Man should know himself:* and this advice was meant experimentally and ontologically, though modern fancy has slighted it and taken every ethnic fable and mythology in a profane sense. And here we are reminded of a difficulty in endeavoring to make these positions respecting the nature of true Being obvious and of drawing them into a form related to sensible intelligence. Every science is difficult to treat of to the uninitiated mind, and this kind of speculation more particularly is irrelevant to many and naturally abstruse. Those to whom nature has granted such a ray of experience in the inner life as would otherwise appear favorable to a more profound investigation, are often indifferent to the rational ground, and remain accordingly satisfied in the dreams and deluding visions of an included imagination; others more awakened to reason on the other hand, but in whom the spirit of inquiry is wholly drawn to externals, disregard as vain every proposition that does not immediately address the senses or pander to some apparent individual interest; even the most reflective and educated class have rare inducements in these days, or permission of leisure sufficient to prosecute studies of an abstract nature. But we have adverted to the independent evidence of Universals in the human intellect by way of introduction chiefly, not on their own account abstractly considered, or so much because the ancients rested their proofs of internal science thereon; but because, having once derived a rational ground of possibility, we may be better enabled to proceed with the tradition of the Hermetic mystery and more tangible effects.

The doctrine of the Hebrew Cabalists is one of absolute Idealism; the whole world was before their eyes as an efflux of Mind, an emanation of the great superstantial Law of Light; and that sublime commentary the *Liber Zohar*, beams with the revelation of the celestial prototype in humanity; and kindling into reminiscence the fire which burns covertly throughout Holy Writ, addresses the Pentateuch to the understanding of mankind.

These Rabbis explain that in pursuance of a certain arcane (though not wholly inexplicable) necessity, creation falls away always for the sake of individual manifestation, from the consciousness of its primal source; that the principle of reunion nevertheless abides in the generated life of individuals and will in process of time operate to a restitution and higher perfection than could have been accomplished if such a fall into this existence had not taken place. Treating of and interpreting as divine symbols, the relations of the Old Testament, they dignify vastly the view of the whole scheme; and placing reason over the head of authority, and inciting man to self-inquiry as the foundation and comprehending identity of every other, they unite in one beautiful system the Religion of Intellect with the Philosophy of Life.

But it is above all by the supreme position which they assign to man in the scale of creation that these Cabalists arrest attention. The Form of man, says the Rabbi Ben Jochai, contains all that is in the heaven and earth—no form, no world, could exist before the human prototype; for all things subsist by and in it: without it there would be no world, and in this sense we are to understand these words, *The Eternal has founded the earth upon his wisdom.* But we must distinguish the true man from him who is here apparent, for the one could not exist without the other; on that form in man, which is the Celestial Prototype, rests the perfection of faith in all things, and it is in this respect that man is said to be the image of God[37]. For there is a wide difference between the idols of the human imagination and the ideas of the divine mind, between man as he is here known, the individualized multiplication of a blind will, and tat Motive Reason which is his life. And all this would appear less extravagant, perhaps, and impractical, if, instead of measuring the surfaces of things, we were to consider principles; if, instead of separating our shrunken understanding to contemplate and compare with the structure of this vast universe, we were to reflect contrariwise upon that wonderful existence which we share in common with all and which is at the basis of every specifical living thing. For there is no reason why man, in that he exists and contains, therefore, within himself the total Cause of existence, should not, if the revelation only were allowed, perceive and understand all, in that all-continental All which is in himself. There is a freedom, and explanatory breadth, too, in these writers that does not bear the impress of mere fancy, with a solemn earnestness of style that breathes only from conviction. That we cannot easily apprehend the magnitude of their doctrine is no criterion in such a case and its objections fail before the inference of reason and supporting experience.

God dwells, says the Jew Philo, in the rational part of man as in a palace; the palace and temple of the great self-existent Deity is the intellectual portion of a man of Wisdom; the Deity could never find upon earth a more excellent temple than the rational part of man[38]. And again, —the Logos, by whom the world was framed, is the seal after the impression of which everything is made and is rendered the similitude and image of the perfect Word of God; and the soul of man is an impression of this seal of which the prototype and original characteristic is the everlasting Logos[39]. And what is Wisdom according to the ancient Hermes? Even the good, the fair, and the blessed Eternity; look upon all things through it, and the world is subject to thy sight. For this Mind in men is God, and, therefore, are some men said to be divine, for there humanity is annexed to divinity[40]; when it is moved into the catholic Intuition of its Source.

Such then was Wisdom, and that high Intelligible which it behooves man to search after the one theme and bulwark of ancient science, which no historical teaching or observance of the accidents of nature could realize or improve—namely, the standard of truth in a rectified intellect. And philosophy was a desire of this kind, an appetition of reason for its antecedent light; and if we may believe these sublime enthusiasts, Intellect does not extend herself towards the intelligible Cause in vain. Quotation were endless, and enough may recur to the memory of those who do not yet despair of philosophy, or limit their faith to the slow evidence of the senses and double ignorance of these days.

Or, if any one should further doubt of this Wisdom, seeing she did not reveal herself in common arts and sciences of more recent human invention, and regard the whole as an abstract creature of the imagination, he will err from the ancient tradition, which makes Wisdom, however far removed from sensibles, to be no inessential thing; but an affirmative operative hypostasis, informing, invigorating, and sustaining all things; in the words of the Stagyrite before cited,—It is essentially, the most essential of that which is most essential.—But Solomon, better than all and most beautifully in his panegyric, describes her: Wisdom, says the wise king, is more moving than any motion, she passeth through all things by reason of her pureness. For she is the breath of the power of God, and a pure influence flowing from the glory of the Almighty; therefore, can no defiled thing fall into her; for she is the brightness of the everlasting light, the unspotted mirror of the power of God, and the image of his goodness. And, being but one, she can do all things, and, remaining in herself, she maketh all things new; and in all ages entering into holy souls, she maketh them friends of God and prophets, for God loveth none but him that dwelleth with Wisdom; for she is more beautiful than the sun and above all the order of the stars; being compared with the light, she is found before it, for after this cometh night; but vice shall not prevail against Wisdom; and if riches be a possession to be desired in this life, what is richer than wisdom which worketh al things? For she is privy to the mysteries of the knowledge of God and a lover of His works[41].

Assuredly, then, is it not our duty and best interest to learn the way, and seek to know every condition of this proffered alliance, since we are not destitute either of rational ground or precedent, nor is this the only place in Scripture where we have a promise with Wisdom of more substantial fruits? But as we observe the outer man to be unbelieving by nature and unpromising for much discovery, with his senses and servile intellect all dark within, we leave him here to work with his own instruments on his own ground; there to calcine, weight, and measure circumferences, from the first to the last round of material possibility; perchance, then, when all has been tried and found wanting to his reason, extremes coalescing, we may meet again.

Meanwhile we, who look directly onward to penetrate the mystery, seek not at random any longer in the outer world where so many before have foundered, albeit extracting their life's blood, and calling the mumial vapor and every element to their aid; but we look within, or rather, that we may learn how to do so, inquire of the wise ancients to direct us about the true method and conditions of Self-Knowledge. For it is this, no common trance or day-dream, or any fanatical vision of celestials, that we propose to scrutinize, but the true psychical experience, catholic, even as the basis of that Law by which we reason, fell, and are one, uniformly living and alike all.

It is into the substantiality of this and for its practical evolution that we must inquire, if we would discover the true Light of Alchemy; and the Alchemists, as we have seen, propose such a reducation of nature as shall discover this Latex without destroying her vehicle, but the modal life only; and profess that this has not alone been proved possible, but that man, by rationally conditionating, has succeeded in developing into action the Recreative Force. But the way they do not so clearly shew, or where nature may be addressed in order to the rejection of her superfluous forms; what was their immediate efficient? Whence and whereon did they direct their fire? These things, with the laboratory, its vessels and various apparatus, they have disguised, as we have already shown, and as a natural consequence, by an incurious world have been misapprehended and despised. For as Geber, with his usual point, observes, men have thought the confection of fold impossible, because they have not know the artificial destruction according to the course of nature; they have proved it to be of a strong composition, but of how strong a composition they have not proven.

And all this because they knew not the verity
Of altitude, latitude, and of profundity[42].

For how should they, who have never glanced even in imagination toward the Causal Truth, believe in any other than remote effects? The well out of which she is drawn is deep, and not therefore to be fathomed by the plummet of a shallow reason; he must ascend in thought who would, descending, hope to penetrate so far as to the superstantial experience of things. For there it is yet hidden, the true light shut up as in a prison, the fountain of Universal Nature separated off from human understanding by the external attraction of it through the gates of sense.

When the soul is situated in the body, says the philosopher, she departs from self-contemplation, and speaks of the concerns of an external life; but, becoming purified from the body, will recollect all those things, the remembrance of which she loses in the present life[43]; and Plutarch, who was well initiated in these mysteries, says, the souls of men are not able to participate of the Divine nature whilst they are thus encompassed about with senses and passions, any further than by obscure glimmerings, and as it were, in comparison, a confused dream. But when they are freed from these impediments and removed into purer regions, which are neither discernible by the corporeal senses, nor liable to accidents of any kind, it is then that God becomes our leader—upon Him they wholly depend, beholding without satiety, and still ardently longing after that beauty which it is impossible for man sufficiently to express or think—that beauty which, according to the old mythology, Isis has so great an affection for, and which she is constantly in pursuit of, and from whose enjoyment every variety of good things with which the universe is filled, is replenished, and propagated[44]. And again, in the opening of the same admirable treatise, he observes, that to desire and covet after the Truth is to aspire to be a partaker of the Divine Nature itself; and to profess that all our studies and inquiries are devoted to the acquisition of holiness; the end of which, as of all ceremonial rites and disciplines, was that the aspirant might be prepared and fitted for the attainment of the knowledge of the Supreme Mind, whom the Goddess exhorts them to search after. *For this Reason is her temple wherein the Eternal Self-existent dwells, and may there be finally approached, but with due solemnity, and sanctity of life.*

But Psellus, in his luminous commentary on the Chaldaic Oracles, further declares that there is no other means of strengthening the vehicle of the sold but by Material Rites; and Plato, in the first *Alcibiades*, calls the magic of Zoroaster the service of the gods; and the use of this magic, in the words of the above Psellus, is as follows:—*To initiate or perfect the human soul by the power of materials here on earth; for the supreme faculty of the soul by the power of materials here on earth; for the supreme faculty of the soul cannot by its own guidance aspire to the sublimest institution, and to the comprehension of Divinity: but the work of Piety leads it by the hand of God, by illumination from thence.*

Synesius, likewise, in his *Treatise on Providence*, bears witness to the efficacy of Divine Works; and the Emperor Julian, in those arguments of his preserved by Cyril, shows that without such assistance the Divine union is neither effected not rightly understood: and all the accounts we read of the Eleusian Mysteries, in addition to the witness of these philosophers, confirms that Wisdom was the offspring of a vital experiment into nature, by certain arts and media producing the central efficient into conscious being and effect. If you investigate rightly, says Archytas, discovery will be easy for you; but if you do not know *how* to investigate, discovery will be impossible.

It is the more to be regretted and wondered at, on account of the importance attached to this discovery, that the Initiated were so profoundly silent upon these means; since mankind in general would seem to have been precisely in this predicament, *they have not known how to investigate;* and were it not for these scattered innuendoes and acknowledgments of an Art, we might well continue in ignorance to despair of their hidden ground: at all events, seeing how far we fall short of the perception in this life; either believing, we might regard the ancients as beings superiorly endowed; or otherwise disbelieving, deny, as many have done, the validity of their assertions. Yet as the case now stands involved in mystery, will it not be unjust to do either? For, being ignorant of the method, how should we presume to test the truth of this philosophy? Equally, also, will it not be incurious to yield an implicit faith? Let us inquire now, therefore, if fortunately a ray of light be left to guide us, whether it be possible to approach to a recollection of this ancient experiment, that we may become better judges of its merits; and lest gaining nothing by a tacit assent, and proving nothing by mere skepticism, we should deny something, and bolt ourselves continuously out from the sanctuary of truth in nature.

And here we would engage the reader's attention for a brief interval (weighing well the substance of philosophical assertion against modern pride an our growing indifference), to consider the ground of this Hermetic mystery, and whether there be still an entrance open, as there was once said to be, to the shut palaces of Mind. Let us descend into ourselves, and believe in ourselves if we be able, that that which we are is worthy of our investigation; and we may discover, as we proceed, by their traditional light unfolding it, that the Wisdom of the ancients was not the outward, adventitious acquisition or vain display which it has been supposed to be, but a very real, substantial, and attainable good.

A spontaneous revelation of truth, if it was ever indeed enjoyed at all without experimental research, after the Hebrews ceased; nor was it longer possible for all, nor at every time, to partake of the Divine communion. This, therefore, as the Platonic Successor remarks, our philanthropic lord and father, Jupiter, understanding, that we might not be deprived of all communication with the gods, has given us observation through Sacred Arts, by which we have at hand sufficient assistance[45].

Here, then, we take up our clue to weave onward as we proceed, unraveling the Mysteries by their traditional light. He objects encountering this research may, as we before said, be appalling to some, nugatory to others, and, at first view, too opposed we fear to the opinions of all; but if, by chance, a less oblivious soul or intellect, more allied than ordinary to antecedent realities, should find familiar scenes recur, thrilling into reminiscence, as of some long past life forgotten; let such a one believe, and his faith will not betray him, the road whereon we are journeying is towards his Native Land.

---

1. See Maria Practica—in fine—Artis Auriferae, vol. 2; Morieni de Trans. Metal. Interrog. Et Resp.
2. See New Light of Alchemy, concluding chapter.
3. Centrum Naturae Concentratum., page 40.
4. Occult Philosophy, Book 3, chap. xxxvi. and xlvi.
5. New Light of Alchemy.
6. Tract. Aur., cap. i and ii.
7. Sum of Perf., Book i.
8. See the Stone of Fire, Kirchringius; Ed. Webster's Hist. of Minerals, the Extract.
9. Crollius' Philosophy Reformed.
10. Tract. Aureus. Text et Scholium, cap.i.
11. Ripley's Admonition of Erroneous Experiments.
12. Centrum Naturae Concentratum pp.80, 81.
13. Phil. Reform, pp. 25 95; Tact. Aureaus, cap. ii.
14. Theat. Chem. Brit. p. 405.
15. De Transm. Metal. Artis Auriferae, vol. i. end
16. See Jacob Böhme on the Generation of the Three Principles.
17. Idem, see Phillip's Lives of the Alchemists, p. 294, etc.
18. Arcanum Liquaris Alkahest Resp. 76, 78.
19. Tract. Aur., cap. ii.
20. Tract. Aur., cap. iii.
21. See Tractatus de Vero Sale, Nuysement, p. 164.
22. Triumphal Chariot of Antimony, by Kirchringius, English edition, p. 146 ; M. Dunstani Tract. Secret. in init.
23. See Böhme's Epistles, and early part of the Forty Questions, and his Discourse of the Three Principles before referred to, containing passages to the same effect.
24. Act xvii: 27, 28.
25. Anima Magia Abscondita, pp. 10, 11.
26. Book iii, cap. xlviii.
27. Epistle to Trithemius at the end
28. Manilius Astronomicon, lib. x.
29. Eléments de Psychologie, etc., Paris 1836.
30. Metaphysics, book I., cap. ii.
31. Ethics, Book x., cap. vii.
32. Metaphysics, Book xii., cap. vii.
33. See the First Alcibiades, page 90; and Proclus on the Theology of Plato, lib. I, cap. iii.
34. See the Fragment given by Taylor in his Jamblichus' Life of Pythagorus
35. Idem, chap. xxix.
36. See the Fragment in Jamblichus' Life of Pythagorus by Taylor, chap. ii.
37. Zohar, part i., fol. 191, recto; part iii. :144, recto
38. De Praemiis et Poenis, vol. ii., p. 428; De Nobilitate, p. 437
39. De Profugis, vol. i., p. 549, l. 49; De Plantatione Noe, p. 332, l. 31.

40. See the Divine Pymander.
41. Wisdom of Solomon, chap. vii.
42. Investig. of Perf., cap. iii.; Russel's Geber; Bloomfield's Camp of Philosophy, v. 27.
43. Plotinus's Select Works; Taylor, page 387, etc.
44. De Iside et Osiride.
45. See Jamblichus on the Mysteries; Taylors' Notes at the end; the Greek extract from Julian's Arguments.

Chapter 2. Of the Mysteries

beginning from the early initiations, to show the imperfection of the natural life and understanding — the artificial means and media employed by the ancients to rectify these — connecting together Alchemy and Mesmerism, also, with those preliminary Rites.

> The Path by which to Deity we climb
> Is arduous, rough, ineffable, sublime;
> And the strong massy gates thro' which we pass,
> In our first course, are bound with chains of brass;
> Those men, the first who of Egyptian birth,
> Drank the fair water of Nilotic earth,
> Disclosed by actions infinite this road.
> And many paths to God Phoenicians showed;
> This road the Assyrians pointed out to view,
> And this the Lydians and Chaldeans knew.
>
> — Oracle of Apollo, from Eusebius

We have shown in our history that the Greeks were not ignorant of the Hermetic Art, which they borrowed with their metaphysics so far indeed as such things may be borrowed which pertain to reason) from the Egyptians and Persians, whose temples were visited by nearly every philosopher of note.

Now the Egyptians, that is the Hermetic Art, or Art of Divine works, was by the Greeks called Theurgy; and was extensively practiced at Eleusis, and more or less in all the temples of their Gods. On no subject has more difference of opinion arisen amongst the learned: the high veneration in which the Mysteries were held, the intellectual enthusiasm with which the Alexandrians speak of them, the philosophic explanations given in detail by Jamblichus and others, concerning the motive and divine nature of the initiatory rites and the spectacles they procured, have puzzled many inquirers who, unable in latter times to account rationally, have disposed of the greater past as a pantomimic show, sanctified by priestly artifice and exaggerated by a wild imagination, natural as it has been supposed to those Ethnic souls. But then the Fathers of our Church, what frenzy should have possessed them, that St Augustine, Cyrillus, Synesius and the rest, should imitate their follies, transferring the very language, disciplines and rites of those "odious mysteries", to their own ceremonial worship as Christians, and that Clemens Alexandrinus should call them "blessed"? This has seemed extraordinary, and the authorities have been quoted and requited and turned in many ways by modern writers each to the support of his own peculiar view or modification, often, as may be recognized, at variance with the original sense in context.

Warburton's bias is negative and singularly misleading: he regarded the whole scheme of the Mysteries as a political fraud, came to the conclusion that the gods were dead men deified, and that the greater mysteries were instituted solely with a view to nullify the lesser[1]. But, as is natural, hw who so shamelessly charged others to be respected as an authority himself, quickly ceased to be respected as an authority himself, and his notions are accordingly quite obsolete. Sainte Croix, whose researches are otherwise the most complete, sets al in an astronomical and eminently superficial aspect[2]. Gebelin and La Pluche see all with vacant agricultural eyes[3]; whilst the author of Antiquity Unveiled, notwithstanding so much learning to his aid, has found out only the foolishness of the ancients, and thinks that the mysteries should be regarded as a depository of the religious melancholy of the first men[4]. Every trifling interpretation in short has been given, and everything imputed to the Mysteries except a discovery of the Wisdom which they professed. For although some with superior minds, as Thomas Taylor for example, have examined philosophically; yet from lack of evidence, and being without a guide from anything analogous in modern times, he too disposes of them as immaterial ceremonies, representations at best of abstract philosophic truths[5].

Now this and all such, like the foregoing opinions, are discordant to our apprehension, and injurious to the spirit of Antiquity, which not alone upholds philosophy, that is to say, Ontological Wisdom, as the true object of initiation, but represents the rites themselves as really efficacious to procure it. As the Platonist and Psellus, before cited to the point, distinctly declare, and Cicero, that they were truly called *Initia*, for they were the beginning of a life of reason and virtue; whence men not only derived a better subsistence here, as being drawn from an irrational and brutal life, but were led on to hope and aspire for a more blessed immortality hereafter[6].

Nor did the ancients promise this indiscriminately, but to those who were initiated in the Greater Mysteries only, as the Pythagoreans and Plato in *Phaedo* assert that by such means an assimilation was induced, and final contact with the object of rational inquiry, which is that identity whence, as a principle, we make our first descent. But Jamblicus more particularly explains that it was by arts divinely potent, and not by theoretic contemplation only or by mere doctrinal faith or representations either of reality; but by certain ineffable and sublime media that Theurgists became cognizant partakers in the Wisdom of true Being[7]. And Heraclitus calls these medicines, as being the help and remedy of imperfect souls; they possessed a power of healing the body likewise, which was extensively practiced in the temples of Esculapius with various minor physico-magical arts, But philosophy, according to Strabo, was the object of the Eleusian rites, and without the initiations of Bacchus and Ceres, he considers the most important branch of human knowledge would never have been attained. Servius, commenting on Virgil, observes that the sacred rites of Bacchus pertained to the purification of souls. *Libris patris sacra ad purgationem animarum pertinebant*; and again, *Animae aere ventilatur, quod erat in sacris Liberi purgationis genus.*—The Greeks conceived that the welfare of the states was moreover secured by these celebrations, and the records refer to them as bestowing that on which human nature stands principally in need, viz., moral enlightenment and purification of life; without the revelation and support afforded by them, indeed, existence was esteemed no better than a living death; the tragedians echoing the sense of the people made the chief felicity to consist therein, as Euripides, by Hercules says,—I was blessed when I got a sight of the mysteries:—and in *Bacchis*, O blessed and happy he who knowing the mysteries of the gods, sanctifies his life, celebrating orgies in the mountains with holy purifications. And Sophocles, to the same purport,—Life only is to be had there, all other places are full of misery and evil[8]. The doctrine of the Greater Mysteries, says Clemens Alexandrinus, related to the whole universe; here all instruction ended; nature and all things she contains were unveiled;—O mysteries truly sacred, O pure light! At the light of torches the veil that covers deity and heaven falls off. I am holy now that I am initiated; it is the Lord himself who is the hierophant; he sets his seal upon the adept whom he illuminates with his beams; and whom, as a recompense for his faith, he will recommend to the eternal love of the Father. These are the orgies of the Mysteries, concludes the bishop, in pious transport, come ye and be initiated. But the usage of the church as not to discover its mysteries to the profane, especially those that relate to the final apotheosis. It is even unwilling to speak of them to the Catechumens, says St Cyrillus, except in obscure terms, in such a manner, however, as that the faithful who are initiated may comprehend, and the rest be discouraged. For by these enigmas the Dagon is overthrown[9].

There was undoubtedly a secret, hanging about these celebrations, both Ethnic and Christian, which no record has divulged or common sense literally succeeded to explain away; the belief in providence and a future state were freely promulgated, and ordinary worship apart with which these mysteries ought not by any means to be confounded; since that might indeed be perpetuated anywhere, and has been without essentially, changing the state of life.

Previous, however, to more fully entering, we are desirous to observe that a few writers on Animal Magnetism, having within these few years became enlightened by that singular discovery, suggest their Trance and its phenomena as a revelation of the temple mysteries and various religious rites. But no one, that we are aware, has developed his suggestion of carried the idea sufficiently above the therapeutic sphere; they appear to have taken a broad view, without particular inquiry into the nature of their rites from the ancients themselves. Had they done this (we speak of the more advanced minds), we are persuaded that with that key in hand, their attention would have been drawn in new directions, and their satisfaction about the modern use of it become much modified by observing the far superior results which, through their Theurgic disciplines, the ancients aspired after, different too, as they were superior to any that we are accustomed to imagine even at the present day.

The ordinary effects of Animal Magnetism, or Mesmerism, or Vital Magnetism, or by whatever other term the unknown agency is better expressed, are now so familiarly known in practice that it will be unnecessary to describe them; they have attracted the attention of the best and leading minds of the present age, who have hailed with admiration a discovery which enables man to alleviate pain and maladies insurmountable by other means, and by benevolent disposition of is proper vitality, acting in accord, to restore health and equilibrate repose to his suffering fellow creatures. And thus it is true we can lull the senses, cure the sick, sometimes to restore the blind and deaf to hearing, sight and utterance; and it is a glorious step in progress, cheering and hopeful, a blessing on our mortal suffering state[10]. But are we to halt here always, or how long? The ordinary phenomena of lucidity, prevision, community of sense, will, and thought, have long been familiar and might have instigated to more important discovery; but years have passed, and the science has not grown, but retrograded rather in interest and power, since De Mainaduc, Puysegur, Colhoun, Elliotson, Townshend, Dupotet and the rest, faithful spirits, first set their fellow men on the road of inquiry.

But the best effects of Mesmerism, if we connect it with the ancients' Sacred Art, appear as trifles in comparison; the Supreme Wisdom they investigated, the Self-Knowledge and perfection of life and immortality promised and said to be bestowed on those initiated in the higher Mysteries, what has mesmerism to do with these things? What wisdom does it unfold? What is its philosophy, or has it yet made an attempt hardly to investigate the subject-being, the cause of its own effects? In common arts, the ingenuity is set to work how it may advance and adapt them to the best advantage; now capabilities are discovered which, put in action, often prove the fruitful source of more; whereas Mesmerism, dwelling together altogether in the *practice* (the same which, from the first, unfolded nature as far as it was able), continues to run on with her in the same commonplace round. Our sleepwalkers are little better than dreamers, for the most part, or resemble children born into a new world, without a guide, unable of themselves to educate their latent talents, or discriminate truth from falsehood in their revelations. And, as respects the Universal Medium, they even, who believe in such a thing, take it as it presents itself naturally, having no knowledge of the capabilities or means of improvement, whither it is able to ascend or descend, or what is its right determination. The few experimental tests that have been instituted hitherto prove nothing but to identify the same Imponderable through all; and if we make trial of the Spirit's instincts, asking for revelations of prophecy and distant scenes or journeyings through the air—and they follow us, those patients of our will, we then go out from them to philosophize, or wonder, or to think no more about it, as the case may be; repeating the same mechanical operations, and witnessing similar effects continually over and over again, until at length the enthusiasm which early characterized the novelty and raised expectation about it, has very generally and naturally died away.

Now this, according to our gatherings, was not the sort of investigation that the ancients followed in their Mysteries; although working in the same material and with similar instruments, on the same ground, yet their practice was different; for it was conducted upon established principles and with a truly philosophic as well as benevolent aim. Theurgists, indeed, condemn the Spirit of the natural life as degraded and incapable of true intelligence, nor did they therefore value the revelations of its first included sphere; but proceeded at once, passing these, as it appears, in the Lesser Mysteries, to dissolve the medium more entirely; and, as they knew how, to segregate the Vital Spirit away from those defilements and imaginative impresses which, by the birth into sense, had become implanted there, obscuring the intelligence and that divine eye which, as Plato says, is better worth than ten thousand corporeal eyes; for by looking through this alone, when it is purified and strengthened by appropriate aids, the truth pertaining to all beings is perceived.

The Neoplatonists wrote largely of the Theurgical art; many are quoted by St Augustine and is contemporaries which are not transmitted, but were destroyed probably through the sectarian malice and short-sighted policy of the later Roman government, which tolerated nothing but luxury and arms.

Yet sufficient remains to evince the nature of the Mysteries since, besides those before named Plotinus, Proclus, Porphyry, Synesius, and Jamblicus especially—all refer to them, declaring also the objects and revelations. And in what the disease of the Spirit consists, and from what cause it falsifies and is dulled, and how it becomes clarified and defecated, and restored to its innate simplicity, may be learned in part from their philosophy; for by the lustrations in the Mysteries, as they describe, the soul becomes liberated and passes into a divine condition of being.

Synesius writes appositely on the early disciplines, showing the phantastical condition also of the natural understanding essence, before it is purified by art and exalted. This Etherial Spirit, he says, is situated on the confines of the rational and brutal life, and is of a corporeal and incorporeal degree; and it is the medium which conjoins divine natures with the lowest of all. And nature extends the latitude of a phantastic essence through every condition of things; it descends to animals in whom intellect is not present; in this case, however, it is not the understanding of a divine part (as in man it ought to be) but becomes the reason of the animal with which it is connected, and is the occasion of its acting with much wisdom and propriety. And it is obvious, he continues, that many of the energies of the human life consist from this nature, or if from something else, (*i.e.*, to say, from reason), yet this prevails most; for we are not accustomed to cogitate without imagination, unless, indeed, some one should on a sudden be enabled to pass into contact with an intelligible essence[11].

That is into the identical apperception of true being; which is not possible under the ordinary conditions of thought in this life; but reason is always more or less debilitated in its energies by the habitual dependence on sense for data and objective proof, and by that modal consciousness which prevents from transcending it. Nor is this the only barrier, since when freed from the encumbrance of the senses temporarily, when in a state of trance they are quiescent, their impressure yet remains, and, as Synesius says, a false imagination, which it is requisite to destroy, as well as to banish all influxions from without, before the understanding spirit can superinduce Divinity.

It is well known that Pythagoras instituted long preparations and ordeals to train the minds of his disciples, previously to admitting them into the deeper mysteries of his school; and his biographer relates how, by divine arts and media, he healed and purified the souls of his followers, and that by constantly holding them allied to a certain precedential good, their lives were preserved in continual harmony and converse with the highest causes. But dense thickets, which are full of briars, says Jamblicus, surround the intellect and heart of those who have not been purely initiated, and obscure the mild and tranquil reasoning power, and openly impede the intellective part from becoming increased and elevated: and again,—It may be well to consider the length of time that we consumed in wiping away the stains which had insinuated themselves into our breasts, till, after the lapse of some years, we became fit recipients for the doctrines of Pythagoras; for as dyers previously purify garments, and then fix in the colors with which they wish them to be imbued in order that the dye may not be evanescent, after the same manner also that divine man prepared the souls of those that are lovers of Wisdom. For he did not impart specious doctrines or a snare, but he possessed a scientific knowledge of things divine and divine[12].

The Egyptian Olympiodorus also speaks of the natural imperfection of the human understanding, and how far its conceptions are adverse to divine illumination. The phantasy, says he, is an impediment to our intellectual conception; hence, when we are agitated by the inspiring influence of divinity, and the phantasy intervenes, the enthusiastic energy ceases; for enthusiasm and the phantasy are contrary to each other. Should it be asked whether the soul is able to energize without the phantasy, we reply, *that the perception of Universals proves that it is able*[13].

As a rational promise to this life of a higher reality, the subsistence of these Universals cannot be too often or too distinctly brought to mind; for not only do they reveal in us a necessity of Being beyond present experience, but, adumbrating, as it were, their antecedent light, assist much, if perspicaciously beheld, to introduce the Idea of that consummate Wisdom, wherein the same reason, becoming passive, receives the substance of her Whole. And the ancients glowingly describe the truth so conceived as an unquestionable experience; one and the same in all, where difference is merged in objective union.

And Jamblicus moreover asserts, that Theurgic rites conspiring to this end were scientifically disposed and early defined by intellectual canons; neither is it lawful to consider these canons as mutable, since they are the natural faith of life, and alone of all creeds catholic and independent.

But to transcend the sensible life in rational energy permanently apart is described as not less difficult than fortunate to attain; hence Plato appropriates the possession of Wisdom to old age, signifying by this Intellect diving intuitively without imaginative error; a Wisdom such as is not worldly, since it by no means belongs to the common life of man, nor is to be hoped for at all either in the early awakening of the life within, but by a transition gradually effected by Art away from the profound strains of a baser affection, it is carried up through the love of truth by faith into vivid contact with its Whole.

And the extremity of all evil in this life consists, according to the ancients, in not perceiving the present evil and how much human nature stands in need of amelioration; and this is a part of that twofold ignorance which Plato execrates, which being ignorant that it is ignorant has no desire to emerge, but may be compared to a body all over indurated by diseases, which, being no longer tormented with pain, is neither anxious to be cured. But he who lives in the consciousness of something better will meditate improvement , and desire is the first requisite; indeed, without desire on our part, art will labor for us in vain, since Will is the greatest part of purgation. And through the means of this, says Synesius, both our deeds and discourses extend their hands to assist us in our assent; but this being taken away the soul is deprived of every purifying machine because destitute of assent, which is the greatest pledge of reconciliation. Hence disciplines willingly endured become of far greater utility, while they oppose vexation of evil and banish the love of stupid pleasure from the soul.

But the phantastic Spirit may be purified, even in brutes, continues this author, so tht something better may be induced: how much will not the regression of the rational soul be therefore base, if she neglects to restore that which is foreign to her nature, and leaves lingering upon earth that which rightly belongs on high? *Since it is possible, by labor and a transition into other lives, for the imaginative soul to be purified and to emerge from this dark abode. And this restoration indeed one or two may obtain as a gift of divinity and initiation.* Then, indeed, the soul acquires fortitude with divine assistance, but it is no trifling contest to abrogate the confession and compact which she has made with sense. And in this case force will be employed, for the material inflictors will then be roused to vengeance, by the decrees of fate, against the rebels of her laws; and this is what the *Sacred Discourse* testifies by the labors of Hercules, and the dangers which he was required to endure, and which every one must experience who bravely contends for liberty, till the Understanding Spirit rises superior to the dominion of nature and is placed beyond the reach of her hands[14].

Hence, and from the foregoing evidence, it may have become probable that modern art has hitherto unfolded but a small and inferior part only of the Spirit's life; nor has experience yet opened into those temptations and trials which the consciousness must necessarily pass through, all the while regressive, before it reaches into the central illumination of truth. Nor does anything occur to us more beautifully suggestive than the whole the passage, from which we here gather, wherein Synesius describes not only the life that is operated upon and, in graceful terms, the artifice, but shows the conditions of desire and will, so indispensable for advancement, the labors and dangers likewise which attend those who aspire to the upper grades of Intellectual Science. And is it not true, as he remarks so far, we do lead for the most part a phantastic life? Nor least they who least suspect it, for it is the shining of truth that makes this visible, as a cloud before her face. Are we not filled too with conceits and roving imaginations and idols, which we are evermore mistaking for the real good? Do we not abound in sects and dissensions, heresies and doubts, so that scarcely two are to be found agreeing on all points? And the causes are obvious; without a standard and sure foundation to build on, we judge, as we are only able, with the rudimentary faculties and senses that are born in us, and of all nature, as through a glass darkly. If, therefore, with this same misunderstanding and infected Spirit, we enter in for the discovery and contemplation of ourselves, it will be useless; we shall not there discern the true hypostasis, but err amongst the turbulent and shadowy impressures of this of this life's birth and sphere of accidents. Thus mingling with the soul of the universe, without purification or any distinction of its light, our vehicle disports herself oftentimes in many mingling forms; as it is with those who dream or make to themselves a fool's paradise with the druggist's gas; since this, even impure as it is and full of folly, being if like nature with our life, coalesces; and would, if allowed to persist, consume its rationality. And on this account we observe the ancients more particularly warn about the treatment of their Spirit, which, though of a higher birth and instinct (as we may observe in the comparison of mesmerized patients and those under the influence of chloroform or common ether), and capable of so much higher, even as they say of the highest intelligence, yet in proportion may suffer also the most fearful degradation. Accordingly if the will incline downwards, persisting to grovel, or evil agencies intervene, then, as the *Sacred Discourse* has it, the Spirit grows heavy and sinks into profound Hades. It is necessary that the mind, once seated in this Spirit, should either follow or draw or be drawn by it. Hence, if growing predominant in folly, she should cease to aspire, the whole identity, being submerged together, would be converted to her life.

For is she not that very Sphinx of the Labyrinth, the devourer of strangers and all who have not the wit to unriddle her and know themselves? At all events, such is said to be the nature of the Phantastic Spirit before it is mundified, that he who enters so far as to be *profoundly* conscious in her essence, will be lost in irrational confusion, if he assume not quickly his intellectual energies and solve, that is comprehend, it on its own ground. For, if reason remains passive, this nature at length prevailing, will ravage and devastate and take possession of the whole mind, destroying its active energies and converting them to herself. Thus Jamblicus, speaking of this mundane spirit, says—it grows upon and fashions all the powers the soul, exciting in opinion the illuminations from the senses, and fixes in that life the impressions which descend from intellect. And Proclus, concerning the same nature, declares that—it folds itself about the indivisibility of true intellect (which is in its center), conforms itself to all formless species, and becomes perfectly everything from which dianoïa and our individual reason consists. And, as it is commonly observed to be a vain labor to infuse doctrine into a perplexed and turbid brain, or for a merely practical unspeculative soul to judge of abstract propositions; just so, no doubt, the best constituted minds would be inadequate to self-inspection on their first entrance into life. For the Spirit understand the affections of the mind, and reflects its image as it is, whether good or evil. But the primary and proper vehicle of the mind, when it is in a wise and purified condition, is attenuated and clear seeing; when however the mind is sensually affected, then this vehicle is dulled and becomes terrene; the instincts are said to be imperfect just in proportion as the perceptive medium is impure, and therefore it needs alternation and solution, as the oracles teach, for the discernment of good and evil, and the proper choice of life.

It is therefore that the Alchemists so much declaim against the vulgar Matter as it is at first made known, full of heterogeneous qualities and notions, as a subject fallen from its sphere and defiled. Hence all those preparations, solutions, calcinations, etc. before it becomes to be the Mercury of the Philosophers—pure, agile, intelligent, living—as they say, in her own sphere, as a queen upon her throne. *Accipe occultum arcanum quod est aes nostrum et lava quod sit purum et mundum. Deinde pone in vase bistro cum sigillo philosophico, regimen initial est perfecta solutio.* Take, says Albertus Mangus, the occult nature, which is our brass, and wash it that it may be pure and clean. The first rule of the work is a perfect solution[15].

All which we understand with reference to the universal Mundane Spirit, as it is at first consciously revealed in the recipient life of humanity; which Aristotle, in his *Metaphysics*, calls *passive intellect*, because capable of receiving and being converted to all—the best pr worst inclination, the highest truth or the most delusive imaginings—of manifesting motives in vital effects, and within certain limits of organizing even and transporting them.

And this we take to be the identical agent which is spread abroad in the present day mesmerizing, the photogenic medium, our New Imponderable, for it is the common soul; also the subject-matter of the Alchemists aforesaid, when they call it a thing indifferent, abject, and exposed in all hands, moving here below in shadowy manifestation, invisibly and unconsciously converted to every will and various use. It is what the world cares not for, as the adept says, but disesteems it; it hath it in its sight, carries it in its hands, yet is ignorant thereof; for it passeth away with a sudden pace without being known; yet these treasures are the chiefest, and he that knows the Art, and the expressions, and hath the medium, will be richer than any other[16]. But, in its natural state, the microcosmic life is not dissimilar from the vitality of the greater world, which is included by respiration in the blood of all creatures, maintaining its perpetual pulsation, as of the wind and waves, their flux and reflux; supplying to all existence the food of life. And how much such a life is in need of melioration, how much it suffers and desires, and how far its beneficence falls short of human hope and identity, may be apparent, and whiteout more evidence that in her Door-keeper, Isis is not revealed.

But so far we have yet advanced only to the gate of the great Labyrinth, where the Sphinx is even now present, rapidly propounding her dark riddles in the world, images of the obscure and intricate nature of the human spirit; which, by the devious windings, delusive attractions and similitudes of its own included sphere, leads imperceptibly, as it were, by an alluring grace, into that Hermetic wilderness and wild of Magic in which so many adventurers have gone astray. This is the Monster and the Eternal Riddle explained to common sense as suits it, but misunderstood to this day; that Compound Simple and ground of the magians' elements —a thing so perplexedly treated of by them, and having about it such a latitude for sophistication, that it is almost impossible to collect or unravel what has been said of it. Or how should reason attempt to define an essence all comprehending, yet separated in each particular, by so great an interval from itself? But this is that Augean Stable that was to be cleansed, that most famous labor of the philosophic Hercules; nor the least of labors, to turn the current of life into another channel, and purify the natural source.

Close upon the revealment of the Medial Life then, as we take it, in order of the Mysteries followed the Purificative Rites, which were designed also to restore the monarchy of reason in the soul, and this not either as an end so much, but preparatory to undergoing the final initiations. We are induced, however, to dwell longer on this first step, and on the necessity of intellectual preparation and auxiliaries; because it may be objected, as we proceed to unfold the ultimate tradition of this Wisdom, that we have no valid witness to our side; that any individual may declare according to the revelations of his mind, and introduce a various imagination to the idea of truth; that even supposing the mind included for a while and entirely free from outward impressions, still, retaining as it must the original bias, not only of sense but of birth and education, its experience will be neither trustworthy nor important to this life: and then nothing of a universal character, such as the ancients speak of, has been observed; or if asserted, how should it be hardly proven? Reason in these days is not content with affirmation; it will have objective response to its faith; all pretensions, therefore, to internal lights and revelations have ceased to attract the attention of mankind. And again, it may be inquired why, if true Being is everywhere totally present, it is not so perceived; and why all things partaking do not enjoy the light of the so-called superstantial world?

In reply to this last objection, we would ask if it be not because that very light is drawn outwardly, and enchanted by sense that it is internally unconscious and oblivious everywhere of the great Identity whence it springs? If that were applied inwardly which now looks out, and every natural impediment removed, experience might then reveal to us the antecedent life. But the former objections recur here: there are impediments; and it behooves us to consider scrupulously, but without prejudice, the possibility and tests of such an experience; for if by this traditionary fall and outbirth, the understanding is so polluted as to be no more able, as Lord Bacon supposes[17], to reflect the total reason to itself, introspection will be useless, and the central mystery remains, as respects humanity, a hopeless problem after all.

None better than the ancients (who profess to have enjoyed the rational life in its most intimate spheres, and to have reaped its most real and lasting advantages), describe the folly and fatal allurements to which they are subjected who trust themselves to remain passively dreaming in the region of the phantasy, with its notions and instincts, often more false, fleeting, and evil that the corporeal images with which sense is conversant. It is for this cause they insist so much that, before any one betakes himself to the inner life of contemplation—before he hopes, we mean, to pass into its Reason—that all else be effectually obliterated, and the mental atmosphere made clear and passive before its objective light. Without this, they promise nothing; with it, all. And on this possibility, namely, of purifying the human Understanding Essence, and developing to consciousness its occult Causality, the transcendental philosophy of the mystics may be observed to hinge entirely and exceed every other.

For that there is a foundation of truth in existence, is as necessary for us to admit as that we are ignorant of it; and the doubt rather remains also about the discovery of means, than the possibility of self-knowledge.

To continue then, partly on the authority of the Greek philosophers and partly on some mother grounds hereafter to be disposed of, we are led to infer that the Hermetic purifications and Mysteries, celebrated in the Eastern temples and by the priests at Eleusis, were real and efficacious for the highest ends that philosophy can propose to itself, namely, the purification and perfection of human life; and that inasmuch as the object was different and immeasurably superior to those proposed by modern Mesmerism, or any other art or science of the present day, so also were the means employed (the particulars of which are further discussed under the Practice), and the administration in proportion purer, holier, and entirely scientific. For does not all our experimentalism and philosophy end in fact where the ancients began, purifying the Vital Spirit in its proper Light?

Or if any one think we have been discussing all the while a mere nothing, and developing a vain imagination, we admit it; suggesting only that, That which is, in his mind, so mere a nothing, become sin that of a philosopher to be the All in all. But who will now conceive the full latitude and substantiality of this principle, or the true metaphysical use thereof? Few, very few, Philalethes said, there were in his day; and who will even inquire now, or believe that it is the very same which solved and resolved, and wisely manipulated, becomes to be the concrete Stone of philosophers; in its pure, passive expanse, a mirror of the catholic reason of nature, and the medium of that holy and sublime experience granted to man alone in the divine alliance—Ex natura et divino factum est, as Reuchlin, in *The Mirific Word,* expresses it—*Divinum enim quia cum divinitate conjunctum divinas substantias facit.*

Take that which is least, and draw it by artifice into the true ferment of philosophers; although our metal is exteriorly dead, yet it has life within, and wants nothing more than that That which in the eyes of a philosopher is the most precious should be collected, and that That which the many set more value on be rejected; and these words are manifest without envy, says the Greek Aristhenes. O, how wonderful different and detract nothing, only in the preparation removing superfluities[18].

From that which is perfect nothing more can be made; for a perfect species is not changed in its nature, neither from an utterly imperfect thing can art produce perfection; but this Universal Spirit is described as a middle substance—passive, undetermined, susceptible of conversion and all extremes. And such accordingly we understand to be the One Thing needful, purifying and to be purified itself by itself, in turn agent and patient, which are the Hermetic luminaries; in their full representative advancement, the Sun and Moon philosophical, passing through many phases from imperfection to perfection in the true magistery.

And the hermetic art would seem to consist simply in the right disposition and manipulation of this our Undetermined Subject, taking her where nature leaves, and by divers operations, to be hereafter noted, as of amalgamation, distillation, filtration, digestion, and lastly by sublimation to the Head of an appropriate Vessel, establishing her in a new and concentric Form of Light.

> *Nor may this seem a fable to the wise,*
> *Since all things live according to their kinds;*
> *Their life is light which in them hidden lies,*
> *Discerned by the eyes of soaring minds,*
> *To them discovered is true nature's map,*
> *By whom produced nothing is by hap:*
> *For she her secret agent doth possess,*
> *Which in the universe is only one,*
> *But is distinct thro' species numberless,*
> *According to their seeds, which God alone*
> *In the beginning did produce, and then*
> *Set them their law, found out my mental men*[19].

But a long interval is between, and all the labors of that Heroic Intellect to be passed through before the rejected Keystone regains her Head place. None but a philosopher ever achieved the work, or for reasons that are imperative, ever will. The idle and vicious are totally excluded, nor are the rewards of Wisdom to be won by fools wanting the very principles of melioration in themselves.—*Nemo enim dat id, quod non habet.*—He only that hath it can impart—and he only has it who has labored rationally in the pursuit. As is exemplified in that saying of Esdras—The earth giveth much mould, whereof earthen vessels are made, but little dust that gold cometh of[20].

> *Non levis adscensus, si quis petat ardua, sudor*
> *Plurimus hunc tollit, nocturna insomnis olivae*
> *Immoritur, delet quod mox laudaverit in se,*
> *Qui cupit aeternae donari frondis honore.*

1. See Divine Legation, vol. i.
2. Sainte Croix des Mystères, 2 vols, 8 vo.
3. Gebelin, Monde Primitif. La Planche des Cieux
4. L'Antiquité dévoilée par ses Usages, etc.
5. Dissertation on the Eleusinian and Bacchic Mysteries.
6. De Legibus, lib. ii, cap. xiv.
7. Jamblicus on the Mysteries; Taylor, p. 109.
8. See Praetextus, Hist. Nov. lib. iv.; Divine Legation, vol. i. P.198 ; Des Septchènes, Chap. ii., p.174, etc.
9. See the extracts rendered by De Septchènes, in his Religion of the Greeks, chap. ii. from Meursius, Eleusines et Cecropia.
10. See Zoist, passim.
11. See Taylor's Proclus on Euclid, the extract from Synesius, vol. ii.
12. Jamblicus, Life of Pythagorus, chap, xvi., xvii.
13. See Porphyry's Aid to Intelligibles, Taylor, p.207, note.
14. See Taylor's History of the Restoration of the Platonic Philosophy in vol. ii. of his Proclus on Euclid. This Synesius was the Christian Platonist, Bishop of Alexandria, before mentioned in the history ; one well experienced, according to his own account, in the Hermetic philosophy, and whose writings on the art of transmutation have in part descended to this day.
15. Secret. Tact. Alberti, in fine; Artis Auriferae, p.130, etc.
16. Aquarium Sapientum, part ii., in fine. Vaughan's Coelum Terrae, p. 80, etc.
17. See his Instauration of the Sciences, sub init.
18. Aristoteles in Roasrio, and in the Lucerna Salis.
19. Eireneus' Marrow of Alchemy, book i.
20. Esdras, cap. iii., Book i.

Chapter 1. Of the Experimental Method and Fermentation of the Philosophic Subject, According to the Paracelsian Alchemists and some others

WHICH INDICATE THE GREATER ORDEALS AND DISCIPLINES WHICH THE VITAL SPIRIT IS MADE TO PASS THROUGH IN THE PROGRESS OF A PHYSICAL REGENERATION BY ART, FROM OUT THE SENSUAL DOMINION OF THE SELFHOOD, THROUGH A TEMPORARY DEATH AND ANNIHILATION TO A NEW LIFE AND CONSCIOUSNESS.

It s necessary that the soul, when purified, should associate with its Generator.

— Porphyry, Aux. to Intelligib.

We have so far developed the nature of the internal life only, as it was at first revealed to the aspirant in the Lesser Mysteries; and this was the only popular initiation open to all. It represented, according to the accounts, a new and fertile field of natural contemplation which every one was at liberty to appropriate, and where each roamed at pleasure without rule or subordination, and without that consent and sympathy which a uniformity of life produces.

Previous to the purificative rites little change, therefore, was effected. It gave a passing experience to the multitude, and in a few awakened the desire and hope of better things; just as amongst us Mesmerism, which of all modern arts is most pertinent to this philosophy as working in the same matter, affords entrance with the imagination of another life. And more than this, in well-conditioned cases, we have proof of the intrinsic intelligence and power of the Free Spirit which can expatiate into the whole circumference of its sphere and reveal hidden things, exhibiting a variety of gifts; it can philosophize also more or less well according to the direction, natural purity, and relaxation of the sensual bond. But not all that men wonder at in the present day, the insensibility, the cures, the mental exaltation, nor much more of the same class which the trance spontaneously develops evening the best subjects, could satisfy the exacting reason of our forefathers; desirous rather to investigate the Thing itself, the subject of so many marvels, they passed the first phenomena to look for Causes, experimenting within.

Volo ovum philosophorum dissolvere et partes philosophici hominis investare, nam hoc est initium ad alia—says the experimental Friar[1]; and to concentrate the whole vitality, to turn the spiritual eye, to purify and analyze the total essence and draw forth the true Efficient and to know it in co-identity, this was their object and the Art of Theurgy. For it is not, as they say, that the Spirit is free from material bondage, or able to range the universe of her own sphere, that guarantees the truth of her revealments, or helps the consciousness on to subjective experience; for this a concentrative energy is needed, and an intellect penetrating into other spheres, rather than discursive in its own.

There are many ways known and practiced of entrancing the senses, and the key of the Hermetic vestibule may be said to be already in our hands, which are able to dissolve the sensible medium and convert it to the experience of another life[2]. But the order in which the next solution, or resolution rather, was operated which was to translate the consciousness underneath this medium by obscuration, towards the Central Source, is known probably to very few in the present day, for it is entirely concealed from the world: they only, amongst the ancients who had fulfilled the previous rites and undergone all the required ordeals, were entrusted with the passport. It discovers a fearful mystery in the opening sensation of power, in a life which, at its entrance, is described as dark, delusive, and dangerous, and more corrupted far than the foregoing, but through which it is quite necessary to pass before inquiry can hope to meet its object in the Elysian light.

> Tenent media omnia sylvae,
> Cocytusque sinu labens circumfluit atro.
> *Betwixt these regions and that upper light,*
> *Deep forests and impenetrable night*
> *Possess the middle space; the infernal bounds,*
> *Cocytus, with his sable wave surrounds*[3].

We are aware that the descent to the Infernal regions and all those highly wrought descriptions of the poets, concerning the riches and powerful allurements of Pluto's kingdom and Hades, have been looked upon, and very naturally, as purely imaginative, and the representations of the same in the mysteries as a pictorial or pantomimic show. But as we have hitherto been enabled to regard the minor celebrations from an esoteric point of view, showing their relationship to more modern experience and the Hermetic art, we hope to continue on our adventure, being not without precedent either or guiding authority over the same ground. For it is not absurd to suppose that men should have philosophized and composed so many excellent and sublime discourses from the contemplation of shadows only?

But setting aside such a notion, neither do we conceive that by Hades, or that profound Lethe, the ancients understood a corporeal nature, or this fleshly existence of ours, or anything in fact with which the whole allusion is to a state of vital submersion in the Mysteries, when the consciousness is artificially drawn about the penetralia of its first life. Nor, if we may credit accounts, is the descent difficult, or so far off, but the infernal gates lie open to mortal men on earth; but because of the arduous nature of the re-ascent and for the sake of securing it, lest unprepared souls, presuming to enter, should be taken captive by deluding and fatal desires, and work irremediable evil there, every precaution has been instituted to keep the way a secret from the world, as well for its own sake as for the cause of justice and divine wisdom about to be revealed; wherefore the Sybil warns Aeneas of the danger of his undertaking in those memorable lines.

> *Facilis descensus Averni;*

> *Noctes atque dies patet atri janua Ditis:*
> *Sed revocare gradum superasque evadere ad auras,*
> *Hoc opus, hic labor est. Pauci quos aequus amavit*
> *Jupiter, aut ardens evexit ad aethea virtus,*
> *Diis geniti potuere*[4].

The grand requirement of the Mysteries after the first purificative rites (the inclination being already freed from the dominion and all the superficial progeny of sense), was that the will should conceive within itself a motive purely rational to withstand the temptations of its next including sphere; that it might be enabled to follow the true path upward, penetrating through darkness, and defilements, and dissolution even, to the discovery of Wisdom in her light abode. To this Aeneas accordingly directed by the Sybil, whom we follow, after her warning already given, to search for that well-distinguished, most mysterious golden bough.

> *Aurus et foliis et lento vimine ramus,*
> *Junoni infernae sacer*[5].

Without which as a propitiation he may not venture on the subterranean research. But it may be asked, why this myrtle branch was represented to be of gold. Not merely for the sake of the marvelous, Warburton tells us, we may be assured. A golden bough was literally part of the sacred equipage in the shows, a burden which the Ass, who carried the mysteries, we may believe, was proud of. But of what kind this branch was, Apuleius partly indicates in his procession of the Initiated into the Mysteries of Isis, where we find it connected with the Mercurial caduceus and treated as a most important symbol in initiatory rites[6]; which we therefore understand ontologically, as a ray of living light, golden and flexible, the true Brancha Spiritualis of Raymond Lully. *Intellectus habens naturam subtilem ad intellignedum res intellibiles*[7];—insinuating by rational penetration alone through the murky circumference of the chloric ether into its own congenial life, which is Proserpine, and that lapsed soul of ours, seated in her dark hypostasis unknown; whose vapor is so subtle and transient that nothing but the glance of its proper intellect by faith can arrest it. And those doves that lead the way too, are they not known to our Alchemists and those chosen seats?

But to be brief; it is only by exceeding zeal and piety of intention, such as is ascribed to Aeneas in search of his father, and a prevailing reason, that the seeking mind becomes fitted for establishment in her essence and percipient of her final duty to separate the good and reject the evil therein by birth allied; that she may know to what she ought to aspire, dismissing every other consideration, where Desires are Images and Will their Act. Thus Plato says, that it is necessary that a man should have his right opinion as firm as adamant in him when he descends into Hades, that there likewise he may be unmoved by riches or any such like evils, and may not, falling into tyrannies and such other practices, do incurable mischief and himself suffer still greater; but that he may know how to shun extremes on either hand, both in this life as far as possible and in the whole hereafter[8]. And again, in the Seventh Book of the Republic—he who is not able by the exercise of his reason to define the idea of the Good, separating it from all other objects and piercing, as in a battle, through every kind of argument, endeavoring to confute, not according to opinion but according to essence, and proceeding through all the dialectic energies with an unshaken reason—he who cannot accomplish this, neither knows he the Good itself, nor anything that is properly denominated the Good. And would you not say that such a one, if he apprehended any certain truth or image of reality, would apprehend it rather, through the medium of opinion than of science; that in the present life he is sunk in sleep and conversant in the delusions of dreams; and that descending into Hades, before he is roused to a vigilant state, he will be overwhelmed with a sleep perfectly profound[9]. To fall asleep in Hades was indeed to be absorbed, without the encumbrance of body, in all its defilements; according to the philosopher, the direst evil that can befall any one; or, as Virgil has it, to be a king in hell.

But with all the earnings of difficulties, and dangers, and death, to be encountered, no hero or great man occurs in the poets, but he sometime descended to the Infernals, and had free egress thereafter to the Elysian Fields; but two are described as suffering for the attempt—Theseus and Pirithous, who, as Proclus admirably explains, were detained there—the one because he was too much a lover of corporeal beauty, the other through his natural inability to sustain the arduous altitude of divine contemplation. In the sixth book of the Aeneid, Virgil has gracefully set forth the whole transaction of his successful hero, with the labors and difficulties, and appalling visions that attended on the outset of his pious research; all which has been shown by Warburton[10] and other learned commentators, to bear close allusion to the Mysteries, in which we have reason also to believe the poet himself was profoundly initiated, and whose allegoric conduct, therefore, we pursue as an inquiry of Intellect after its Paternal Source.

To continue, then, in order of the tradition: after the ordeal rites had been undergone, and the few who were found fit, selected for further initiation, the concession of more arcane mysteries succeeded.

> *Gressus removete prophani*
> *Jam furor humanus nostro de pectore sensus*
> *Expluit[11].*

As the consciousness passing the middle region, clear and rational from out the *Aquaster*, enters the *Fire World*, and the Sybil leads her hero to the dark descent.

> *Spelunca alta fuit, vastoque immanis hiatus,*
> *Scrupea, tuta lacu nigro nemorumque tenebris;*
> *Quam super haud ullae poterant impune volantes*
> *Tnedere ita pennies: talis sese halitus atris*
> *Faucibus effundens supera ad convexa ferbat,*
> *Unde locum Graii dixerunt nominee Aornum[12].*

And what does all this imagery point at, but the thickening darkness of the nether air verging to the chaos of matter flowing out from the perpetual motion of the first life; destitute of elasticity, *Aornus*, heavy like that of an enclosed cave, and vast; dangerous, as it is said by some, giving forth a murky odor, like that of graves. It is the Black Saturn of the adepts, and that appearing corruption that precedes the mystical death and regeneration into new life: as describing the same ens, they call it *lapis niger, vilis, foetens, et dicitur origo mundi et oritur sicut germinantia.* Sendivogius calls it Urinus Saturni, with which he waters his lunar and solar plants; and another,—*Ex mari meo oriuntur nebulae, quae ferunt aquas benedictas et ipsae irrigant terras et educant herbas et flores.* With this allusion, the Alchemists also call the Ether their mineral tree; for they were not so careful to hide this in general, seeing the true species was laid asleep in sense, and doubly locked up, as it were, within both corporeal and spiritual confines, and how far the world was off from the art of unfolding or profiting by it. The reception of Aeneas in Hades is next described.

> *Ecce autem, primi sib lumina et ortus,*

> *Sub pedibus mugire solum, et juga coepta moveri*
> *Sylvarum, visaeque canes ululare per umbram,*
> *Adventante Dea*[13].

And Claudian, to the same effect, poetizes the tremendous advent.

> *Jam mihi cernuntur trepedis delubra moveri*
> *Sedibius, et claram dispergere fulmina lucem*
> *Adventum testate dei : jam magnus ab imis*
> *Auditur fremitus terries, templumque remugit*
> *Cecropium; sanctasque faces attollit Eleusin;*
> *Angues Triptolemi strident, et squamea curvis*
> *Colla levant attrita jugis Ecce procul ternas*
> *Hecate variata figures Exortur*[14].

And all this, extravagant and fanciful though it should appear, has been echoed by philosophers, and the Greek descriptions agree in each remarkable particular. Plato, amongst others, likens the descent of the soul into these oblivious realms of generation to an earthquake and other strong convulsions of nature. Psellus, in his valuable commentary, describes the apparitions procured by the Chaldaic rites as of two kinds: the first called *superinspection*, when he who celebrates the divine rites sees a mere apparition, as, for instance, of light in some *form* or figure, concerning which the oracle advises, that if anyone sees such a light, he apply not his mind to it, nor esteem the voice proceeding thence to be true; sometimes, likewise, to many initiated persons, there appear lights in various forms and figures. These apparitions are created by the passions of the soul, in performing divine rites, mere appearances, having no *substance*, and therefore not signifying anything true[15]. Which vaporous estate of universal-being, the poets also fabulously concealed under the satiric form of Pan, who exhibited himself in every variety of atrocious disguises of wild beasts, and monsters, and demoniacal appearances, that he might affright those who would captivate him.

> *Corripit hic subita trepidus formidine ferrum*
> *Aeneas strictamque aciem venientibus offert.*
> *Et ni docta comes tenues sine corpore vitas*
> *Admoneat volitare cava sub imagine formae,*
> *Irruat, et frustra ferro diverberet umbras*[16].

For it is the imaginative spirit which is the maker of these images, as in dreams, only more intense. As moisture condensed in the air constitutes clouds, which the wind disposes in various forms, so our pneumatic vehicle, becoming humid and condensed beneath her heaven, presents many formidable apparitions to the inner sense, and all the race of demons, so much celebrated by antiquity, appear to have their origin in a life of this kind, viz., from an included vapor of the imagination: nor these, individually belonging, were seen only; but, as it is recorded, each by rapport in this state becomes conversant with the whole phantasmagoric universe of his sphere; hence the platitude of the descriptions and poetical crowding of images to the individual sense. Proclus, commenting on the First *Alcibiades* of Plato, asserts that material images, assuming the appearance even of things divine, constantly attended on the Mysteries, drawing towards them souls not yet sufficiently purified, and separating them from truth. And that such actually appeared to be the *Mustai*, during the evaporative process of purification, and before the lucid vision of the light within, is further shown in the following passage of the same experienced theologian. In the most holy Mysteries, says he, before the presence of the god, the impulsive forms of certain terrestrial demons appear, which call the attention off from undefiled advantages to matter, And again,—as in the most holy Mysteries, the mystics at first meet with the multiform and many-shaped genera which are hurled forth before the gods; but on entering the interior part of the Temple, unmoved and guarded by the sacred rites, they genuinely receive into their bosom divine illumination, and divested of the Divine Nature, the same method takes place in the speculation of Wholes[17].

For the reason of this life imitates, inasmuch as it is able, and obeys instinctively its motive light; and as the natural intellect is liable to error, so the spiritual also, not et perfected, is liable to be caught in the traps of these exterior spirits, which being, as Basil Valentine, in his *Alchemical Chariot*, observes, endowed with senses and understanding, know Arts, and have in themselves an occult operative life; giving testimony also of their virtue in the art of healing and other secrets, by which they deceive and detain the unwary from the search of better things[18].

The writings of the middle ages abound likewise with descriptions of these demoniacal natures; regular descriptions of them are given by Agrippa[19]; and Trithemius[20]; and Psellus[21]; Proclus[22]; Jamblicus[23]; and Porphyry[24], allude to their material efficacy and operation in Divine Works, where desire, entering into those aerial forms, is said to vivify them; and the Chaldaic oracle even persuades that there are pure demons. —*Natura suadet esse demonaspuros, et malae materiae germina utilia et bona,*— and that the germinations even of evil matter are of use[25]. Synesius mentions them also as the progeny of matter, and as having an energetic virtue, but at natural war with the truth-seeking soul[26]; and Proclus, in his Hymn to the Sun, desecrates them as

> *Demons who machinate a thousand ills,*
> *Pregnant with ruin to our wretched souls,*
> *That merged beneath life's dreadful sounding sea*
> *In body's chain they willingly may toil;*
> *Nor e'er remember in the dark abyss*
> *The splendid palace of their sire sublime.*

And it is the dread of such an oblivion there below that the oracle announces to intellect in those solemn tones—*Ducat animae profunditas immortalis oculosque affatim,*—*Omnes sursum extende.* Let the immortal depth of thy soul be predominant, and all thy eyes extend upwards; incline not to the dark world whose depth is a faithless bottom and Hades dark all over, squalid, delighting in images, unintelligible, precipitous, and a depth always rolling full of stupidity and folly[27].

> *Umbrarum hic locus est, somni noctisque soporae*[28].

If the soul on its departure, says Porphyry, still possesses a spirit turbid from humid exhalations, it then attracts to itself a shadow and becomes heavy; and a spirit of this kind naturally strives to penetrate into the recesses of the earth, unless a certain other cause draws it in a contrary direction: as, therefore, the soul when surrounded with this testaceous and terrene vestment necessarily lives on the earth, so likewise when it attracts a moist spirit, it is necessarily surrounded with the image. But it attracts moisture when it continually endeavors to associate with nature, whose operations are effected in moisture, and which are rather under the earth: when however the soul earnestly *desires* to depart from nature (*i.e.,* strives to penetrate centrally without exploring the intermediate spheres), then she becomes a dry splendor from exhalation[29]. Hence that renowned saying of Heraclitus, that *a dry soul is the wisest,* for the soul looking at things posterior to herself beholds the shadow and images of her vaporous vehicle; but when she is converted to herself, she evolves her proper essence and irradiates the whole circumference with her own abundant oxygenating and dispersive light[30]. Thus Hermes: Extract from the ray its shadow and its obscurity, by which the clouds hang over it, and corrupt and keep away the light; by means of its constriction, also, and fiery redness it is burned; take, my son, this watery and corrupted nature, which is as a coal holding the fire, which if thou salt withdraw so often until the redness is made pure, then it will associate with thee, by whom it was cherished and in whom it rests[31].

> *Visitabis interiora terrae rectificando, invneies*
> *Occultum lapidem, veram medicianam.*

Visit the interior of the earth rectifying, says the sage, and thou shalt find the hidden Stone, the true medicine: not the feculent dead soil, but our dark divulsed chaotic life from sense, which opened and rectified, dissolved and reunited, is changed from an earthly to a spiritual body, by rapport divine. In such a process it would seem the Alchemists discovered the hidden principles of nature, as, experimentally passing thought the animal and vegetable into the mineral circulation of her Law, they describe the life of all things here below to be a thick fire imprisoned in a certain incombustible aërial moisture;—*Ignis rubber super dorsum ignis candidi*—which moisture in its native state, before it is purified by the inflowing light of reason, is that Hades we are treating of, the Purgatory of the wise, wherein the consciousness, becoming artificially wrapped by the Mysteries, continues for a while in a state of solicitude and painful amazement, unable of itself to discover, through so great a cloud of darkness, that Hypostatic Reality towards which it is instructed evermore to aspire. And until this attraction is found and finally established in union, the opposive powers display their mutual forces in discordant dissolute array, as the Alchemists, with all who have been profoundly experienced in this ground, relate each in his own instructive way, warning about the conduct through it, and the many real, though chimerical horrors and enticing phantoms that haunt around, guarding the secret chamber of their mineral soul. For, as the sage in Enoch declares it, lead and tin are not produces from earth as the primary fountain of their production; but there is an angel standing upon it, and that angel struggles to prevail[32].

Vaughan notes the same in the *Regio Phantastica* of his Hieroglyphic, and elsewhere, speaking of the mineral nature or First Matter, he says, The eye of man never saw her twice under one and the same shape; but as clouds driven by the wind are forced to this and that figure, but cannot possibly retain one constant form, so is she persecuted by the fire of nature[33]; as, by the re-entering Light of Reason in the Mysteries, which is that Sulfur of adepts, causing all this manifold scenery in the disruption of life. O Nature! The most wonderful creatrix of natures, cries Hermes, which containest and separatest all things in a middle principle. Our Stone comes with light and with light it is generated, and then it brings forth the clouds, and darkness which is the mother of all things[34]. Raymond Lully, also, in his *Compendium of Alchemy*, calls the first principles of the Art, *Spiritus fugitives in aere condensators, in forma monstrorum diversorum et animalium etiam hominum, qui vadunt sicut nubes, modo hinc modo illuc*; that is to say, certain fugitive spirits condensed in the air, in shape of divers monsters, beasts, and men, which move like clouds hither and thither.

In an outward acceptation such an announcement of principles would be absurd, or what possible interpretation could afford them a place in commonsense? Or whence, if they be true (and Lully's name sands well for their defense), were they so probably brought to the cognizance of the philosopher, as from the self-inspection of them in life? But Lully, indeed, calls these chaotic forms first principles; not because they are permanent or their essence rational, in that unctuous dark condition, but because within the material extreme of this life, when it is purified, the Seed of Spirit is at last found: which the adept further describes as a decompounded ens, extremely heavy, shining through the darkness like a fiery star, being full of eyes like pearls or aglets. For it is the whole Demagorgon, as yet not actually animated by contact of his own returning light. The father of it, says Vaughan, is a certain inviolable mass, for the parts of it are so firmly united you can neither pound them to dust, nor separate them by violence of fire[35]. This is the rock in the wilderness, because in great obscurity and difficult to find the way of, compassed about with darkness, clouds, and exhalations, as it were dwelling in the bowels of the earth.—Our viscous soul, as Synesius calls it, circulating in the midst of all her Adamical defilements, and which Plato compares to that marine Glaucus so deformed by the foreign weeds and parasites that had grown about him, that in every respect he resembled a beast rather than what he really was[36]. In such a deplorable condition is the divine germ of humanity said to be beheld under the thousand evils of its birth.

Monstrum, horrendum, informe, ingens, cui lumen ademptu.

There is a curious figurative account given in a letter circulated under the name of the Brethren of the Rosy Cross, which appears to have reference to this passage of initiatory progress in the Mysteries. It may be rendered thus: —

There is a mountain situated in the midst of the earth or center of the *world*, which is both *small* and great. It is soft, also above measure, hard, and strong. It is *far off, and near at hand*; but, by the providence of God, it is invisible. In it are hidden most ample treasures, which the world is not able to value. This mountain, by envy of the Devil, who always opposes the glory of God and the felicity of man, is compassed about with very cruel beasts and ravenous birds, which make the way thither both difficult and dangerous; and therefore, hitherto, because the time is not yet come, the way thither could not be sought after by all; but only by the worthy man's self-labor and investigation.

To this *mountain* you should go in a *certain night*, when it comes most *long and dark*; and see that you prepare yourself by *prayer*. Insist upon the way that leads to the mountain, but ask not of any man where it lies; only follow your guide who will offer himself to you and will meet you in the way[37].

This guide will bring you to the mountain at midnight, when all things are silent and dark. It is necessary that you arm yourself with a resolute heroic courage, lest you fear those things that will happen and fall back[38]. You need no sword or other bodily weapon, only call upon you God, *sincerely and heartily seeking Him.*

When you have discovered the mountain, the first miracle that will appear is this: a most vehement and very great wind that will shale the whole mountain and shatter the rock to pieces. You will be encountered by lions, dragons, and other terrible wild beasts; but fear not nay of these things[39]. Be resolute, and take heed that you return not, for your guide who brought you thither will not suffer any evil to befall you. As for the treasure, it is not yet discovered: but it is very near. After this wind will come an earthquake which will overthrow those things which the wind had left. Be sure you fall not of. The *earthquake* being passed, there shall follow a fire that will consume the earthly rubbish, and discover the treasure: but as yet you cannot see it[40]. After all these things, and near daybreak, there shall be a great calm, and you shall see the day-star arise, and the darkness will disappear; you will conceive a great treasure; the chiefest thing, and the most perfect, is a certain exalted tincture with which the world, if it served God and were worthy of such gifts, might be tinged and turned into most pure gold.

And thus much of the concordance of these famous Christian philosophers who, if they had not promised gold, and proclaimed prodigies after an entertaining Arabian Nights fashion, would never, probably, have been thought of by the world, or inquired after, as they were, over Europe during the last century, but without success. For they who have this knowledge know where and how likewise to bestow it, discerning betwixt the lovers of mammon and of truth. Fearing the dangerous curiosity of the vulgar herd also, we observe, the Greeks pass by in silence the physical revealments of these Tartarean realms, or, poetizing the great experience, evaporate in fancy, as it were, the teeming life therein opened with its overflowing spirit and light of increase.

> *Let none admire*
> *That riches grow in hell; that soil may best*
> *Deserve the precious bane; and here let those*
> *Who boast in mortal things, and wondering tell*
> *Of Babel and the works of Memphian kings,*
> *Learn how the greatest monuments of fame*
> *And strength and art are easily outdone*
> *By spirits reprobate*[41].

And further, how these again maybe surpassed and vanish, as Aladdin's rapid castle into air, before the discriminate radiance of celestial light. And as in the pursuit of other sciences and arts, though, and persevering labor and experience are required to ensure success, so should those delusive visions and errors which occur during the conscious transference to a more excellent condition of being be considered, in like manner, not as derogatory or casting a doubt at all upon the ultimate truths of divine science, but as obstacles rather contrary to it, and detersive as evil is to good everywhere adverse.

We do not, therefore, linger here any more to consider the different allotments, the longer or shorter periods which engage pure or impure souls in Hades, their habits or the triple path arising from their essences, all which is indicated in the Platonic discourses, and most of which is abound with symbolical theories and poetical descriptions concerning the descent, ascent, and intermediate wanderings, expiatory punishment and sacrifices and things of a similar import, which the rites enjoined, before the aspirants, by the Greeks called *Mustai*, were passed on by the Hierophant of the inner temple to its immortal abode: for such was Tartarus, the next beyond Hades, according to the Ethics, the alone eternal hypostasis to be redeemed from thence, from the oblivious realms of generation, into the Elysiam recollection of Wisdom in the highest consciousness. But the soul is said to be in Hades all the while that her hypostasis continues in darkness; that is, we would say, whilst she regards her image objectively, before attaining to the experimental knowledge. And here the Lesser Mysteries ended; the soul as it were, on the borders of the Stygian lake in view of Tartarus, which Euripides has elegantly styled also "a dream of death".

And the conformity between death and this next initiation, is strikingly exhibited in a passage preserved by Stoboeus from an ancient record; it has been well rendered by Dr Warburton, and runs thus:—The mind is affected and agitated in death, just as it is in initiation into the Grand Mysteries. And word answers to word, as well as thing to thing: for τελευτάν is to dies, and τελείσθαι is to be initiated; the first stage is nothing but errors and uncertainties; laborings, wandering, and darkness. And no, arrived on the verge of death and initiation, everything wears a dreadful aspect; it is all horror trembling, sweating, and affrightment. But this scene once over, a miraculous and divine light displays itself, and shining plains, and flowery meadows, open on all hands before them. Here they are entertained with hymns and dances, and with sublime and sacred knowledges, and with reverend and holy visions. And now become perfect and initiated, they are free, and no longer under restraint; but crowned and triumphant, they walk up and down in the regions of the Blessed[42].

But all, during the transition, is described as wearing a fearful aspect; and dread fills the sould about to relinquish her natal bond in life; neither may it be irrelevant to call in mind that repeated advice of Solomon, that —the fear of God is the beginning of Wisdom;—as the spiritual regard in the mysteries, already involuted, and drawing towards its end, with awe, begins to perceive itself in that Identic Source. And shall we not believe that it was out of the same intimate experience that the son of Dirach, inciting men to search after the Divine Wisdom, confesses, that—at first she will walk with him by crooked ways, and bring fear and dread upon him, and torment him with her disciplines, until she may trust his soul, and try him by her law? Then she will return the straight way unto his, says the Divine teacher, and comfort him, and show him her Secret. The root of Wisdom, is to fear the Lord, and the branches thereof are long life; strive for the truth, even unto death, and the Lord shall fight for thee[43]. So, likewise, we read, that there is in Alchemy a certain noble body, which is moved from one Lord to another; in the beginning of which there is suffering with vinegar; but, in the end, joy with exaltation. O happy gate of Blackness! Cries the adept, which art the passage to so glorious a change! Study, therefore, whoever appliest thyself to this art, only to know this secret; for to know this, indeed, is to know all, but to be ignorant of this, is to be ignorant of all. Take away, therefore, the vapor from the water, and the *blackness* from the *oily tincture*, and death from the *faeces*; and by *Dissolution* thou shalt possess a triumphant reward, even that in and by which the possessors live[44].

In the beginning of *Phaedo*, Plato, by Socrates, asserts, that it is the business of philosophers to study how to be dead. Plotinus, at the same time reprobating suicide, has the same doctrine; but Porphyry, in his *Auxiliaries to the Perception of Intelligible Natures*, explains the meaning of these others; for there is, says he, a twofold death, the one indeed universally known, in which the body is liberated from the sol; but the other peculiar to philosophers, in which the soul is liberated from the body: nor does the one entirely follow the other. That which nature binds, nature also dissolves; that which the soul binds, the soul likewise can dissolve: nature, indeed, binds the body to the soul, but the sol binds herself to the body. Nature therefore liberates the body from the sol, but the soul may also liberate herself from the body[45]. That is to say, if she know how, and have the right disposition awarded, she may dissolve her own disposition awarded, she may dissolve her own conceptive vehicle, even the parental bond, and return consciously (the elementary principles remaining, nor yet suffered to depart) under the dominion of another law to life. That was the "precious death", spoken of by the Hebrews and Academics, this the "happy gate of blackness" celebrates by the old adepts, the "head of Hermes' crow", which is in the beginning of the work; that which was fixed, viz., the sensual compact, is dissolved, and that which is dissolved is renovated, and hence the corruption and evil of mortality is made manifest in the ultimate circulation of the matter to be renewed, and on either side it is a signal of Art. And all without destruction to the mortal body (if perhaps some one values this), the willing life was made to pass out of its present oblivious fall, through regeneration, into the reminiscent consciousness of her Causal Source. As the truth-telling Oracle again declares that,

Mary Anne Atwood

If thou extend the fiery mind to the work of piety,
Thou shalt preserve the flexible body likewise.

Even through death, re-entering into and fortifying it with the elixir of an immortal life. *Orandum est ut sit mens sana in corpore sano.*

Seek thou the way of the soul,
Whence and by what order, having served the body,
He same from which thou dost flow, thou must return
And rise up again, joining action to sacred speech[46].

Suppose any one beginning at the top of an artificial edifice, should undertake to decompose it stone by stone, setting all aside, with the dirt and rubbish, as he proceeds, he would at last come to the earth which is at the foundation, and have space to build up anew; and thus it would appear to be in the Hermetic process. If any one should take the natural life as it presents itself, opening and analyzing the parts thereof, spiritually and wisely, one from another, graciously, as the mandate runs,—*Terra ab igni, subtile a spisso, suaviter cum multo ingenio,*—he would arrive finally at the basement, wherein is hidden the true alkaline original of life in this threefold essence separately contained. And this, the adept tells us, is the syllogism it best behooves us to look after; for he that has once passed the Aquaster, and entered the Fire World, sees what is both invisible and incredible to common men. He shall discover the miraculous conspiracy that is between the Prester and the Sun, the external and internal fire of life, the thing desiring and the thing desired. He shall know the secret love of heaven and earth, and why all influx of fire descends against the nature of fire, and comes from above downwards, until having found a body, it reascends therewith in perpetual interchange. He shall know, continues the adept, and see how the Fire Spirit has its root in the spiritual fire earth, and receives from its root in the spiritual fire earth, and receives from it a secret influx upon which it feeds. A body immarcessible, than which ther is nothing more ancient, vigorous, and young. The Salt of Saturn, that most abstruse principle of the Stone—the most ancient Demagorgon—*aethero dempto*—deprived of light, whose perpetual motion emanates the first material universe, and is the mineral soul, This is the earth, distinguished by Anaxagoras, which abiding durably in the center, "hands loftily", but its Being is Tartarus;

> *And the light hating world, and the winding current*
> *By which many things are swallowed up.*
> *Stoop not down, for a precipice lies below in the earth;*
> *Drawing thro' the ladder which hath seven steps,*
> *Beneath which is the throne of Necessity.*
> *Enlarge not thou thy destiny,*
> *The soul will, after a manner, clasp God to herself*[47].

As Porphyry, in our motto head, declares that—it is necessary that the soul when purified should associate with its generator; and the virtue of its after this conversion is said to consist in a scientific knowledge of true Being, which cannot be obtained either otherwise or without such a conversion.

> *O beatam quisque felix gnarus*
> *Dei Sacroorum, vitam piat;*
> *Ac animam initiat Orgyris Bacchans in montibus,*
> *Sacris purus lustrationibus*[48].

But, perhaps, inquisitive reader, you will very anxiously ask, what was said and done? I would tell you, replies the Epidaurian, if it could be lawfully told. But both the ears and tongue are guilty of indiscretion. Nevertheless, I will not keep you in suspense with religious desire, nor torment you with a long continued anxiety. Hear therefore, but believe what is true; The priest, then, all the profane being removed, taking me by then, all the profane being removed, taking me by the hand, brought me to the penetralia of the temple. *I approached the confines of death, and, having trod the threshold of Proserpine, I returned from it, being carried through all the Elements. At midnight I saw the Sun shining with a splendid light; and I manifestly drew near to the gods above and beneath, and proximately adored them.* Behold I have narrated to you things of which, though heard, it is nevertheless necessary that you should be ignorant[49].

By no explanation, nor any familiar analogy do we here presume to aid the natural intellect to a conception that transcends it, and which can only be attained through the identical experience. Yet reason may, does perceive it, and which can only be attained through the identical experience. Yet reason may, does perceive it, but abstractly only as an inference; yet it is her true Hypostasis, for which, as Isis for Osiris, she is constantly seeking, her objective reality in the Great Unknown. The rude, uneducated reason, however, which serves sensibles without reflection, will not understand; but that only which, seeing something more in causation than mere antecedence, can imagine into the intelligible substance of her Law. For there the true Efficient is to be found, which is not externally developed; but, becoming conjoined in consciousness, the soul knows herself as a Whole which before knew but a part only of her human nature; and proceeding thus, by theurgic assistance, arrives at her desired end, and participating of Deity, perceives then and knows, as Plotinus gratefully expresses it, that the supplier of life is present; and free from all external perturbation and desire, percipiently included in the circular necessity of her Law, believes its revelation which is her very self.

This is the *Introspection* which Psellus speaks of, as distinguished from the *Superinspection* which takes place in Hades. When the initiated person sees the Divine Light itself without any form or figure; this the oracle calls Sacro Sancto, for that is seen with a beauty by sacred person, and glides up and down pleasantly through the depths of the world. This will not deceive; but as the Oracle in fine advises,

> When thou seest a Fire without Form,
> Shining flashingly through the depths of the World,
> Hear the voice of Fire[50].

The same solemn and articulate instruction is given in an Indian record, translated by Sir William Jones, as follows:—Except the First Cause, whatever may appear or may not appear in the mind, know that to be the mind's maya (or image or delusion) as of light or darkness; as the great elements are in various beings entering, yet not entering, thus AM I, in them and yet not in them; even thus far may inquiry be made by him who seeks to know the principle of mind in *union and separation*, which must be every were and always[51]. And in the book of Deuteronomy, fourth chapter, the unfigured form of the Divine Essence, is noted in several places; and in the book of Zohar, it is explained, that before the descent into creation the Divine Nature has no form, and therefore it was forbidden to represent Him under any image whatever, even so much as a letter or point, and in this sense we are to understand the mandate,—Take good heed unto yourselves, for ye saw no manner of similitude on the say that the Lord spake unto you in Horeb out of the midst of the fire[52].

But then the revelations we have here gathered (and which are but a small part indeed of what has been described of the visions, and awful accompaniments which took place in the celebration of the Greater Mysteries) have been explained away as trifling exhibitions; orreries, as some say, contrived after the fashion of Walker's or Lloyd's Eidouranion; by those unfigured lights, it has been argued, were meant asteroids, whilst the figured are supposed agreeably to represent constellations of stars, grouped together in a more defined form. The whole, in fact, has been regarded as a moving panorama and illusory display of lights. But what extreme of trifling or fantastic folly has not modern imagination ascribed to the ancient mind? And how commonly mistaken and useless do not its best relics remain, for want of a corresponding intelligence in latter times? Allegories of recondite experience, truthful fables, symbols replete with instruction and refined emblems of art, have been either trivially interpreted, or condemned as futile without appeal; even those life-bound mysteries, those disciplines, purifications, sacred and primordeal rites have gone for nothing, or as good for nothing, whilst Astronomy has been the imputed spirit of the whole.

On risk of some ridicule, therefore, and diletanti scorn, we continue by our clue, leaving the darker scenes of life's drama, to look beyond, even upon that beautiful sun-lit horizon of the Mandeurentian, rising to intellectual radiance, as of the real life. Thus Proclus says, that to the wise indeed all things possess a silent and arcane tendency; and Intellect is excited to the Beautiful with astonishment and motion; for the illumination from it and its efficacy, acutely pervade through every soul, and as being the most similar of all things to the Good, it converts every soul that surveys it. The soul also, beholding that which is arcane, shining forth as it were to view rejoices in and admires that which sees, and is astonished about it. And as in the most holy Mysteries, prior to the mystic spectacles, those who are initiated are said to be seized with astonishment and dread, so in Intelligibles, prior to the participation of the Good, Beauty shining forth astonishes those that behold it, converts the soul to itself, and being established in the vestibules (of the good) shows what that is which is in the adyta, and what the transcendency is of occult being. Through these things, therefore, concludes the philosopher, let it be apparent whence Beauty originates, and how it first shines forth, and also that Animal (life) itself is the most beautiful of all intelligibles[53]. But Apuleius no less directly indicates the nature of his own mysterious revelation where, speaking of the Intellectual contact which the wise have proved, when they were separated from body, through the energies of mind, he says (calling his divine master also to witness), that this knowledge sometimes shines forth with a most rapid coruscation like a bright and clear light in the most profound darkness[54]. And Plato himself, speaking in like manner of the Intellectual Intuition, in his seventh Epistle, writes from long converse with this thing itself, accompanied by a life in conformity to it, on a sudden a light, as it were a leaping fire, will be enkindled in the soul, and will there itself nourish itself[55]. And heaven, he adds in another place is the kindled intelligence of the First Intelligible, and sight looking to things above is heaven[56]. And the sense of sight is celebrated by all these, therefore, as not only beautiful and useful for the purposes of this life; but as a leader in the acquisition of Wisdom. For it is not that very light which in us looks out beaming on our eyes that, directed within, and being purified also, and scientifically inquiring, discovers at last that other light which is the substance of its own, until light meeting light apprehends itself alone?

> *While thro'the middle of life's boiserous waves,*
> *Thy soul robust the deep's deaf tumult braves,*
> *Oft beaming from the god's thy piercing sight,*
> *Beholds in paths oblique a sacred light.*
> *Whence rapt from sense with energy divine,*
> *Before her eye immortal splendors shine,*
> *Whose plenteous rays in darkness most profound,*
> *Thy steps directed and illuminated round.*
> *Nor was the vision like the dreams of sleep,*
> *But seen whilst vigilant you brave the deep;*
> *While from your eyes you shake the gloom of night,*
> *The glorious prospect bursts upon your sight*[57].

Open the compound creature; look up the elements; divide the elements, and you shall find the quintessential nature: open this, continues the adept, and you shall conceive the subtle altereity of the angelical spirit in which is the divine act, and immediate beam or Wisdom from God. In this work, therefore, there concurreth in the separation of the first, a sensible aspect, in the other we behold with *intellectual eyes*, so that you may observe how all is in everything, and everything in all. As Hermes alludes: *Qui fornacem cum vase nostro construit, novum mundum conflat.* He that maketh a furnace with our glass to it maketh a new world[58];—a new hypostasis, and a new stone, —even that Stone of the Apocalypse, the true crystalline rock without spot or darkness, that renowned Terra Maga in aethere clarificata, which carries in its belly wind and fire. Having got this fundamental of a little new world, says Vaughan, unite the heaven in triple proportion to the earth, and then apply a generative heat to both, and they will attract from above the starfore of nature. So hast thou the glory of the whole world, therefore let all obscurity flee before thee[59]. This is the true Astrum Solis gotten and conceived, the internal spiritual Sun which is the Perpetual Motion of the Wise, and that Saturnian Salt which, developed to intellect and made erect, subdues all nature to his will. For it is the whole Demagorgon, now actually animated, which before was made visible without its subject light; but at length becoming ignited, reflects from out the dark abyss of being, as a luciferous wheel, with its radiant sections, all comprehending in their law, as the Oracle again bespeaks,

> *Fire, the derivation and dispenser of Fire,*
> *Whose hair pointed is seen in his native Light:*
> *Hence comes Saturn.*
> *The Sun Assessor beholding the Pure Pole.*

And this we take to be that midnight Sun of Apuleius, the ignited Stone of Anaxagoras (for which that philosopher has suffered such abundant disrepute, under error that his allusion was to the luminary of this world). This is the triumphal Chariot of Antimony, the Armed Magnet of Helvetius turned swiftly about the current axle of life, which is the Wheel of Fire signalized in Ezekiel, seen by the Hebrew prophets, Moses, David, and Zachariah, the Fiery Chariot of the Cabal, called Mercaba, in which all things are transfigured; and this is the Stone with the new name written in the Revelation and that Salt which the Savior orders that we should have it in ourselves; and is the same with the Prester of Zoroaster which in the Chaldean sense means the Fire Spirit of Life, and is that Identity in all which sustains all by the efflux of His power—the supernatural center of every living thing, the infinitely powerful and all-efficient making power.

In the beginning was the Word, and the Word was with God, and the Word was God. The same was in the beginning with God. All things were made by Him; and without Him was not any thing made that was made. In Him was Life; and the Life was the Light of men. And the Light shineth in Darkness and the Darkness comprehended it not[60].

And that Light shining in darkness, if men had never known, how should they have asserted, or do theologians invent such things in the present day? Neither did they formerly invent, but what they knew and had seen, declared.—To as many as received the Spirit to them gave He power to become the sons of God, which were born not of blood, nor of the will of the flesh, nor of the will of man, but of God.—This therefore is that Power which is hidden in man, the true Light which lighteth every man that cometh into the world, if haply one might feel after Him and find Him. An enchanted treasury known only to the wisely simple who have subdued their will to the Law of Wisdom, as Abraham did, as soon as he had gotten the creature into his hands[61].

We omit many things here relating to the mystical death and regeneration, which may be better understood when we come to treat of the manifestation of the Philosophic Subject; adding merely at present, in conclusion from our doctors, that the grand perfection of their Art was to multiply the Prester and place him in the most supreme Ether, which is that Augean palace already prepared for him in the beginning; where, as in a suitable habitation, he abides shining, not burning as below, or wrathful; but vital, calm, transmuting, recreating, and no longer a Consuming Fire.

INTELLIGE IN SCIENTIA ET SEPIAS INTELLIGNETIA: EXPRERIRE IN ILLIS, ET INVESTIGA ILLA, ET NOTA, ET COGITA, ET IMAGINARE, ET STATUE REM INTEGRITATE ET FAC SEDERE CREATORM IN THRONO SUO[62].

---

1. Roger bacon, De Mirab. Potest. Artis et naturae, Ars Aurifera, vol ii., p. 342
2. We adopt the term *dissolve* here in accordance with the old doctrine; varying theories have been proposed to explain the change that takes place in the vital relationship of the patient in the mesmeric trance: some have thought the sensible medium is drawn away by a superior attraction to life in the agent; others, that it is overcome, or included, or arrested, or destroyed; but the Alchemists, with one accord, say it ought to be *dissolved*; and, I default of better authority, shall we not suppose it so to be dissolved, or that it ought to be, the alkali by the acid, the dark dominion of the selfhood by the magnetic friction of its proper light, the sensible or animal into the vegetable, the cerebral into the ganglionic life? *Corpora ubi quid vult purgare oportet fluxa facere*, says the author of the Rosarium, that the compact earthy body of sense may be rarified and flow as a passive watery spirit. The beginning of the work, says Albertus Magnus, is a perfect solution; and all that we teach is nothing else but to dissolve and recongeal the spirit, to make the fixed volatile and the volatile fixed, until the total nature is perfected by the reiteration, both in its Solary and Lunar form.—Alberti, Secret. Tact.A rtis Auriferae, p.130.
3. Dryden's Aeneid, lib. vi.:130
4. Aeneid, lib. vi.:126.
5. Idem Aeneid, lib. vi:136
6. Metam., lib. xi.
7. Arbor, X, Scientiae Humanalis, p.99.

8. Republic, Book x.
9. Idem, Book vii.
10. Divine Legation, vol.i. p.345, etc.
11. Claudian de Paptu Proserpineae, sub initio.
12. Aeneid, lib. vi.:237.
13. Aeneid, lib. v:255.
14. De Raptu Prosepinae, sub init.
15. Pesllus de Oraculs, 14, 19. See also Oraculis Chaldaeorum Deomes Sacrificia...
16. Aeneid, lib. vi.:290.
17. Proclus on the Theology of Plato, vol. i., p.9; De Anima et Demone, throughout.
18. Triumphal Chariot of Antimony, Kirchringius, Engl. edit. p.16.
19. Occult Philosophy, book ii.
20. De Spetem Intelligneti, etc.
21. Michaele Psello de Demonibus.
22. Excerpta M. Ficini ex Graecis Procli Com. in Alcibiad.
23. De Mysteriis Aegypt-Chaldeor.
24. De Divinis atque Demonibus.
25. Oracula Zoroastri.
26. De Somnii.
27. Zoroastri Oracula Anima, Corpus, Homo.
28. Aeneid, lib. vi.:389.
29. Auxil. To Intelligib., sect. 1
30. Proclus on the Theology of Plato, book i,cap. iii.
31. Tract. Aur., cap.ii.
32. Book of Enoch, chap. lxiv. 7,8.
33. Lumen de Lumine, Introd. Coelum Terrae, p.90.
34. Tract. Aur., cap. iii.
35. Lumen de Lumine, p. 68.
36. Republic, book vii.
37. Themistus relates how, when entering the mystic dome, the initiated is seized at first with solicitude and perplexity, unable to move a step forward, at a los to find the entrance to that road which is to lead him to the place which he desires; till the conductor laying open for him the vestibule, he enters, etc. See Warburton's Divine Legation, the Extract, col. 1. The adepts, many of them, are at some pains to denote the peculiar disposition and appearance of this guide, and the Chaldaic oracle promises that the mortal, approaching the fire, will have a light from divinity.
38. Nunc animis opus, Aenea, nunc pectore firmo. Aeneid, lib. vi.:260.
39. Idem Aeneid vi.:285.
40. Through fire the divine oracles more plainly teach, that those strains are all finally obliterated that accede to the soul from generation and which conceal the immortal principle in unconscious oblivion for the sake of vivifying the mortal sense. But the inquisitive light once entering as a ferment combats meeting its proper pole, and conjointly kindling with it, absorbs, transmutes, and occultates the surrounding medium into its own abyssal life.
    See. Tract. Aureus, cap. iv.
    See Eccles. iv.:28; 1 Kings xix.:11-12.
41. Milton's paradise Lost, i.:676
42. Divine Legation i.:342
43. Eccles. i. v.20; chap iv. v.17, 18, 28.
44. Hermes, Tract. Aur., cap. ii.; Ripley Revived, 5th Gate, p. 357.
45. Aux. to Intell., sect. 1, 8, 9.
46. Oracula Chaldaica.
47. Oracula Chaldaica.

48. Euripides in Bacchis.
49. Apuleius Metam., Book xi.
50. Quando videris forma sine sacram igneam
    Collucentum saltatim totius per profundum mundi,
    Audi Ignis Vocem.
    Oracula Chaldaica, infine
51. Asiatic Researches, vol. i., p.241.
52. Deuteronomy iv.:15; Zohar, part ii.
53. Proclus on the Theology of Plato, Vol. i., Book iii., Chap. xviii.
54. On the God of Socrates, in int.
55. Epistle vii.; Taylor, vol. v.
56. The Cratylus, and in Timaeus.
57. Porphyry's Hymn to Plotinus, Select Works, Preface.
58. See Fludd's Mosaica, circa medio.
59. Anima Magia, p.50. ; Tabula Smaragdina Hermetis
60. St. John's Gospel, chap.i.
61. Zephir Jezirah, in fine.
62. Idem., Liber de Creatione, Authore Abraham, cap. i.

Chapter 4. The Mysteries (Concluded)

WITH A VIEW OF THE ULTIMATE OBJECT OF THESE INITIATIONS TO PROVE THE PERFECTION, PURITY, AND INTEGRAL EFFICIENCY TO WHICH THE HUMAN SPIRIT MAY ARRIVE BY DIVINE ASSIMILATION COMING IN VITAL CONTACT WITH ITS SOURCE.

It behooves thee to hasten to the Light, and to the beams of the Father from whence was sent to thee a soul clothed with much mind.

— Zoroastri Oracula, Anima, Corpus, Homo.

It is known concerning Hercules, that he performed his last labour in the Hesperidian region, and Olympiodorus, in his Commentary on the Gorgias of Plato, informs us what we are to understand by this, It is necessary to know, says he, that islands stand out of, as being higher than the sea; a condition of being, therefore, which transcends this corporeal life and generation is denominated the Islands of the Blessed; and these are the same with the Elysian Fields. Hence Hercules is said to have accomplished his last labour in the Hesperidian region; signifying by this, that having vanquished an obscure and terrestrial life, he afterwards lived in open day[1]. For he dragged up Cerberus from hell, that is to say, he liberated the whole individual entity through a threefold evolution from the bond of its earthly geniture, and established it finally in the most exalted life. And those golden apples were a part also of the regard of his arcane and telestic labours; which Theseus, before him, was unable to finish, being detained by his passions in the sea of sense. So Proclus understands the allegory, where he says that, being purified by sacred institutions and enjoying undefiled fruits, Hercules at length obtained an establishment among the god.

> *Felix, qui potuit rerum cognoscere Causas,*
> *Atque metus omnes et inexorabile Fatum*
> *Subjectitpedibus, strepitimque Acherontis avari!*

Nature indeed, as a beneficient mother, offers the rich treasury of life to all, and the universal Father, it is said, keeps the gate of the fatal cavern open for the convenience of mankind. The descent, therefore, is allowed on all hands to be easy; but the ascent otherwise; the gate indeed being so narrow, close, and difficult to discern, that there be few, and they immortals only, that are able to pass through. The allusion to these gates is frequent in antiquity, and that of Homer in the thirteenth book of the Odyssey, describing the cave in Ithaca has been the subjects of many comments.

> *A lofty gate unfolds on either side,*
> *That to the North is pervious to mankind,*
> *The sacred South t' immortals is consigned.*

That the poet does not narrate these particulars from historical information or misinformation either is very evident. For neither if there had been any geographical ground for such a description, could he have hoped to gain belief for the persistent allegory, thus artificially opening up a path to god and men in the region of Ithaca. But the wise Porphyry, after combating many erroneous opinions, explains that whereas the southern gate pertains to souls descending into the realms of generation, and the southern to souls ascending to divinity; we ought to observe, on this account, that Homer does not say indeed that this last is a passage of the gods but of immortals: signifying by this, souls which are *per se*, that is to say, essentially immortal[2]. For nothing but the subtlety of an immortal essence, and that by regeneration, can pass into immortality. And here we may better conceive, perhaps, the value of that Golden Branch, which, attracted from the first to its native soil, indifferent to every other lure, through death and darkness enters; and taking root at last, gathers strength to germinate and blossom, as a radiant flower, overspreading and illuminating the surrounding wilderness of life. The sudden transition from the horrid realms of Tartarus, forms an admirable contrast in that part of the Aeneid where the hero, having passed the Stygian border, goes forth to meet his father in the Elysian Fields.

> *Devenere locos laetos, et amoena vireta*
> *Fortunatorum nemorum, sedsque beatas*
> *Largior hic campos Aether et Lumine vestit*
> *Purpureo: solemque suum, sua sidera norunt.*

This divine ethereal purpled verdure, this meadow of Divine Ideas, or Pratum, as the Oracle denotes it, is a place well known to philosophers; the Alchemists in general call it their garden, but Flammel, in his Summary, includes the Mountain of the Seven metals, saying,—the philosophers have indeed a garden where the sun as well morning as evening remains with a most sweet dew; whose earth brings forth trees and fruits which are transplanted thither, which also receive nourishment from the pleasant meadows. And if thou wouldst come hither and find good, betake thyself to the mountain of the Seven, where there is no plain, and look down from the highest downward to the Sixth, which you will see afar off; in the topmost height, you will find a royal herb triumphing, which some call mineral, some vegetable, some saturnine[3]. For it is either and all, which Vaughan describes as the rendezvous of all spirits, where Ideas as they descend from above, are conceived and incorporated. But it is a delicate and pleasant region, he says, as it were in the suburbs of heaven. Those seven mystic mountains, whereupon grow the roses and lilies, are the outgoings of paradise mentioned in Esdras, and the Planetary Sphere of Sendivogius, and that most famous tincture of the Sapphiric Mine: which is in truth the cleansed Augean, the already prepared medial receptacle of the newborn light; no sooner does this arise than all the vegetable colours, before obliterated in darkness, return to neutralize their poison and restore the suspended circulation to a conscious equilibrate accord. This is Elysium, the enclosed garden of Solomon, where God condescends to walk and drink of the sealed fountain; the true Terrestrial Paradise, which some have called *nox corporis,* the night of body or corporeal sleep, a term made more intelligible by the apposite saying of Heraclitus, concerning souls in that condition, that *we live their death and die their life.* In these meadows therefore the souls of the dead are said to inhabit, souls dead indeed to this life, yet more alive in that. For converted to externals, we desert our best life unconsciously as Empedocles says,

Mary Anne Atwood

Heaven's exiles straying from the orb of light.

But philosophers are said continually to have visited this place, as we read for instance concerning the habitation of R.C., *Vidi aliquando Olympicos domos, nonprocul a fluviolo et civitate nota quas Sanctus Spiritus fontem aperuit perennis aquae adhuc stillantem, in quo Diana se lavat, cui Venus ut Pedissaqua et Saturnus ut anteambulo, conjunguntur. Intelligenti nimium inexperto minimum hoc erit dictum.* To clear the prospect a little, therefore, Vaughan adds this description to the Indian Brachman's abode. I have seen, says Apollonius, the Brahmans of India dwelling on the earth and not on the earth; they were guarded without walls invisibly, and possessing nothing, they enjoyed all things[4]. In such a place the oracle told Amelius the soul of Great Plotinus was,

> *Ubi Amicitia est, ubi cupido visu mollis,*
> *Purae plenus laetitiae, et sempiternis rivis*
> *Ambrosiis irrigatus a Deo; unde sunt amorum*
> *Retinacula, dulcis spiritus et tranquillus*
> *Aether Aurei generis magi Jovis.*

By such clear and rapid rivers of supernal light the adoring Sybil drew her inspiration, and by such, according to the Orphic poet, the god Apollo even loved to contemplate.

> *Omnia quae Phoebo quondam meditante beatus Audiit Eurotas,*
> *&c...*

There are three modes of human vision recorded by St Augustine; the first external, and belongs to the outward eye; the second that of imagination, by which representations are visible to the internal sense; the third is anagogic, and an intellectual sight, drawn above, by which intelligible species are beheld, as a pure infusion of light to the understanding. The first mode is familiar, the second has already been discussed; but this third vision of the light is in Elysium: where the eye of mind, no longer as heretofore looking from without inwardly, beholds its object through the atmosphere of the natural life; but contrariwise, having passed through this, purifying to the center, is converted and raised; and, as a Unit, now regards the circumference transitively, including it as an understanding or reflector, as it were, to the focus of her light. Porphyry beautifully resembles this mode of being to a fountain, not flowing outwardly, but circularly scattering its streams into itself. And thus there is an assimilation established, as near as may be in *consciousness*, of the self-knowing and the self known; yet with this motion of the soul, time is consubsistent, as changing her conceptions, she passes from one to another according to the self motion of her essence, and through her eyes being directed to the survey of the different forms which she contains, and which have the relation of parts to her whole essence; but eternity is consubsistent only with the permanence of intellection itself[5]. And thus, though there is a grade above; yet this is the Intellection in Elysium where the exemplary Image of the Universal Nature also is revealed as in that Athanor of Hermes before mentioned, or furnace having a glass to it, that singular fundamental of his small new world.

And the life of the intelligible world consists thenceforth in intellectually energizing, and this energy, distinguishing, desiring, understanding within itself simultaneously, generates Light through a perpetual tranquil and quiet contact with the Principle of things. And the calm delight of Being there in universal harmony, the truthful visions, scenery, occupations and integral intelligence are pictured with all the vivid colouring of that experienced poet's soul; and will be rightly understood as an unfolding of the embryo life, the nourishment and education of the understanding vehicle now standing in open presence before its Archetypal Light; according to which also it Archetypal Light; according to which also it perfects all the new-born attributes, as of justice, beauty, charity, hope, every faculty, sentiment and desire in orderly relation under the dominion of reason; and evolves the total harmony of nature, and all specific variety in her originating source.—The sun shines but for us, exclaims the chorus of the Initiated in Aristophanes; we alone receive the glory of his beams; for us alone the meadows are enameled with flowers; even for us, who are initiated and who have learned to perform all acts of piety and justice[6]. Nor is it without reason that the river Eridanus is said by Virgil to pass through those celestial abodes; for this indicates the prolific flow of spirit which accedes spontaneously from the occult energy of such a life. Taylor has admirably set forth these particulars of the poet in his *Dissertation*; and that the most abundant spectacles and powers are belonging to those Elysian fountains is shown by Proclus, in his fourth book *On the Theology*, in which also he relates that Theurgists placed their chief hopes of salvation: for the plain of Truth, he says, is intellectually expanded to intelligible Light and is splendid with the illuminations which proceed from thence; and as the one (subjective identity) emits by illumination intelligible light so the intelligible (objective entity) imparts to secondary natures a participation *productive of essence.* But the Meadow is the prolific power of life, according to Plato, and of all various reasons, and is the comprehension of the First Efficient causes of life and the generation of Forms: for the meadows also which are here, continues the great exponent, are productive of all various forms and reasons and *bear water* which is the symbol of vivification[7]. And here the metaphysician accords with the ancient physiologists and alchemists, who, experimentally searching, were said to prove the Universal Identity of Nature on the ontological ground; reproducing the whole material principle to sense and visibility from the dissolution of the spirit in its proper kind without alloy. But intending to speak of these material rewards of initiation hereafter, and of this Water especially, we pass onward for the present to introduce the self-conspicuous and prolific goddess herself, according to Apuleius' most eloquent announcement, appearing in the Eleusian Fane.

Moved by thy prayers, O Lucius! Behold, I am come! I, who am nature, the parent of all things, the Queen of all the nature, the parents of all things, the Queen of all the elements, the primordial progeny of ages, the supreme of divinities, the sovereign of the spirits of the dead, the first of celestials, and the uniform resemblance of gods and goddesses; I, who rule by my nod the luminous summit of the heavens, the salubrious breezes of the sea, and the deplorable silences of the realms beneath; and whose one divinity the whole orb of the earth venerates under a manifold form, by different rites and a various of appellations. Hence the primordial Phrygians call me Pessinuntica; the Attic Aborigines, Cecropian Minerva; the floating Cyprians, Paphian Venus; the arrow-bearing Cretans, Diana Dyctynna; the three-tongued Sicilians, Stygian Proserpine; and the Eleusinians, the ancient Goddess Ceres. Some also call me Juno; others, Bellona; others, Hecate; and others, Rhamnusia. And those who are illuminated by the incipient rays of that divinity, the Sun, when he rises, viz., the Ethiopians and the Arii, and the Egyptians skilled in ancient learning, worshipping me by ceremonies perfectly appropriate, call me by my true name, Queen Isis. Behold then, I, commiserating thy calamities, am present, favouring and propitious; dismiss now tears and lamentations, and expel sorrow; for now salutary day will shine upon thee. Listen therefore attentively to these my mandates. The religion which is eternal has consecrated to me the day which will be born of this *night;* on which *day* my priests offer to me the *first fruits* of *navigation,* dedicating to me a *new ship,* when now the *winter tempests* are mitigated and the *stormy waves* of the *deep* are appeased, and the *sea* itself has now become *navigable.* That sacred ceremony you ought to expect with a *mind* neither *solicitous* nor *profane.* For the priest, being admonished by me, shall bear *a rosy crown in his right hand adhering to the rattle,* in the precinct of the *pomp.* Without delay therefore cheerfully follow, confiding in my benevolence. When you approach the priest, gently pluck the *roses* as if you intended to kiss his hand, and immediately divest yourself of *the hide of that worst of beasts,* and which for some time since has been to me detestable[8]. Nor should you fear anything pertaining to my concerns as difficult—only remember and always retain it deposited in the penetralia of your mind, that the remaining course of your life must be dedicated to me, even to the boundary of your latest breath. Nor is it unjust that you should owe your whole life to that goddess by whose assistance you will return to the Human Form. But you will live happy, and you will live glorious under my protection: and when, having passed through the allotted space of your life, you descend (once more) to the realms beneath, there also in the subterranean hemisphere, you dwelling in the Elysian Fields, shall frequently adore me whom you now see, and shall there behold me shining amidst the darkness of Acheron, reigning in the Stygiam Penetralia, and being propitious to you. Moreover, if you shall be found to deserve the protection of my divinity, by sedulous obedience, religious services, and inviolable chastity, you shall know that it is possible for me to extend your life beyond the limits appointed to it by fate.

The venerable Oracle being thus finished, adds the philosopher, the invincible goddess receded into herself; and without delay, I, being liberated from *sleep,* immediately arose, seized with fear and joy, and in an excessive perspiration, and in the highest degree admiring so manifest a presence of the powerful goddess; having sprinkled myself with *marine dew,* and intent upon her great commands, I *revolved* in my mind the *order* of her mandates; shortly after too the *sun* arose, and put to flight the *darkness* of black night[9]. The dragon shuns the sun's beams which look through the crevices, and the dead son lives—and the new vessel, purified and holy, is brought into the Eleusinian temple, to be consecrated in Light. Not, as some have imagined, a crystal night-lamp or magic lanthorn, cleansed for the consumption of the best olive oil, to dazzle the ignorant or instruct beholders with artificial emblems of natural science;

but a far more pellucid gas-lamp, an infallible gasometer, able to hold and sustain and measure simultaneously, even within itself to kindle a perpetual flame, shining in equilibriate constancy about the sufficient fuel of all life. As Apuleius further apostrophizing the same divinity, continues —Thou rollest the heavens round the steady poles, dost illuminate the sun, govern the world, and tread on the dark realms of Tartarus. The stars move responsive to thy command, the gods rejoice in thy divinity, the hours and seasons return by thy appointment, and the elements reverence thy decree[10].

All which is readily admissible of the Universal Nature; and, if we may believe the experienced, we are not cut off from this fountain, but attracted out from it; which supplies all things with life perpetually, so that we are what we are by its influence; but in turn receiving the impressure of foreign forms, passions, accidents, and evil generations, the passive purity is defiled and obscured, and unconscious of that inner light which lives in reality; of which the present life is a mere vestige and a comparative diminution of existence, an imitation, as it were, of that which is absolute and real; whose spontaneous revelation in a purified soul imparts virtue with understanding, and universal knowledge, health of body, and long length of days; riches as from the Causal fountain of all things, and felicity in communion with all. It also emits light accompanied with harmony of intellection, and finally exhibits a form of such rarified effulgence that the eye of mind, all the while regarding, is drawn to contact suddenly, unable longer to sustain itself alone. This is the method and arcane principle of SelfKnowledge, and the narrow way of regeneration into life; and so great is the tenuity and attractive subtilty of the Divine Nature, says Jamblichus, that the initiated, when surveying it, are affected in the same manner as fishes, when they are drawn upwards from the dark and turbid waters into the diaphanous clear air; becoming languid as soon as they perceive it, and deprived of the use of their co-nascent spirit[11]. For to this spirit the vision in Hades is allied which is born be through without much disturbance of the common life; but, when the central magnet moves to the ascent, this expiration is described as taking place; a liberation is effected through agony, as it were of death, the circulation oscillates, and the soul, coalescing with its vehicle, transcends free from corporeal hindrance into the elysian light. That was the rosy crown of which the Hierophant was to assist Apuleius' Lucius to partake, when he was enabled to put off the hide of that worst of beasts, and reenter into the Divine Form of humanity. Wherefore, O ye asses!

Cries Agrippa, in condemnation, which are now with your children under the commandment of Christ by his Apostles, the messengers and readers of true Wisdom in his Gospel, be you loosed from the darkness of the flesh and blood, ye that desire to attain to true Wisdom; not of the tree of the knowledge of good and evil, but of the tree of life: setting apart all traditions of men and discourse of the flesh and blood whatsoever it be; entering not either into the schools of other philosophers, but into yourself, ye shall know all things, for the knowledge of all things is compact in you: even as God hath created trees full of fruits, so hath he created the soul as a reasonable tree full of forms and knowledges: but through the sin of the first parent all things were opened; and oblivion, the mother of ignorance, stepped in. Set you then now aside who may, continues the magician, the veil of your understanding, who are wrapped in the darkness of ignorance: Cast out the drink of Lethe, you which have made yourselves drunken with forgetfulness, and wait for the True Light ,you which have suffered yourself t be overtaken with unreasonable sleep; and forthwith, when your face is discovered, ye shall pass from the light to light[12], and from glory to glory, as the Apostle says—from the light of the senses to the illumination of reason, and from reason through its topmost faith into the substantive glorification of all.

> *'Twas in a golden cup*
> *That Helius passed,*
> *Helius, Hyperion's son.*
> *O'er floods and oceans wafted far away.*
> *To Erebus he went, and the sad realms of night*
> *His aged parent there he found,*
> *And the kind consort of his better days,*
> *And all his blooming offspring.*
> *Then to the sacred grove he sped,*
> *The sacred grove of laurel.*

And this strain brings us to the final purpose of Aeneas who, going forth to meet his *father* in the Elysian fields, has the whole *Epopteia* opened to him—the Pantheistic revealment of the Universal Nature, her secret foundation, the soul's essence, origin, hindrances, and proper end.

> *Principio caelum ac terras camposque liquentis*
> *Lucentemque globum Lunae, Titaniaque astra*

Mary Anne Atwood

Spiritus intus alit, totamque infusa per artus
Mens agitat molem et magno se corpore miscet.
Inde hominum pecudumque genus, vitaeque volantum,
Et quae marmoreo fert monstra sub aequore pontus.
Igneus est ollis vigor et caelestis origo
Seminibus, quantum non noxia corpora tardant,
Terrenique hebetant artus moribundaque membra.
Hinc metuunt cupiuntque, dolent gaudentque, neque auras
Respiciunt, clausae tenebris et carcere caeco.
Quin et supremo cum lumine vita reliquit,
Non tamen omne malum miseris nec funditus omnes
Corporeae excedunt pestes; penitusque necesse est
Multa diu concreta modis inolescere miris.
Ergo exercentur poenis, veterumque malorum
Supplicia expendunt. Aliae panduntur inanes
Suspensae ad ventos : aliis sub gurgite vasto
Infectum eluitur scelus, aut exuritur igni;
Quisque suos patimur Manes. Exinde per amplum
Mittimur Elysium, et pauci laeta arva tenemus :
Donec longa dies, perfecto temporis orbe,
Concretam exemit labem, purumque relinquit
Aethërium sensum atque auraï simplicis ignem.[13]

This initiation to the Paternal abode which, according to the Alexandrian Platonists, opens the whole of the divine paths and media by which the soul becomes finally fitted for establishment under the celestial circulation of her Law, exhibits in progress likewise the self-splendid appearances of the true gods, which are both entire and firm, and expand likewise the self-splendid appearances of the true gods, which are both entire and firm, and expand to the mystic inspection of all intelligibles; as Socrates explains in Phaedrus: For *telete* precedes *muesis*, and *muesis*, *epopteia*. Hence, says he, we are initiated (*teleioumetha*) in ascending by the perfective gods. But we view with closed eye, *i.e.*, with the pure soul itself (*muoumetha*) entire and stable appearances, through the connective gods, with whom there is the intellectual wholeness and the firm establishment of souls. And we become fixed in, and spectators of (*epapteuomen*) the intelligible watch-tower, through the gods who are collectors of wholes; we speak, indeed, of all these things as with reference to the intelligible, but we obtain a different thing according to a different order. For the perfective gods initiate us in the intelligible through themselves; as the collective monads are through themselves the leaders of intelligibles. And there are indeed many steps of ascent, but all of them extend to the Paternal port and the Paternal Initiation[14].

> *To find the Hero, for whose only sake*
> *We sought the dark abodes and crossed the bitter lake.*

For the paternal is the first source of life, and the last into which the conscience is initiated; and the rebirth and recreation of this principle in the Free Ether, prepared for it, is the end and plenitude of initiatory rites.

In Taylor's notes to his Pausanias we find an extract from an ancient writer, Ascelpius Trallianus, wherein the etymon of σοφία, Wisdom, is derived from τοσφες, the conspicuous and the clear. Thus—what is Wisdom? We reply, that it is a certain *clearness*, as being that which renders *all things conspicuous*. From whence was this word clearness denominated? We reply, from *light*. Since, therefore, the clear is accustomed to lead into light and knowledge things concealed in the darkness of ignorance; on this account, concludes the writer, it is thus denominated. Thus, also, Minerva is sometimes called Phosphor, as being the bearer and measure of the Demiurgic Fire. And what are all the gods but manifestations of this same Fire germinating through the projecting energy of Intellect distinct in Light? In its lucid understanding, stable expanse, Minerva; in its golden radiance and ideality, Apollo; shining forth in beauty, warmth, and infinite attraction, Venus; in its concentrated flashing force, Mars; in compact impenetrable purity, the chaste Diana; penetrating in all the variety of perspicuous thought and imagination, the winged Mercury; in its universal fabricative virtue and beneficience, the Demiurgic Jupiter; and thenceforth downward and upward from the last to the first ineffable Phanes, before Saturn, or that ancient Cybele, proceeded to manifestation by will in time.

> *Then nor the sun's swift members splendid shone*
> *But in dense harmony established lay*
> *Concealed; eternity's revolving sphere*
> *Rejoicing round its center firm to roll.*

Until, as a poet goes on to explicate, by the fanning of the celestial ether set in motion,

Then all the members of the god appeared[15].

And the nourishing cause of these gods is said to be a certain intelligible union, comprehending in itself the whole intellectual progression, and filling the Ethereal Hypostasis with acme and power. All the gods, says Plotinus, are beautiful, and their splendour is intense. What else, however, is it but Intellect through which they are such? And because intellect energizes them in so great a degree, as to render them visible by its Light. For they are not at one time wise, and at another destitute of wisdom, but they are always wise, in an impassive, stable, and pure Intellect; seeing such things as Intellect itself sees, they occupy and pervade without ceasing the whole of that blissful region. For the life there is unattended with labour, and Truth is their generator and nutriment, their essence and their nurse[16]. Plato also by Socrates narrating the mode of ascent to the Intelligible Beauty, and how, following the divine leaders they became partakers of the same, concludes.—It was then lawful to survey splendid Beauty, where we obtained together with that happy choir, this blessed vision and contemplation; and we indeed enjoyed this felicity, following the choir together with Jupiter. But others in conjunction with some other god; at the same time beholding and being initiated in those mysteries which it is lawful to call the most blessed of all mysteries. And these divine orgies were celebrated by us while we were perfect and free from those evils which awaited us in a succeeding period of time; *we likewise were initiated in and became spectators of entire, simple, quietly stable, and blessed visions, resident in a Pure Light; being ourselves pure and liberated from this surrounding vestment, which we denominate body, and to which we are bound like an oyster to its shell.* And beauty, continues the divine narrator, shone upon us during our progression with the gods: but on our arrival hither, we possessed the power of perceiving it, through the clearest of our senses[17]. Not, let us believe with Dr Warburton, "a mere illuminated image, which the priest had purified", for indeed his while account of the institution is absurd; but when we consider to what Plato really alludes, by those *simple and blessed visions resident in a pure light*, we can no longer wonder why the initiated were conjoined with the total deity and intellectual perfection of their leaders, and were replenished with the divine essentiality. And the being entire is derived to souls from equilibrate circulation in their Ether; which contains, and is connective of all the Divine genera. Everything, however, which in the whole contains parts, comprehends also that which is divided, and collects that which is various into union and simplicity. But the quiet, stable, *and simple visions, are* unfolded to souls supernally; as Proclus explains from the supercelestial place. And so those gods and those powers that follow the gods reveal themselves each in his particular form or essence of light, but by no means extend themselves as figured phantasms, such as the mind before beheld in Hades from its own self-shadowing creative fancy. For wherefore should they be supposed to exhibit these? Is it not evident that their characteristic would be far better expressed by their simple idea living in the understanding, than by any other figured light or representation? By no means therefore, says Jamblichus, does Divinity either transform himself into phantasms nor extend these from himself to other things, but emits illuminations, true representations of himself in the true manner of souls. And truth, he adds, is coexistent with the god, in the same manner as light with the sun. For as all other things, such as are principal, primarily begin from themselves, and impart to themselves that which they give to others; as for instance, in essence, in life, and in motion; thus also the natures which supply all beings with truth primarily proclaim the truth themselves, and precedaneously unfold the essence of themselves to the spectators. Hence likewise they exhibit to Theurgists a Fire which is itself, to itself, visible[18]. Let no one therefore wonder, says Proclus, the gods being essentially in one simplicity according to transparency, if various phantasms are hurled forth before the presence of them; nor if they, being uniform, should in their appearance be multiform, as we have learned in the most perfect Mysteries. For nature and the demiurgic intellect extend corporeal formed images of things corporeal, sensible images of things intelligible, and those without interval, since all things are an emanation from these[19]. And thus the soul, when looking at things posterior to herself, beholds the shadows only and images of true being; but, when she converts herself to herself, she evolves her own Essence, and the vivific reasons which she contains. And at first, indeed, she only as it were perceives herself; but, when she penetrates more profoundly for the examination of herself, she finds in herself both understanding and the Reason of created beings. When, however, she proceeds into her interior recesses and into the Adytum of Life, as the great theologian declares, she perceives, with the eye closed, as it were, the genus of the gods, which are the unities of all being: for all things are in us psychically, that is to say, in the efficient Reason of our life, and through this, when it is developed, we are capable of knowing of all things, by exciting the images and powers of the Whole which we contain. And this has been said to be the best employment of our energy, to be extended to a Divine nature, and having our individual powers at rest, to revolve harmoniously round it, to excite all the multitude of the soul to this union; and laying aside all such things as are posterior to the One, to become seated and conjoined to that which is ineffable and beyond all things[20].

It is satisfactory to observe how these ancients, with one accord, dismiss all visions which take place during the imperfect self-activity of the human mind as arbitrary and untrustworthy; how well they had learned to discriminate, and how very absolute and clear a line they draw between enthusiasm and fanaticism, between the shadowy world of imaginative vision and the light of the true gods; nor will any one, profoundly considering their assertions, doubt about the origin or respect due to these divinities, which, as an emanative splendour from the Causal Fountain, make manifest in energy its Intellectual Law.

> *What though in solemn silence all*
> *Move round this dark terrestrial ball*
> *In Reason's ear they all rejoice,*
> *And utter still their glorious voice,*
> *For ever singing as they shine,*
> *"The Hand that moves us is divine"*[21].

Or, as the mathematician paints it,

> *En tibi Norma Poli—! en divae Libramina Molis!*
> *Computus en Jovis! Et quas dum primordial rerum*
> *Conderet, omnipotens sibi leges ipse Creator*
> *Dixerit, et Operis quae Fundementa locarit.*

And here again we take occasion to observe that it is indeed by divine Media, and not a mere conception of the mind or metaphysical abstraction, either, that Theurgists are conjoined to the Divine nature; since, if this were the case, what would hinder those who philosophize theoretically from participating of this union? Which they do not; but the perfect efficacy of ineffable works, says Jamblichus, which are divinely performed, in a way surpassing all ordinary intelligence and the power of inexplicable symbols which are known only to the gods themselves, impart Theurgic union. Hence we do not perform these things through intellectual perception; since, if this were the case, the intellectual energy of them would be imparted by us, neither of which is true: for when we do not energize intellectually (all preparative conditions having been fulfilled), the *Synthemata, i.e.,* the Theurgic aids and media themselves, perform by themselves their proper work; and the ineffable power of the gods itself, knows by itself its own images. It does not however know them, as if excited by our intellections; but it is requisite to consider these and all the best dispositions of the soul, and also the purity pertaining, *as certain concauses*; the things which properly *excite* the Divine will being the *Divine Synthemata* themselves; and thus things pertaining to the gods are moved by themselves, and do not receive from an inferior nature (*i.e.*, to say, from the regardant subject) the principle of their energy[22]. As the Chaldaic Oracle likewise in its own operative language declares:

> *And these things I revolve in the recluse temples of my mind:*
> *Extending the like fire sparkling into the spacious air,*
> *To put into the mind the symbol of variety,*
> *And not to walk dispersedly on the empyreal channels, but stiffly:*
> *For the king did set before the world an intellectual incorruptible*
>   *pattern,*
> *This print through the world, he promoting, accordingly appeared,*
> *Beautified with all kinds of Ideas of which there is one Fountain,*
> *Intellectual notions from the Paternal Fountain cropping the*
>   *Flower of Life —*
> *And to these Intellectual Presters of Intellectual Fire all things are*
>   *subservient by the persuasive will of the Father.*
> *Having put on the completely armed vigour of resounding Light,*
>   *with triple strength, fortifying the soul and the mind.*
> *O how the world hath Intellectual guides inflexible!*[23].

So did Theurgic rites, by the medium of the passive Ether, unfold the embryo vigour of her newly conceived life; awakening intellect into reminiscence and filling it with the conscious reasons of things manifest and occult; and as it were by an obstetric hand and action, bringing forth the total nature and ornamenting it with Light. For Wisdom here enacts the apart of a discreet mother, who having educated her son and furnished him with understanding, bids him use it, exercising him in every virtue and theoretic discipline for the final conversion and accomplishment of his soul. And if the education has been complete and the discipline perfect, says Porphyry, the whole inferior powers will range in harmonious concord about their proper rule, and will so venerate this Reason, as to be indignant if they are at all self-moved, in consequence of not being quiet when their master is present; and will reprove themselves for them imbecility, so that the motions themselves will be *dissolved* through their proximity to the reasoning power[24].

So did Theurgic rites, by the medium of the passive Ether, unfold the embryo vigour of her newly conceived life; awakening intellect into reminiscence and filling it with the conscious reasons of things manifest and occult; and as it were by an obstetric hand and action, bringing forth the total nature and ornamenting it with Light. For Wisdom here enacts the part of a discreet mother, who having educate her son and furnished him with understanding, bids him use it, exercising him in every virtue and theoretic discipline for the final conversion and accomplishment of his soul. And if the education has been complete and the discipline perfect, says Porphyry, the whole inferior powers will range in harmonious concord about their proper rule, and will so venerate this Reason, as to be indignant if they are at all self-moved, in consequence of not being quiet when their master is present; and will reprove themselves for their imbecility, so that the motions themselves will be dissolved through their proximity to the reasoning power.

But the government of the natural life is oligarchical, almost an anarchy, where there is no permanently accepted leader of the whole; but each motive rising, as it were, becomes a usurper of a vacant throne; and external institutions imaged from thence accordingly are selfish, conflicting, and unhappy. Yet observing how the faculties of each tyrant motive, as it accedes, and how the highest are thus often made to subserve the lowest ends, how covetousness, ambition, and envy, and pride will erect and manifest themselves in the circumstances of individual and social life, and stamp their character on nations, and obscure the perception of every other good; we may gather from thence a passable though faint conception of the Almighty force that moves about the Rational Magnet, and how the Presters of Intellectual Fire follow in radiant order the will of their First Cause. Under such a monarch indeed, when once he is established, no dissensions would be likely to arise, but the inferior powers will so venerate his leading motive that they will move only according to his movement, pursuing constantly in observant order his infallible rule.

Fire, says the adept philosopher, is the purest and most worthy of all the elements, and its *substance* is the finest of all; for this was first of all elevated in the creation with the throne of Divine Majesty. This nature is of all the most quiet and like unto a chariot, when it is drawn, it runs; when it is not drawn, it stands still. It is also in all things indiscernibly. In it are the reasons of life and understanding, which are distributed in the first infusion of man's life, and these are called the rational soul, by which alone man differs from other creatures and is like to God. This soul was of that most pure fire, infused by God into the vital spirit, by reason of which man, after the creation of all things, was created into a particular world or microcosm. In this subject, God, the Creator of all things, put his seal and majesty, as in the purest and quietest subject, which is governed by the will and infinite wisdom of God alone. Wherefore God abhors all impurity; nothing that is filthy or compounded, or blemished may come near Him, therefore, no mortal man may come near Him, therefore, no mortal man can see God, or come to Him *naturally*. For that Fire which is carried the seal and majesty of the Most High, is so intense, that no eye can penetrate it; for Fire will not suffer anything that is compounded to come near to it: but is the death and separation of everything that is compounded. We have said that it is the most quiet subject; so it is, or else it would follow that God could not rest; but it is of a most quiet silence in itself more than any man's mind can imagine. Thou hast an example of this in the flint, in which there is fire, and yet is not perceived, neither doth appear until it is *stirred up by motion,* and kindled in it that it may appear. So the Fire in which is placed the sacred majesty of our Creator, is not moved unless it be stirred up by the proper will of the Most High, and so is carried where His holy will is. There is made by the will of the Supreme Maker of things a most vehement and terrible motion. Thou hast an example of this, when any monarch of this world sits in state; what a quietness there is about him, what a silence, and although some one of his court doth move, the motion is only of some one or other particular man, in an order which is not regarded. But when the Lord himself moves, there is a universal stir and motion, then all that attend on him move with him. What then, when that Supreme Monarch, the King of kings, and Maker of all things (after whose example the princes of this world are established) doth move in his own majesty? What a stir! What a trembling, when the whole guard of this heavenly army move about him! But some one may ask, how do we know these things, since heavenly things are hid from man's understanding? To whom we answer, that they are manifest to philosophers into whom the incomprehensible Deity has inspired his own Wisdom[25].

For the total Reason is in this life of ours hidden, as the fire in fuel that is not kindled, or as gold in the dark ore unseen—our Iron, our Red Earth, our Loadstone, celeberrimus ille microcosmos et Adam, in which we are all now as dead; nor can be awakened to reminiscence without a resolution of the whole circulatory confine, when I arises identically reverse, perfect, and alone. This is the *Sal Sepientum et Mercurius Philosophorum; their Secretu, Secretorum et Pons Asinorum;—Scire etiam tibi convenit, O bone rex, quod hoc magisterium nihil aliud est, nisi Arcanum et secretum secretorum Dei altissimi et magni; Ipse enim hoc secretum prophetis commendavit: quorum scilicet animas suoparadiso collocavit*[26].

We learn, finally, that the souls of the Initiated, being made perfect in every telestic accomplishment and virtue, and having passed orderly through the whole progression of Intelligible Causes, by the Greeks called gods, were next promoted to a contemplation of their Highest Unity. For having vanquished every irrational and gravitating inclination, the soul, holding the circle of reason complete, as it were, and paramount over all, and possessing all, except her own identic essence, desires this now alone and above every other good, her final Cause and consummation in the Absolute so long deprived.

I open a secret to the *Initiated,* but let the *doors be shut.* And thou, O Musaeus, *offspring* of the *bright Silene,* attend carefully to my song; for I deliver the truth without disguise: suffer not therefore former prejudice to debar thee from that *happy life* which this *knowledge* will procure unto thee. But studiously contemplate the *divine oracle,* and persevere in *purity* if mind and heart. Go on in the right way, and contemplate the sole Governor of the World. He is *One* and of Himself *alone,* and to *that One* all things owe their Being. He operates through all, was never seen by mortal eyes, but does Himself see every one[27].

His contemplation, then, of the indwelling Unity was the final preparative to translation; but it has been supposed, from the concluding passage, that He was never seen by mortal eyes, and others of like import, that the Initiated, therefore, did not behold Him. But it should be remembered, that the initiated were nowhere considered as mortal men, in respect of their souls, which were regenerate, and so fortified by assimilation and proximity, that, whether in union or separation, their regard was not extraneous but hypostatical, as of like to like. No mortal can see God or come to Him naturally; for if that light which is in the circumference be so intense that nothing corporeal can sustain it, and previous unions, which were but partial and instantaneous, as it were, tried the ethereal vehicle to its utmost susceptibility, how much less, therefore, can the compound creature, approaching to the Fiery Centre, live? Neither is it said to be lawful for the pure to be touched by the impure, and the uninitiated are for this reason totally debarred, as it were, by a threefold barrier of sense, ignorance, and disinclination, from the discovery of truth. But neither let it be imagined, do the Initiated self-actively comprehend the life of Deity; for that would be indeed in inversion and a submerging of the Creator in the creature; but Plato beautifully unfolds the passive method of the Divine Intuition, and the three elevating causes of love, hope, and faith, to those who do not negligently read what he has written. For what else than love conjoins the soul to beauty? And where else is truth to be hoped asks the philosopher, except in this place? And what else than faith is the cause of this ineffable muesis? For muesis, in short, is neither through intelligence nor judgment, but through the uncial silence imparted by faith, which is then better than every Gnostic energy (when it surpasses this) and which establishes both whole and individual souls in the ineffable Unknown[28]. But, lest we prolong the transcendental theme; that which is most externally remarkable in the theurgic mandates for this translation is, that the whole body should be buried, except the hear; sublimely signifying that the total life, with exception of that which is intellectual, should be buried in profound oblivion; alone elevating, in Platonic phrase, the head of the charioteer to the place beyond the heaven, where he is filled with the Demiurgic Wisdom and an empyreal life.

And it is necessary, says Proclus, that the soul thus becoming an Intellectual World, and being as much as possible assimilated to the whole intelligible universe, should introduce herself to the Maker of the Universe, and, from this introduction, should, in a certain respect, become familiar with him, through a certain intellectual energy. For uninterrupted energy about anything calls forth and resuscitates our dormant Ideas, But through this familiarity, it is necessary that we should become united to Him. For discovery is this,—to meet with him, to be united to Him, and to see Him Himself— the Alone with the Alone; the soul hastily withdrawing herself from every other energy to Him; for then, being present with her father, she considers scientific discussions to be but words, banquets together with Him on the Truth of Real being, and in pure splendour is purely initiated in entire and stable vision. Such, therefore, is the Discovery of the Father; not that which is doxastic, or pertaining to opinion; for that is dubious and not very remote from the irrational life; neither is it scientific; for this is syllogistic and composite, and does not come into contact with the intellectual essence of the Intellectual Demiurgus. But it is that which subsists according to Intellectual Vision itself: a contact with the Intelligible, and a union with the Demiurgic Intellect. And this may properly be denominated difficult, as Plato alludes, either as how to obtain, presenting itself to souls, after every evolution of life, or as to the true labour of souls For after wandering about generation, after the purification and the light of science; intellectual energy alone, by the Intellect that is in us, shines forth; locating the soul in the Father, as in a port, purely establishing her in fabricative intellections, and conjoining Light with Light.—Not such as was with science, or that vision that was in Elysium, but more beautiful, more intellectual, and partaking more of the nature of the One than this. This, then, is the Paternal Port and the discovery of the Father, according to Proclus, viz., an undefiled union with him[29].

And with what magnificence of thought and diction does the Platonic Successor recall the Initiated Reason to the contemplation of her end, as ablating everything else in gradual approach. Calling together the whole voluntary accord, he exhorts us. Now, if ever, to remove from ourselves multiform knowledge, exterminate all the variety of life, and in perfect quiet approach near to the Cause of all. Let not only opinion and phantasy be at rest, not the passions alone, which impede our anagogic impulse to the First, be at peace; but let the air and the universe be still (within us), and let all things extend in us with a tranquil power, to commune with the Ineffable. Let us also, standing there, having transcended the Intelligible, and with nearly closed eyes, adoring, as it were, the rising sun, since it is not lawful for any being whatever intently to behold Him, let us survey that Sun whence the Intelligible gods proceed, emerging, as the Poets say, from the bosom of the ocean; and again from this divine tranquility descending into Intellect, and from Intellect, employing the reasonings of the soul, let us relate to ourselves what the natures are from which, in this progression, we shall consider the First God exempt. Let us, as it were, celebrate Him, not as establishing the earth and heavens, nor giving subsistence to souls and the generations of mortals; for these things He produces indeed, but amongst the last of things. Prior, rather, let us celebrate Him as unfolding in Light the whole Intelligible Universe and intellectual genus of gods, together with all the super-mundane and mundane divinities; as the God of all gods, the Unity of all unities, and beyond the First Adyta; as more ineffable than all silence, and more Unknown than all recondite essence, as Holy amongst the holies, and concealed amongst the Intelligible gods.

Such was the theology of the wise Ethnics, such their piety, and with such an energetic expansion of their whole unfettered will and understanding, did they seek to prove Reality in the Great Unknown — unknown, because concealed in this life—unconscious, even whilst yet in Elysium, the soul looked out through all her imaged light. But returning from thence into herself with all her beams concentrated, addressing the Great Archetype, He becomes known; yet not as in the individuated consciousness, things are said to be known apart; nor as before, either in separation of subject and object; but absolutely, in Identity; as passing from herself the soul no longer sees or distinguishes by intellection nor imagines that there are two things, but, consubstantial, becomes herself the ultimate object as she was before the subject in simultaneous accord. And thus the Divine Oracle ratified the platonic instruction to inquire.

> *There is something Intelligible which it behooves thee to understand with the Flower of thy mind.*
> *For if thou inclinest thy mind thou shalt understand this also,*
> *Yet understanding, thou shalt not comprehend this wholly:*
> *For it is a Power of circumlucid strength glittering with vehemence of intellection.*
> *But with the ample flame of the ample mind which measureth all things,*
> *Except this Intelligible:*
> *But it behooves thee to understand this also; not fixedly but having a pure turning eye,*
> *Extend the empty mind of thy soul towards the Intelligible,*
> *That thou mayest learn the Intelligible, for it exists beyond the mind.*

Such is the condition and metaphysical alienation which ancient experience sublimely proved, as passing to deification; which the natural reason echoes, but by a necessity of faith only, since it cannot pass into the superstantial proof. Theoretic contemplation, sensible attraction, continuity of active thought, all are alike inadequate; Without the Pontic Medium, without Theurgic assistance we are unable to transcend the consciousness of this life, and so are prevented from carrying metaphysics or of proving existence on the ontological ground. But this desiring faith of reason by which she has persisted and still persists, occasionally to inquire and infer, respecting causes which are both beyond and behind her natural grasp, has, we think, been aptly compared to the perception which the eye has of light and colours for as sight, observing believes, yet can affirm nothing absolutely about the reason, reflecting abstractedly, perceives a necessity of subsistence within itself, yet, unable to know, can affirm nothing with respect to it. For affirmation implies a doubled testimony in subject and object, or as a logician might say, affirmation implies a doubled testimony in subject and object, or as a logician might say, affirmation arises out of that which is composite from a subject and a predicate. If therefore Intellect should by any means be enabled to come into visive contact with its vision, as if begetting an experience, it would then assert; and the assertion, as respects itself, would be true; and the disbelief of other who had not proved the same, would be to it as if some one having slept away his life dreaming in this world, should on awakening to outward sense, persist in those dreams with which he had been so long conversant, denying the reality of the appearing world; and as his infatuation would be obvious, and his denial disregarded by mankind, so is the blindness of the sensible life described as obvious and lamentable by those who have passed into a more profound and convictive experience.

But not reason, nor enthusiasm, nor ardent desire, nor an intellectual conception, nor abstraction, as we are taught, conjoins theurgist with the One; but these are preparatory steps only to the self-oblivious amplitude of conception which precedes Him moving in the ultimate reccessure of life.

He comes, says Plotinus, suddenly alone, bringing with him his own empyreal universe and total deity, in one. And all things in that ultimate circulation are diaphanous, nothing dark or resisting, as of subject and object remaining in the mind; but everything is apparent to every faculty intrinsically throughout. For light everywhere meets light, as thought its understanding in the all, continental all, resident in each particular, perfect with all; and the splendour there is infinite, for everything there is great, even that which is small, for it has the great. The sun which is there is all the stars, and again each star is the sun, and all the stars, as ideas are in the mind everywhere, and the same mind in all; only in each a different quality is dominant, yet all are comprehensible in each, and transmutable one into another, as thoughts arise and are displaced without disorder or opposive persistence. Motion likewise there is perfectly harmonious, for the motion is not confounded, as in the world it is, by a mover different from itself; but the seat of each thing is that which the thing itself is; but the seat of each thing is that which the thing itself is, and concurs and proves itself to be what it is by its own self-evidence, proceeding constantly towards that whence it originated. Thus that which thinks and understands, and the thing understands, and the thing understood are one, co-eternal and co-equal, and their substance is intellect, and Intellect according to these philosophers is the subsistence of all.

But in the sensible world the circulation of things is altogether different; for though this has been proved also to be an outbirth from the same universal center, yet the equilibrium of being is broken everywhere at the circumference for manifestation; one thing does not subsist by another, but each part or individual remains alone in contrariety of conscience; nor does the devious wheel of life obey her axle any more, until returning into it, she perceives her error and the transgression that was made in self-will, for the sake of this experience, from the great Law of Light, from plenitude of Power, from immortal Harmony, and that high Exemplar which is before all things, and the Final Cause of all; which seeing only is seen, and understanding is understood by him, who having a sight like that of Lynceus, penetrating all centers, discovers himself in That finally which is the source of all; and passing from himself to That, transcending, attains the end of his progression.

Ille deum vitam accipiet, divisque videbit
Permixtos heroas, et ipse videbitur illis.

And this was the consummation of the Mysteries, the ground of the Hermetic philosophy, prolific in supernatural increase, transmutations and magical effects. And thus it is said to be lawful for the Vital Spirit to descend and ascend in successive circulations until she terminated her flight in the Principle of things. And this was the life of the gods and of divine happy men, who rising in voluntary abnegation above the evil and sensual habitude of this life and many sufferings to which body is allied, obtained together with a liberation from these, a foretaste simple, beatific, and secure, of the life which is eternal; when, by exciting the divine virtue within, they became simultaneously elevated, and proceeding through Intellect to Wisdom, they arrived at the First Principle; and again descending thence, increasing in divine virtue by each ascent, until the total life was irradiated from the ample recess of light.

Tunc ire ad mundum archetypum saepe atque redire
Cunctarumque patrem rerum spectare licebit
—Cujus tunc Co-operator effectus potest Omnia.

But there are many degrees of Divine illumination; nor were the rites of Eleusis found to be equally efficacious for all; since the souls are not of equal capacity or bias towards intellectual education: but as philosophers agree that preceding initiations are preparatory to those in a subsequent order, so the possession of the best habits of thought in this life, and natural inclination, render the Spirit better adapted to sublime. Plato, accordingly, cites the records of the Mysteries, to witness that there are many more thrysus bearers than Bacchic souls; which is to say, that many had the fire indeed, and were able even to perceive it, who were without the power to discover and draw it forth to manifestation. For, in the thrysus, Prometheus is fabled to have concealed the fire he stole from heaven; but Bacchus, persisting through the whole course of life allotted, returned,. As the orphic verse denotes him, triumphant, and appearing in splendour to mortals.

Bacchus, ipse totus igneus et fulgidus apparet, qui nudis oculis
tolerari non posset.

So Osiris appeared in shining garments, as Apollo, all over radiant; so Socrates his mighty genius once freed, in ecstasy shone forth, as it is related, to the beholders, more dazzling than the luciferous wheel of the meridian sun, diffusing itself from the freed center outwardly center outwardly until it moved the dark circumference

of sense itself[30].
So great Alcides, mortal mould resigned;
His better part enlarged and all refined;
August his visage shone; Almighty Jove
In his swift car his honored offspring drove.

So Orpheus, and divine Achilles shone refulgent in his armour; and Jason, on his return from Colchis, with the Golden Fleece.

But, say the expounders, all this splendid delirium and transfiguration in the Mysteries was the effect of narcotic liquors, which were administered to the Mystae before the shows commence, causing a confusion of their intellects, and the strange and miraculous appearance of the objects exhibited to them. But this is all a mistake; arising naturally enough out of the tendency of common sense, Procrustes like, to accommodate things to the limitation of its own sphere, which comprehends but a small part, however, of the things which are. The light exhibited in the Eleusinian msteries, *i.e.*, in the true initiations as is plainly to be gathered from the sense of the ancients, was the Light of Life which these could kindle and fortify, and the total drama was Divine. Let ignorance believe, and impiety reprobate, as long as they are able; those Theurgic associations were neither futil nor unholy; nor were the visions or gods attending on those Mysteries dead images, nor mere symbols, nor impotent, nor idle, nor invisible, though unseen. For are we not taught by the highest philosophic authorities to believe that by Theurgic rites, an ascent was made through appropriate media and a gradual assimilation, which without these could not be effected, to the knowledge of the First Cause; and that not theurgic only, but actual in co-efficiency of being and universal intellection?

And here, if any agree with us, he will readily appreciate that mandate of the Mysteries which forbids that divine things should be divulged to the uninitiated. For beyond the early danger to unpurified souls, there remains this objection, that such things cannot be understood by the multitude, nor rightly by any but by those only who were fortunately enabled to perceive them. But it is not possible, following their descriptions, the sublimely articulate relations of the Greek and Alexandrian Platonists, or those no less profound and earnest mystics of the middle ages, concerning the divine hypostasis and the last conjunction of the contemplative soul and its immortal experience, to maintain an indifferent spirit, or without being in a degree moved to a responsive sense of their reality. And he who, being endowed with a percipient mind and liberal, will take pains to examine those writings, or even those of the reputed enemies of their faith—the enlightened Fathers of the Christian Church—may be persuaded by very much evidence. Too much to intrude in this place, that the Eleusinian rites alluded to, and the objects attained, were of a nature widely differing from those which have been generally reported. And if, as must be indeed admitted, they became latterly disgraced in impure hands, yet this ought not by any means to detract from our esteem of the original institution, to which those latter orgies were diametrically opposed That the Mysteries were instituted pure there is no doubt, since it is universally allowed; early Christians concurring with the wisest Ethnics in declaring that they proposed the noblest ends, and by the worthiest means attained them; where not only everything within was conducted with decorum, but utmost care was taken to secure the same for those passing without the Fane, where misbehavior, even of the eye, was accounted criminal, and indiscretion was punished, and profanation by death. That all was a mere machination and priestly lure, or the visions of men of obscured intellects, is an assumption arising out of the double ignorance of modern times; all those immortal fables and glowing descriptions of poets, philosophers, saints and historians belie the folly, and reflect it on those who, from regarding objects of sense only, with a trifling imagination, have obscured the high reality and light of better days.

But is is then, as Epictetus says, that the idea of the Mysteries become truly venerable, when, believing the ancients, that all things therein were provided by them for the improvement and perfection of human life.

Thus far we have endeavored to sketch through the order of the Mysteries of their consummation; for the sake of affording a ground to the pursuit of our inquiry, to indicate the connection of the Sacred Art and Alchemy, and inasmuch as modern revelation would permit, the nature of that Art and proper Subject of this philosophy. In the progress of this Vital Experiment, it may not be difficult to imagine that powers would be disclosed and particular secrets of nature in the substance of her Whole. These intermediate fruits and fragments, having been exhibited at intervals to the world, without a discovery of their source, have given rise to much astonishment of common chemistry after the elixir and gold. Both of which are vital products, as we shall proceed to elucidate with the method and metaphysical origin of the Philosopher's Stone.

---

1. See Taylor's notes to his *Pausanius*, Vol. iii., p. 215, the extract.
2. Porphyry on the Cave of the Nymphus, sub init.
3. Falmmelli *Summula*, in fine, and Maria *Practica*.
4. *Famma et Confessio*, R.C. Preface by Vaughan.
5. See Porphyry's *Aid to Intelligibles;* Taylor, p.237.
6. In *Ramis*, Act i.
7. Proclus, on The Theology of Plato, Book. iv., Cap. vii. Tractatus Aureus, cap.iii.
8. It will be remembered that Lucius entered upon this initiation under the guise of an ass, into which he had been previously transformed, which guise the oracle also had announced should not depart from him until he eaten of some flowering roses.
9. Apuleius, *Metam.*, Book xi.; Taylor, p. 263,etc.
10. Apuleius, *Metam.*, Book xi.
11. Jamblichus on the Mysteries, Taylor, p. 100.

12. Vanity of the Sciences, in conclusion.
13. Aeneid, Lib. vi.: 724
14. Proclus on The Theology of Plato, Book iv., Chapter xxvi.
15. Empedocles, Physics.
16. Plotinus on the Beautiful and the Three Hypostases.
17. Phaedrus, Taylor, Vol viii., p. 327, and following
18. Jamblichus on the Mysteries, Chap. x.; Taylor, p. 106.
19. On the Theology, Book I., Chap. xx.
20. Idem., Chap. iii.
21. Blackwell's Mythology, lett. 8.
22. Jamblichus on the Myst., Chap xi.; Taylor, p. 109.
23. Oracula Chaldaica.
24. Aids to Intelligence, Sect. ii.
25. Sendivogius, New Light of Alchemy, Element of Fire, p. 99.
26. Morieni, de Trans, Metal; Ars Aurifera, vol ii., p. 27.
27. See the Orphic Fragment in Warburton, vol. i.
28. Proclus, on the Theology, Book iv., Chap. ix.
29. On the Timaeus of Plato, Vol. i.; Taylor, p. 254.
30. Agrippa Occult Phil., Book iii., where are given several notable examples in this kind; and Apuleius on the Demon of Socrates.

Part Three
Concerning The Laws and Vital Conditions of the Hermetic Experiment

Chapter 1. Of the Experimental Method and Fermentation of the Philosophic Subject, According to the Paracelsian Alchemists and Some Others

Whereby the Principles of the Art are yet more intimately unfolded, and the methodical order in which the experiment was conducted to discover that hidden Light which is the specific form of Gold — how to educate this and multiply it by the ethereal conception until it is made concrete and substantially brought forth.

> *Naturam in primisimitabere in arte, magister.*
> *Hanc massam exterio tentum calor excitat ignis;*
> *Aethereo interior sedperfecit omnia fot.*
>
> — *Tractatus Aureus*—Scholium,
> cap. i.

It is no less a tendency of the Greek philosophy to substantialize life, than to free the conscious being from corporal dependency; in considering mind apart from its material organs, they by no means make it appear therefore as an abstract conception, or inferential only, as with modern metaphysics is the case; but as an absolute substratal matter also of existence.

In just such a foundation do the Alchemists establish their Free masonry; claiming like extreme attributes and miraculous origin for their first matter, as do the Greeks, for that ethereal hypostasis we were before discussing. A few also profess, with the same admirable earnestness, to have observed in the experimental development of their whole internal being, the whole procedure of the occult nature into evidence, with her universal efficient by the Light of Wisdom thenceforth revealed. In ignorance of the means by which such a spectacle was obtained, they may continue unaccredited, for their assertion is at variance with the judgment of common sense, neither does it belong to the natural order of mental experience; nevertheless, since the whole of the Hermetic philosophy, and every tradition of occult science, depend immediately therefrom, for our understanding's sake, it will be requisite to consider this, their Initial Principle, more particularly, and how possibly it became known in its first arcane descent and emanation.

We have already endeavored to prepare a way in part, showing the imperfection of the natural Spirit in his world, the occultation of its Light, and the vital alteration that was deemed necessary and operated in the Mysteries upon those who were desirous of wisdom and immortality in the awakening conscience of a divine life within. Let us examine yet further into the Method of this Vital Experiment, that, before proceeding to infold the Art in actual practice, we may understand the Principles; and be enabled, from out the many clouds of sophistry in which it is enveloped, to distinguish that Light and virtue of true Chemistry, by which the ancients were assisted:—that deformed and limping Oedipus for example; so that he was able to vanquish the Metaphysical Monster, and enter I with her to the Temple of Truth.

And here, preliminarily, we may remark with how much propriety the Egyptians placed the Sphinx in the vestibule of Isis, who is the same with Minerva and that Wisdom we are investigating; for what the natural intelligent Spirit is in man, that Ether is in the universe; and this intelligence, phantasic as it is and drawn without, may be called the vestibule of Reason, which is, as it were, the temple of that Intellectual Ilumination which proceeds, when the conditions are duly offered, from the Divinity within. In our vestibule, therefore, the Phantastic Spirit, which is the natural vehicle of our life, is situated; and in a similar manner the commonly diffused Ether is as a vestibule or vehicle in respect of the universal soul of the world, which is occultly suspended in Nature, and may be called her temple; as an outward shadow, guarding the Light within if both world, so is that Ether then the Sphinx of the Universe.

And she is all things passively which the internal light is impassively. By her animal form, combined with the human face and summit, is indicated the twofold capability and diffusion of such a life; for she is the summit of the irrational mind relying on instinct, and the basis whereon o build the rational and transcend opinion in indivisible science. Her winds are images of the elevating power which the imagination possesses, by which likewise she is rendered capable of divine assimilation and of returning within and upward to a region of vivid intellection everywhere resplendent with light[1].

Such was the Door-keeper of the Egyptian Mysteries; agreeable also do we find the art of Alchemy directed upon the same enigmatical source.

> *A nature to search out which is invisible,*
> *Material of our Magistry a substance insensible.*

This Material, whilst yet immanifest, they worked, and worked with by itself alone; joining self to self, as the advice runs—*vita vitam concipit, natura naturam vincit ac superat, patefacit, gignit et renovat; item natura natura laetatur et emendetur*[2]; as men also now prove, mesmerizing one another but without the important knowledge how to alter and amend the Thing. This Mesmerism, in respect of our Mystery then, may be regarded as a first key which, opening into the vestibule, affords a view within the sense's prison, but of the labyrinth of life only. Facts vary at the circumference, and appear often so contradictory that reason is at a loss, even if otherwise admitted capable, for stable materials whereon to base judgment; and each succeeding theory yields to some unforeseen diversity of the Spirit's manifestation. If the ancients had known the inner life only as it is now known, if they had mistaken dreams for revelations, instinct for intellectual vision, and insensibility for the highest good, and so left Nature to dream on and take her rest without exerting a thought to probe or prosper her ability, then they would have been just such inconsiderable heathens as the world has taken them for; the Sphinx had never owned her mastery or yielded to theirs her wary wit; then they would have been, as we, servants, not masters; plodding interpreters of effects, without power or prescience. But it was all otherwise, as will one day be perceived; their philosophy as far exceeded ours in substance and objective certainty, as it does avowedly is scope, beauty and intellectual promise.

It may be considered that the discovery of Vital Magnetism is young, and has had no time to grow up into a science; that it is the business of a philosopher to observe and gather facts from without patiently and compare experiences; and we do not object but admit that it is a way; but whether it is the best way, or surest, to find the truth eventually we doubt: a long way we all know it to be —laborious and not very cheering, if we regard the point to which has hitherto attained in the most intelligent and experienced hands. Or how should they attempt to theorize about a revelation that is above their own? ; as well might we presume to estimate the worth of a treasure that is unseen, as to judge of spiritual causes from remote effects. Is not experience the basis of true knowledge, and rational experiment the proper road to attain it? How then can we hope for an understanding of spiritual causes without entering in upon the proper ground of their experience? Verily, says the adept, as long as men continue to lick the shell after their fashion, presuming to judge of hidden celestial things which are shut up in the closet of the matter, and all the while perusing the outside, they can do no otherwise than they have done; they cannot know things substantially, but only describe them by their outward effects and motions, which are subject and obvious to every common eye[3].

But be the modern method of experimenting as it may, right or wrong, according to opinion, the ancients did not choose it; but adopted a different one in their philosophy; which we, observing the imperfect fruits of the inductive sciences generally, and that facts accumulated about them for ages, having failed in every instance to yield the satisfaction which reason requires, are more particularly desirous to examine at the present time, if peradventure philosophy might hope with advantage to return with her instruments to work as formerly on the a priori ground. It has lain a long while uncultivated, and indigenous weeds and briars have sprung up over, so that it is difficult, on first view, to believe that it ever yielded foreign fruits; but patience, and the possibility granted, we will endeavor to clear a path, by the help of evidences that yet remain, many and curious, about the riches of Wisdom and those living waters that abound in Paradise, compassing about too that land of Havilah where good gold is[4]; the Tree of Life also, and Knowledge, and other precious things wonderfully adumbrated about the penetralia of True Being.—Surely there is a vein for the *silver*, says Job, and a place for *gold* where they *fine* it. *Iron* is taken out of the *earth*, and *brass* is molten out of the *stone*. As for the *earth*, out of it cometh *bread*: and *under* it is turned up as it were *fire*. And the *stones* of it are the place of *sapphires*: and it hath *dust of gold*. There is a path which no fowl knoweth, and which the *vulture's eye* hath not seen: the *lion's whelps* have not *trodden* it, nor the fierce *lion* passed by. He putteth forth his *hand* upon the rock; he overturneth the *mountains* by the roots. He cutteth out *rivers* among the *rocks*; and his eye seeth every precious thing. He bindeth the *flood* from overflowing; and the *thing that is hid* bringeth he forth to *light*. But where shall *wisdom* be found? And where is the place of *understanding*? Man knoweth not the *price* thereof; neither is it to be found in the *land of the living*. Whence then cometh Wisdom? And where is the place of understanding? Seeing it is hid from the *eyes* of all *living*, and kept close from the fowls of the air. God understandeth the way thereof. For he looketh to the *ends of the earth*, and seeth *under the whole heaven*; to make the *weight for the winds*; and he weigheth the *waters* by *measure*. When he made a decree for the *rain* and a way for the *lightning* and *thunder*: *then* did he *see* it, and *declare* it; he *prepared* it, and *searched* it out. And unto *man* he said, Behold, *the fear of the Lord, that* is *Wisdom*; and *to depart from evil is understanding*[5].

Let us then, investigate a means for the discovery of Wisdom, as the ancients declare to be right and profitable, and believe that he spoke well and summarily who said, that "the first step of philosophy is to set the mind a-going".

As we are informed that the conduct of the Mysteries was uniform and entirely scientific; so likewise philosophers insist that, in the Hermetic art, theory ought to precede practice; and that, before the Spirit can be expected to yield any rational or pure effects, she must be made to *conceive* them: the right way and object of investigation being well understood.—Dwell not altogether in the *practice*, says the adept, for that is not the way to *improve* it: be sure to add *reason* to thy experience, and to employ thy *mind* as well as thy *hands*[6]. So wrote Vaughan in 1650; and to the same effect, artists of every age: and, in the sequel of this inquiry, we may understand *Why*; and why we have no such miracles as those which are related of the saints and apostles in former times who *received* the gift of healing from their Lord. Is it not obvious to common sense, that he would heal others, or hope to impart any superior efficacy, should first of all heal or be healed himself? Take first the beam from out thine own eye, and then thou mayest see clearly to take out the mote that is in thy brother's eye: and again, is it not written,—Physician, heal thyself; Prepare thy work without, and make it fit for thyself in thy field; and afterwards build thy house[7]. If, ten, we go out at once to throw our common lives to common lives, what wonder we have only common results? That much depends on the quality of life imparted, general observation teaches; and with what sure corresponding consequences the moral heaven is attended may be understood, in a degree, by the recipient in the mesmeric trance. But the spontaneous fermentation which the Vital Spirit undergoes, and the change that is thereby effected in the Passive Subject, is not taken advantage of in modern practice, or pushed to the uttermost; much less is understood, that exact art of grafting and transplanting which the ancients practiced, and by means of which a growth and sublimation of the Spirit was effected, even to a third, fourth, and fifth degree of concentrated essentiality in as many representative vessels or forms.

The true medicine, according to the Paracelsians, is bound in man, shut up as it may be milk, within the hard and solid nut: and as fire which lies hidden in fuel, unless it be ignited, is good for nothing, so our fire of life (called Antimony by adepts) can effect nothing comparatively excellent whilst it is immured. When, however, by a due purgation, the pure life is separated, as metal from the dark and sordid ore, it will flow forth, as is declared, "a pure panacea from the god of Light".

> *Whose fragrant locks distill ambrosial dews,*
> *Drop gladness down and blooming health diffuse;*
> *Where'er the genial panacea falls,*
> *Health crowns the state, and safety guards the walls.*[8]

As all things are proved by fire, so also, are we told, the trial of the knowledge of physic is to be made by fire; physic and pyrotechny, says Crollius, cannot be separated; for the natural inbred chemist teaches to segregate every mystery into its own reservacle, and to *free the medicine* from those scurvy envelopes wherein naturally it is wrapped, by a due separation from the impurities and filthy mixtures of superficial external elements; that the *pure crystalline matter* may be administered to our bodies; and therefore a physician should be born of the light of grace and spirit of the invisible divinity[9]. Wherewith a man no longer asks, What is it? How can this be? Or whence come such salutary effects? For it feels itself move in conscious virtue from its own source being allied, as an efflux of that living light which can move mountains to its faith.

To find this Light, and to free it from captivity, was the practice of physicians on the middle periods, for curing bodily ills, and administering to the defects of age. But the Theurgic Art professed a power of purifying and informing the Mind much more beneficial and lasting than this pertaining to the mortal body, and far advanced beyond that object; approaching more nearly, as it would seem, to a fulfillment of the perfect doctrine of regeneration preached by Jesus Christ and his apostles, than any other known; for, by an effectual baptismal purification, they also prepared the way, and by a gradual subjugation of the passions and adaptation of the subordinate powers to reason, the whole hypostasis was converted finally through faith into the identity of substant light within.

And it appears that, in order to discover this Reason, men had in former times the faith to put the question to Nature rationally: not rudely indeed, or, as is with modern chemistry the fashion, to demolish her edifices and burn her out of life and home; and they knocked as was bid them, and the doors being opened from within, they enjoyed and took advantage of their entrance as lawful guests: and, when all was ready, and they were admitted to the inner chamber, we observe them still, not much engaged in noting phenomena, or looking about for facts to furnish private judgment; but more becoming inquisitive, addressing themselves to nature, and admitting there where they found her happily exalted above them, sphered in the magian circle of her own light: not stupidly gazing either, but speculative now they might approach nearer and become worthy of the knowledge and familiarity of that light. For they were not content with first phenomena, nor did Theurgists disturb the divine intellect about trifling concerns; but they consulted it about things which pertain to purification, liberation, as Jamblicus tells us, and the salvation of life. Neither did they studiously employ themselves in questions which are indeed difficulty, yet useless, to mankind; but on the contrary, they directed their attention to things which are beneficial to life, and such as tend towards the discovery of truth[10].

No man enters the magian's school, it seems, but he wanders awhile in the region of chimeras; and the inquiries which he makes before attaining to experimental knowledge are many, and often erroneous[11]. But investigation, once begum in a right rectifying spirit, enters; as adepts who having set the chain of vital causes in action, succeeded in tracing them to their last efficient link in Deity; whence surveying, they were enabled, under the divine will, to work such perfection in things below as are supernatural to this life, and greater than the natural intellect is able to conceive. For the Central Light and Wisdom was all their aim, and the way to it was all the revelation they valued or asked for, until the hidden Divinity was moved into experience and made manifest in effect and power.

But what say our Oedipus distillers of this Ether, the instructive Alchemists? Lay the *line* to thy thoughts and examine all *patiently*, and *infer* from *experience*, and thou art in the *way* to become *infallible*. Take hold of that Rule which God hath given thee for direction, by which thou mayest discern the right from the wrong. Seek not for that in *nature* which is an effect beyond her strength; you must help her, that she may exceed her common course, or all is to no purpose; for the *Mercury of the Wise* comes not but by help of ingenuity and industry[12]. But he that devoteth himself to philosophy, says Crollius, and shall sincerely and as he ought come to the inner rooms of nature by a holy assiduity of preparations, joining thereto diligent *contemplation* of natural causes, and withal shall refuse no pains or difficulties to get *experience* by the industry of his handy work, he shall, if the grace of the most high be infused into him, bring forth far greater things out of this open bosom of nature than they seem to promise at first sight[13]. To the same effect Van Helmont writes, that the attainment of the Tree of Life is laborious, and the fruit of intellectual research[14]. Excellent, also, is this advice of Basil Valentine, and instructive to the point: Learn and look for the first foundation, says the monk, which nature holds concealed; search for it even with thine own eyes and hand, in order that thou mayest be able to philosophize with judgment and build upon the impregnable rock; but without this discovery, thou wilt continue a vain and phantastic trifler, whose discoursings, without *experience*, are built upon sand. Let not any one imagine either that we can be satisfied with mere words, who rather exact documents proved by experience, in which we are bounden to have faith[15].

Such are a few of the preliminary lessons of adepts, in which they all agree that the way to Wisdom is by patience and rational inquiry. Some scattered specimens of the kind we have remarked in the writings of Lully, and Michael Mayer and others, to which in the Practice we shall have occasion to allude. That they did not investigate trifling matters is indeed obvious, but diligently, from the first, concerning the intimate causes of things; and how they might themselves enter into the fundamental experience, their anxiety is manifest and the truly philosophic inclination of their mind.

But the contemplation which absolves the *Second* part of our admonition is *celestial*, continues the monk Basil, and to be understood with *spiri-*

tual reason; for the circumstances of everything cannot be perceived any other way than by the *spiritual cogitation* of man, considering how nature may be helped and perfected by *resolution* of itself, and *how* the *destruction and compaction* are to be handled, whereby under a just title, without sophistical deceits, the pure may be separated from the impur[16]. For it is no graft from this life that enters into the divine foundation, nor any arbitrary instinct; natural reason, even the most acute, is dull here comparatively, and inoperative, and stands in the Philosophic Work, albeit necessary, as a mere circumstantial aid on the threshold of the divine inquiry, as it were an iron key, intended to unlock the golden treasury of light within. And no sooner, we are informed, has it done this, and, further extricating itself, helped to introduce the *spiritual intellect* into *self-knowledge*, than this latter, returning with power upon the life without, proceeds to analyze and revolutionize, proving all, as may be said, chemically by the fiery essence of its newly conceived Law. It is this vital perscrutinator, *the internal fire of the sulfur of thy water*, as Eireneus calls it, that, investigating scientifically, operates the whole change. And it is happily provided against intruders, lest the casket should be rifled of its rich offering, that they only who have obtained this passport can attain to the Magistery of life; since they only, literally speaking, can enter in through the narrow gate, as in the Mysteries we have already described. And the discovery is difficult, and reputed tedious by many who have spared no labor either of body or mind in the research—*reclusa resedit longius*, as the poet says; it is far off, gotten in the penetralia, as it were, the flower of human intellect, triply imprisoned in the dark body's hold. This it is the business of the philosopher to open and set free; and this is the security, that he must be a lover of Wisdom who can set her free.

Our *fire* is the *true sulfur of Gold*, says Eireneus, which in the hard and dry body is imprisoned but by the mediation of our water it is set loose, by rotting the moles of the body (*i.e.*, of the ethereal body) under which it is detained; and after separation of the elements (of the same body) it appears *visibly* in our *Third Menstrual*. But the means to discover this is not a light work, it requires a *profound meditation*: for this is the *seed of gold*, involved in many links, and held prisoner, as it were, in a deep dungeon; he that knows not our *two first menstruals* is altogether shut out from attaining to the *sight* of this Third and last: yet he who knows how to *prepare the first water*, and to join it to the *body* in a just pondus, *to shut it up in its vessel philosophically*, until the *infant* be formed, and, what is greater than all, to govern his *fire dexterously*, so as to cherish *internal* heat with *external*, and can wait with patience till he sees *signs*: he shall perceive the *first water* will work on the *body* till it hath opened the pores and extracted partly the tincture of *Sol*. Take counsel; be not so careful of the fire of the *Athanor* as of your *internal* Fire. Seek it in the *house of Aries*, and draw it from *the depths of Saturn*; let *Mercury* be the *interval*, and your signal the *Doves of Diana*[17].

On some such errand, we may remember, the Sybil sends Aeneas, that, from out many entanglements and obscurity, he may discover and bring to her the Golden Bough, well directing him how to look from beneath upwards, and take it in hand.

> Alte vestiga oculis: et rite repertum,
> Carpe manu; namque Ipse volens facilisaque sequetur,
> Si te fate vocant; aliter, non viribus ullis
> Vincere, nec duropoteris convellere ferro[18].

So Orpheus, in his *Argonautics*, leading to the Cave of Mercury, exhorts mankind how they ought to act and study there.

> At quaecunque virum ducit prudnetia cordis
> Mercurii ingedier speluncam plurima ubi ille
> Deponit bona, stat quorum praegrandis acervus
> Ambabus valet hic minibus sibi sumere, et ista
> Ferre domum, valet hic vistare incommoda cuncta.

He, therefore, who wishes to partake of many goods, let him approach to the Cave of Mercury, which, according to the Hermetic interpretation, is Taenerus, the most hidden vapor of life: let him enter with a prudent motive, well understanding and allied to what he seeks; and that which he shall bear away from thence, Centaur-like, in both his Hands, will be the *mineral radix* and *true mater* of the Hermetic Art. But if he have not a right mind, and unless the predestined conditions and the order of operation be observed, all will be in vain; for the power will remain hidden, despite of every effort, in a pusillanimous uncongenial soul. *Nescit Sol comitis non memor esse sui; Ignire ignis amat, non aurificare sed, aurum.* Fire loves fire, say they, not to make gold, but to assimilate it. Take, therefore, that body which is gold (not a brazen ferment), and throw it into Mercury—such a Mercury as is bottomless, or whose center it can never find, but by discovering its own[19].

This is the art of Oedipus which, well conducted with the Sphinx ends in her subjugation; in other words, the Ethereal Spirit abandons her phantasy, and yields the clear light of understanding to him who, having been duly educated and singled out, knows how and wherewith to investigate her peculiar essence. Thus, Synesius says—Intellect above all things separates whatever is contrary to the true purity of phantastic Spirit; for it attenuates this spirit in an occult and ineffable manner, and extends it to Divinity[20]. But the natural Intellect cannot do this, neither comprehending properly, or being conceived of the Spirit; neither is its essence so acutely penetrative as to operate the change required. Salt is good, but if the Salt have lost its savor wherewith shall it be seasoned?

And here the common difficulty ensues, as language becomes less and less adequate to convey to the natural understanding the truth alleged. To conceive at once the free perspicacity which experience and long study bestowed on those men, their assertion of the magic action of mind in her own spheres, the efficient force of an individual freed will upon the vehicle of its motive cause, separating, refining, and transmuting it from an impure, dull consistency to the clear light of universal intelligence, is arduous to the unaccustomed mind; and in this age, which is without a witness, without experimental knowledge, we should say, of true causality, most especially adverse; yet it will be necessary, having so far ventured, to discuss the point; and, as well as we may be enabled, to substantialize without deforming this Intellectual Science.

It may be remembered, in a former citation from his book to the Athenians, Paracelsus saying, that SEPARATION *is the greatest miracle in philosophy, and that magic the most singular by which it is effected; very excellent for quickness of penetration and swiftness of operation, the like whereof Nature knows not.* Now this Separation, of which he speaks, and of which all the Hermetic Masters speak appears to be identical with that which is described as taking place in the Mysteries, when the great ordeals are passed through during the decomposition and death of the natural life. The analogy bears throughout from the beginning in suffering, succedent dread, dissolution, and corruption, to the final resurrection of the pure Ether into Light. This Separation is indeed the primary object of the Art which, continues our doctor, if it were divinely done by God alone, it would be to no purpose to study after it; but there is a free power in the creature to its mutual affection and destruction; and again —The free will flourisheth and is conversant in virtue, and is either friend or foe in our works; but that is the sequestatrix, which gives to every thing its form and essence[21]; which is the part especial of Intellect, that same perscrutinating Intellect which Hermes speaks of[22], and where in the *Smagardine Tablet* it is written—*Separabis*, THOU shalt separate the earth from the fire, the subtle from the gross, gently, with much sagacity; it will ascend from earth to heaven, and again descend from heaven to earth, and will receive the strength of the Inferiors and of the Superiors: this is the strong fortitude of all fortitudes, overcoming every strong and penetrating every solid thing: therefore let all obscurity flee before thee; so the world was created, and hence are all wonderful adaptations of which this is the manner[23]. So passing wonderful is it related by the same reputed author, in the *Asclepius*, that man should be able not only to find the Causal Nature but to effect it[24].

Nor ought we, therefore, taking into consideration the human agency, to understand this decomponency of life in a mechanical sense, or in any ordinary way of dissolution, but according to the literal wording of the Table, we observe Mind to be the true Separator, the efficient as well as the regimen of the work, into which, as before shown, no foreign admixture is allowed to enter. And thus we are given to understand that the knowledge of the elements of the ancient philosophers was not corporally or imprudently sought after, but is through patience and Wisdom to be discovered according to their causes and their occult operation; for their operation truly is occult, since nothing is discovered except the matte be decomposed, and because it is not perfected unless the whole introversion is passed through.—Auditor, understand, reiterates the great Master; let us use our Reason—consider all with the most accurate investigation, the whole matter andknow to be One only Thing[25].

And as folly, and phantasy, and passion are modes of being of the One Thing, and Reason is another; and as the phantasy, if suffered to prevail, will convert all to her own folly in the internal life; so may we judge contrariwise, that this Reason gaining the ascendancy, would gather all up, as a ferment, into the superior essence and traction of her own Light. This Lully intimates; and Arnold, and Bacon, and Geber, with the rest, abundantly celebrating the virtues of their Head Stone[26].

But if anyone should be further disposed to question their doctrine or demur about the physical efficacy of this Reason, let him for a plea only regard the image of it in this life. What else is it but reason, that enables us to analyze and judge opinion, to govern our passions, and separate facts from falsehood in the understanding? And with the logical faculty, is there not a universal evidence which subsists by faith, an independent standard by which all things are measured and proven in life? Considering this standard of our common faith, abstractedly a prior necessity of being also, will be understood, an infinite sufficiency, magnitude and eternity of duration; and thus obtaining a glance only of the antecedent, we find less difficulty in imagining the superior virtue of that which is the Reason of our Rule; well remembering that it is of this the ancients speak, calling it Wisdom, Intellect, Gold, Sol, Sulfur, *Tincture, Intellectus naturam habens subtilem ad intelligendum res intelligibles, participans, cum entibus intensis et cum entibus extensis, viz., cum intenso calore corporis, cum quo conjunctus est et cum intense bonitate sustentata in suis intensis concretis*[27]. For it is Light indeed, and an occult splendor of existence transcendentally pure; and as the luminary of the sensible world purifies and subtilizes the gross parts of matter, and by a natural chemistry sublimes and converts the varied elements of earth, so are we taught to conceive of the Intellectual sun; for these things which the natural reason as an image enacts theoretically, this supernatural reason is said to do as an archetype essentially; separating and rejecting the false forms and elementary qualities which supervene through generation, assimilating the whole inferior life by continual trituration of its foreign tincture, perfection to such faculties as are indigent by pure infusion of Itself to the passified Spirit throughout, even as light through the open atmosphere is everywhere seen diffusing itself invigorating and manifesting all. The following remarkable extract from the last works of Anaxagoras, one of the earliest of the Greek hermetic School, further exemplifying the nature of such an Intellect, confirms what has been said above of its efficient operation. The passage, as preserved by Simplicius, is given in a note to Aristotle's *Metaphysics*, by Taylor, page 7, and runs thus:

—Intellect is infinite and possesses absolute power, and is not mingled with any thing; but is alone by itself. For if it were not by itself, but were mingled with something else, it would participate of all things, for in every thing there is a portion of every thing; and things mingled together would prevent it from having a similar dominion over things, as when alone by itself. For it is the most attenuated and pure of all things. It likewise possesses an universal knowledge of every thing, and is in the highest sense powerful. Whatever soul possesses greater or lesser, over all these Intellect has dominion. Every thing, too, that comprehends or contains is subject to its power; so that it even comprehends the Principle itself. And first of all indeed, it began from that which is small to exercise its comprehending power, but afterwards it comprehended more and more abundantly; Intellect also knew all that was mingled together, and separated and divided, together with what they would in future be, what they had been, and what they now are. All these Intellect adorned in an orderly manner, together with this circular enclosure which is now comprehending by the stars, the sun, and the moon, the air and the ether, which are separating from each other. But this comprehending Intellect made things to be *separated*; and separated the dense from the rare, the hot from the cold, the lucid from the dark, and the dry from the moist. There are many parts indeed of many things; but in short no one thing is singular by itself except Intellect. Every Intellect too is similar, both the greater and the lesser; but no other thing is similar to another[28].

That is to say, no other faculty is universal, or of itself alone consciously distinguishable, but this root of reason which is truly catholic; and so by the microcosmic experiment into It, the knowledge if the macrocosmic Cause also was derived. For in the hermetic process they are seen to cooperate; and all that Anaxagoras here speaks of as relatively past, has been described as present by philosophers on the internal ground. Else, how should men have asserted such things about Intellect and the rational faculty as by no means belong to the natural revelation of it, if they had not known another and proved the work divine? No one could assert them now. Few believe, indeed, that mind is anything really but an elaboration of the brain, a resulting phenomenon of organization. Sensible evidence favors such an opinion, for life is nowhere seen apart by itself, but follows constantly as a result of material generation in order of effect of cause; and human reason, as a ray of light, reflected apart from its originating focus, is halting and impotent in respect of nature, and unconscious of its First Source.

There is a piece of Egyptian mythology, related by Eudoxus in Plutarch, concerning Jupiter, that his feet had grown together and that he was forced to live in solitude, and ashamed of himself as it were; until at length Isis, pitying his forlorn condition, succeeded in cutting them asunder, and so restored him to himself and society. And this, continues the scholar, is designed to represent to us that the mind and reason of the Supreme God, which in nature is invisible and dwelling in obscurity, by being put in *motion* becomes known, and proceeds to the production of other beings[29]. And this, too, is an allegory of the Art, in which the purified spirit or intelligence, that is Isis, by dissolving the vital medium, opens the occult source, and draws the Voluntary Efficient upward into intellectual reminescence. And this is the one thing needful which ought to be consummated, that man may know himself; whence, what for, and whereto, he is allied.—All is one soul, says the Magian, but reason, unless it be illuminated, is not free from error, and Light is not given to reason except God impart it; for the first Light is in God, far exceeding all understanding[30]. And Aristotle says, *That* Intellect must be assumed which is most perfectly purified; the knowledge of which must be sought for in spirit or spirits, by him who aspires to obtain it. For this indeed is pure, and possesses an ineffable beauty, because it is nothing but Intellect. For the beauty of Spirit is the highest beauty when it energizes intellectually, without error, and purely; and it knows things as they are unfolded by the Divine will[31]. The Alexandrian Plotinus also speaking of such Intellect, describes the material of it as beautiful, and as far surpassing ordinary intelligence, as paradigms are wont to do the images which represent them; and the sol receives with it, he says, a sudden Light, and this Light is from Intellect, and is also It[32].

It would be mere perplexity, and evince a want of rational perception, to regard this Reason therefore as inessential; or as arbitrary, either in operation or event; since, in our mere individual consciousness it is the foundation of all law—the only unerring necessity of faith in this life; the luminous revelation of which in a purified human intelligence, is that perfect beginning of Wisdom, which is half of the perfect whole.

Dimidium facti qui bene coepit habet, says the philosopher; for a small grain of the metaphysical ferment leavens the whole lump. And as the grain of wheat is putrefied in the earth, and afterwards by the nourishment of water becomes growing wheat, terminating and multiplying in the fermental form inbred, so the metaphysical graft, already purified and passed the fire, re-enters to redeem its congenital life, and finally by assimilation transmutes all into the substance of its own Aurific Light.

During the process of working this leaven, many phenomena arise, and those wonders which, having been variously observed, are described and poetized; for this acute discriminative sulfuric Spirit occasions a putrefaction of the philosopher's Mercury, *i.e.*, of the impure vapor of life, into which it enters, so that all the elements are in commotion, raging, swelling, and rolling like a tempestuous sea; darkness, made visible by the appearing light, shrinks more and more condensing; and falsehood, as it were, trembling for her kingdom, puts on every sinister guise, to combat and eclipse the living truth, as, increasing in power and armed with bright effulgence, it arises, threatening to dissipate the total fabric, and dissolve its very foundation.

So did the armor of Achilles, while yet far off he only showed himself, dismay the assembled hosts of Troy; that shield so ominous in its device, breastplate, and helmet's crest of gold, forged by Vulcan, at Thetis's prayer for her hero in Olympus; wherewith he single-handed overcame them all—gods, men, and rivers—triumphant in the divine fury which roused him to the fight[33]. And here the poetic allegory likewise is apparent; Achilles does not appear at all in arms, nor has he these, until after Patroclus, his bosom friend, is slain; just as Misenas' funeral rites must be celebrated before Aeneas is allowed to journey to the infernal shades[34]. Peculiar too the rites are, which the Sybil enjoins, and the sacrifices to be made to those remains, as at the pile of Patroclus, set on the seashore. Let it not be believed that Virgil on this or on any other occasion was so servile an imitator, or that either poet is relating events of human history, or magnifying the heroes of a common fight; but Virgil and Homer agree in this, that they adopted the same theme, had witnessed the same heroic conflict, the same summary action of Divine vengeance and mysterious metamorphosis of life; their warriors, therefore, are demigods divinely tutored and sustained—free from the dilemma of earthly difficulties, and in their strength and use of it sublime. If tradition was useful to supply their imagery, the incidents are nevertheless woven into a mystical accord, and natural probability and the relations of time are unscrupulously sacrificed to the report of Truth. And they who have partaken of the same mystic knowledge from the Greeks—Plato, Proclus, Porphyry, to Faber, Tollius, and Michael Mayer, the golden chain of Hermetic philosophers—unanimously tracing even through minutest incidents their allusion—have claimed those poets for their own. Skillfully, doubt not, they have delineated the most poetical of Arts; and the admiring world has listened, but without understanding; and may long continue to do so:—Yet we will proceed: —

For the friends of those heroes must die indeed, as they are said to do—those bosom friends—and he lamented; for the celestial medial life which, in the order of divine rites, precedes the heroic work, is by necessity cut off, even in its prime; when perfected at all points, is shut up and buried; all but the hallowed memory burning to retrieve. Thus the excellent poet Manzoli, whose assumed name of Palingenius denotes one regenerated, divulges the artificial method in the few following lines, which have been rendered thus:

Take this Arcadian slippery lad that's apt to fly.

> *And in the glittering Stygian lake, drowned let him die,*
> *Then set on Hyales's lap, let Lemnos'*
> *God Take him to feed, and crucify the lad.*
> *Then in a warm womb placed, his taint dissolve,*
> *Whose dropping limbs a spirit shall devolve,*
> *To him and penetrate; and strangely so,*
> *Dead by degrees, shall bring to life anew*
> *All clad in robes of gold and silver hue.*
> *Cast him again on hot coals, Proteus like*
> *He'll be renewed, and all he touches make*
> *Most perfect; nature's laws and promises excel,*
> *Species he'll change and poverty repel.*

Nothing is done radically to meliorate the Vital Spirit previous to this dissolution of the first medial life; so Hyanthe died, so Hylas at the fountain, Adonis, Misenas, Elpênor, Patroclus, too, before the heroic virtue was brought into act. It needs a motive and excitation; and this is given by artifice of the Divine Law depriving it when in full vigor of its Understanding Light. So Eurydice was lost to Orpheus and Proserpine by Pluto's stratagem, whom the goddess Ceres too bewails; for the identical dilemma is common to these all, who personate the wanderings and anguish of Intellect so artificially isolated on the plain of Truth.

> *'Tis not in fate th' alternate then to give,*
> *Patroclus dead, Achilles hates to live.*
> *Let me revenge it on proud Hector's heart,*
> *Lest his last spirit smoke upon my dart;*
> *On these conditions will I breathe, till then*
> *I blush to walk among the race of men*[35].

Nor all in vain was that vindicative will conceived or those heroic tears, though Pope has rendered them unavailing. Not so the master. Nor is anything, we believe, in that so lengthened Iliad of woes unpurposed, or with all its inconsistencies, untrue: but in those particulars above all suggestive, which are to common sense least bent; such weeping warriors, so much brave reserve, such radiant armor, such a magic strength of hand, and eye, and voice, to kill and terrify whole armies and convulse the elements, belongs but to one race, one cause, one conflict; Divinity mingles but in one, the war of life. And for this cause the Heroic Will enters in, self-sacrificing, and stirs the bitter waters, to redeem and reinstate the kingdom lost. But Achilles, too, must die and suffer, as was predestinated, before the fatal gates, as Aeneas leaves the dedicated bough in Tartarus. For how otherwise should that which is sown be quickened unless it die? Does not the grain putrefy in the moist earth before it springs? So each succeeding life must die, as transplanted in the next, it dissolves, corrupts, and rises into a better form. For when thou sowest, as the great Apostle says, thou sowest not that body that shall be[36]; but it is the Law especial of spiritual generation that the parent is bettered in the offspring, even to the fourth generation, or fifth, if this happily should be attained.—There is an earthly body and there is a spiritual body—the terrestrial is bettered in the celestial, and the celestial, descending and overcoming, is conceived into the divine. *No man ascends up into heaven but he who came down from heaven, even the son of man which is in heaven.* This is the true Light which lighteth man that cometh into the world, which is in the Savior was perfected; one ray of which is able to cleanse this leprous life of ours, and convert it to the purest spiritual extreme.

> Cujus de lumine lumen
> Omne micat; sine quo tenebrescunt lucida, de quo
> Lucescunt tenebrae atque inamimae noctis imago.

Speaking of the Intellectual Essence, Plotinus writes to the effect that we should not at first hope to obtain the universal subject, but through the medium of an image, and be satisfied—such is his expression—with a certain portion of gold, as a representative of universal gold[37], and therefore Anaxagoras says, it begins from that which is small to exercise its comprehending power. Ramus, non arbor—The bough, not the whole tree, is to be taken. For, in however small a proportion, if the reason be but pure, it will penetrate according to its purity, and gather growth; but if it be not pure, in other words, if the motive be not universal, it must be returned, to work, and resolve, and meditate, and prove, until it finds experience at length in the supreme Unity of its Law. To find the true Separator is described, in fact, as the greatest difficulty[38]; as we may remember also in Virgil, the tree is hid.

> Hunc tegit omnis
> Lucus et obscures claudunt convallibus umbrae

The tree of life covered over, indeed, with the dark oblivion of this natural outbirth, is latent and difficult to find, even for him who has already passed the turbulent waters of the senses' medium and sees within. For it lies not in art merely, or in natural cunning, but with the celestial instinct only to reveal; that subtle Maternal; intelligence which originally conceived it, and can alone lead into the yet more central, antecedent Paternal, light of life.

> Materna agnoscit aves laetusque precatur
> Este duces, O si qua via est, cursumque per auras
> Dirigite in lucos, ubi pinquem dives opacat
> Ramus humum[39].

Thus has the premeditation of the Divine Art been poetized; and the discovery of that heroic, separable, triply refined intellectual purpose, which has been so often and under so many names personified—Hercules, Jason, Lyncaeus, Perseus, Cadmus, Oedipus, Dionysius, Achilles, Bacchus, Amphiaraus, our Son, as Hermes calls him, born a king who, taking his tincture from the fire, passes through darkness, and death and Stygian waters. This is that prolific Mustard-seed, and Light of divine Faith, which being the proper substance of the thing hoped for, penetrates into the yet unseen reality of life; it is this, which, visiting the interior rectifying, discovers the occult Stone—the hidden Medicine. Such was the Caduceus of Hermes—the Golden Bough, the ferrying Cup of Hercules, and all the golden passports admitting to those realms, so dangerous to folly, and delightful; to Wisdom recovering her lost Efficient in the Light of life.

This vertical separated Light then we take henceforth to be the true alternative principle in the Divine Art,—The Alchemists are excessively wary in speaking of it, as they are indeed concerning the human circumstances of the mystery throughout. For as we may be by this time perceive, it is no common light that enters into Divinity, but a congenial ray; a Power which glancing forth from the capable will of such, as are divinized only, is essentially Divine. The persevering Trevisan worked for upwards of half a century in vain, until he found this; and Pontanus in his *Epistle* confesses how he erred two hundred times, experimenting even after he had attained a general knowledge of the *matter* and method of its use, never correctly diving the Identity of the singular Identity of the singular thing itself. Seek therefore, he says, writing to his friend, seek to know this Fire with all thy soul, that so thou mayest attain to thy desire; for it is the key of all the philosophers which they have never openly revealed. But profound meditation alone can give it to thee so thou mayest discern, and not otherwise[40]. Other examples we have in Zachary, and in Flammel; who, after he was conversant in the *matter*, and had both fire and furnace indicated to him by Abraham the Jew, wandered in the wilderness of uncertainty for three several years. Madathan, another celebrated adept, practiced for five years together unsuccessfully, until at last, he says, after the sixth year, I was entrusted with the Key of Power, by a secret revelation from Almighty God[41]. Contemplate therefore and observe, says basil Valentine, these things diligently, for in the preparation of *Antimony* consists the Key of Alchemy, and this principal key is of great concern. Be it known, moreover, that our stone of Fire (which is Antimony) ought to be boiled and matured with the corporeal fire of the microcosm, for at the farewell, or ne plus ultra, of the operative fire of the macrocosm, the fire of the microcosm doth begin the production of a new species of generation; and, therefore, let no man wonder at this coction[42]. And believe not only Basil, says Kirchingius, but me; with the same faith and sincerity, affirming to you that this key is the principal part of the whole Art; this opens the first gate, this will also unlock the last, which leads into the palace of the king. Believe not only, but consider and observe. Here you stand in the entrance; if you miss the door, all your course will be in error; all your haste ruin; and all your wisdom foolishness. He who obtains this key and knows the method, which is called Manual Operation, by which to use it, and hath strength to turn the same, will acquire riches, and an open passage into the mysteries of chemistry.

Sophistry, it will be observed therefore is no leader in this Art, or avarice, or ignorance,; but he who presumes without the revelation of the Divine Light to introduce his own blind purpose, instead of conditionating and inquiring patiently, will be in danger of falling into infinite snares. The Law of Nature, being simple and harmoniously framed, will baffle him and rise up in judgment against his generation, and condemn him to wander in the labyrinth alone. Hence, all the care that is taken to train the true Inquisitor, that he may obtain the passport clear, as we have shown it; that he know what, and where, and how he ought to obey, and inquire, and will, and hope.

And it therefore declared to all lovers of Art, says Jacob Böhme, whose Separator is an artist of great subtlety in them, that they first seek God's love and grace, and resign up themselves to become wholly one with that:

else all their seeking is but a delusion, or a courting of a shadow, and nothing is found in any *fundamental worth, unless one doth entrust another with somewhat*. The which is forbidden to the children of God in whom the grace is revealed, that they cast not pearls before swine, upon the pain of eternal punishment; only it is freely granted to them to declare the light, and to show the way of attaining the pearl; but to give the divine Separator into the bestial hand is prohibited, unless a man knoweth the way and will of him tat desires it[43].

We do not see either that it is exactly possible to give into such possession that which is divine; except, indeed, the Theosophist alludes to a *mediate* occupation. And this brings us to consider more particularly the representative understanding, measure, and guardian of the Light; for, as we may remark in the fables, the heroic adventurer with all his divine equipment, though he loses his first companion, never goes through the labors alone; but is aided by stratagem and wise counsel in the way. Without Ariadne's conduct, Theseus could not have tamed the Minotaur; or Jason, but for the ready counsel and assistance of Medea, have obtained the fleece; Eurystheus set Hercules to the performance of each separate labor; his mother aids Achilles; Elpênor, Ulysses; and the Sybil accompanies Aeneas through the infernal shades. In Alchemy too, the Moon is singularly honored, for it is the Passive Intelligence which, freed by art and set in conjunction, responds to the Will of her seeking Reason; discovers the way of progress, unraveling the context of each involuted thought, and setting aside obstacles with utmost discretion, passes with him through the abyss, as it were the very kingdom of confusion, triumphant over all and unconfounded. It is from within that the knowledge springs together with the true efficient, springs (which are indeed one in principle, but in their practical operation and for the sake of offspring are distinguished and separately represented in the Art), revealing at the same time their origin, essence, and destination. The mode of analysis however is directed, and the means for the most part provided by the Passive Understanding gotten in transcendental contemplation of herself.

ISTUD EST VAS HERMETIS, QUOD STOICI OCCULTAVERUNT, ET NON EST VAS NIGROMANITICUM SED EST MESNURA IGNIS TUI[44].

Both therefore have to be prepared—the spiritual agent and the spiritual patient—according to those words of the Smagardine Table; That which is above is as that which is below, and that which is below is as that which is above, for performing the miracles of the One Thing whence all the rest proceed by adaptation. It is not lawful therefore, in this work, to conjoin unlike natures; but, in order to bettering in the offspring equal Spirits are allied; as Hermes says, both need the help one of another, for the precepts demand a medium[45]; that as the crude natural life was in the first place bettered in the natural, so the supernatural may be so much further advanced within themselves, even to the order of bodies permanent, being changed from a corporeal to a spiritual extreme:

> Ouvrier, sur tout aye cure
> Que 'art imite la nature
> L'externe feu de charbon
> Rend la matière alterée,
> Mais l'interne et l'artherée
> Faira ton ouvrage bon[46].

The fire of the natural life stirs up and, being manumitted, alters; but the internal alone is able, being purified, to perfect the work begun; according to that other saying of the sage—*Si pariat ventum valet auri pondera centum*—if wind be made of gold it is worth a hundredfold. Let us be careful therefore to distinguish, in our conception, the pure from the impure, the rectified spirit of universal reason and its intelligence from the gross ether and perplexed understanding from the gross ether and perplexed understanding of this mundane sphere. For there cannot come of any thing that virtue which it has not; though that which it has indeed may be improved and magnified. And therefore it behooves us to mortify two Argent vives together, says Hermes; both to venerate and to be venerated, viz., the Argent vive of Auripigment and the Oriental Argent vive of magnesia[47].

SOL MEUS ET RADII SUNT IN ME INTIME, LUNA VERO PROPRIA MEUM LUMEN EST, OMNE LUMEN SUPERANS; ET BONA MEA OMNIBUS BONIS MELIORA SUNT. PROTEGE ME ET PROTEGAM TE, LARGIRI, VIS, MIHI MEUM UT ADJUVEM TE[48].

These are they which sound the depths together; the Sun and Moon, philosophical. And as the influence of the Moon, says Plutarch, seems to *reflect* the *works* of reason, and to proceed from Wisdom, so the operations of the Sun are seen to resemble those *strokes* which by mere dint of strength and force bear down all before them. You also have been initiated in those Mysteries in which there are two pairs of eyes, and it is requisite that the pair which are beneath should be closed when the pair which are above them perceive, and when the pair above are closed those which are beneath should be opened. Think therefore, says Synesius, explaining the same Egyptian Mythology of Isis and Osiris, that this is an enigma indicative of *contemplation and action*; the intermediate nature alternately energizing according to each of these[49]. Proclus, also dividing the Apollonical Intellect, remarks that the prophetic power unfolds the simplicity of truth and takes away the variety of that which is false; but the *arrow-darting* power exterminates everything, furious and wild, and prepares that which is orderly and gentle to exercise dominion, vindicating to itself Unity[50].

Power alone, indeed, if destitute of the ruling aid of Wisdom, would be borne along with violence, mingling and destroying all things; yet nature will not move by mere theory either, and Intellect is therefore useless for the purposes of action when deprived of the subserviency of the Hands. But these two concurring, Wisdom with Power in subtle and firm texture of divine splendor and prophetic companionship, the Will may descend in safety to the abodes of Power. A wise man is strong, says the wise king, and knowledge increaseth strength. Two are better than one, because they have a good reward for their labor; as in water face answers to face, so the heart of man to man[51].

> *By mutual confidence and mutual aid*
> *Great deeds are done and great discoveries made,*
> *The wise new prudence from the wise acquire,*
> *And one brave hero fans another's fire*[52].

And as the Rational Efficient, armed with a bright intelligence, discovers the evil of its first conception, now appearing manifold within the veil, it proceeds even to a dissolution of the vital bond, continually imaging its revelation in act.—Beloved brother, advises the experienced and earnest Böhme, if you would seek the Mystery, seek it not in the *outward* spirit; you will there be deceived, and attain nothing but a glance of the mystery; enter in even to the *Cross*, then seek gold and you will not be deceived. You must seek in another world for the pure child that is without spot; in this world you will find only the drossy child, that is altogether imperfect; but go about it in the right manner; enter I even to the cross in the Fourth Form, there you have Sol and Luna together; bring them through an anguish into death, and bruise that composed magical body so long until it becomes again that which it was before in the center of the will; and then it becometh magical and hungry after nature. It is a longing in the eternal desire, and would fain have a body; give it Sol, viz., the soul, that conjoining they may conceive a body according to that soul. So the Will springs up in Paradise with fair golden fruits. We speak not here of a glass or image, but of gold, whereof men vaunt themselves, their idol god[53].

In such few words does the Theosophist comprehend the end and beginning of the Sacred Art, the sum of the divine Intention and its vital fruits; for by death and contrition of the agent in the patient, and vice versa, the old life is finally crucified; and out of that crucifixion, by reunion of the principles under another law, the new life is elicited; which life is a very real and pure Quintessence, the Mercury so much sought after, even the Elixir of Life; which needs only the corroborative virtue of the Divine light which it draws, in order to become the living gold of the philosophers, transmuting and multiplicative—the concrete *form* of that which in the dead metal we esteem. O Nature, the most magnanimous creatrix of natures! Cries the Master, which containest and separatest all things in a middle principle! Our stone comes with Light, and with Light it is generated; and then it brings forth the clouds, or darkness, which is the mother of all things[54].

Let us pause here, then, to consider what it was the philosophers really searched for and discovered in this Stone; that we may be prepared to learn some more definite particulars of their practice, and in what condition the vital elements are placed during their experiment and recreation. We have seen that, next to the first preliminaries, the object was to produce an alteration in the Vital Spirit and that this was operated by a true Rational Analysis, which, repeatedly passed through, leads on to a dissolution of the whole natural born hypostasis, and is the condition proper to induce a new life and growth into consciousness. That which they sought after, and profess accordingly to have discovered, therefore, is this miraculous principle of regeneration; by which the relationships of the vital elements are exchanged; the sensible medium, which in this present birth is dominant, being made occult; and the occult supernatural reason of life, which is catholic, also becoming manifest in the self-evidence and power.

And this is the true way and means by which the metaphysical body of gold will be made profitable, and in no other way, as the adepts teach; but by taking that body, when it is found, and joining it with a spirit that is *consanquineous* and proper to it, and circulating these two natures one upon the other, until one have conceived by the other.—Pinge duos Angues, cries Cornelius Agrippa; or, to proceed in the more suggestive language of his ingenious disciple—Take our two serpents, which are to be found everywhere on the face of the earth; they are a living male and a living female (understand in relation to the spirit always without all corporeal allusion); tie them in a love knot and shut them up in the *Arabian Caraha*. This is the first labor; but the next is more difficult. Thou must *incamp* against them with the *fire of nature*, and be sure thou dost bring thy *line* round about. Circle them in, and *stop* all *avenues*, that they find no *relief*. Continue this *siege patiently*, and they turn into an ugly venomous black *toad*; which will be transformed to a horrible devouring *dragon*, creeping and weltering in the bottom of her *cave*, without *wings*. Touch her not by any means, continues the adept, not so much as with thy hands, for there is not upon the earth such a vehement transcendent poison. As thou hast begun so proceed, and this dragon will turn into a *swan*, but more white than the hovering virgin snow when it has not yet *sullied with the earth*. Henceforth I will allow thee to *fortify* thy *fire*, till the *Phoenix* appears. It is a *red bird* of a most deep *color* with a *shining fiery hue*. Feed this *bird* with the *fire* of his *father* and the *ether* of his mother; for the first is *meat*, the second is *drink*, and without this last he attains not to his *full glory*. Be sure to understand this secret; for *fire* feeds not *well* unless it be *first fed*. It is of itself *dry* and choleric, but a *proper moisture* tempers it, gives it a *heavenly complexion* and brings it to the *desired exaltation*. Feed thy *bird* then as I have told thee, and he will *move* in his *nest*, and rise like a *star* of the *firmament*. Do this, and thou hast placed nature in the horizon of Eternity. Thou hast performed that command of the Cabalist, *Unite the end to the beginning as the flame is united to the coal; for the Lord is superlatively one and admits of no second*[55]. Consider that it is you seek: you seek an insoluble, miraculous, transmuting, uniting union; but such a tie cannot be without the first unity. For to create and to transmute *essentially* and naturally without violence is the proper office of the *first power*, the *first wisdom* and the *first love*. Without this *love* the elements will never be *married*; they will never *inward and essentially unite*; which is the *end* and *perfection* of magic[56].

Thus Vaughan: the italics, copied from the original, serve well to denote where a latent meaning is implied and those analogies which are aptly referable throughout the process. The following verses translated from the *Aquarium Sapientum* of about the same period, may help to elucidate the subject further and lead on the discerning mind.

> *The Spirit is given to the body for a time,*
> *And that refreshing spirit washes the soul by art;*
> *If the spirit suddenly attracts the soul by art;*
> *Then nothing can separate it from itself;*
> *Then they consist in Three and yet abide in one seat,*
> *Until the noble body is dissolved, and putrefy and separate from them;*
> *Then after some time the spirit and soul come together*
> *In the extreme or last heat, and each maintains its proper seat in constancy.*
> *Then, nothing wanting, an entire sound estate and perfection is at hand,*
> *And the work is glorified with great joy*[57].

This is the constant doctrine and rule of the regeneration of light out of darkness, of life from death; the solution of the sense-born spirit and its subsequent sublimation, by a preponderant affinity artificially endowed, into the transparent glory of its prototypic form. And thus we learn from adepts, though particulars vary, that nature was not proved by them at random; for neither does she move by theory only or mere mechanic art, but by rational experiment and the light of faith, which, entering, stirs up in the inward oppressed fore of the chaotic natural-born life, and endeavors to convert, as it were, by a pure conscience, moving at length penetrating to meet the self-willed Identity within, is arrested, and the contest of good and evil commences in the soul, each striving for the ascendant, until the later prevailing for a period (and such being the necessitous decree) an eclipsation of the light takes place, and a dissolution of its body, as was before shown. And, as we read in the fable, Typhon killed Osiris, his uterine brother, and scattered his members to the four winds, and usurped his rightful throne; but Isis, recollecting, hides them in a chest: just so the ethereal hypostasis is divided against itself and brought to a separation even as these three; the soul, the spirit, and the body principle; the paternal, maternal, and proceeding substance of life; sulfur, mercury, salt. The sulfur, which is the soul and golden ferment, being dislocated in its purpose by the oppressive will, is carried aloft to float upon the ethereal waters, whilst these continue to tear, decoct, and soften the sensual dominant and make it more fit for the returning reason and understanding to work upon; for it is brought to an extremity indeed, and made to feel the want of the light it had rejected. The light moreover does not ascend but it carries with it a fermental odor of the body, which by the divine Art also is so contrived in order that the soul may not depart altogether into the region of nonentity. Thus Hermes—Take, my son, the flying bird and drown it flying, then divide and cleanse it from its filth which keep its in death; expel this and put away all pollution, that it may live and answer thee, not by flying away indeed but truly by forbearing to fly[58]. And all the while, during this period of the severation, a wonderful coction is described as going on, the *earth* is overflown with *waters*, the *two great lights* are eclipsed, the *air* is darkened, and all things are in confusion and disorderly relation, by reason of the successive passion and prevalence of the vital principles one over another; for the balance is so maintained that they can neither be said properly to die or live according to that descriptive Prosopopoeia of the Stone.

> *Non ego continué morior dum spiritus exit,*
> *Jam redit assidué quamvis et saepe recedit*
> *Et mihi nunc magna est anima, nunc nulla facultas.*
>
> *Plus ego sustinui quam corpus debuit unum,*
> *Tres animas habui, quas omnes intus habebam;*
> *Discessere duae, sed Tertia paene scenta est, &c.*
>
> *I am not dead although my spirit's gone,*
> *For it returns, and is both off and on,*
> *Now I have life, now I have none;*
>
> *I suffered more than one could justly do,*
> *Three souls I had, and all my own; but two*
> *Are fled; the third had almost left me too*[59].

Unremitting care and attention are enjoined at this critical juncture, lest either of the dissolute elements should escape from its legitimate attraction, and the property of the Spirit, which is at yet indifferent to life or death, should by force of too strong a fire, as Lully explains, be dissevered from the body, and the soul thenceforth depart into the region of her own sphere. And therefore he says,—Let the heavenly power or agent be such in the place of generation, or mutation, that it may alter the humidity from its earthly complexion to a fine transparent form or species[60].

But we are not proposing to exhibit the Practice, but only to understand it. Previous, therefore, to the birth and fruits of spiritual increase, it may be expedient briefly only to consider the intermediate stages of the abyssal regeneration and contest of the metaphysical Embryo before it is born into the conception of the eye of sense. Entering it for the dissolution, adepts describe it indeed as the greatest poison—the contrary will of the whole dissolving life is loosened by it, which actuates it exceedingly, the one being natural and the other a fire against Nature; conjoining together, they make a conflagration more fiercely consuming than any elemental flame; and being of equal origin, they prey upon each other incombustibly, and by so much the more increasing as they draw together in might. And as the fable further relates of the Egyptian monarch, that his hair was suffered to grow whilst yet he tarried in Ethiopia; so this fire is suffered to grow profusely, shooting forth all his Satanic radiance in personality and act, until the time for his mortification is ripe and ready at hand. Adepts call him the Green Lion, Typhon, Firedrake; or during the mortification, he is their venomous Black Toad; for the newly roused Efficient is exceeding wrathful, as we before hinted, reducing the foreign body of Light, which is Osiris, to a mere vapor, called by the philosophers, on account of its origin, the *Four Winds*, which, condensing together at the top of the vessel in the form of drops, runs down continually, day and night, without ceasing[61]. So Sendivogius, in witty discourse of his, relates that Sal and Sulfur meeting together at a certain fountain began to fight, and Sal gave Sulfur a mortal wound, out of which, instead of blood, came forth, as it were, most white milk, and it became to be a great river[62].

> *For first the sun in hys uprising obscurate*
> *Shall be, and passe the waters of Noa's flude,*
> *On erth which were a hundred days continueate*
> *And fifty, away or all thys waters yode,*
> *Ryght so on our waters, as wise men understode,*
> *Shall pass: that thou, with David, may say*
> *Abierunt in sicco fluminae, &c*[63].

This is commonly called the Gate of Putrefaction, and its entrance is described as dark, with Cimmerian windings, and continual terrification of the Spirit; but the cause of the dissolution appears to proceed from the action of the vital heat stirred up artificially within the blood, and which being so continuously triturated, ignites and opens for itself a passage, endeavoring forthwith to absorb the circulating light by the efflux of its own abundant chloric spirit being transfixed. And all this while it is that the powers of the Philosophic Heaven are so wonderfully shaken and defiled; for, as the French adept phrase it, the two dragons do bite one another very cruelly, and never leave off from the time they have seized one another, till by their slavering venom and mortal hurts they are turned into a gory blood, and then, being decocted totally in their own venom, are turned into a Fifth Essence.

> *To Saturn, Mars with bond of love is tied,*
> *Who is by him devoured of mighty force,*
> *Whose spirit Saturn's body doth divide,*
> *And both combining yield a Secret Source*
> *From whence doth flow a Water wondrous bright*
> *In which the Sun doth set and lose his light*[64].

There is a profound mystery couched in these light word; for as there was darkness upon the Abyss when the Divine Spirit moved upon the Water's face, so in the hyperphysical work is it seen to be, when the swifter current of the Infernal motive wheel surmounts and eclipses the Divine Light in the circulation. And, moreover, there is the tempter Evil of the Son of Man made manifest, and all in reality the original Sin with a more appalling possibility, to be met only by voluntary sacrifice and humiliation of the Selfhood under the exemplary cross of Christ. For is it not written, He shall overflow the *channels*, and go over all the *banks*: and he shall pass through *Judah*; he shall overflow and go over, he shall reach even to the neck; and the stretching out of *his wings* shall fill the breadth of thy *land*, O Emanuel[65]?

There is, say the Alchemists, nothing of an unclean nature that enters into the composition of the Stone, except One thing, which is the Instrument moving the gold to putrefy; and in this respect (for it is the very grave of the rational light) it is called by them Typhon, Satan, Aquafoetida, Ignis Gehanna, Mortis Immundities, etc. And because the philosophers are obscure concerning this principle, lest the rational inquirer should be led into troublesome error by their sophistication, we are induced to dwell rather and explain at length that, though impure in the beginning, and manifestly evil, it is nevertheless a necessary ingredient, and when finally brought through the natural Alembic, and returned, it constitutes the natural Alembic, and returned, it constitutes the force and integral perfection of the Divine Superstructure. And although Sulfur and Mercury, says the Adept, should be already described and known, yet without Salt no man can attain to this Sacred Science[66]. Hermes, alluding to the same, says—The Dragon dwells in all the threefold nature, and his houses are the darkness and blackness that is in them; and while this fume remains *they are not immortal*. But take away the cloud from the water, the blackness from the sulfur, and by dissolution thou shalt obtain a triumphant gift, even that in and by which the possessors live[67]. And although Hermes does not speak of it openly, because the root of this Science is a deadly poison, yet I protest to you, says Maria laconically, that when this poison is resolved into a subtle water, it coagulates our Mercury into most pure silver o all tests[68]. But whilst it remains in the natural state, in the evil of its original conception, no good can come until it is overtaken and resolved.

> *Then lyke as sowles after paynes of purgatory*
> *Be brought into Paradyce, where ys joyful lyfe,*
> *Soshall our stone after hys farknes in purgatory*
> *Be purged, and joined in elements without stryfe*
> *Rejoicing in the beauty and whytenes of his wife,*
> *And pass fro' the darknes of purgatory to lyght*
> *Of Paradyce, in whytenes Elixir of great might.*
> *And like as yse to water doth relent,*
> *Whereof congealed it was by violence of greate cold,*
> *When Phoebus yt smyteth hys beams influent,*
> *Ryght so to water minerall reduced ys our gold,*
> *As wryteth plainly Albert, Raymond and Arnolde*
> *Wyth heat and moisture by Crafte occasionate*
> *Wyth congelation of the Spyrite*[69].

By crafte occasionate, he says, because, it is by the attractive grace of the connate spirit that the self-willed agent is finally seen to be subdued and betrayed to self-mortification, as it were, by a conscience moving contrite in the Law of her Light; here, therefore, Sol being eclipsed, the Lunar Vulcan acts a principal part, as Isis in the Mysteries, where she is also called Athena, to express that self-motion and intelligence with which this Spirit is endowed. In like manner they gave to Typhon, in this predicament, the name of Seth, Bebo, and like words, as Plutarch explains, importing a certain violent, forcible restraint, contrariety, and subversion, all which Osiris, *i.e.*, the Divine Light, suffers in passing through the voluntary axle in the regeneration; but tempered by the benign offices of Isis, he is likewise gradually enthralled, and the opposive principles are, through her artful intercession, finally reconciled, and remain together, circulating with her in equilibriate accord.

Canst thou draw out Leviathan with an *hook*? Or his tongue with a *cord* which thou lettest *down*? Canst thou put an hook into his nose? Or bore his jaws through with a *thorn*? Will he make many *supplications* unto thee? Will he speak *soft words* unto thee? Will he make a *covenant* with thee? Wilt thou take him for a *servant for ever*? Wilt thou *play* with him as with a *bird*? Wilt thou *bind* him for thy maidens? Shall the *companions* make a *banquet* of him? Shall they *part* him among the *merchants*? Canst thou fill his *skin* with *barbed hooks*, and his *head* with fish spears? LAY THY HAND UPON HIM, REMEMBER THE BATTLE AND DO NO MORE. Behold, the hope of him is in vain. Yet shall not one be cast down even at the sight of him? None is so fierce that dare stir him up: who then is able to stand before ME? Who hath prevented me, that I should *repay* him? Whatsoever is made *under the whole heaven* is mine. I will not *conceal* his parts nor his comely *proportion*. Who can discover the face of his *garment*? Or who can come to him with his *double bridle*? Who can open the *doors* of his face, his *teeth* are terrible all about. His *scales* are his *pride*, shut up together as with a *close seal*. One is so near to another, that *no air* can come between them. They are *joined* one to another, they *sick together*, that they *cannot* be sundered. By his *neesings a light* doth shine, and his *eyes* are like the eyelids of the morning. Out of *his mouth go burning lamps, and sparks of fire leap out*. Out of his *nostrils* goeth *smoke*, as out of a seething pot or cauldron. His *breath kindleth coals*, and a *flame* goeth out from his *mouth*. In his *neck* remaineth *strength*, and *sorrow* is turned into *joy* before him. The *flakes* of his *flesh* are *firm* in themselves; they cannot be moved. His *heart* is firm as a *stone*; yea, as hard as a piece of the *nether millstone*. When he *rouseth up himself*, the *mighty* are *afraid: by reason of the breakings they purify themselves*[70]. *The sword of him that layeth at him cannot hold: the spear, the dart, nor the habergeon*. He esteemeth *iron as straw*, and *brass as rotten wood*. The *arrow* cannot make him *flee*, *sling stones* are turned with him into *stubble. Darts* are counted as stubble. Darts are counted as stubble; he laugheth at the *shaking of a spear. Sharp stones* are *under* him: he spreadeth *sharp pointed things upon the mire*. He maketh the *deep* to boil like a pot: he maketh the *sea* like a pot of *ointment*. He maketh a *path to shine* after him; one would think the deep to be hoary. Upon *earth* there is not his *like*, who is made without *fear*. He *beholdeth* all high things: he is a king over all the *children of Pride*[71].

Much might be added, and innumerable similitudes belonging to this rebellious Principle and that identical representative of him which the Divine Art requires, in order that his stolen forces may be drawn forth and spent in the sanquinary conflict which he provokes in life. Just as in the Egyptian relics he is so frequently seen depicted with all the emblems of grace and power in human semblance, fiercely seated between his circumventing foes. For the Orient Animal must be stripped of his skin, not with arrows or clubs, but with the Hand, as Adepts say; the whole garment of Light must be dissected, shorn, and the signal of victory be heroically transferred. Animal de Oriente pelle sua leonine spoliari debet ejusque alae evanescere atque tum simul ingredi magnum oceani salum cumque pulchritidine iterum egrdi, &c[72]. But we must proceed; giving only, by way of recreation, this Philalethean Lion Hunt from Malden in part, and the Cosmopolite Eireneus.

HUNTING OF THE GREENE LYON.
All hail to the noble Companie
Of true Students in holi Alkimie,
Whose noble practice doth them teach
To veil their art with mysty speech;
Mought yt please your worshipfulnes
To heare my idle soothfastnes,
Of that stronge practise I have seene,
In hunting of the Lyon Greene,
And because you may be apaid,
That ys truth, that I have said;
And that you may for surety weene,
That I know well this Lyon Greene:
I pray your patience to attend
Till you see my short writt end,
Wherein Ile keepe my noble Masters rede,
Who while he lived stoode me in steede;
At his death he made me sweare hym to,
That all the secrets I schould never undoe
To no one Man, but even Spread a Cloude

Mary Anne Atwood

Over my words and writes, and so it shroude,
That they which do this Art desire,
Should first know well to rule their Fyre:
For with good reason yt doth stand,
Swords to keep fro mad Mens hand:
Least th'one shoul, kill th'other burne,
Or either doe some fore shroud turne:
As some have done that I have seene,
As they did hunt thys Lyon Greene.
Whose collour doubtles ys not soe,
And that your wisdomes well doe know;
For no man lives that each hath seens
Upon foure feete a Lyon colloured Greene:
But our Lyon wanting maturity,
Is called greene for unripenes trust me,
And yet full quickly he can run,
And soone can overtake the Sun:
And suddainely can hym devoure,
If they be both shut in one towre:
And hym Eclipse that was so bryght,
And make thys redde to turne to whyte:
By vertue of hys crudytie,
And unripe humors whych in hym be,
And yet wything he hath such heate,
That whan he hath the Sun up eate,
He bringeth hym to more perfection,
Than ever he had by Natures direccion.
This Lyon maketh the Sun sith [fith] soone
To be joined to hys Sister the Moone:
By way of wedding a wonderous thing,
Thys Lyon should cause hem to begett a King:
And tis as strange that thys Kings food,
Can be nothing but thys Lyons Blood;
And tis as true that thys ys none other,
Than ys it the Kings Father and Mother.
A wonder a Lyon, and Sun and Moone,
All these three one deede have done:
The Lyon ys the Preist, and the Sun and Moone the wedd,
Yet they were both borene in the Lyons Bedd;

And yet thys King was begott by none other,
But by Sun and Moone hys owne Sister and Brother.
O noble Master of pardon I you pray,
Because I did well-neere bewray
The secret which to me ys so deare,
For I thought none but Brothers were here:
Than schould I make no doubt,
To have written plainley out,
But for my fealty I must keepe aye,
Ile turn my pen another way,
To speake under Benedicite Of thys noble Company:
Wych now perceives by thys,
That I know what our Lyon ys.
Although in Science I am noe Clerke,
Yet I have labour'd in thys warke:
And truly wythouten any nay,
If you will listen to my lay:
Some thing thereby yow may finde,
That well may content your minde,
I will not sweare to make yow give credence,
For a Philosopher will find here in evidence,
Of the truth, and to men that be Lay,
I skill not greatly what they say.
For they weene that our Lyon ys
Common Quicksilver, but truly they miss:
And of thys purpose evermore shall fayle,
And spent hys Thrift to ltle availe,
That weeneth to warke hys wyll thereby,
Because he doth soe readely flie;
Therefore leave off ere thou begin,
Till thow know better what we meane;
Whych whan thow doest than wilt thou say
That I have tought thee a good lay,
In that whych I have said of thee before,
Wherefore lysten and marke well my lore.
Whan thow hast they Lyon with Sol and Luna well fedd,
And layd them clenly in their Bedd;
An easie heate they may not misse,
Till each the other well can kisse;

Mary Anne Atwood

And that they shroude them in a skin,
Such as an Egg yelke lyeth in:
Than mus thow draw from thence away,
A right good secret withouten any nay:
Wych must serve to doe thee good'
For yt ys the Lyons Blood:
And therewith must be the King fedd,
When he ys risen from the dead:
But longe tyme it wilbe,
Or ere his death appear to thee;
And many a sleepe thow must lack,
Or thow hym see of Collour black.
Take heede yow move hym not with yre,
But keepe hym in an easy fyre;
Untill you see hym separate,
From hys vile Erth vituperate;
Wych wilbe black and light withall,
Much like the substance of a fusball:
Your magnet in the midst wilbe,
Of Collour faire and white trust me;
Then whan you you see all thys thing,
Your fire one degree increasing;
Untill yow well may se thereby,
Your matter to grow very dry:
The yt ys fit wythout delay,
The excrements be tane away;
Prepare a Bed most bryght and shine
For to lodge this young Chylde in:
And therein let hym alone lye,
Till he be thoughly dry;
Than ys tyme as I doe thinke,
After such drouth to give him drinke:
But thereof the truth to shew,
Is greate secret wekk I know;
For Philosophers of tyme old,
The secret of Imbibition never out tould;
To create Magnesia they made no care,
In their Bookes largely to declare;
But how to order it after hys creacion,

The left poore men without consolacion;
Soe many men thought they had had perfeccion,
But they found nothing in their Projeccion:
Therefore they mard what they had made before,
And of Alchimy they would have no more.
Thus do olde Fathers hide it from a Clearke,
Because in it consisteth the whole subtill warke;
Wych if ye lift of me to know,
I shall not faile the truth to shew.
Whan your pure matter in the glasse is fitt,
Before that you your vessell shitt;
A portion of your Lyons sweate
Must be given it for to eate:
And they must be grounded so well together,
That each fro other will flee now whither;
Then must you seale up your Glasse,
And in hys Furnace where he was,
You must set them there to dry.
Which being done then truly,
You must prepare like a good Phisitian,
For another Imbibition:
But evermore looke that you dry
Up all hys drinke, that none lye by,
For if yow make hym drink too free,
The longer will your workeing be,
And yf you let hym be too dry,
Than for thirst your Child may dye;
Wherefore the meane to hold is best,
Twixt overmoyst and too much rost [roft];
Six tymes thy Imbibtions make,
The seaventh that Saboath's rest betake:
Eight dayes twixt ilke day of the six,
To dry up moist and make it fix;
Then at the nynth tyme thy Glasse up seale,
And let him stand six weeks each deale:
With his heate tempered so right,
That Blackness passed he may grow white;
And so the seaventh weeke rest him still,
Till thow Ferment after thy will;

Mary Anne Atwood

Which if thow wilt Ferment for Whyte,
Thereby thow gainst noe greate prifitt;
For I assure thee thow needest not dred,
To proceede with fire till all be Redd;
Than must thow proceede as did Philosophers old
To prepare thy Ferment of peure Gold,
Which how to doe though secret that it be,
Yet will I truly teach it thee.
In the next Chapter as erst I did say,
That soe the truth finde yow may,
Therefore of Charity and for our Lords sake,
Let noe man from my writings take
One word, nor add thereto,
For certainly if that he doe,
He shall shew malice fro the which I am free,
Meaning truth and not subtilty;
Which I refer to the Judgement
Of those which ken the Philosophers intent:
Now listen me with all your might,
How to prepare your Ferment right.
O noble Worke of workes that God has wrought,
Whereby each thing of things are forth aye broght;
And fitted to their generacion,
By a noble Fermentacion;
Which Ferment must be of such a thing,
As was the workes begyning;
And if thow doe progresse aright
Whan thow hast brought the worke to whight;
And than to stay is thy intent,
Doe after my Comandement;
Worke Luna by her selfe alone,
With the blood of the Greene Lyon:
As earst thow didst in the begining,
And of three didst make one thing,
Orderly yeilding forth right,
Till thy Magnet schew full whyte;
Soe must thow warke all thy Ferment,
Both White and Red, else were yt shent.
Red by yt selfe and soe the White,

With the Lyons Blood must be deight;
And if thow wilt follow my lore,
Set in thy Ferment the same houre,
Of Sol for Redd, of Luna for White,
Each by himself let worke tight;
Soe shall thy Ferment be ready edress,
To feed the King with a good mess
Of meates that fitt for his digestion,
And well agreeing to his Complexion;
If he be of Collour White,
Feed hym than with Luna bright;
If his flesh be perfect Red,
Than with the Sun he must be fedd,
Your Ferment one fourth parte must be,
Into your Magnet made evenly,
And joyne hem warme and not cold,
For raw to ripe you may be bold
Have disagreement soe have heate and cold:
Therefore put hem warme into thy Glasse,
Then seale it up even as it was:
And Circle all till yt be wonne,
By passing degrees every each one:
Both black and whyte, and also redd,
Than of the Fire heere have noe dread;
For he will never dreade the fyre,
But ever abide thy desire.
And heere a secret to thee I must shew,
How to Multeplie that thow must know,
Or else it wilbe over micle paine
For thee to begin thy worke againe:
I say to thee that in noe fashion,
It's so well Multeplied as with continuall Firmentation:
And sure far it will be exalted at the last,
And in Projeccion ren full fast:
Therefor in the fyre keepe Firment alway,
That thy Medicine augment mayst aye;
For yf the maid doe not her leaven save, (crave;
Then of her Neighbours sche must needs goe
Or sche must stay till sche can make more,

Remember the Proverbe that store is no sore:
Thus have I tought thee a lesson, full of truth,
If thow be wicked therefore my heart is reuth:
Remember God hys blessing he can take,
Whan he hath given it, if abuse any you make,
For surely if thow be a Clerke,
Thow wilt finde trewth in thys werke:
But if so be that thow be lay,
And understond not what I say,
Keepe Councell then and leve thy Toy,
For it befitts no Lymmer loy,
To medle with such grete secresie:
As ys thys hygh Phylosophy.
My Councell take, for thow schalt finde it true,
Leave of seeking thys Lyon to pursue,
For hym to hunt that ys a prety wyle,
Yet by hys Craft he doth most Folke beguile,
And hem devour and leave hem full of care,
Wherefore I bidd thee to beware.
And Councell give thee as my frend,
And so my Hunting here I end.
Praying God that made us we may not myss
To dwell with hym in hys Hevenly blyss.

 The evil of the Original Sin being overcome by so many subtle stratagems, the New Life thence arises whose quintessential virtue, imperishable and perpetually victorious, is the Corner Stone or first Material foundation of the Hermetic Art: known, as the Adept says, only to the Wise, because they alone can know it who have it in themselves. The irrational and frivolous-minded cannot Receive this truth, because it depends exactly upon the knowledge of That which is most abstruse in them. The example given of Cadmus, from the Greek fable, identified him with Jason, Orpheus, Aeneas, and the rest, who represent the Rational Ferment; the associates are taken to signify the other faculties of the mind originally attendant on this, but which are drawn away afterwards into the vortex of the Opposive Principle, rapidly attracting them when it is freed, and reveling with which, it becomes satiated and more easily ensnared. As it is told of Saturn, likewise, that he was inebriated when he was bound in fetters by his son; and by the advice of the goddess, too, according to Orpheus, the subtle stratagem was contrived.

> *When stretched beneath the lofty oaks you view*
> *Saturn, with honey of the bees produced,*
> *Sunk in ebriety; fast bind the god.*

For the Saturnian Will, being allowed to revel without limitation or rational restraint, throughout te subordinate faculties, becomes intoxicated; his desires are more than satisfied, and, as the image runs, from the effect he sleeps. It is then the watchful eye of Intellect, well advised and able, prepares to cut him off, and drawing forth all his brazen strength, plants it in the newly-furrowed soil, whence springs another armament, which, still rebellious, contending with each other for the self-same Stone, are by it once more annihilated and again raised up. So the Bath of Diana is prepared out of the blood of many battles, where the innocents suffer for the guilty, and many barbarous images befall, until the Identical Spirit arises, pure, bright, and contrite, from its primaeval eleemtn, and free in legal subordination only to its own perfect Law.

> *The matter first of metals Mercury*
> *A moisture is which wetteth no the hand*
> *Yet flows, and therefore is named water dry,*
> *The vulgar is at every one's command,*
> *But this is not the water we desire,*
> *For in our water is our secret fire.*
> *This Matter while its life it did retain,*
> *Was apt all metals e'en to procreate,*
> *The life when gone, then dead it doth remain*
> *Till a new soul shall it reanimate.*
> *This Matter is to metals all of kin*
> *All which do hide a Mercury within.*
> *He then who knows the parts of Mercury*
> *And can it superfluities decrease And with true sulfur it can*
>   *vivify;*
> *For dead it is, though, fluent, he with east*
> *May gold unlock and after recongeal*
> *Both to an Essence which all griefs canheal.*
> *Lo! Here a spring of wealth, a Tree of Life,*

Mary Anne Atwood

No wealth so great, no sickness here is rife,
Here in a map, thou seest the creatures all
Abridged, and reduced to their perfection.
Here thou beholdest in a Subject Small,
From this world's isery a full protection.
O Mercury, tou wonder of the world!
How strange thy nature is and how compact!
A body dost possess which doth enfold
A Spirit inexpressible to act,
Our mysteries; this only we desire,
This is our water, this our secret fire.
For Argent Vive is gold essential
Only unripe, which, if thou canst prepare
By art, it gives the secret menstrual:
The mother of our Stone which is so rare.
Our oil, our unguent, and our marchasite;
Which we do name also our fountain bright.
O crystal fountain! Which with fourfold spring
Rubs down the valleys with its pearly drops
Distilling, with which our noble king
Is wshed ad carried to the mountain tops,
Where he the virtue of the Heavens receives,
Which never after him, when fixed, leaves.
This our May-dew which our earth doth move
To bring forth fruit, which fruit is perfect gold:
This is our Eve, whom Adam doth so love,
That in her arms his soul, stange to be told,
He doth receive, who erst as dead was seen,
And quickened first appears in colours green.
How this? Even thus, in Saturn there is hid
A soul immortal which in prison lies,
Untie its fetters, which do it forbid
To sight for to appear, then shall arise
A Vapour shining, like pearl orient,
Which is our Moon and sparkling Firmament[73].

By such a vital and mysterious process is the First Matter of the adepts said to be generated and produced by an emancipation of the Fontal Source; and this is Diana, and that refulgent Light which eclipses every other light but that of its proper Reason, and strikes the irrational intruder blind. For she is the wholeness of the Fundamental Nature at once personified, the knot and link of all the elements o being, inferior as well as superior, which she contains within herself.—A light more splendid than the Sun and gold, and more beautiful than the Moon or silver, and more diaphanous than the purest crystal; inasmuch transcendant, says the acute Helvetius[74], that that most recreant Beauty can never be blotted out from my mind, though it should be rejected by all, and disbelieved by fools and the illiterate. For though our Art is unknown, we do assert, according to experience, that this mystery is to be found; but only with the great Jehovah saturninely placed in the center of the world. There, within most intimately, the Abyss of the Spoagyric artifice is disclosed; there, as in a crystalline diaphanity, the Miracle of the whole world. There, in that region, no longer fabulous but by art made natural, is seen the Salamander casting out the ethereal waters, and washing himself in the flames; there the river Numitius, in which Aeneas, bathing, was absolved from his mortality, and by command of Venus was transformed into an immortal god. There, also, is Eridanus, and that Lydian river Pactolus transmuted into gold as soon as Mygdonian Midas had washed himself in the same. Also, as in a beautifully pictured series, there is displayed every mythological antique device; Apollo and the Muses, and Parnassus and the Fountain struck from Pegasus, and the fountain of Narcissus, even Scylla washing in the flood, beneath the fervent rays of the meridian sunbeams; there, too, the blood of Pyramis and Thisbe, which turned the white mulberries to a deeper die. The blood of Adonis transformed by Venus into an anemone rose; that blood too, of mighty Ajax, out of which sprung the fairest hyacinth flower. There are also the drops of water decocted by Medea, out of which such a verdure sprang up suddenly to cover the bleached earth; and that potion which the enchantress boiled out of so many herbs gathered three days before the full moon, for the healing of Jason, when that hero had grown infirm. The gardens of the Hesperides, also, are in Elysium; and here Hippomanes runs the race with Atalanta, and vanquishes by stratagem of the golden fruit. Here, too, magnanimous Hercules, having burnt all his maternal body upon a pile of wood, revives entire and incombustible, as the Phoenix on her pyre, and is changed into the likeness of an immortal god. Such are a very few of the games and choice spectacles which tradition commemorates as instituted by Wisdom, for the benefit of souls emerging from Lethe and Egyptian darkness to the glorious liberty of the Freed Will in life, And it is that kindling of Divine Ecstasy, in connection with this Source, that attracts the whole phenomenon of nature to its desire, and works the total miracle of the Hermetic Art in life, exalts Mind by the understanding of Causes, and confirms it. But in the summary language of the Greek saint (since here it becomes us not to assert): Know, says Synesius, that the Quintessence and hidden thing of our Stone is nothing else than our viscous celestial and glorious soul, drawn by our magistery out of its mine, which engenders itself and brings itself forth, and that Water is the most sharp vinegar, which makes gold to be a pure spirit—nay, it is that Blessed Nature which engenders all things; but by usurpation, in each particular universally and without return.

These plain words, supporting the evidence which has gone before, will leave less doubt, if we yield them credence, with respect to the method and true basis of the Hermetic experiment; reason, aided by a perspicacious imagination, will attain readily to the idea, and research may further assist the faithful to confirm it. We cannot, however, quit a subject, the preliminaries of which are so important to establish, without adverting to certain Cabalistic and other Greek concordances, in the hope that their separate witness may tell favorably in conclusion to this Material of Mind.

---

1. See Taylor's notes to his Pausanius; an admirable extract from Laus Hermonaeus concerning the Sphinx, vol. iii.
2. Arnboldi Rosarium, Democritus, et al., in Turba Philosophorum; De Lapidis Physici Condit., cap. iii.
3. Vaughan's Anima Magia Abscondita, p. 8.
4. Genesis ii. Ver. 10, and following.
5. Job, chap. Xxviii.
6. Vaughan's Lumen de Lumine, p. 18.
7. Wisdom of Solomon, and Proverbs, chap. xxiv.
8. Callimachus's Hymn to Apollo, by Dodd.
9. See Crollius' Philosophy, The True Physic, chap. i.; also B. Valentine's Chariot of Antimony, p. 42, &tc.
10. See Jamblicus de Mysteriis, sect. vii., cap. viii.
11. See Vaughan's Lumen de Lumine, p. 40 ; B. Valentine's Chariot sub initio; Norton's Ordinal, c. iv., &c.
12. Lumen de lumine, p. 39 ; Lullii Theoria et Practica, cap. lxviii and lxxxviii
13. See the Admonitory Preface of Oswald Crollius, page x.
14. Oreatrike, p. 631, 710, &c. 4to.
15. Disce igitur, disputator mi, et inquire primum fundamentum ipsis oculis et manu, quod natura secum fert absconditum: sic denùm prudenter, et cum judicio inexpugnabilem Petram aedificare poteris. Sine hoc autem vanus et phantasticus nugator manebis, cujus sermones absque illâ Experientiâ supra arenam solum fundadi sunt. Qui autem sermocinationibus suis et nugis me aliquid docere vult, is me verbis tantum nudis non pascat, sed

Experientiae factum documentum simul sit praesto oportet, sine quo non teneor verbis locum dare, fidemque iis adhibere, &c.
16. B. Valentine's Chariot of Antimony sub initio.
17. Ripley Revived, pp. 263, 266, 69.
18. Aenid, lib. vi.:145
19. See Ripley Revived, p. 206; Maieri Atalanta Fugiens, Emblem xviii.; Lumen de Lumine, p. 97
20. See the extract from Synesius de Somniis, in Taylor's Proclus on Euclid.
21. First Book of the Athenians, text 9 and 10.
22. Tract. Aureus, cap. ii.
23. Tabula Smaragdina Hermetis.
24. Asclepius, cap. xiii.
25. Tract. Aur., cap. iv.
26. See Lullii Theoria et Practica, et Arbor Scientiae, Brancha Human; Arnoldi Speculum, Geber Invest. of Perf.; and again in Manget, Sumantur Lapis in capitulis notus, &c.
27. Lullii Arbor X., Scientiae, p. 99 de Intellectu qui est Bracha Spiritualis Arborio Humanalis. See also in Plotinus' Select Works, a very beautiful treatise on the Gnostic Hypostasis.
28. Aristotle's Metaphysics, note, page 7.
29. See the Treatise De Iside et Osiride.
30. Agrippa's Third Book of Occult Phil., chap. xliii.
31. This passage is taken from one of those singularly instructive treatises attributed to Aristotle by his Arabian compilers, as rendered by Taylor, from the Latin of Albertus Magnus in his Dissertation, book iii.
32. Plotinus, Select Works, On the Gnostic Hypostasis, etc.
33. See Iliad, Book x., Apollon; Rhodius Argonaut., Lib. ii.:
    So the gloomy god
    Stood mute with fear to see the golden rod, &c.
34. Aeneid, Lib. 6:149
35. Pope's Homer's Iliad, book xviii.; See also Fawkes' Apollonius Rhodius Argonautics, Book. I. *He too Alcides, &c.*
36. St. Paul to the Corinthians, 1s ep. xv. 37.
37. Select Works; Ennead v, Lib. viii.
38. L. Comitibus Metallar. Nat. Oper., lib. iv., cap. vii.; Chrysopaea, lib. ii.
39. Aeneid, lib. vi. 138, 193
40. See Pontanus Epistle in Theat. Chem.
41. Post sextum annum clavis potentiae per arcanam revelationem ab omnipotente Deo mihi concredita est, &c. ; See Lumen de Lumine, p. 67.
42. Chariot of Antimony p. 24.; Stone of Fire pp. 160, 168 ; Idem p. 24; also Dyou. Zachary Opusculum, part ii.; Lucerna Salis, p. 64 &c.
43. See Böhme's Epistles; and to the same effect on The Turned Eye; printed with the rest of his works, in 4to.
44. Maria Practica, in fine.
45. Tract. Aureus, cap. ii.
46. Tract. Aur., Scholium, cap. i.
47. Tract. Aur., cap. iii.
48. Idem, cap. iv.
49. See Extracts from his treatise on Providence, at the end of Plotinus' Selct Workd, by Taylor, p. 531; and Plutarch, Isis and Osiris, circa mediam.
50. Proclus on the Theology of Plato—Scholia on the Cratylus.
51. Proverbsm chap. xxiv. xxvii. ; Eccles. iv.
52. Iliad, book x.: 265
53. Turned Eyes Quest. 17, &c.

54. Tractatus Aureus, cap. iii.
55. Liber Jezirah, cap. i. Fige finem in principio sicut flamman prunae conjunctam, quia Dominus superlative unus, et non tenet secundum.
56. Vaughan, Lumen de Lumine, p. 62 and following.
57. Aquarium Sapientum, in Mus. Herm. The Enigma
58. Tract. Aur., cap. ii.
59. Theatr. Chem., Tome iii., p. 764; Processus Chimica, Carmen Elegans v. x; and xi. ; Vaughan's Magia Adamica.
60. See his Theoria et Practica, and in the Testament; Sal Lumen; Nuysement, p. 133, &c.
61. See Ripley, Second Gate, of Solution, and in Ripley Revived.
62. New Light of Alch.,; Discourse of Sulphur.
63. Ripley's Fifth Gate, Of the Putrefaction, v. 12
64. Eireneus, Marrow of Alchemy, Book iii., v. 35.
65. Isaiah, Chap. viii., ver. 8; See the book of Jehior of the Fire and its Mystery, chap. xi.
66. Sendivogius, New Light; Discourse of the Three Principles.
67. Tractatus Aureus, cap. ii.
68. Maria, Practica, circa finem.
69. Ripley's Fifth Gate, Of the Putrefaction.
70. See Maieri Atalanta Fugiens, Emblema xi. Dealbate Latonam et rumpite libros, &c.
71. Job chap. xli.
72. Maieri Hierog. Egypt. Graec., p. 222
73. Eireneus, Marrow of Alchemy.
74. Vitulus Aureus.

Chapter 2. A Further Analysis Of The Initial Principle, And Its Eduction Into Light

comprising the Metaphysics of the Matter; gathered more particularly from the Greek Ontologists and Cabalists, to show the progress of the consciousness through the various stages of purification and dissolution until the rectified ferment, overwhelming, becomes established in life.

Deus, cum solus fuisset in principio, creavit unam substantiam; hanc primam materiam nominamus.

— Mylius Phil. Reform, pars. vi. Lib. i.

The philosophy of the Cabal, as delivered in the only genuine Hebrew remains and their commentaries, is eminently comprehensive and sublime; and these characteristics are mainly dependent on its very great simplicity. All things therein are psychically derived: and, according to the doctrine of an essential emanation, the whole physical universe is extended and corporified, as it were, by a multiplication of the indeficient unit into its parts, under the intelligible Law of its own proceeding Light. Into the Method of this Philosophy, or the many beautiful particulars arising out of its material, space does not allow us to enter; they who are desirous may conveniently examine for themselves, either in the Latin editions of Rosenroth[1]; or to begin with, Franck's very excellent history of the Cabal, which contains, besides numerous translated passages from the Hebrew, commentaries and notes, that we have read with no less instruction than delight[2].

The Initial Principle, however, which we have been discussing, and to which it will be necessary to confine inquiry for the present, is in the *Zohar* designated by the name of *Wisdom*, or the *Supreme Crown;* that is to say, after it has become into manifest Being; but in the Beginning, for reasons metaphysically explicable, the divine hypostasis is distinguished by the epithet of *Unknown,* and described according to its negative absoluteness, in the sum of two or three paragraphs, as follows:

All things before they became manifested were concealed in the unknown and incomprehensible Infinite, and this subsistence, whence all proceeded, was but as an *interrogation,* an imperceptible sufficience, having neither mind, nor figure, nor self-comprehension, or Being, properly so called; but when the Unknown would manifest himself, he begins by producing a point; but, whilst the point of Light remains within subjective and inseparate, he is unknown, and as the Unity of things to be developed only by the separation of them in Himself: in this sense he is called the Ancient of Days, the White Head, the Old Man by excellence, the Mystery of Mysteries, Which is before all things—whose emanation is All[3]. And thus the hypostatic vision is more prominently delineated. He is, says the Rabbi Ben Jocahi, speaking of the same, the Mystery of Mysteries, and most unknown of the unknown; yet he has a form or idiom which belongs to him; but, under this form by which he is *seen*, he remains still *unknown.* His clothing is white, and his aspect that of a countenance unveiled... From his *head* he shakes a *dew* which awakens the *dead,* and brings them to *new life;* wherefore, it is written, *Thy dew is the dew of light.* It is this which nourishes the most exalted saints, the manna which descends into the field of sacred fruits; the *aspect* of this *dew* is *white,* as the diamond is white, the colour which contains all[4].

This white appearance of the primeval splendour in the abyss, is very constantly notified; thus we reading the Apocalypse, of the White Stone with the new name written upon it; and in the vision of the Son of Man, of the snowy whiteness of his glory, whose hair was like wool, and white as snow[5]. And I beheld, says the prophet in Enoch, the Ancient of Days, whose head was like wool, etc.[6]. But these, and all such revelations, will be esteemed fanciful or figurative, perhaps, or arbitrarily, since they are not commonly conceivable, and the worldly mind is shut out from the imagination even, of occult truth. They only who have entered experimentally within to know themselves, have been satisfactorily able to recognize the ground; and they only who are gifted with an approximately faith, to discriminate their universal testimony from amongst so many fanatical delusions, will be inclined, or able either, to advance to the contemplation of their proofs.

But to continue. As all colours in their prismatic unison are white, just so is the Universal Nature, described as appearing in the evolution of her Fontal Light; and Paracelsus gives it as a reason, that there should be a simple ground of all diversity without confusion whereon to recreate: —*Omnia in Dei manu alba sunt; is eas tingit ut vult:*—all things in the hand of God are white, says the Magian, that He may colours them according to His pleasure. Agreeably, the author of the *Lucerna Salis* writes:—he matter will become white like a hoary man, whose aged complexion resembles ice; it will also whiten more afterwards, like silver. Govern your fire with a great deal of care, and afterwards you shall *see* that *in your vessel* your *matter* will become white as snow. Then is your elixir perfect as to the white work. This agrees with the descriptions of Arnold, Lully, Artefius, and the rest cited in the *Theory*, which, in the original verse, runs thus: —

> *Acquiret canitiem viri senis,*
> *Albicabitque fere ut argentums,*
> *Summa dilignetiâ ignem rege*
> *Videsbisque sequenter materiam in vitro*
> *Albere omnino candore nivali*
> *Et tum confectum est elixir ad album*[7].

The same Sendivogius, in his *New Light*, call the Water of our Sea, the Water of Life, not wetting the hands; and believe me, he says, for I saw it with my eyes, and felt it—that water was as white as snow[8]. And Eireanaeus, but we will not enlarge; for is not this the Matter already defined so often by the old Alchemists, saying, it is no common water, but an unctuous mineral vapour, universally subsisting? Bodies, therefore, say they, are to be turned into such a vapour, and this vapour is the Stone known and proven in the Book of Life—Sumatur lais in capitulis notus;—Such is the subtle phrase of the Arabian; and this is the Matter everywhere alluded to, and so often denoted in the Mysteries; which in demoniacal forms is at first in vision made apparent, nor known until the eye of mind, regardant and purifying, meets its First source. For are we not all verily, "such stuff as dreams are made of"? Yet the discovery of it is no dream, if we may believe the experienced; but, on the contrary, every phantastic desire and imagination is alienated and merged in intellectual contact of the Thing itself, which is our Identity. This is the true Hermetic material, which is celebrated by all is disciples; that recommended by Orpheus to be taken in the cave of Mercury, and carried in both hands away; and this is the power borne by the Centaur Cheiron, the monster tutor of heroes, cloud-begotten, sprung from out of the nebulous impure ether, with a duplicate real, and promise of a more perfect life to come. The same in Silenus is satirically personified the most venerable preceptor of the God of Wine; and this is Pan, and the foundation of the great Saturnian Monarchy of the Freed Will, which was once circumscribed in Intellect, for the manifestation of its Light.

This same, the Arabians call *Flos Salis Albi*—the Flower of White Salt, and thus the substant hypothesis is said very truly to be designated; and this is the white sand, *Quellum*, which Van Helmont speaks of as manifesting itself forth in a vivid vital soil, which spade or mattock never pierced[9].

This is the true magic earth wherein is the recreative fire, even that "Land of Havilah, where good gold is"; and this fire binds the parts thereof spontaneously to himself, coagulates them, and stops their flux; and this salt is the Water that wets not the hands; and that identical Magnesia that was exhibited in the Mysteries; the White Island of Vishnu; the Lord of Radha; the White Paradise, which the author of the *Round Towers*, with an exclusiveness, pardonable for its enthusiasm, mistook for his Emerald Home[10].

The Platonists have declared true Being to be white, and all that Plato says, in *Phaedo*, about Tartarus is, according to Olympiodorus, to be understood ethically and physically: ethically, in that Tartarus is the place of the soul's trial, where the balance of existence is struck, and imperfections are made manifest; physically, in that it is the *wholeness of existence.* And what is written about rivers and seas by Plato, which is ridiculous in an external sense, is to be psychically understood, as when he says that the taste and colour of these waters is according to the quality of the earth through which it flows; this also indicates, adds our exponent, that souls, in which reason does not preside as a charioteer, are changed according to the subject temperament of the body; but when reason has the dominion, the soul does not yield, but, contrariwise, assimilated herself to the Supreme virtue[11]. And her *first motion* towards this from her ultimate artificial recessure is the true *origin of matter*, according to these philosophers, and the primary cause of all, when the generative virtue is drawn up into intellectual alliance with the medial life and light.

In the third book of Reuchlin, *De Arte Cabalistica*, we read, *Nihil est in principio nisi Sapientia.*—Nothing is in the beginning but Wisdom, or Sapience.—It is this which we are accustomed to call the Three Persons in Divinity, the which is an *Absolute Essence*, which, whilst it is retracted in the Abyss of darkness, and rests still and quiet, or, as they say, having respect to nothing, is for this cause termed by the Hebrews, *Ain, i.e.,* to say, *Nihil quoad nos;* nothing or no entity as respects us. Because we, being affected with inability in the conception, do judge and imagine of those things which do not appear immediately as if they were not at all. But when it has showed itself forth to be somewhat indeed, and that it does really in the human apprehension exist, them, continues the Cabalist, is dark *Aleph* converted into light *Aleph;* as it is written, The night shineth as the day, the darkness and the light are all alike to Him:—*Tenebrae sunt ei sicut ipsa lux.*

> *Si tu, Deus meus, illuminaveris me*
> *Lux fiant tenebrae meae.*

So Paradise was opened in the Seer, and by that kindling of Divine enthusiasm in conjunction with its source, the soft lenient Light was created, which he celebrates, and whence all things are said to emerge, and whither they return; but without our cognizance, who are chained to these exterior surfaces, content with the bare tradition of a life to come. But in that Place, whither he was snatched up, the prophet describes them, and what he beheld of the Radical Essence, and the manifold glories of that mystical Adamic Soil. And this I beheld, says he, the secret of Heaven and of Paradise according to its divisions, and there my eyes beheld the secrets of thunder and lightning, and the secrets of the winds, how they are distributed as they blow over the earth. The secret of the winds and of the clouds; there I perceived the place whence they issues forth, and I became saturated with the *dust of the earth.* There I saw the wooden receptacles (the vegetable or medial life) out of which the winds became separated, and the receptacles of the *snow, and the cloud itself which continued over the earth before the creation of the world*[12].

This nebulous apparition of the Catholic Embryo before its birth, some modern Cabalists have explained to be an absolute concentration of Divinity within its original identity; which, as a cloud before the falling shower, gives birth to the primitive Ether, which is the pure attracting vacuum, or understanding whereby the central efficient is drawn forth to will and operation. Dionysius styles it *caligo divina*, because, as he says, it is obscure and humanly incomprehensible, though visible indeed. The author of the *Lumen de Lumine* calls it, from the Cabalists, *Tenebra activae*, and describes it as beneath all degrees of sense and imagination—a certain horrible, inexpressible chasm[13].

> Non-being, which nor mind can see
> Nor speech reveal; since, as of being void,
> 'Tis not the object of the mental eye;
> But there thy intellectual notions check
> When in this path exploring[14].

For its End is infinite; as the Oracle forewarns,—Stoop not down, for a precipice lies below in the earth;—it is nothing as respects the consciousness before it is conceived. Nothing, as Dionysius adds, of those things that are, or of those that are not, in an empty destructive sense; but it is that only True Thing of which we can affirm nothing, whose theology is negative; but to be in the perfect possession of the most happy life. This Böhme also declares—God, incomparably good and great, out of *nothing* created *something*, and that something was made *one thing* in which all things were contained, both celestial and terrestrial. And this first something was a certain cloud or darkness, which was condensed into water; and this water is that One Thing in which all things are contained[15].

Now here we do not read either that all things came of nothing absolutely, but that *God* of nothing created something which was made that one thing in which are all. And this One Thing appears to be nothing less or more than that Identity which is made in the regeneration by the reprocedure into experience out of the dissolute void of life artificially induced. As respects the creature, therefore, it may be considered as the first divine manifestation out of the abyss, when the Spirit is brought forth into a new circulatory confine, displaying its universal properties internally according to the magnetic virtue, action, and passion of the Microcosmic Heaven. And there is in the Celestial Light, continues the same author, a Substance like water which yet is no water, but such a spirit or property: but it burns more like a kindred oil, and is called by many the Tincture. And this Tincture is the source of the material world, and gives to all essences virtue to grow: it is also in all metals and stones; it causes silver and gold to grow, and without it nothing could grow, but with it, all things: amongst all the children of nature it only is a virgin, and has never generated anything out of itself; neither can it generate, yet it makes all things that are to be impregnated: it is the most hidden thing, and also the most manifest; it is the friend of God and playfellow of virtue; it suffers itself to be detained of nothing and yet it is in all things; but if anything be done against the *right* of nature, then it readily flies away: it continues in no kind of decaying of anything, but abides constantly with life. The way to it is very near, yet no language can express it: nevertheless it *meets* them that seek it *aright in its own way*. It is powerful, yet of *itself* does nothing; when it goes out of a thing it comes not into it again *naturally*, but it stays in its ether. It is not God, but it is God's friend; for it works not of itself. It is in all things *imperceptibly*, and yet *it may well be overpowered and used*, especially in metals: there it can of itself, being pure, make gold of iron or copper, and makes a little grow to be a great deal. For it is as subtle as the thoughts of ma, and his thoughts do even arise from thence. All things are thence arisen through the *Divine Imagination* and do yet stand in such a birth, station, and government. The four elements have likewise such a ground or original; but the understanding and capacity is not in nature's own ability without the Light of God; but it is very easy to be understood *by those who are in the Light, to them it is easy and plain*[16].—I have myself seen this knowledge, continues our author in another place, with those eyes wherein life generates in me, for the new man speculates into the midst of the astral birth or geniture, and thus, he adds, in explication the method of his experience.—At last when, after much Christian seeking and desire, and suffering of much repulse, I resolved, he says, rather to put *my life to the utmost hazard* than to give over and leave off; the gate was opened to me, so that in one quarter of an hour I saw and knew more than if I had been many years at the University; at which I did exceedingly admire, and knew not how it happened to me; and therefore, I turned my mind to praise God for it. For I saw and knew the Being of beings, the Bysse, or ground or original foundation; and the Abysse, that is without ground, or fathomless or void;

also the birth or eternal generation of the Holy Trinity, the descent and original of this world and of all creatures through the Divine Wisdom, and I knew and saw in myself all the Three Worlds, viz., first, the divine angelical, or paradisiacal; and then the dark world, being *the original of nature by the fire*; and thirdly, the eternal and visible world, being a procreation or extern birth or, as it were, *a substance expressed or spoken forth from the internal and spiritual worlds*. And I saw and knew the whole Being, and *working essence* in the evil and in the good, and the mutual original and existence of each of them; and likewise how the pregnant generatrix or fruitful bearing womb of eternity brought forth, so that I did not only greatly wonder at it, but did also exceedingly rejoice. Albeit, I could very hardly apprehend the same in my external man, and express it with my pen. I saw as in a great deep in the Internal; for I had a thorough view of the universe as in a chaos wherein all things are couched and wrapped up, but it was impossible then for me from time to time, as a young plant, and came forth into the external principle of my mind... And thus I have written not from instruction or knowledge received from men, nor from the study of books, but I have written out in my own book which was opened in me, being the noble similitude, the book of the most noble and precious image of God; and therein I have studied as a child in the house of its mother, which beholdeth what the father doth. I have no need of other books, my book hath only *three leaves*, the same are the Principles of Eternity. Therein I can find all whatsoever Moses and the Prophets, Christ and his Apostles have taught and spoken. I can find therein the foundation of the world and mysteries; and yet not I but the Spirit of God doeth it according to the measure as he pleaseth[17].

Here we have modern testimony agreeing in all particulars with the most ancient Cabal and profound experimental divinity; nor this alone, but other favoured individuals, amongst whom Van Helmont relates, how by a mysterious hand he was led along into a perception of the simple element of nature.—And while I variously wandered that I might view the Tree of Life, says the physician, at length without the *day* and beyond the beginning of the *night*, I saw, as in a dream, the whole face of the earth even as it stood forsaken, and empty or void at the beginning of the creation; then afterwards, how it was, while, as being fresh, it waxed on every side green with its plants; again, also, as it lay hidden under the *flood*. For I saw all the species of plants to be kept under the *waters*: yet presently after the flood, that they did all enter into the way of interchanges enjoined to them, which was to be continued by their species and seeds, etc. For in the sky of our Archaeus, aspectual Ideas are deciphered as well from the depth of the starry heaven of the soul itself, as those formed by the erring or implanted spirit of the seven bowels[18].

> *Here is this sphere those mighty wonders are,*
> *Which, as the sporting of the Deity,*
> *Themselves display; wonders indeed they are*
> *Which do exceed man's comprehending far*
> *Here 'tis that God himself t' himself displays,*
> *From whence the sense arises up in joys,*
> *A thousand things for aye arise,*
> *Eternal waters and eternal skies*[19].

Basil Valentine also, before proceeding to a description of the Philosophic Matter, opens his discourse to the effect as follows:—When at a certain time an abundance of thoughts, which my internal fervent prayer to God suggested, had set me loose and wholly free from terrene business, I purposed in myself to attend to those spiritual inspirations of which we have need for the more *accurate scrutiny* of nature. Therefore I resolved to *make myself wings*, that I might *ascend* in high and inspect the *stars* themselves, as Icarus and is father Daedelus did in times past. But when I soared too near the *sun*, my *feathers* with its vehement heat were consumed, and I fell *headlong* into the depths of the sea. Yet to me, in this *my extreme necessity*, invoking God, *help* was sent from *heaven* which freed me from all peril and present destruction. For *one* hastened to my assistance who commanded the *waters* should be *still;* and instantly in that *deep abyss* appeared a most *high mountain* upon which at length I ascended; that I might examine whether, as men affirmed, there was indeed any friendship and familiarity between *inferiors* and *superiors*, and whether the *superior stars i.e.*, Ideae Divinae Mentis have acquired strength and power from God, their Creator, to *produce* any one thing *like to themselves on earth*. And having searched into things, I found, *viz.*, in the metaphysico-chemical analysis that whatsoever the ancient masters had so many ages committed to writing and delivered to their disciples, *was true as truth itself* In very deed, that I may expound the matter in a few words, I found all things which are generated in the *bowels* of the *mountains* to be infused from the *superior stars* as *light,* and to take their *beginning* from them in the *form of an aqueous cloud, fume, or vapour*: which, *for a long time fed and nourished,* is at length *educted* into a *tangible form* by the *elements.* Moreover this vapour is dried, that the *wateriness* may lose its *dominion*, and the *fire* next by help of the air retain the ruling power—of water, fire; and of fire, air and earth are produced; which notwithstanding are found in all things consisting of body before the separation of them: but this *water* therefore *containing all*, which by the dryness of its fire and air is formed into *earth*, is the *first matter* of all things[20].

In this allegory the whole metaphysico-chemical analysis of the Universal Subject is displayed—the separation, introspection and reunion of the vital elements in their ethereal accord. And for this reason adepts have concluded this Identic Salt to be the true grain, since it cannot be annihilated, but survives the wreck of the whole dissolute Being throughout—the seed not only of this world but o the next. For all things, whether organized or otherwise, decay and pass away into other elements; but this mystical substance, this root of the world, returning immediately upon the dissolution of its parts, renews them; nor will then be quiet, but Proteus-like runs from one complexion of light into another, and from this colour to that, transmuting himself before the regardant eye into a strange variety of forms and appearances, exhibiting the universal phenomenon of nature in recreant display as he runs forth from green to red and from red to black, receding thenceforth into a million of colours and transmigrating species.

> *Verum,ubi correptum minibus, vinclisque tenebis;*
> *Tum variae illudent species, atque ora ferarum;*
> *Fiet enim subito sus horridus, atraque tigris,*
> *Squamosusque draco, et fulva cervice lana:*
> *Aut acrem flammae sonitum dabit, atque ita vinclis*
> *Excidet aut in aquas tenues dilapsus abidit.*
> *Sed quanto ille magis formas se vertet in omnes*
> *Tanto, gnate, magis contende tenacia vincla*[21].

And when he has departed from the fragile labyrinth through which he was dispersed, says the adept, and is moreover purified from every impurity, he raises himself likewise into an infinity of forms: one while into a vegetable, and then into a stone or into some strange animal; now he transmutes himself into the sea, becoming a pearl, or a gem or a metal, beautifully shining with red flames, and iridescent with myriads of colours; and thus he lives perpetually the worker of miracles, an indefatigable magian, by no means wearying in his labour but growing young evermore and increasing daily in vigorous display and strength[22]. And these miraculous alterations will not cease, as Democritus alludes, until the Matter has worked out its own restitution and is brought by Art into the supernatural fixity of its Final Cause; and that mode of binding is said to be best which makes use of manacles and fetters; as Hermes also says— The philosophers chain up their matter with a strong chain or band when they make it to contend with fire[23].

> *Nam sine vi non dabit praecepta, neque illum*
> *Orando flectes: vim duram et vincula capto*
> *Tende. Doli circum haec demum frangetur inanes*[24].

To arrest this imaginative flux of freed vitality, we may well conceive that it need the whole voluntary force of the central magnet; and that this alone, which is its proper reason, can compel it to repose. As Reuchlin, concerning the two catholic natures contained in the mirific Word, alludes saying,—One nature is such that it may be seen with the eyes, felt with the hands, and is subject to alteration almost at every moment: you must pardon, as Apuleius says, the strange expression, because it makes for the obscurity of the thing. This very nature, since she may not continue one and the same, is accordingly apprehended of the mind under such her qualification more rightly as she is than as she is not; namely, as the thing is in truth, that is, changeable; the *other* nature or principiating substance is incorruptible, immutable, and always subsistent[25].

And this, adds an ancient and much esteemed Adeptist, is the work which I have sometimes seen with a *singular* and most *dear* friend; who showed me certain large *furnaces*, and those *crowned* with *cornues of glass*. The *vessels* were *several;* having, besides their *tripods*, their *sediments or caskets;* and within was a holy *oblation* or present, dedicated to the *Ternary*. But why should I any longer conceal so divine a thing? Within this *fabric* (i.e., the consecrated vessel), was a *certain mass moving circularly,* or driven round about, and representing the very figure of the *great world.* For here the *earth* was to be *seen* standing of itself in the *middest of all, compassed about with most clear waters,* rising up to several *hillocks* and craggy rocks, and bearing many sorts of *fruit,* as of it had been watered with showers from the *moist air.* It seemed also to be very fruitful of *wine, oil, and milk,* with all kinds of *precious stones and metals.* The *waters* themselves, like those of the sea, were full of a certain *transparent salt*—now white, now red, then yellow and purpled, and, as it were, chamletted with various colours, which swelled up to the *face of the waters*. All things were actuated with their own *appropriate fire;* but in very truth imperceptible as yet, and ethereal. But one thing above the rest forced me to an incredible admiration, namely, that so *many* things, and diverse in kind, and of such *perfect particulars*, should *proceed from one only thing;* and that, with very small *assistance:* which being *strengthened and furthered by degrees*, the *artist* faithfully affirmed to me that all those *diversities* would settle at last into *one body*. Here I observed that *fusil kind of salt* to be not different from *pumice stone*, and that quicksilver, which authors call *mercury*, to be the same with Lully's Lunaria, whose water gets up against the *fire of nature*, and shines by *night*, but by *day* has a glutinous, viscous faculty[26].

Here we have the whole Hermetic laboratory—furnace, fire, matter, and vessels, with their mysterious germinations, subtly depicted and set apart. For this clarified hypostasis (shall we not believe in it?), is the stage of all Forms, and here they are spontaneously produced, not in mere imagination, or as we might conceive imaginatively, or, as in a dream, shadowly; but as the true Genesis of Light.

> *Haec dedit Argenti Rivos, Aerisque metalla*
> *Ostendit venis, atque plurimafluxit*
> *Haec genus aere virum; Marsos Pubemque Sabella*
> *Assemtuque; Malo Ligurem volcosque verutos*
> *Extulit; Haec Decios Marios, magnosque Camillos;*
> *Salve Magna Parens frugum Saturnia Tellus*
> *Magna virum!*

And though these images, with the rest, may appear extravagant, and Virgil refers all the compliment to his native soul; yet the truth, gathering strength by detail, may plead through the whole accord. Such are a few only of the remarkable declarations of individuals who, by an experimental ingress, as they acknowledge, to the Vital Radix, have discovered the catholic original of nature, intellectual and material, with the ground of every phenomenon, through the arising spectacle of the Creative Majesty within themselves. Many might be added of good repute and accordant; but numbers would not ensure more credence for them, who ought, on their own authority, to be believed; and have been and will be always by those who are able to glance freely, without imaginative hindrance, into the capability of mind; and, by analogy of their own clear reason, can judge of that fontal revelation which, when entertained in consciousness, becomes efficient, and in consciousness, becomes efficient, and, in its simultaneous energy, divine. Hence, they will perceive and from no idle dreaming the conviction of those sublimated souls arose, who were not alone superior to the dictation of folly, but were freed moreover from the liability of error which besets ordinary minds: for they had passed the turbulent delusions, not of sense only but of the selfhood, and having combated every sinister disguise in opposition, were proved and reproved, previous to being admitted to the apperceptive vision of the Causal Truth which they describe, when Light meeting Light, apprehends itself alone; and develops the triple mystery of its creative Law throughout, from the infernal motive wheel which is the origin of the mineral kingdom, through the whole intermediate paradisiacal vegetable growth, up to the final concord of the Divine Image in man. For as Life passes through the philosophic fermentation, its substance is entirely transmuted, and the threefold property is developed, with a dividing of the heterogeneous parts, by an extinguishing of the forms and properties of the Medial Spirit. And not only is it resolved into these three principles, which Van Helmont also calls Salt, Sulphur, and Mercury, but there is a procedure towards a radical destruction, almost annihilating the components of the former life, which at length, in its extreme exigence, draws a new seed to begin a New Generation.—Ands this is the way of the recedure to the Night of Hippocrates, leading thenceforth into the Day of Orpheus.

It is not a little remarkable that the same ideas, and even to their expression, are to be founding the metaphysics of modern Germany as in the Cabalistic commentators and mystics of the middle ages. Yet the surprise which this might otherwise awake is diminished, when we consider the *universal* characteristic of Reason; whence it happens accountably that that truth which common logic arrives at by abstraction as an inferential necessity, is the same which the Rabbics, ontologically experimenting, and guided by the same Law, affirm out of their own more proving observation and experience. And thus we may illustrate the point.

All things, says the German philosopher (Hegel), have their commencement in *pure Being*, which is merely an *indeterminate thought*, simple and immediate; for the true commencement *can* be nothing else: but this pure Being is *no other* than a *pure abstraction*, it is a term *absolutely negative*, which may also in its immediate conception be called *non-Being*[27].

Such is the conclusion rationally arrived at by sensible abstraction; Kant, Fichte, but more especially Schelling whose intellectual penetration appears to have passed beyond these two, carried metaphysics into the same void non-entity at last. Hence the skeptical result of their transcendental labours, which, too far surpassing sense and its phenomena to accept their proof, stopped short nevertheless of objective realization on their own ground; there being arrested, faithful and as it were in view, without a means of passage to the promised shore. Yet so it is, that very hypostasis which bounds reason in transcendental abstraction, when met by contact of the inquiring light within, is that Absolute Identity which it seeks after, which, before all duality of consciousness, is the fortitude and life of all. But let us revert to the learned Rassbi's advice concerning the true nature of Divine Inversion; for Ben Jochai and his disciples also affirm that God created all things out of *nothing*, and this not dubiously, *sed quasi auctoritatem habens;* but in what sense this *nothing* is to be understood, we are thus, differently than by the German, informed.

When the Cabalists affirm that all things are drawn forth from nothing, they do not intend, says the Rabbi, from nothing in the commonsense acceptation of that word; for Being could never be produced from non-Being (deficiently understood), but by non-Being they mean *that which is neither conceivable as cause nor as essence*, but yet is in fact the Cause of causes: it is that which we call the primitive non-Being; because it is anterior to the universe: and by it we do not signify corporeity either, but that Principle or Wisdom on which it is founded. Now if any one should ask what is the essence of Wisdom, and in what manner she is contained in non-Being, no one can reply to this question: *because* in non-Being, there is no *distinction* (as of subject and object in the consciousness by which it can be truly said to be known), no mode of true existence; neither can we, therefore, *comprehend*, so to say, how Wisdom becomes united to life[28].

Now this doctrine is precisely in accordance with the Hermetic philosophy, and these definitions of the primitive non-being, perfectly corresponding with the Platonic theology, and Aristotle's discourses concerning the origin of things and incomprehensible nature of the objective contact in Identity. And as to the dogmas of the rest, as of Thales, Pythagoras, Anaxagoras, Parmenides, Empedocles, and others, which men have been accustomed neglectfully to run over; it may not be amiss, as Lord Bacon advise, to cast our eyes with more reverence upon them[29]. For, although Aristotle, after the manner of the Ottomans, thought he could not well reign unless he made away with all his brethren; yet, to those who seriously propose to themselves the inquiry after truth, it may not be displeasing to regard the positions of those various sages, touching the nature of things and their foundation. Nor ought we, in this our state of inconceptive ignorance, to conclude, as many have done, that these men spoke ill, or arbitrarily, imagining causes whereof to make a world, for it was not so: their elements, atoms, numbers, mathematics, physics, and metaphysics, or by whatever names their principiating ideas were distinguished—all their philosophy, in short, was confessedly established, and belonged to an experience and method of observation, unknown to the profane multitude. For they discovered, and have asserted, that there are methods by which an ascent may be affected from the oblivious bondage of this existence, and, through a gradual assimilation, to a survey more or less immediate of the Causal Source.

And thus, neglectful though it has seemed in general of facts, and common-sense observation, these Greeks too derived nature mediately from a certain Intellect in energy, but without distinction, fixing her true Being in the Law of Universals. Those even who appear to differ, as for example, Thales, and the physiologist Empedocles—substituting elements as principles, do so in the choice of expression chiefly, and in the manner of regarding; for the substance alluded to by them all is the same; for the substance alluded to by them all is the same; for the substance alluded to by them all is the same; as we may judge by their definitions, which agree not with any material of elements, or intellect, or atoms, that we discern or understand at all; but we they speak, as before said, out of another perception of tings, exhibiting the phenomena of the superstantial world. It may not be improper here to delay a short time, in order to point out to the more studious, how it happens, that so many mistakes have arisen about their doctrine, and that language apparently divergent, may, nevertheless, harmonize at its source.

For that these philosophers have discoursed variously, is very certain; some saying indeed of the Initial Principle, saying that it is one and finite, others infinite; some, as Heraclitus, according to essence, have denominated it to be *fire*; another, as Thales, looking to the first material manifestation, teaches that all beings have their beginning from *water*; whilst Timaeus, with no less reason or authority, mentions a certain *earth* as antecedent, and the most ancient element; but Anaxagoras, rather regarding the perfection and origin of the One Thing in consciousness, calls it *Intellect;* as Plato likewise, in the *Parmenides,* derives all things transcendentally, proving the perpetuity of Being in itself. But whilst these celebrate Mind as precendential, and those desire to indicate the subsistence of Matter, in either case it is the same; for the mind is not without the matter (the universal element we mean), nor that matter without the mind; but all things, however various in manifestation, are consubstantial in their Cause.

And with respect to the number of principles and elementary transmutations, we may plainly perceive that it is not the common elements, or abstracts either, they contend about; but their investigation concerned the prior Elements of Life; which some, openly distinguishing, call the Celestial Elements; as Plato, in *Phaedo,* speaking of *earth,* for instance, calls it *the most ancient element within the heaven*; and Proclus informs us what we are to understand by the heaven;—Heaven, he says, is the *intellectual contact with the intelligible,* for there is an intelligible which may be conjoined to intellect, and is its true end[30]. But this is in allusion to the highest sphere of ethereality, which Aristotle triply distinguishes, first, *as the essence of the ultimate circulation of the universe*; second, *as that which is in continuity with it;* and third, *as that body which is comprehended by the last circulation.* For, he says, we are accustomed likewise to call *that* heaven, which is composed from every natural and sensible body[31]. That is the arising Spirit of the Universal nature which, persisting separately, bounds as it were, by an invisible summit, every corporeal subsistence, and in the conscious alliance only becomes known .The same is called by Hermes, a Quintessence; and the Hermetic philosophers, speaking of their *earth,* locate it even as Plato does, within their heaven; and in order to distinguish from the feculent dead soil, call it magical, the Earth of the Wise, Olympus, Our Earth, etc., and of the other elements the same, as we have shown already in our *Exoteric Theory,* and elsewhere. Which the initiated poet, in his *Metamorphoses,* neither unaptly signalizses in the arising circulation of Mature from the four concentering winds.

> *Haec super imposuit liquidam et gravitate carentem,*
> *Aethera, non quicquam terrenae faecis habentum*[32].

But Plato yet more plainly alluding to the Etheral Quintessence, in *Timaeus,* says, that *of four elements the Demiurgus assumed One Whole from wholes, in all things perfect and free from old age and disease*[33]. As Aristotle again, where he says, that *the world, being composed from all sensible matter, is one alone and perfect;* cannot mean this world, which is neither uniform nor free from age or disease, or perfect in any way; what other, therefore, should they either mean but the ethereal; which art once taught them to segregate, and establish upon the ruins of this mortal and dislocated existence?

That Empedocles likewise taught a twofold order of natural procedure —the one intelligible, and the other sensible;—deriving the latter as an image from the former as an exemplar, is evident, from the whole tenor of his *Physics*. For he identifies all things in respect of their source; making elements there to subsist as qualitative virtues, which, multiplying into being, become distributive powers, of which the sensible elements and this world are the remote subjects and emanation; contrariwise, also, receding from effect to cause, he shows how the universal frame is borne along in perpetual interchange.

> *How many things to one their being owe,*
> *Fire, water, earth and air immensely high,*
> *And each with equal power is found endued,*
> *And friendship equalized in length and breadth.*
> *All things in union now thro' love conspire,*
> *And now thro' strife divulsed are borne along,*
> *Hence, when again emerging into light,*
> *The One is seen, 't is from the many formed.*
> *All mortals, too, so far as they are born,*
> *Of permanent duration are deprived;*
> *But, as diversified with endless change,*
> *Thro' this unmoved for ever they remain,*
> *Like a sphere rolling round its center firm*[34].

Anaxagoras, and certain others of the early Greek school, alluding to this absolute subsistence of things, assert, that *matter* likewise is the *progeny* of *mind*; and the Alexandrians go so far as to explain the manner of its descent and efflux; as if they too in alliance had known these things, and by analogy, through their own, the structure of the universe; observing so many fine distinctions and such a subtlety of ontological operation as was extremely difficult to delineate by words, or consistently in writing to unfold, Many, therefore, adopted fables, symbols, similitudes, enigmas, and the license of poetry they also called in aid, as well on this account, as to veil their meaning from vulgar misprision and debate. But Aristotle preferred an abstruse style of diction to every other disguise, that he might be comprehensible to the profound only; as, when writing to Alexander about the publication of his *Acraomatic Ethics*, he avows that none but his own pupils would be able to understand them[35].

And with respect to those strictures on the writing of his predecessors, we are disposed to take them in a particular application only; his most erudite translator, Thomas Taylor, having also shown that their reference has been alienated and widely misunderstood. The Aristotelian philosophy is built on similar grounds, and arrives at the same conclusion as those whom it rebukes; but the method is different, and herein the Stagyrite lays claim to superiority, rather than by professing any new basis of argument or superior knowledge. The differences that arose in philosophy owing to men regarding the same nature from diverse points of view, and the contradictions that occur in language, offended his accurate genius; and he was desirous that they should harmonize in the expression of that truth in which they, by co-knowledge, were agreed. That thereas, for instance, Pythagoras would explain essence in number and define it by mathematical reasons, as Plato by Ideas, mingling these with geometric symbols; Parmenides and others, by atoms, elements, and by so many various ways; he complains that they deliver nothing clearly, nor carry their principles duly and comprehensively through their whole system; but shift from one assertion to another, that is apparently, varying their speech. Thus, in the beginning of his *Metaphysics*;—There are some, he says, who have discoursed about the universe as if it were indeed one nature; yet all of them have not discoursed after the same manner: but their assertions are of a different nature; for the physiologists who contend that Being is one, when they generate the universe, at the same time add motion; but these men assert that the universe is immovable. Thus, Parmenides appears to have touched upon the One according to Reason; but Melissus, according to Matter; hence the former asserts that the universe is infinite; but the latter that it is finite. But Xenophanes, who was the first that introduced this doctrine, did not assert anything clearly, nor does he appear to have apprehended the nature of either of these; but looking to the whole heaven, he says, the One is God. These men therefore are to be dismissed, two of them indeed as being a little too rustic,—viz., Xenophanes and Melissus, but Parmenides appears to have seen more than these where to speak[36].

Such like defect of method and incorrectness of diction does the Stagyrite complain of, sparing none of his predecessor; but his opposition is uniformly directed to the letter rather than to the spirit of their doctrine; for he was strenuous in asserting the causality of mind, and praises those as in the highest degree gifted who perceived this; in his *Metaphysics* throughout, evincing a magnificent appreciation of the Intellectual ground. But he was desirous, as we have said, to methodize philosophy; and accordingly undertook, by establishing a system of universal logic, to correct the imperfection of common thought and speech. The design was noble, and carried out to the original intention and on its own intimate basis, was no doubt valuable to fix experiment and assist in defining and unfolding, by means of the categories, as by a congenial channel, the birth of the Divine Intellect into life and manifestation.

That was the syllogism so important to be sought after, which also is according to Aristotle the true object of philosophy; in the universal terms of which every other science is implicated, and without which nothing permanent is said to be endued. When, losing this substantial ground and aim therefore, the *Organon* began to work upon itself, it grew weak and wore out gradually, as Bacon observed it in his day becoming worse than useless, since it occupied an intellect that might have been better employed, and substituted for truth the least salutary kind of satisfaction in the display of scholastic subtlety and aimless dispute.

The same has happened with the Pythagoric numbers, and those mathematics which had all their original keystone in the Arch of Heaven; or how else should numbers have been established as the causes of things if they had not been allied in idea to something better than themselves? All things naturally produce their similars, numbers beget numbers, letters and words constitute phrases, and lines superficial forms only. They may, by composition, be made, in their way, to represent degrees and kinds of things; but this is the utmost of their abstract capability. They cannot produce themselves, or anything else, into substantive appearance. We may exhaust all their combination, divide, add up, and multiply figures to infinity, we shall have figures and nothing more; nothing solid, long, short, or square, not the smallest grain of sand without the Efficient which is in all.

This being obvious therefore, we judge that when the ancients established numbers as the causes of things and derived from them the gods themselves, with all their hosts of power and material dependencies, they had some very different idea attached from that which modern theorems or their probations supply. Or shall it be believed that Pythagoras was so wanton and vain-glorious as to sacrifice a hecatomb, when he discovered that the subtendent of a right-angled triangle is equivalent to those parts which contain it; or that Thales, when, as is related, he did something of the same kind about the inscription of the circle, gained nothing more than a flat demonstration for his pains? Or are not rather the hecatomb, and the theorem separately symbolical, and alike relating to the discovery of that miraculous Psychical Quintessence, known to the wise as the *Tincture of the Sapphiric Mine* which, being in its own threefold segregated essentiality equal to the whole dissolute compound whence it arises, cast off the superfluity, sacrificing the old nature to begin anew? Charon does not ply the Stygian Lake without a recompense, neither are the secrets of the highest causes approached without a mean of expiation; but the vicarious dedication of huge beasts will not avail whilst their Prototypes remain feeding and fattening in the Philosophic Field.

The habit of exhibiting points of abstruse philosophy by mathematical reasons has been general in every age; but in order to derive from them or from numbers anything substantive, it is necessary that the point or unit should be established as something absolute; that every dependent partaking, whether multiplied, added, or divided amongst each other, may be essentialized in the same. Hence Zeno said (of Elea, not the stoic) *that if any one should undertake to demonstrate the philosopher's Unit, he would unfold Being.* For the One of these philosophers is the Fountain of all being; and just as there is a descent from unity into multitude, and all that multitude is implied in the One; and this furthermore fills all and each of its dependent multitude—as one is in two, and two in three, and three in four, and four in five—and still that unit, which is in the beginning, is implied in all and all in each, and every part of each in all, from the equilibriate eternal center to its infinite extremes. And as the smallest fragment of the loadstone remains perfect in two poles, and each particular spark of fire contains the principle and developing force of the entire kindred element, so may we not conceive every portion of existence to be continent and comprehended proportionally of the Great Whole?

All those amongst the Greeks who have written concerning this Whole, and who appear to have arrived at an experimental conception of its reality in the self-knowledge, unanimously assert that it is simple, and not so much therefore an object of reason as of contact and intuition. They contend moreover, with the Alchemist, that there is a certain *pure matter* subsisting about Intelligibles which is universal, and the proved origin of every vital and corporeal existence; that though occult in nature, it can be made manifest to sense even, and exhibited in divine and practical effects. But it was forbidden by the mandate of the Mysteries that their revelation should be communicated to the profane; and the modern Alchemists are, with few exceptions, silent respecting the metaphysics of their Art; the Neoplatonists were, however, more communicative, since forbearing direct allusion to the Practice, they feared less to speak of Principles and the procedure of mind. Their writings appear indeed as so many auxiliaries to the perception and images are admirably adapted to stimulate that faith, dormant as we now are in the corporeal darkness, glows notwithstanding responsive to the truth within.

If we desire to investigate principles and the highest causes, let us inquire now therefore of them briefly, how we may begin to learn; and concerning this Intelligible Mater whether it is, what it is, and after what manner it ought to be conceived of, what the perception of it resembles, and what relation it bears in general to the reasoning power, and finally how it comes forth our of the Causal fountain to be in effect? The following summary gathered from the scientific conduct of Plotinus and Porphyry may not be acceptable to the philosophically inquisitive reader.

That it is necessary there should be a certain Subject of bodies which is different from them, is sufficiently evinced by the continual mutation of corporeal quantities; for nothing that is transmuted is entirely destroyed; since if such were the case there would be a certain essence dissolved into nonentity; and this persisting, there would be no remaining ground of generation. But change arises, from the departure of one quality and the essence of another; the subject-matter however—that which receives the forms and reflects them—always remains the same and proceeding and receding continually into itself.

This therefore Corruption manifests (especially the artificial), for corruption is of that which is composite, and so each sensible thing is made to consist of matter and form and their union in corporeality. This too Induction testifies, demonstrating that the thing which is corruptible is composite. Analysis likewise evinces the same thing, as if for example an tin pot should be resolved into gold, but gold into water; and the water, being incorruptible, will require no analogous process[37].

But the elements, continues Plotinus, are neither form, not matter, but composite and therefore corruptible; and since everything manifest is corruptible, and yet a certain subsistence remains, it is necessary there should be a *Nature primarily vital which is also formless, indestructible and immortal, as being the principle of other things*. Form indeed subsists according to quality and body in manifestation; but *matter* according to the subject which is indefinite, because it is note form. This Indefinite is not therefore everywhere to be despised, not that which in the conception of it is formless, if it applies itself to things prior, *i.e.,* to the divine exemplaries, and the most excellent life. Neither should it be considered by any one as incredible that *there is a certain pure and divine Matter mediately subsisting between primary and secondary causes* and their gross effect; but it is rather requisite to be persuaded by philosophical assertion that such is the case, and that by means of the Theurgic Art it is made *manifest* and imparted through arcane and blessed visions. So far do the ancients likewise extend matter even to be gods themselves; and no otherwise according to them can a participation of superior Being be effected by men who dwell on earth, unless a foundation of this kind be first established. For this Matter, as Jamblichus relates, being connascent with the gods by whom it is imparted, will doubtless be an entire and fit receptacle for the manifestation of Divinity. He moreover adds, that an exuberance of power is always present with the highest causes; and at the same time that this power transcends all things, it is nevertheless present with all in unimpaired energy. Hence, the first illuminate the last of things, it is nevertheless present with material natures immanifestly[38].

Since then, it becomes necessary simply to refer Being to all things, and all things sympathize thereby internally with each other; but consciousness in this natural life of ours is separated off from the antecedent essentiality, so that we perceive in reality nothing of our true selves; hence the ancients have declared this life to belittle better than a diminution of existence; for by no ordinary process of rational contemplation is the mind able to conceive of this nature or the infinitude of true Being. But if any one wish to discover the One Principle he must become first assimilated to it, as Proclus in the sixth book, on the *Parmenides* of Plato directs—he must raise himself to *that* which is most united in nature, and to its flower and *that* through which it is Deity; by which it is suspended fro its proper foundation and connects and unites and causes the universe to have a sympathetic consent with itself.—I have also, says Plotinus, investigated myself, as one among the order of beings, and the reality is testified by reminiscence; for no one of real being subsists out of intellect nor as sensibles in place; but they always abide in themselves, neither receiving mutation nor corruption[39]. And again in his treatise treatise concerning the *Descent of the Soul*, the same author relates,—Often when by an intellectual energy, I am roused from body and converted to myself, and being separated from externals, retire into the depths of my essence, I then perceive an admirable beauty, and am then vehemently confident that I am of a more excellent condition than of a life merely animal and terrene. For then especially, I energize according to the best life and become the same with a nature truly Divine; being established in this nature I arrive at that transcendant energy by which I am elevated beyond every other intelligible, and fix myself in this sublime eminence as in an ineffable harbour of repose. But after this blessed abiding in a Divine Nature, falling off from Intellect into the discursive energy of reason, I am led to doubt how formerly and at present my soul became intimately connected with a corporeal nature; since in this deific state she appears such as she is herself, although invested with the dark and overflowing vestiment of body. And since there is a twofold nature, one intelligible and the other sensible, it is *better* indeed for the soul to abide in the intelligible world; but *necessary* from its condition that it should participate of a sensible nature; nor ought it to suffer any molestation because it obtains only a *middle* order in the universality of things; since it possesses indeed a divine condition, though it is placed even as in the *last gradation* of an intelligible essence, bordering, as it were on the regions of sense. For our souls are able alternately to rise from hence, carrying back with them an experience of what they have known and suffered in their fallen state; from whence they will learn how blessed it is to abode in the Intelligible world; and by a comparison, as it were of contraries, will more plainly perceive the excellence of a superior state. For the experience of evil produces a clearer knowledge of good, especially where the power of judgment is so imbecile that I cannot without such experience obtain the science of that which is best[40].

These things supposed then, we proceed to amore intimate consideration of the Material Principle which, according to these philosophers, the Divine experience imparts; that we may judge how far they agree or whether they differ at all in their definitions from those of the foregoing Hermetic philosophers and adepts.

These Greeks wishing indeed to exhibit, as well as words might enable, the peculiarities of this Matter when they assert that it is one, immediately add that it is all things, by which they signify that it is not some one of the things with which sense brings us acquainted; and in order that we may understand that the Identity of every Being is something uncompounded, and that the mind should not fall into the error of coacervation, they say it is one so far as one; depriving the idea of multitude and dual, *i.e.*, reflective, contemplation. When likewise they assert that it is everywhere, they add incontinently that it is nowhere; so on endeavoring by means of contrary peculiarities to gather the mind up into a neutrality about itself; at one and the same time exhibiting these in order to exterminate from the apprehension those notions which are externally derived, and such ordinary reasoning as tends to obscure rather than elucidate the essential characteristics of real Being. Neither is there any absurdity in their conduct of the understanding so far, or even in an external sense considering one thing to be many, since every center bears a circumference of radii, and each dependent number differs from the One.

But since the ethereal element is described by so many ablative characteristics, since they assert it is neither form, nor quality, nor corporeal, nor reason, nor bound; but a certain Infinity; how therefore ought we to conceive, asks Plotinus, of that which is infinite? What is its idiom in the intellection, or how is such an image to be entertained by the reasoning power? Shall we say it is indefiniteness? For if the similar is perceived by the similar, the Indefinite also will be apprehended by the Indefinite: Reason however in such an apprehension, will become bounded about the Indefinite, that is to say, will pass out from itself into an undefined void of thought. But if everything is known by reason and intelligence, and not otherwise, and here reason is bounded so that it cannot be said to have intelligence; but as it were, a deprivation of intellect is implied, how shall we conceive such a state of being to be genuine, or believe it even to be at all? Yet Plato, in *Timaeus*, informs us that Matter is indeed to be apprehended, and that by a sort of defective or ablative reasoning; and Aristotle has been at some pains in his *Metaphysics* to explain the conceptive idiom of Materiality. I mean, he says, by Matter, that which of itself is neither essence nor quantity, nor any one of those things, by which Being is defined. For there is something of which each of these is predicated, and from which Being and each of its predications are different; but Matter, being the last of things (extant without identity), has neither essence nor quantity nor anything else in its perception, at least of those things which subsist according to accident. Or if any one from this suppose Matter to be essence, he will err; for a *separate* subsistence as this or that particular thing especially belongs to what we call essence, (that is to say, composition of subject and object is necessarily implied in the idea of true intelligence), which is both posterior and anterior to the subject sought; which therefore is in a certain respect manifest only, being one and void in respect of other things; Matter, therefore, concludes the logician, is made veritably manifest only be negation and in defect of true Being; so that, to pass into contact with it, is to be in a certain respect ignorant[41].

Since, then, they assert this subject-matter to be somewhat; and real, notwithstanding all its inverse and irrational characteristics; ought we not to analyze yet more profoundly therefore, not slighting reason indeed, but passing through it, beyond every bound and finite probability in order to conceive that kind of ultimate ignorance, which is the Infinity of Life? Whether shall we conceive it to be an allperfect oblivion, or such an ignorance as in the absence of every knowledge is present? Or does the indefinite consist in negation simply, or in conjunction with a certain interrogative affirmation? Or shall we suppose it to be like darkness to the eye, obscurity being the ground of every visible colour? Or to this, also, the wise ancients have compared the estate of Being verging to annihilation: and as the sensual eye without light sees nothing but darkness, becoming in a certain respect and for the period one with it; so the mental eye, observant of no attracting object, thought, reflection, and all that in sensibles resembles light being submerged, and not being able or having the motive to bound that which remains, is said to become wholly into that obscure oblivion which is the Original of Life: a crass, obscure vacuity—as the *Descent* Virgil describes it—vast, endless, horrible—and Parmenides and the rest cited to prove the same initial nonentity of all; having the same relation to true Being, indeed, as silence to sound, as night to day, or as body rude or misshapen bears to any artificial form with which it may afterwards become endued. And as body rude or misshapen bears to any artificial form with which it may afterwards become endued. And as that which is above all degrees of intelligence is a certain infinite and pure light, so is this darkness, therefore, to be conceived at the opposite extreme of the magnetic chain, which is extended *a non gradu ad non gradum:* and this is that ladder of Celsus and of Zoroaster which reaches from Tartarus to the highest Heaven. Just as in the ascending series of causes, it is necessary to arrive at something which is the Final Cause of all; so in descending analytically it is equally necessary to stop at the contrary conclusion, which is this proved, in the experience, to be the last and lowest effect, in which all the attributes of the First Cause are not only deficient but reversed.

When therefore the mind is in the Night of Matter, shall we suppose that she is affected in such a manner as if she understood nothing? By no means, says the philosopher—but when she beholds Matter she *suffers such a passion as when she receives the being of that which is formless*; and her perception of the Formless Subject is obscure, and vast, and infinite, as we have shown, where descending into the bosom of the Mysteries, Intellect, having already analyzed and separated the component parts of Being, becomes dismayed about the sensation of her extreme life. Then indeed she understands obscurely, and sinking into the Abyssal Subject, feels, but understands not her intellection any more; until, pained with the void of the retreating infinitude (such being the divine decree), and as if afraid of being placed out of the order of things, the soul retracts, rallying about her last deserted Unit, and not enduring any longer to stop at nonentity, becomes into true Being. So true is it, that Death is the way of Life, and that the fear of God is the beginning of Wisdom.

For Self-knowledge is impossible unless every other knowledge is deprived; as this selfhood likewise is obliterated in the overwhelming attraction, which raises it into the First Cause. And thus extremes are said to be present at the new birth, when Light springs forth to manifestation out of the abyssal Darkness, which is then alone before its Creator; and is brought forth by Him for a *First Matter* to give contrasting substance to his revelation, and understanding to His Act.—As the motto simply expresses it—Deus, cum solus fuisset in principio, Creavit unam substantiam, Hanc primam materiam nominamus.

And since it is given us in theory to understand that such an hypostasis is in the *beginning* without all affirmation, being neither in life, nor intellect, nor reason, nor bound, for it is infinite; nor power from itself, but falls off from the consciousness of all these; sought we therefore to conceive of the First Matter, which cannot either receive the appellation of Being, since it is not known in energy, but flies from him, indeed, who wishes intently to behold; for the thought, as circumscribing boundary, eludes the *Infinite*, and thus the desire it, in this instance, diametrically opposed to the *presence* of the thing desired. When therefore, as the Platonist and the Cabal teach, it is unknown, or known as nothing; it is rather probably present, but is not perceived by him who strives selfactively to comprehend it. And this the poets signify in the story of Actaeon, who for his presumptuous intrusion was disgraced by the goddess and hunted thereafter by his own distracted thoughts; but to the sleeping Endymion she vouchsafed her willing presence, and the vast benefits of her love.

Quaeres multum et non invenies;
Fortasse invneies cumnon quaeres.

When you have assumed to yourself an Eternal Essence, says Prophyry, infinite in itself according to power; and begin to perceive intellectually an hypostasis unwearied, untamed, and never failing, but transcending in the most pure and genuine life, and full from itself; and which, likewise, is established in itself, satisfied with and seeking nothing but itself; and which, likewise, is established in itself, satisfied with and seeking nothing but itself; to this essence, if you add a subsistence in place, or a relation to a certain thing, at the same time you diminish this essence, but you separate yourself from the perception of it, by receiving as a veil the phantasy which runs under your conjectural apprehension of it. For you cannot pass beyond, or stop, or render more perfect, or effect the least change in a thing of this kind, because it is impossible for it to be in the smallest degree deficient. For it is much more sufficient than any perpetually flowing fountain can be conceived to be[42]. If, however, you are unable to keep pace with it, and to become assimilated to the whole Intelligible Nature, you should not investigate anything pertaining to real Being; or if you do, you will deviate from the path that leads to it, and will look at something else; but if you investigate nothing else, being established in yourself and in your own Essence, you will be assimilated to the Intelligible Universe, and will not adhere to anything posterior to it. Neither therefore should you say, I am of a greater magnitude; for omitting this idea of greatness, you will become universal, as you were universal prior to this. But when, together with the universe, something was present with you, you became less by the addition; because the addition was not from truly subsisting Being, for to that you cannot add anything. When, therefore, anything is added from non-being (*i.e.*, from the subjective selfhood) a place is afforded to poverty as an associate, accompanied by an indigence of *all things*. Hence, dismissing *non-being*, you will then become sufficient; for when any one is present with that which is present in himself, then he is present with true Being, which is everywhere; but when you withdraw from yourself, then likewise you receded from real being: of such great consequence is it for a man to be present with that which is present with himself, that is to say, with his *rational part*, and to be absent from that which is external to him[43].

Add to this, that contraries are always consubsistent in the Divine Original—the small, the great, the deficient, and the exceeding; for as a mirror is, to external images, passive, neither able to itself to withhold, nor yet to pass away, so is this ethereal glass to intellect, subsisting according to processure and in defect of all imagination. Hence, every imagination concerning it will be false, either that it should appear in the conception as any particular thing, or contrariwise as nothing; for it is both; and the subsistence, which is the reality of it, may be felt indeed, not known—but as an escape of consciousness into its primal source without ideal limitation. Thus it is said to be formless, variable, incorporeal, infinite; neither mere power, or perfect action, but a weak superstantial prolific nature, as it were nothing in the Idea yet in Being all things—whence every form of life, increase, and materiality also are derived. And Ideas, as they enter into and depart from it, are seen as images which pervade without dividing, like shadows in water, or more exactly as in a dream; or as if we should conceive imaginations sent into a percussive mirror or reflective vacuum on the understanding.

And the Passive Nature ought indeed to be a thing of this kind, pure and indeterminate; that it may reflect, without self-hindrance or refraction, the Divine Light throughout; that there may be no falsehood or commixture of images, but the Truth only, and alone, and by itself should be made manifest in life. Such was the Matter so often celebrated by the Alchemists, the Quintessence of Plato, the Water of Thales, the Non-Being of Parmenides, and that Abyss of the Cabalists, styled also by them Unknown, Void, Nothing, Infinite, until returning by its Rational Boundary in the Freed Will to consciousness, t makes manifest the Life, Wisdom, Plenitude, and Supreme Cause of all. And concerning this matter ecclesiastics of different orders are happily agreed: Pierce the Black Monk, with the Benedict Valentine; the experimentalist Friar Bacon, with the Greek Divine; Synesius, with the Canon Ripley, Morien, Lully, and Albertus Magnus; the Mahomedan princes Calid, Geber, and Avicenna, with Paracelsus and the Christian brotherhood of the Rosy Cross, who, having searched into Nature by their proper Reason experimentally, found Her's; and used it; giving thanks, and adoring the perfection of the Almighty Creator in his discovered Light.

For in the natural world there is no such Matter to be found; but the purest is defiled with the imagination of Forms externally introduced. Nothing therefore is generated truly; *i.e.*, we mean, simply so as to represent the Formal Agent alone; or can be; for Nature is bound magically, nor is she able of herself to loosen the bond of coagulation by which her Inner Light and principle of perfection is everywhere shut up. She cannot enter into the True Light; for, as the adept says, she has no hands[44], nor intellect sufficient, nor a free will to vindicate her final purpose in life. It is therefore she proceeds to generate in monotonous retrogression, always circulating into herself. If indeed things beheld in nature were such as the Archetypes, whence they are derived, it might be said that matter is passive to their reception; but that which is seen as that which sees is falsified, and nothing possesses a true similitude; all is mixture and an adulterous manifestation, so far as the phenomenon of the external Nature is concerned. Without the magical solution and human aid to fortify, the Spirit is not able to forsake her extraneous forms even, much less can she conceive herself singly in the Universal anew. Wherefore she reads this important lesson to Madathan, who thinking, in his ignorance, to make the Philosopher's Stone without dissolution, receives this check: —*An tu nunc cochleas vel cancros cum testis devorare niteris? An non prius a vetustissimo planetarum coquo maturari etpreparari illos oportet?* Dost thou think, says she, to eat the oysters, crabs, shells and all? Ought they not first to be opened and prepared by the most ancient cook of the planets?

If any one now, therefore, by hazard should lightly propose to himself to probe this Matter; yet without risking anything, or devoting his life, as philosophers did formerly, to the pursuit; but thinks the times are altered, and that his mind, being on the alert, will discover it, or that some entranced sleepwalker will reveal the truth to him, if there be any, without delay; let him be advised by these monitions; since Life and nothing but Life, and no other Fire but that of Intellect, sublimed and fortified in its efficient source, discovers the True matter of the adepts; and this, as we are abundantly instructed, by a dissolution of the Vital Spirit and alienation of its natural bind—Flesh and blood cannot enter into the kingdom of heaven, neither doth corruption inherit corruption; the sting of death is sin, but the strength of sin is in the Law of dual generation.

> *Debit modo ergo Lapidem solvas,*
> *Et nequaguam sophistico,*
> *Sed potius secundum mentem sapientûm,*
> *Nullo corrosivo adhibito;*
> *Nusquam denim aqua aliqua est*
> *Quae solvere posti lapidem nostrum*
> *Praeter unicum fonticulum purissimum et limpidissimum,*
> *Sponte scaturientem, qui latex ille est*

Ad solutionem idoneus;
Sed omnibus ferè absconsus,
Incalescens quoque per se
In causa est, ut lapis sudet lachrymas;
Lentus calor externus ei expedit,
Id quod memoriae probe mandabis.
Adhuc unum tibi aperire libet,
Quod nisi videris funum nigrum
Inferius, superiusque albedinem existere
Opus tuum sinistre peractum est
Et lapidem erronè solvesti
Ex hoc signo potes static cernere,
Si vero rectè procedis,
Apparet tibi atra nebula,
Quae fundum sine mora petet,
Spiritu albedinem assumente.[45]

All that is performed in the Proto-chemic artifice may be comprehended in three terms—solution, sublimation, and fixation.. Solution dissolves and liquifies the included Spirit; sublimation volatilizes and washes it; and after calcinations there is a reunion into a more permanent form of Being. And these processes are reiterated many times, and many labours of body and mind have to be undergone, as in the *Practice* will be demonstrated; and as Hermes himself assures, that to obtain the blessed Lunary of Diana, he had suffered much, and toiled incessantly. For the spirit is in the beginning, even in the seat disposed subjects, terrestrial, heavy, fantastic, and proves rebellious everywhere at its Source. And, as in the Sphinx's fables, we read that when vanquished, she was carried within the temple upon the back of an ass, this is to signify the simple estate of Being to which such a nature is to be reduced by deprivation of all passion, will, imagination, purpose, or reflective thought. Neither, perhaps, is the patient suffering that has afterwards to be endured, in bearing and bringing forth the burden of the divine mystery, unaptly represented under this same guise of an ass; for it is not until the conquered elements return under the humiliating cross of dissolution that the catholic Wisdom is made manifest, and brought to hand. Agrippa, in his *Vanity of the Sciences*, has written many things in favour of this asinine condition, which is very necessary, he says, for a disciple of Wisdom to undergo; for this beast is an example of fortitude, patience, and clemency, and his influence occultly depends on *Sephiroth, i.e., Hochma*. He liveth on *little forage*, is *contented* with *whatsoever* it be; is ready to endure *penury, hunger, labour, stripes, and persecution;* is of a very *simple, indifferent* understanding, yet withal has an *innocent, clean heart*; without *choler*, and peaceful, bearing all things *without offense*; as a reward for which virtues, he wanteth lice, is seldom sick, and liveth longer than any other beast.—So runs the parallel according to the magician's mind; and the ass, he goes on further to observe, does also many labours above his part; for *he breaketh the earth with the plough, draweth many heavy carts and water in mills, grinds corn, etc.;* and these things willingly, for against his will he does not go. All which qualifications are, in their similitude, very applicable and necessary to be found in the Philosophic Subject; and without which it does not serve to carryout into operation the Divine behests. But many wonderful stories are related of this allegorical ass in former times, and of his qualifications, which the familiar quadruped is no more known to exhibit; nor is he even treated with that kind of consideration which tradition has secured in certain instances for things less celebrated and as unworthy. For did not the Saviour signalize this beast above every other, making choice of it on the occasion of his greatest earthly triumph? Of Abraham, too, the Father of the Faithful, we read that he constantly traveled with his asses; and that one, ridden by the prophet Balaam, was notoriously clear-sighted and, more discerning than his master, intelligibly spoke. A story, little less astonishing, is related of Ammonius, the philosopher, that he admitted an ass daily to be the auditor of his lectures, and join in fellow scholarship with Origen and the Greek Porphyry. Who would believe it? Yet this same ass has been accounted a worthy companion of the wise in all ages, and has borne the burden of the mysteries from time immemorial. Jews, Ethnics, Christians, have in turn, identifying, honoured him; neither, perchance, had Apuleius honoured him; neither, perchance, had Apuleius of Megara been admitted to the mysteries of Isis, if he had not first of an inquisitive philosopher been turned into an ass. There is no creature, concludes the panegyrist, that is so able to receive divinity as an ass, into whom if ye be not at length turned, ye shall in no wise be able to carry the divine mysteries[46]. For nothing that is defiled by information, or inconstant, or impassive, or selfish, or impure can attract Divinity. All mixed unguents are hateful to Minerva.

The goddess scorns

All mixture of her pure and simple oil⁴⁷.

And, as in the mysteries, the Aspirant entering into the interior to behold the Adytum, leaves behind him all the statues in the temple; so must the mind be prepared to depart from all images and intellections, whether self-originating or impressed, before it can entertain the simple Unity of Light within. The wise hierophants indeed appear to have signified by these illustrations the order in which Divinity is perceived. For, as when returning after the association within, which was not with a statue or mere mental image (but with the reality which these images represent), the statues again present themselves as secondary objects to view; so likewise, subsequent to the Divine Union, there recurs That also which was in the mind prior to the union, exalted and multiplied. *And that which thus remains to him who passes beyond all things, is That which is prior to all things, and the First Matter.* For the soul does not willingly accede to that which is entirely non-being, but running back from thence in a contrary direction, but running back from thence in a contrary direction, it arrives not at another thing but at itself. And as in the Divine conjunction, whilst it lasts, there are not two things as of subject and object in the consciousness, but the life understanding and the light understood are one; whoever thus becomes One by mingling with the Efficient, will have a remnant of it with himself; according to the eloquent tradition of Plotinus, where, discussing this union, he treats it as no mere spectacle or theoretical figment, but as a true experimental ingress of the understanding essence to its source. And the light and energy which are there, he says, are of the First Light shining primarily in itself, which at one and the same time illuminates and is illuminated. But if any one should inquire what the nature is of this First Light, which is the foundation of every intellect and primarily knows itself, such a one should first become established in Intellect, when he will e able through it, as an image, to behold the Archetype. And this, continues the philosopher, may be effected if you first separate body from the man and its defilements; *and That which becomes generated of intelligence, after everything foreign is removed, is the original of all.* For this primary motion of the ebbing life from its ultimate recessure recreates and so the Generative Virtue, which was alienated, becomes reunited to mind.

And here we observe the rule of thought to be invariable, whether theoretic or in actual operation; whether, according to strict analysis, reason becomes bounded about its own inversion, as with common logic is the case; or, experimentally proving, it effects that inversion, strictly followed either way, it arrives at the same Truth, though in different relations, the one in light, the other in life, the one by inference, the other in Absolute Identity, proving the First Source. The differences and inconsistencies that occur in the ancient writers and those faults which now to verbal writers and those faults which now to verbal critics are most apparent, vanish for the most past in their right understanding, and might cease to be regarded as such, could we but for an interval only enter into their original light. The proud spirit of modern science might then be taught to venerate the Wisdom it has so long in ignorance despised; even to honour the very contradictions, which not from levity or indistinctness of thought arose, but from such an excessive subtlety and refinement of reason rather, as, seeking to find utterance, was blurred by inadequate reception, and the duplicity of common speech.

---

1. Kabbala Denudata, seu Doctrina Hebraeorum Transcendentalis et Liber Zohar Restitutus. Franckf. 1684.
2. La Kabbale, ou Philosophie Religieuse des Hébreux, par Ad. Franck. Paris, 1843.
3. Zohar, part i., Franck's Translation, pp. 175, 185, &c.
4. Zohar, part iii., fol. 12, 8 recto in Franck., p. 170.
5. Revelation of St. John, chap. i. v. 14; chap. ii. v.17.
6. Book of Enoch, chap. xlvi. v. 1, &c.
7. Lucerna Salis, p. 153, 12 mo.
8. Philosophical Parable.
9. Oreatrike, chap. ix.
10. See the Round Towers of Ireland; an estimable work, by H. O'Brien, chap. xxii., p. 327.
11. See Taylor's Dissertation on Aristotle, Book ii. p. 319.
12. Book of Enoch, chap. xlvi. and xli.
13. Lumen de Lumine, the chapter on Matter, in int.
14. From the Fragments of Parmenides, given at the end of Taylor's Dissertation on Aristotle.
15. Generation of the Three Principles.
16. See Böhme's Works, Vol. i., p. 97, 41 fol.
17. See Böhme's Works, Turned Eye, in Vol. ii.
18. Oreatrike, Chap. lx. and xcvi.
19. Pordage, Mundi Explicatio, p. 320
20. B. Valentine, Stone of Fire, in int.
21. Georgicor., Lib. iv.:405.
22. Fama et Confessionis, R.C., Preface. Ubi vero spiritus excessit, &c.
23. Tract. Aur., cap. iii.
24. Georgic, lib. iv.:397.
25. Reuchlin de Verbo Mirificao. And in the Coelum Terrae of Vaughan.
26. See, in Lumen de Lumine, the Extract, p. 69. Also, the Parable of Sendivogius, and Paracelsus' account of the magical separation of the Elements, and vision, in their native place. Helmont's Imago Mentis, in the beginning; and his Tree of Life. Genesis ii., Deut. viii., ix., etc.; and, in Exodus, Moses' Description of the Promised Land. Job xxviii., &c.

27. Das reine Seyn macht den Anfang, weil es so wohl reiner gedanke, als das unbestimmte einfache unmittelbare ist, der erste Aufang...—*Encyclopédie des Sciences Phil.* 86 and 87. See M. Franck's observations on this point, and *La Kabbale*, p. 187, etc.
28. See *La Kabbale*, p. 214. Comment. Abram ben Dior on the Zephir Jezirah, p. 67, &c.
29. Adv. of Learning, lib. iii., sec. 5.
30. On the Theology of Plato, pp. 236, 240, &c.
31. See his Treatise on the Heavens, Book i.
32. Ovidii *Metam.,* lib. i.:67.
33. Proclus on the Theology of Plato, Book v., p. 365.
34. Empedocles, Physics, cap.i.
35. See the Commentary of Simplicius in Plutarch's Life of Aristotle, and the note, p. 4, to Taylor's Dissertation.
36. Metaphysics, sub init.
37. Here Plotinus doubtless makes an allusion to the mystical analysis; drawing his comparison also from thence. For by no other analysis either is a pot resolved into gold, or gold into a water which is indissoluble. But what he says is perfectly conformable to the hermetic doctrine, both in an internal and in an external sense; for, by a reducation of the iron spirit in the blood, it becomes cleansed from its foreign oxide and aurified—that is, illuminated by contrariation of its Form. The radical moisture of the metal likewise, obeying the fermentive virtue of such a test when applied, may be made to pass away, as the tradition runs, from its own Form into that which is more integral and perfect. All things may be reduced to gold according to this doctrine, as Albertus Magnus in his book *De Minerabilis* asserts, and where also he is cited by Beccher in his *Physica Subterranea*, p. 319:—Light, which is the formal essence of all things, and most abundant in gold, is found in the ultimate alchemical analysis of every existing thing.—that all metals, likewise, may be reduced into water, that is, into their first pure matter, is the doctrine of Plato and his disciple, Aristotle. See Taylor's Translation of the Timaeus of the former, and the Meteors of the latter, and the Select Works of Plotinus, p. 38, note.
38. Jamblichus on the Mysteries, chap. xxiii., sect. v., and Plotinus' Select Works—of Matter, and of the Impassivity of Incorporeal Natures.
39. Select Works, p. 294.
40. See Plotinus on the Descent of the Soul, last of the five treatises rendered by T. Taylor.
41. Aristotle's Metaph., Book ix., p. 221; Book x., p. 237, 154, &c.
42. The Mind of Divinity, says Trismegistus, which becomes known by the Divine Intention in the understanding, is most like unto a torrent running with a violent and swift stream from a high rock, whereby it glides away also from the understanding of such as are either hearers or dealers in it.—Asclepius, cap. 1 end. See also Vaughan, Lumen de Lumine, where, discoursing with nature in her mineral region, the artist describes the same Matter as if he had been an eye-witness of the whole supernal procedure from its source.—A fat mineral nature it was, he says, bright like pearls, and transparent like crystal; when I had viewed it and searched it well, then it appeared somewhat somewhat spermatic; and herupon I became informed that it was the First Matter and very natural true sperm of the greater world. It is invisible in nature and therefore there are few that find it; many believe that it is not to be found (for the world is made up of many divers dark and particular and contrary qualities, and the first unity is occultated in its generation and does not appear). But that stream was more large than any river in her full channel; and notwithstanding the height and violence of the fall, it descended without any noise, the waters were dashed and their current distracted by the saltish rocks, but for all this they came down with a dead silence like the still soft air. Some of the liquor, for it ran by me, I took up to judge what strange woolen substance it was that did steal down like snow. When I had it in my hand, it was not common water but a certain kind of oil of a watery complexion.—Lumen de Lumine, pp. 7, 8, etc. This same, Sendivogius in his

New Light, calls the water of our sea, the water of life, not wetting the hands; and believe me, he says, for I saw it with my eyes and felt it, that water was as white as snow, etc.
43. Porphyry's Auxil. to the Perception of Intelligibles, sec.iii.
44. Filium Ariadne, p. 61.
45. Lucerna Salis Phil, p. 36, cap. iii.
46. Vanity of the Sciences, chapter next in conlusion. Apuleius, Metapmorphoses, or Golden Ass.
47. Callimachus' Hymn to Minerva.

Chapter 3. Of the Manifestation of the First Matter, and its Information by Light

EXHIBITING HOW, WHEN, AND WHERE THE INVISIBLE SPIRIT OF NATURE IS BY ART MADE VISIBLE AND BROUGHT THROUGH A VITAL DISTILLATION INTO SUBSTANTIVE EFFECT — WITH POWER AND WILL TO TRANSFUSE ITS LUMINOUS AURIFIC VIRTUE AND DRAW THE UNIVERSAL LIFE OF NATURE TO ITS HOMOGENEAL ACCORD.

> *Wisdom is poured forth like water, and glory faileth not before Him for ever.*
>
> — Book of Enoch, c. xl., v. 1.

Let us now conceive the Vital Spirit theurgically purified and freed through sacrifice of all foreign attractions, revolving about its center and having power active and passive in hypostatic union always about to generate the infinite fullness which it contains and draws; as even now we approach, carrying along with us the body of our Sphinx, subdued and contrite, to the gate of the first Adytum; where we would contemplate awhile, in the vestibule, admiring at the Tears of Isis, even that blessed Water which nature sheds divinely for the sins of the world. For not all was vaporous vision, as we have shown, or mere ideality on the internal ground; but experience there was present with power and effect in substance to bear it witness.

> *It was scarce day when, all alone,*
> *I saw Hyanthe and her throne;*
> *In fresh green damasks she was drest,*
> *And o'er a saphir globe did rest.*
> *This slippery sphere when I did see,*
> *Fortune, I thought it had been thee;*
> *But when I saw she did present*
> *A majesty more permanent,*
> *I thought my cares not lost, if I,*
> *Should finish my discoverie.*
> *Sleepy she looked to my first sight,*
> *As if she had watched all the night.*
> *And underneath her hand was spread*
> *The white supporter of her head:*
> *But at my second studied view,*
> *I could perceive a silent dew*
> *Steal down her cheeks; least it should stayne*
> *Those cheeks, where only smiles should reign,*
> *The tears streamed down for haste, and all*
> *In chains of liquid pearl did fall.*
> *Fair sorrows; and more dear than joys,*
> *Which are but emptie ayres and noise"*[1]

When divine Causes and human Conditions which are assimilated to them are coordinate to one and the same end, the perfection of such works overflowing returns a pure and most bright reward.

> *Ite profani! Fanum est fanum*
> *Nihil ingreditur profanum.*

For thought does not move, passing its own essence into feeling in vain; but mercy imparts the benefits and gifts of the most exquisite sacrifice.

Nor less instructive than elegant is the following Prosopoiae of the Stone.

> IN NOMINEE DEI VIVENTIS ET VIVIFICANTIS.
> *Terra mihi corpus, vires mihi praestitit ignis:*
> *Alta domus quaero, sedes est semper in imo:*

Mary Anne Atwood

Et me perfundit qui me cito deserit humor

Sunt mihi sunt lacrymae, sed non est causa doloris;
Est iter ad coelum, sed me gravis impedit aer:
Et qui me genuit, sine me non nascitur ipse.

Pulvis aquae tenuis, modico cum poudere lapsus,
Sole madens, aestate fluens, in frigore siccus,
Elumina facturus, totas prius occupo terras ;

Mira tibi referam nostrae primordia vitae :
Nondum natus eram, nec eram tum matris in alvo,
Jam posito partu, natum me nemo videbat.

Non possum nasci, si non occidero matrem:
Occidi matrem, sed me manet exitus idem.
Id mea mors patitur, quod jam mea fecit origo.

Vita mihi mors est, morior si caepero nasci.
Sed prius est fatum lethi quam lucis origo;
Sic solas manes ipsos mihi duco parentes.

Magna quidem non sum, sed inest mihi maxima virtus,
Spiritus est magnus, quamvis in corpore parvo,
Nec mihi germen habet noxam, nec culpa ruborem.

Ambo sumus lapides, una sumus, ambo jacemus
Quam piger est unus, tantum non segnis it alter;
Hic manet immotus non deserit ille moveri.

Findere me nulli possunt, praecidere multi:
Sed sum versicolor, albus quandoque futurus
Malo manere niger, minus ultima fata verebor.

Nulla mihi certa est, nulla est peregrina figura.
Fulgor inest intus, radianti luce coruscus,
Qui nihil ostendit, nisi si quid viderit ante.

Non ego continuo morior dum spiritus exit.

> *Nam redit assiduè, quamvis et saepe recedat:*
> *Et mihi nunc magna est animae, nunc nulla facultas.*
>
> *Plus ego sustinui quam corpus debuit unum.*
> *Tres animas habui, quas omnes intus habebam.*
> *Dicessere duae, sed tertia poene secuta est.* ²

This marvelous subsistence of the Vital Principles in their extreme separation by Art has been already noticed, and will be in the *Practice* more particularly hereafter. It may be sufficient for the present to observe, that great care and diligence is needed at this juncture to apply the threefold secret of the Art; so that the hypostatic principles of attraction and repulsion and circulation may be brought into a perfect equilibriate accord, the one no more acting than the other is resisting in the ethereal bond. —Seek Three in One, and again seek One in Three, dissolve, congeal: and remember, says Kuhnrath, most carefully to observe the animated spirit cannot be conjoined to the body, nor, in the other hand, will the body be reunited to the spirit. Which process, however, being rightly gone through from the beginning—the new Chaos of the Universal Nature of the of the new world will then appear to be unfolded and separated. Apply nomanual labor, but when you shall have enacted the separation,—(*cum percepcris motum in te expieris internum et pro gaudio, lachrymabis!*)—thou wilt surely understand that the original sin has been removed—separated by the Fire of Divine love in the regeneration of the three principles—body, soul and spirit. I write not fables: With thy hands thou shalt touch, and with thy eyes thou shalt see Azoth! The Universal! Which alone, with the internal and external fire in harmonious sympathy with the Olympic Fire, is sufficient for thee: by inevitable necessity, physicochemically united for the consummation of the Philosopher's Stone.³

When in the last extreme of tribulation and departing life, the returning faith and desire of the Passive Spirit attracts the Soul again into herself, the first link in the chain of the magnetic series moves: then the Divine Fiat comes mercifully to bless the union, and a new hypostasis is created out of the darkness to abide: the fiery soul suffers itself again to be imprisoned, as by a lawful magic in the liquid crystal of the understanding ether; and the light which is in her then streams forth brightly rejoicing in her Paradise Regained. Then it is *Lux manifeste et visibilis ad* oculum, as the adept says, in which state it is first made subject to the artist.

Mars et Venus, ou plutôt mars par Venus, en fait une fort noble medicine et précieuse, qui a le grain fixe solaire ; et ces deux font ensemble le mariage si célèbre auprès des amateurs de la sagesse :pendant leur Conjonction, il s'élève une vapeur très spiritueuse et nécessaire à un grand ouvrage : il faut prendre cette vapeur avec des filets bien subtils : dans le reste, on trouve un vitriol bien beau, dont on tire par des opérations fort subtiles et de difficulté découverte, un soûphre solaire ou or philosophique vivant[4].—Which subtle device of Vulcan most profoundly hidden unless the artist shall have rightly conceived either by spiritual aid or himself experimenting in a triune furnace spherically round, his labours are declared to be vain, even though working in the right material, if he cannot cause it to *appear*. If the horse's strength be yet denied, in vain he will strike upon the mountain, the flinty conscience yields no chalybeate, feels no contrition, but by the fiery well-tempered steel.

> Haud licet latices haurire salubres
> Cui scelerum viru mens moribunda tumet:
> Divino calice abstineat, ne cordis ad arcem
> Pervehat arcanam potio iniqua luem.
> Diffluat in lacrymas vehemens quas fervor amoris
> Elicit, et fletu diluat antè scelus.
> Culpa ciens lacrymas non tota est conscia, viru
> Gemma oritur, foedi filia pulchra patris.
> Gutta fluens oculis velut Indicus unio fiet
> Ut medicina reo, sic pretiosa Deo.
> Post lacrymas é fonte potest haurire salutem:
> Qui non flet moritur, ne moriare, fleas[5]

All is sown under the cross and completed in its number—Darkness will draw over the face of the Abyss, Night, Saturn and the Antimony of the Wise will be present, Obscurity and the Head of the Crow in the various hours of conjunction; and all the colours of the world will be apparent; also Iris, God's messenger, and the tail of the peacock; as the rainbow through the falling drops, reflects the sunbeam in the apparent ether after the storms are overpast and the dark clouds are dispersed, the same beautiful token of reconciliation is made apparent in the Microcosmic Heaven; the fire and water are commingled, and, falling together under the cross, germinate, and the beautiful Ideal of Harmony is born of the Spirit.

IN CRUCE SUB SPHERA VENIT SAPIENTIA VERA.

This is the union supersentient, the nuptials sublime, Mentis et Universi; the Thought solitary unites itself to the non-being, or simple Understanding of its ether, and proceeds into simultaneous subsistence with exuberance of power This is the marriage, by the ancients so many times prefigured, of Peleus and Thetis, of Earth and Heaven, when the gods, attended with all their attributes, come together in divine hilarity; of Bacchus and Ariadne; of Jason with Medea, when after many trials and risk of life, he gained with her the golden fleece from Colchos. Lo! Behold I will open to thee a mystery, cries the Adept, the bridegroom crowneth the bride in the North!—In the darkness of the North, out of the crucifixion of the cerebral life, when the sensual dominant is occultated in the Divine Fiat and subdued, there arises a Light wonderfully about the summit, which, wisely returned and multiplied according to the Divine blessing, is made substantive in life.

> *In Arsenic sublimed there is a way straight,*
> *Wyth Mercury calcined, nyne tymes hys weight,*
> *And grownd together with the Water of Myght,*
> *Which beareth ingression of Lyfe and Light.*
> *And anon, as thye together byne,*
> *Alle runnyth to Water bright and schene;*
> *Upon this fire they grow together*
> *Till they be fast and flee no whyther:*
> *Then feed them forth with thine own Hand,*
> *With meat and bread, tyll they be strong,*
> *And thou shalt have a good Stone*[6]

Our golden water, says the adept, is not found in wells, nor in profundities, but in higher places, and as the inhabitants of the Canary Islands draw sweet water from the tree tops, so is ours taken from the higher parts of the world; for Mercury, being ripe, arises to her superior habitation[7]. Exalt her, and she shall promote thee: she shall bring thee to honour when thou dost embrace her; she shall give to thy head an Ornament of Grace; a Crown of Glory shall she deliver unto thee[8]. Return then, O my son, reiterates the Hermetic Master, the coal being extinct in life, as I shall note to thee; and henceforth thou art a Crowned King, resting over the Fountain and drawing from thence the Auripigment, dry without moisture: now I have made the heart of the hearers hoping in thee to rejoice, even in their eyes beholding thee in anticipation of that which thou possessest. Rejoice now, therefore, O son of Art! who hast the Sun for thy Diadem and the Moon Crescent for thy Garland[9].

Ce qui a été attiré doit être cuit si long temps d'une certaine manière de répétition, jusqu'à ce qu'il montre les couleurs de l'arc-en-ciel ; signe de grâce et de reconciliation ; et que les goutes pesantes tombent dans le fond du vase récipient ; quasi comme un mercure commun distille : ce qui vous donnera un Ophtalmique et Antiépileptique merveilleux ; et même quelque chose de plus si le Seigneur vous ouvre les yeux. Cet ouvrage s'appelle Aimantique[10].

Lastly, says Kuhnrath, after the ashy colour, and the white, and the yellow, thou shalt behold the Stone oft eh Philosophers; our King and Lord of hosts go forth from *the chamber* of his *glassy sepulchre*, into this mundane sphere, in his glorified body, regenerate and in *perfection* perfected; as a shining carbuncle, most temperate in splendour; and whose parts, most subtle and most pure, are inseparably blent together in the harmonious rest of union into one[11].

It is an adopted maxim with the Adepts that they who sow in tears shall reap in joy. For he that reenters liberated and with the prepared Light of intellectual faith, mourning, and, like another Achilles, conscious of self-sacrifice, to besiege the fortress of Self-Will in life, prevailing at length through death and every obstacle, the Divine Will favouring, is not only promoted through the whole hypostatis, and converted to the proper virtue and perfection of its root; but there, likewise, to increase, triumph, and multiply, according to the hermaphroditic virtue of its conceived Law. So life is perfected in Wisdom, and the Will springs up in Paradise with fair golden fruits.

> *Corpus solutum est aqua perennis congelans*
> *Mercurium perpetua congelatione.*

Never grudge, then, that thou hast destroyed thye gold, says Eireneus, for he that thus destroys loseth it not, but soweth good seed in good earth, from whence he shall receive it again with one hundred fold increase[12]. Whereas he that saves his gold, that is to say, remains satisfied in the first fruits of his reason, loses his labour, and is deceived, like

Midas, and dismayed for want of understanding and faith in the destination of Causes.

But if any one here demand, how that which is destroyed should be capable of increase, and how the newly implanted motive takes root in life? The Apostle has best answered it; as concerning the mystery of the resurrection, he shows, by the common analogy of nature, the Law to be such. Behold, says he, that which is sown is not the body that shall be, but mere grain, as it may be of wheat or any other grain.—The germ of all Being is indeed corrupted before it is brought forth, and seeds spring up not as seeds merely, but into a perfect semblance of their developed stock; yet it is not anything the more bettered in its kind, but the process of vital melioration is further exemplified in the fermentive art, where, by a contrition and fretting of their elementary particles, natures are transformed, and their bodies spiritualized and preserved by the assimilating must or leaven. So in man,—there is a natural body and a spiritual body. Howbeit that is not first which is spiritual, but that which is natural, and afterwards that which is spiritual.—The Rational Light, once discovered and set in motion, actuates the Spirit, and the Spirit, in its turn penetrating, overcomes the corporeal, which is the sensual dominant, in the regeneration; and so swallows up the same, that it is glorified and transfigured, occultating the body in more luminous manifestation.—Know ye not how a little leaven leaveneth the whole lump? Purge out therefore the old leaven, that ye may be a new lump, as ye are unleavened[13].

SOLVE ET COAGULA, reiterates the Benedictine Monk, Dissolve and Coagulate; after putrefaction succeeds generation, and that because of the *incombustible sulphur* that heats or thickens the coldness and crudities of the *quicksilver*, which *suffers* so much thereby, that at last it is united to the *sulphur* and made one body therewith. And these, viz., the fire, air and water, are contained in one vessel in their earthly vessel, *i.e.*, in their gross body or composition; and I take them and then I leave them in one alembic, where I decoct and sublime them, without the help of hammer, tongs, or file; without coals, smoke, or fire, or bath; or the alembics of the sophisters. For I have my *heavenly fire*, which excites and stirs up the elemental one, according as the matter *desires* a more becoming agreeable Form[14]. And the Light is made manifest in great darkness, viz., in the contrition or distress of the sensible nature in the conscience, where a peculiar motion is present; even then, as Jacob Böhme says, cometh the Power of Christ in the midst of such a motion. And, further, of the noble tincture arising in the light, he says—It cometh forth from anguish into the meekness of the light and springeth forth afresh through the mortifying anguish[15], *as a life having another property*, where the property of the fire is a desiring, and thereby it *attracteth the virtue of the Light* unto itself, and maketh it an essence, viz., WATER.—Common chemistry is not without an analogy of this kind, by the condensation of light producing it into a fluid form, But herein are the two forms: one according to the source of the fire, which is red, and therein the virtue, viz., sulphur is: and the other is like a thin meekness, yet having co-essentiality, is water, which is the desiring tincture; and both of which contracting together into one, are converted into Blood. Now the original in the blood, viz., fire, which is its warmth, is life; and in the virtue of the warmth, the Thin Water of Life proceedeth; one virtue proceedeth forth from another, and the virtue doth always re-assume that which goeth forth. And this is the true Spirit which is born of the Soul, wherein is the Image of God, and the Divine Virgin of God's wisdom consisteth. For all understanding and knowledge lieth in this Spirit; it hath the senses and the noble life, which uniteth it with God: for this Spirit is so subtle that it can enter into God, if it resigneth itself up to Him; and, casting away the cunning fire of its own soul, putteth its will into God; then it dwelleth with Him in *power*, and is *clothed* with the *Divine Essentiality*[16].

And this Essentiality it is which qualifies the true Adept; which sanctifies even as it qualifies, infusing true goodness into every life it has once adorned. It is this material of the Corner-Stone which links reason to Divinity, Theology to the subtle philosophy of the middle ages, and made the vulgarly contemned Art of Alchemy to be honoured and holy.—It is sown in corruption, it is raised in incorruption; It is sown in dishonour, it is raised in glory; t is sown in weakness, it is raised in power; It is sown a natural body, it is raised a spiritual body. The first man is of the earth, earthy; the second man is the Lord from heaven[17].

And this is that great and miraculous mystery of our Image, which it behooves us to reflect into, rather than profanely to discuss; that we may know our true selves, and what Adam, even our Father is; and what the Son; and, without error or presumption, that Holy Spirit which fabricates all things, and sustains all by the Word of his power. —

> *Non poterit ilia dare qui non habet : habet autem nemo, nisi qui jam cohibitis elementis, victa natura superatis coelis, progo suos Angelos, ad ipsum Archetypum isque transcendit ; Cujus tume Cooperator effectus potest Omnia.*

For the soul, being in such a condition, associates with her Efficient, and he who perceives himself so to associate will have a similitude of It with himself. And if he surpasses from himself as an image to the Archetype, he will then attain the end of his progression. And when falling off from the vision of God, if he again excites the virtue which is in himself and perceives himself to be perfectly adorned, he will again, says the Platonic Successor, be elevated, through virtue proceeding to Intellect and Wisdom, and afterwards to the Principle of things.

Vaughan, in his *Anima Magia*, has well described the Hypostatic Metamorphoses; and how the Light, striking in a rapid coruscation from the center to the circumference, depends from the solitary unit through the surrounding vapor, in a vital magnetical series; where the celestial nature, he says, differs not in substance from the aerial spirit but only in degree and complexion; and the aerial differs from the aura or material efflux of the soul in constitution only and not in nature; so that These three, being but One substantially, admit of a perfect hypostatic union, and may be carried by a certain hypostatic union, and may be carried by a certain intellectual Light into the supreme horizon, and so swallowed up of immortality.—Behold I show you a mystery, says the Aristotle, we shall not all *sleep*, but we shall be *changed*; in a moment, in the *twinkling of an eye*, at the last *trump* (for the trumpet shall sound) and the dead shall be raised incorruptible, and we shall be changed. For this corruptible must put on incorruption, and this *mortal* must put on *immortality*[18].

And know, says Roger Bacon, that it is impossible for you to attain this immortal essentiality, unless you become sanctified in mind and purified in soul, so as to be united to God, and to become one spirit with Him. But if you revolve these my instructions in your mind, you may obtain the knowledge of the beginning, the middle, and the end of the whole work. And you will perceive such a *subtlety of Wisdom*, and such a *purity of matter*, as shall amply *replete your soul*, and fill you with *satisfaction*. And when you shall appear thus before the Lord, He will open to you the gates of His treasure, the like of which is not to be found on earth. Behold, I show you *the fear of the Lord*, and *the love of Him*, with unfeigned obedience; nothing shall be wanting to them that fear the Lord, who are *clothed* with the excellency of His holiness: To whom be all praise[19].

For as in the Beginning there was said to be one only matter of all things, so in this imitative process all diversities of things are seen to proceed from and return to this only One; which is called a conversion of the elements, and a conversion of the elements in this respect is just to make active passive and passive active; the occult becoming manifest and the manifest occult in inverse order of conception. And he, says Sendivogius enigmatically, who knows how to congeal water with heat, and to join a spirit thereto, shall certainly find out a thing more precious than gold, and everything else. *Let him therefore cause that the spirit be separated from the water, that it may putrefy and be like a grain. Afterwards, the faeces being cast away, let him reduce and bring back the spirit again from the deep into the water and make them be joined again, for that Conjunction will generate a branch of unlike shape to its parents*[20].

In such a process it was that the Quadrature of the Circle was supernaturally demonstrated; which naturally it cannot be; and in no other way but by a transmutation of the hypostatic relations, as in a circulating medium making passive active and active passive. In the first conjunction the Spirit predominates; in the second the Soul, *i.e.*, its Light; which two are, by adepts, called Mercury and Gold, and the activity of mercury over gold in the first place is because the formal virtue of Sol is sealed; his sulphur is imprisoned, so that he is not aware of it, does not feel or know himself, as we may say, until penetrated by the mercurial Spirit, then he sends forth his Light; to which the Mercury, in turn becoming passive, conceives and bears an offspring more perfect than either parent. And when that light is again taken and given to a proper recipient, it is made a thousand times more fit and apt to bring forth excellent and abundant fruits.

> *Fac ex mare et foemina circulum; inde quadrangulum; hinc triamgulum, fac circulum, et habebis lapidem philosophorum*[21].

For beyond all the four precedent degrees of perfection there is made a Fifth Essence, which neuter from all, yet partaking of all in perpetuity of union, the Ethereal Quadrangle becomes a Circle of golden light in eternity; being advanced into the order of spirits permanent, which, though they have bodies, yet are not subject to those laws of gross corporeity which fetter bodies unregenerate. And therefore the philosopher's Mercury is a system of wonders ponderous, fixed, and, as a petrification from water is, exquisitely compact; yet penetrative withal and communicative of tincture; for it can pass, as it were, in the twinkling of an eye to the very center, and, projected on the imperfect metal of any life, dissolves, drawing away the foundation into itself. Thus the author of

Lucerna Salis describes the gold of the Wise to be by no means vulgar gold; but it is a *certain water clear and pure,* on which is borne *the lightning of the Lord*; and it is from thence that all things receive their life. And this is the reason, continues he, why our gold is become spiritual; by means of the spirit it passes through the *Alembic,* its earth remaining black, which however did not appear before, but now dissolves itself and becomes a *thick water.* The which desires a more noble life, to the end it may be able to *rejoin itself.* By reason of the thirst it has, it dissolves and is dissevered, which benefits it very much; because if it did not become water and oil, its spirit and soul could not unite and mingle with it, as it then does; and in such a manner that of them One Thing is made which rises to a consummate perfection; the parts thereof being so firmly joined together that they can never after be separated[22].

This then is the Conjunction in which all the mysteries of the Microcosm have their consummation—the true circulated Form of Gold; the Conjunction, by Ripley called *tetraptive,* that so highly commended fountain of Pythagoras, and Divine *Tetractys.*

> *Whence all our Wisdom springs, and which contains*
> *Perennial nature's fountain, cause, and root*[23].

Tetractys, fourfold, drawn from three heads by the obstetric hand of the physico-chemical Art and without possibility of dissolution any more; for those principles so joined together of God, man cannot any more put asunder.

> *There is no light but what lives in the Sun,*
> *There is no sun but which is twice begot;*
> *Nature and Arte the parents first begonne:*
> *By Nature 'twas but Nature perfects not.*
> *Art then, what Nature left, in hand doth take,*
> *And out of one a twofold worke doth make.*
>
> *A twofold work doth make, but such a work*
> *As doth admit Division none at all,*
> *(See here wherein the secret, most doth lurke,)*
> *Unless it be a mathematical.*
> *It must be two yet make it one and one,*
> *And you do take the way to make it none.*

> *Lo here, the primary secret of this Arte,*
> *Contemne it not but understand it right,*
> *Who faileth to attain the foremost part,*
> *Shall never know Arte's force or Nature's might.*
> *Nor yet have power of one and one, so mixt,*
> *To make by one fixt, one unfixed fixt*[24].

Here again the geometric method of procedure with the Metaphysical Embryo, through its complex parts, is epigrammatically symbolized by Michael Mayer.

> *Feomina masque unus flunt tibi circulus, ex quo*
> *Surgat habens aequum forma quadrata latus.*
> *Hinc Trigonum ducas, omni qui parte rotundam*
> *In sphaeram redeat:* TUM LAPIS ORTUS ERIT.
> *Si res tanta tuae non mox venit obvia menti.*
> *Dogma Geometrae si capis,* OMNE SCIES[25].

He therefore who discovers the Quadrature, and on this ground is able to demonstrate it, will have a reward sufficient without the University patronage or a more laborious proof. For having resolved all sorts and ideas of things, all thoughts, passions, and actions to one and the same Principe, he will not alone have that Principle, and be able to compose and renumerate every former particular out of the same; but, according to the philosophic report, he will be percipient of the most beautiful and Universal Mystery of Nature; having before himself, as in a glass, the great Archetypal Law of Light, in which are all things causally ranged in the order in which they were originally distributed and set apart. As, in the *Pimander and Book of Wisdom*, we read,—The whole world is before thee, O God! As a little grain of the balance, as a moment of the little tongue in the weights and scales, and as a drop of the dew that falleth in the morning upon the earth[26].—Perfect in the Microcosmic Unit as in the total Deity of the Great World. For no sooner, it is said, does the Divine Light pierce to the *bosom* of the *matter*, but the pattern of the whole universe appears in those Subject Waters, as an image in a glass, conceived and divided forth in all the vastness of ideal distinction and effulgence upon that glorious metaphysical height where the Archetype shadows the intellectual spheres.

> *Tu cuncta superno*
> *Ducis ab exemplo pulchrum pulcherrimus ipse*
> *Mundum mente gerens, similique in imagine formas*[27].

Tell me, ye celestial powers! How first the gods and world were made? The rivers and boundless sea with its raging surge? How the bright shining stars and the wide stretched heaven above, and all the gods that spring from them, givers of good things? First of all existed Chaos; next in order of the broad bosomed Matter; and then Love appeared, the most beautiful of the Immortals. Of Chaos sprung Erebus and dusky night, and of Night came Ether and smiling Day[28].

The theogony of Hesiod, though long esteemed a mere poetical fiction, was accepted by the ancient philosophers, who quote his language; and the Epic Cycle is said, by the Platonists, to include the true philosophic secret of the creation. And when set in comparison with the Alchemical descriptions, the above passage appears indeed to be very regular and correct; as also the continued imagery of the poet, indicative of the several estates of the Ethereal Quintessences arising one above another, called forth by the light and heat of the superincumbent mind, as posterity from a common parent. Indeed, the more closely we compare the cosmogonies of the ancients, the more consistent do they appear one with another, and less so with the commonplace imagination of things: insomuch that the learned have judged them to be copied from some one original, or that the Mosaic was the only revealed truth of all. We are not disposed to rest anything on our own assertion, but neither should we be less inclined to reverence the received Scripture, if it should prove, at any time, that those agreeing with it, were not borrowed; but all originated from the same divine source.

In the Beginning—in that inane Identity—from that silent dead obscurity—when as yet nothing is fashioned in the dissolute chasm of life—the Divine Will, then alone operating, says the Cabalistic Interpreter, produces itself into a material form and recreation.—Behold, I deliver thee of an awful birth and progeny of the ever living god, revealed only to the favourites of Heaven and ministers of His Mysterious Will[29].

And these were a part of the lesson taught by the Memphian prophet to the young Aspirant to the priesthood, even the most hidden mysteries of God's creation. And how did he teach? By words merely, or signs, or traditional authority? Or, if none of these can truly reach the understanding; shall we say, more probably, by passing it inwards to the evolution of its proper mystery, thence to emanate and recreate? When the initiated poet Ovid sat down to write his Fasti, he was inspired, as he declares, by that same universal deity of the two-faced Janus.

> *ME CHAOS antiqui, nam res sum prisca, vocabant.*
> *Adspice, quam longi temporis acta canam.*
> *Lucidus hic Aër, et, quae tria corpora rcstant,*
> *Ignis, aquae, tellus, unus acervus erant.*
> *Ut semel haec rerum secessit lite suarum,*
> *Inque novas abiit massa soluta domos ;*
> *Flamma petit altum ; propior locus aëra cepit :*
> *Sederunt medio terra fretumque solo.*
> *Tunc Ego, qui fueram globus, et sine imagine moles,*
> *In faciem redii dignaque membra Deo.*
> *Nunc quoque, confusae quondam nota parva figurae,*
> *Antè quod est in me, postque, videtur idem.*
> *Accipe, quaesitae quae caussa sit altera formae ;*
> *Hanc simul ut nôris, officiumque meum;*
> *Quidquid ubique vides, coelum, mare, nubila, terras,*
> *Omnia sunt nostra clausa patentque Manu*[30].

When the primeval parent of CHAOS, hoary, as the Egyptian figure runs, with unnumbered ages, was first moved by the breath of EREBUS, she brought forth her enormous first-born HYLE, and, at the same portentuous birth, the amiable EROS, chief of the Immortals. They were no sooner come to Light than they produced an infinite offspring, various and undefined at first, but afterwards fountains of Being. And know, consecrated Youth, adds the metropolitan of Memphis, that ere this fair universe which thou beholdest appeared; ere the sun mounted on high, or the moon gave her paler light; ere the vales were stretched out below, or the mountains reared their towering heads; ere the winds began to blow, or plants had sprung forth out of the earth; while the heavens yet lay hid in the mighty mass, or ere a star had darted to its orb; the various parts of which this wondrous frame consists lay jumbled and inform, brooding overwhelmed in the Abyss of Being. There it had lain for ever, if the breath of the tremendous spirit that dwells in the Darkness had not gone forth and put the lifeless mass in agitation.

> *Sire hunc divino semine fecit*

> *Ille opifex rerum, mundi melioris origo:*
> *Sive recens tellus seductaque nuper ab alto*
> *Aethere, cognati retinebat semina coeli;*
> *Quam satus Iapeto mistam fluvialibus undis*
> *Finxit in effigiem moderantum cuncta deorum*[31].

It was then the congenial poets began to *dissever* from their *heterogeneous* associates, and to seek a mutual embrace: *Matter appeared*: and inseparable from it attraction instantly began to operate. O! who can unfold or sufficiently declare the strife ineffable, the unutterable war, that attended their operation[32].—To whom hath the root of Wisdom been revealed, or who hath known her wise counsels? Unto whom hath the knowledge of Wisdom been made manifest? And who hath understood her great Experience? There is One Wise and greatly to be feared, the Lord sitting upon his throne. He created her and numbered her, and poured her out upon all his works. She is with all flesh according to his gift, and he hath given her to them that love him[33].

And Solomon, with matchless eloquence and beauty that remains unrivalled, celebrates the revelation of that Living Light which became known to him, with the mysteries of universal creation, not by outward teaching or rational inference from effects, but by the Conscious Intuition, as he relates it, of only might. God hath given to me, says the Wise King, a certain knowledge of the things that are, namely, to know *how the world was made, and the operations of the elements.* The beginning, ending, and midst of the times; the alterations and turning of the sun; and the changes of the seasons. The circuits of years and position of the stars. The natures of living creatures and the furies of wild beasts, the violence of winds and the reasonings of men; the diversities of plants and the virtues of roots. And all such things as are either secret or manifest, them I know. For *Wisdom*, which is the Worker of all things, taught me. In her is an *understanding spirit*—holy, only begotten, manifold, subtle, lively, clear, undefiled, plain, not subject to hurt, loving the thing that is good: quiet, which cannot be letted, ready to do good, kind to man, steadfast, free from care, having all power, overseeing all things, and going through all understanding, pure and most subtle spirits[34].

And such a Wisdom (shall we not believe it?) was the worthy object of all Hermetic Philosophy, and the miraculous substance of its transmutative Stone. Or what, do we ask, is the Philosopher's Stone? The philosopher's stone, says the mysterious adeptest, is *Ruach Elohim*, which moved upon the *face of the waters*, the *firmament* being in the midst, conceived and made *body*, truly and *sensibly*, in the virgin womb of the greater world, viz., that Earth which is *without form and water*. The *Son*, born into the light of the macrocosm, mean and of no account in the eyes of the vulgar, consubstantial nevertheless, and like his father the lesser world, setting aside all idea of anything individually human: universal, triune, hermaphrodite; visible, sensible to hearing, to smell, *local* and finite; made *manifest by itself regeneratively by the obstetric hand of the Physico-Chemical Art*: glorified in his once assumed body, for benefits and uses almost infinite; wonderfully salutary to the microcosm in universal triunity. The Salt of Saturn, the Universal son of Nature, has reigned, does reign, and will reign naturally and universally in all things; always and everywhere universal through its own fusibility, self-existent in nature. Hear and attend! Salt, that most ancient principle of the Stone; whose nucleus in the *Decad* guard in holy silence. Let him who hath understanding understand; I have spoken it—not without weighty cause has Salt been dignified with the name of Wisdom; than which, together with the Sun, nothing is found more useful[35].

But what explanation is this?, it will be objected; a baffling about of terms, *ignotum per ingotius*. Truly, and thus it has been the custom of philosophers to ring the changes from Wisdom to their Stone, and from the Stone to Wisdom, through every imaginable note and echoing cadence in variation, round to the same again: but the world has become no wiser for their song. For how hardly should words avail, even the most significant, to convey a tangible idea of that which is beyond and inverse to all sensible experience; which is neither hard nor soft, not tangible nor visible, nor comprehensible by common sense, until thought, by understanding (as light by the focus of the familiar lens, producing combustion), has brought it forth into effect and flame?

Thus considering the inverse problem, analogically however, we arrive at a more familiar conception as reason assists the imagination to a solution to its own intimate mystery in life.

The centre of every Being is a spirit from the original of the world; and the separation of this is constantly enacted in generation, whence every creature is brought through experience into life and operation. And so far we stand even now in the great mystery, in the Mother of all beings; but by the corporeal, *i.e.*, the sensual principle which is predominant in the mundane conception, the divine original is obscured and separated off from the consciousness; and the individual subsists, as a distinct selfspiration, severation, or outbirth, as it were, from that Fontal Reason whence it springs. But in the regeneration this Reason is said to be discovered, as, upon the dissolution of the natural life, it arises through the self-perceivance, with creative attributes and powers. Let us hear the testimony of Hermes concerning his own intimate experience in the divine Poemander, figuratively set forth as follows: —

My thoughts, being once seriously busied about the things that be, and my understanding lifted up, —all my bodily senses being entirely holden back; methought I saw once of an exceeding great stature, and infinite greatness, call me by name, and say to me, What wouldst thou hear and see? And what youldst thou understand to learn and know? Then said I, Who art thou? I am, quoth he, Poemander, the Mind of the Great Lord, the most mighty and absolute Emperor. I know what thou wouldst have, and I am always present with thee. Then, said I, I would learn the things that are, and understand the nature of them, and know God. How? Said he. I answered, that I would gladly hear. Then, said he: *Have me again in thy mind*, and whatsoever thou wouldst learn, I will teach thee.

When he thus said, *he was changed in his Idea or Form, and straightway*, in the *twinkling of an eye*, all things were opened to me; *and I saw an infinite Light, all things were become Light, both sweet and exceeding pleasant*. And I was wonderfully delighted in the beholding it. But after a little while, there was a *darkness* made in part, coming down obliquely, fearful and hideous, which seemed tome unto me to be *changed* into a certain *moist nature unspeakably troubled, which yielded a smoke*, as from *fire*; and there proceeded *a voice unutterable*, and very mournful, but *articulate*: insomuch, that it seemed to have come from the *Light*. Then from that Light a certain holy Word joined itself unto Nature, and *out flew the pure and unmixed fire from the moist nature upward on high*. It was exceedingly light, *sharp, and operative withal*, and the *air*, which was also light, followed the spirit, and mounted up with the Fire (from the earth and water created below) insomuch as it seemed to *hang and depend on it*; and the *earth* and *water* stayed by themselves, so mingled together, that the earth could not be seen for the water; but they were moved because of the Spiritual Word that was carried upon them.

Then said Poemander unto me, Dost thou understand this, and what it meaneth? I shall know, said I. Then said he, *I am that Light, the Mind, they God, who am before that moist nature*, that appeareth out of the *darkness*, and that bright and lightful *Word from the Mind is the Son of God*. How is that? quoth I. Thus, replied he, understand it. *That* which, in thee, seeth and heareth the Word of the Lord, and the Mind, the Father, God, *differ not one from another*, and the union of these is life. I thank thee: But first, said Poemander, *Conceive well the Light in thy Mind, and Know It.*

And when he had *thus* said, for a long time, *we looked steadfastly one upon the other*, insomuch that I *trembled at his Idea or Form*: But when he *nodded* to me, I beheld in my mind the Light that is *innumerable*, and the truly *indefinite ornament or world*, and that the fire is *comprehended* or contained in and by a most great Power, and constrained to keep its station.

These things I understood, seeing the *Word of Poemander*, and when I was mightily *amazed*, he said again unto me; hast thou seen that *Archetypal Form*, which was before the interminated and infinite beginning? But whence, quoth I, or whereof are the elements of nature made? *Of the Will and Counsel of God*, he answered, *which* taking the *Word and beholding* the beautiful world in the Archetype thereof, *imitated it*, and so made this world by the same principles and vital seeds, or soul-like *production of itself*. And straightway, God said to the Holy Word, increase increasingly, and multiply in multitude, all ye my creatures, and workmanships. And let him that is endued with *Mind know himself to be immortal*; and that the cause of death is the love of body, and let him learn all things that are of which he is made. If therefore thou learn in this way, and *believe* thyself to be of the Life and Light, thou shalt pass back into Life.

But tell me more, O my mind! How shall I go into Life? God saith, let the man endued with mind, mark, consider, and *know himself well*. Have not all men a mind? Have a heed what thou sayest, for I, the Mind, mark, consider, and know himself well. Have not all men a mind? Have a heed what thou sayest, for I, the Mind, come into men that are holy and good, and pure and merciful, and that live piously and religiously, and my presence is a help unto them; and forthwith they know all things, and lovingly, they supplicate and propitiate the Father, and *blessing* Him; being ordered and directed by filial affection and natural love; and before they give up their bodies to the death of them, *they hate their senses, knowing their works and operations*; or, rather, I, that am the Mind itself, will not suffer the works or operations which belong to the body to be finished in them; but being the Porter and Door-keeper, *I shut up the entrance of evil*, and cut off the thoughtful desires of filthy works. But to the foolish, and evil, and wicked, and envious, and covetous, and murderers, and profane, *I am far off*, giving place to the *revenging Demon*, which, applying unto him the *sharpness of fire*, tormenteth such a man sensibly, and armeth him the more to all wickedness, that he may obtain the greater punishment, that he may obtain the greater punishment; and such a one never ceaseth unfulfillable desires, and insatiable concupiscences, and always fighting in darkness; for the *Demon* afflicts and torments him, continually increasing the Fire upon him, continually increasing the Fire upon him more and more.

Thou hast, O Mind, said I, most excellently taught me all things, as I *desired*; but tell me moreover, after the *return* is made, what then? First of all, in the resolution of the material body of sense, this body itself is given up to *alteration*, and the form which it hath becometh *invisible*; and the *idle manners* are permitted and left to the *Demon*, and the senses of the body return into their *fountains* (in the circulation); being parts, and are again made up into operations; and anger and concupiscence remain lowest in the irrational life, and the rest strive upward by harmony; until, being naked of all operations, it cometh to the eighth sphere, which is Intellect, having its proper power and singing raises to the Father, with the things that are. And all they that are present rejoice and congratulate the coming of It, begin made like to Him with whim it converseth; it heareth also the powers that are above the eighth nature, singing praises to God in a certain voice that is peculiar to them, and them in order they return to the Father and to themselves.

When Poemander had thus said to me, he was mingled *among the Powers*, but I, giving thanks, and blessing the Father of all, rose up and being enabled by Him, and taught the nature of the Whole, and having seen the greatest Spectacle, I began to preach unto men the beauty, and fairness of piety and knowledge; and becoming a guide unto many, I sowed in them the words of Wisdom. And in myself I wrote the bounty and beneficence of Poemander, and being filled with what I most desired, I was exceedingly glad.—For the sleep of the body was the sober watchfulness of the mind; and the shutting of my eyes the true Sight; and my silence great with child and full of good; and the pronouncing of my words the blossoms and fruits of good things.—And thus it came to pass, and happened unto me by Poemander, the Lord of the Word, whereby I became inspired by God with the Truth. For which cause with my soul and whole strength, I give praise and blessing unto God the Father.—Holy is God the Father of all things! Holy is God whose will is performed and accomplished by His own Powers; Holy is God that determineth to be known; and is known of his own, and those that are His! Holy art thou, that by thy Word hast established all things! Holy art thou, whom nature hath not formed! Holy art thou, that art stronger than all strength! Holy art thou, that art grater than all excellency! Holy art thou, that art better than all praise! O thou unspeakable! Unutterable! To be praised in silence. I beseech thee that I may never err from the knowledge of thee; look mercifully upon me and enable me, and enlighten with thy grace all that are in ignorance, the brothers of my kind, but thy sons. Therefore I beseech thee, and bear witness, and go into the Light and Life. Blessed art thou, I Father! Thy man would be sanctified with thee, as thou hast given him all Power[36].

To such testimony we are unable to add anything that would render the operative revelation of Intellect more obvious, or its experimental knowledge more credible to the uninitiated. They who cannot imagine will disbelieve without experience; but others there may be, at this day even, in whom the flame of thought burns broad and clear, who having within them a substantial evidence of the thing hoped for, will believe and know too, long before sensible observation shall have forced the many to a faith which, in the Intuition alone, is blessed. But if any one wish to discover the First Principle, according to the doctrine of the ancients, he must be theurgically prepared, and pass through many preliminary ordeals, corrosive tests, and fiery solutions and dissolutions refining, in order to raise himself to That which is the most united in nature, and to its Flower, and That through which it is Deity; by which it is suspended from its proper fountain, and connects and causes the Universe to have a sympathetic consent with Itself. —And if it called them gods unto whom the Word of God came, and the Scripture cannot be broken, say ye of Him whom the Father hath sanctified and sent into the world, thou blasphemest, because I said I am the Son of God[37]. Does not all our unbelief, as the common faith, arise in ignorance? For at present there is no profound understanding of the Scriptures; nor does any look, as Agrippa says, under the Bark of the Law. But even unto this day, when Moses is read, the veil is upon their heart. Nevertheless, when it shall turn to the Lord, says the Apostle, the veil shall be taken away. For the Lord is that Spirit, and where the Spirit of the Lord is, there is liberty. We all, with open face beholding, as in a glass, the glory of the Lord, are changed into the same image from glory to glory, even as by the Spirit of the Lord[38]. Unhappy, truly therefore he is said to be, who regards the law as a mere simple recital, or in the light of an ordinary discourse, for, if in truth it were nothing more than this, one could even be composed a this day more worthy of admiration. In order to find such mere words, observes the cabalist, we have only to turn to the legislators of this world, who have frequently expressed themselves with more grandeur and grace. It would suffice to imitate them, and make expedient laws after their fashion. But it is not thus; each word of the Law has a meaning and cloaks a mystery entirely sublime. The story of the Law is the vestment of the Law; unhappy he, who mistakes the vestment for the Law itself. The wise attend not to the outer clothing of things, but to the body which it covers; the sages and servants of the Supreme King, those who dwell on the heights of Sinai, are occupied only about the Soul, which is the basis of all rest; which is the Law itself; so that they may be prepared at length to contemplate and know that Soul which breathes in the Law[39]. Without which nothing is truly known; whose Experience is All. Moreover, says St. Paul, I would not that ye should be ignorant, how that all our Fathers were under the cloud, and all *passed through* the *sea*; and were all *baptized* unto *Moses* in the *cloud* and in the *sea*; and did all eat the same spiritual meat, and did all drink the same *spiritual drink*: for they drank of that *spiritual rock* that followed them: and that *rock* was *Christ*[40].

And I advise thee, my son, says the Saint Synesius, to make no account of other things; labour only for *that Water* which burns to blackness, dissolves and congeals. It is that which putrefies and causes germination, and therefore I advise thee that thou wholly employ thyself in the coction of this water, and demur not at the expense of time; otherwise thou shalt gain no advantage. Decoct it *gently* by little and little, until it have changed its false tincture into a perfect form of light; and have great care at the beginning, that thou burn not its flowers and its vivacity, and make not too much haste to come to an end of thy work[41]. *Shut thy vessel* well that it may not breathe out, so that thou mayest bring it to some *effect*[42]; and not that to dissolve, to calcine, to tinge, to whiten, to renew, to bathe, to wash, to coagulate, to imbibe, to decoct, to fix, to grind, to dry and to distill are all one, and signify no more than to decoct nature until such time as she be *perfected*. Note further, that to extract the soul, or the spirit, or the body, is nothing else than the aforesaid calcinations in regard they signify the operation of Venus. It is through the fire of the extraction of the soul that the spirit comes forth gently; understand me, the same also may be said of the extraction of the soul out of the body, and the reduction of it afterwards upon the same body; until the whole be drawn to a commixion of the four elements, and so that which is below, being like that which is above, there are made *manifest two luminaries*, the one fixed, the other not; whereof the fixed which is the male remains below, and the volatile remains above, moving itself perpetually, until that which is below rises upon that which is above, and all being substantiated, there then issues forth an incomparable Luminary[43].

That was the Experiment that led our Fathers into Experience, and illumination in the Divine Antecedent of all life. And if experience be truly, as it is said to be, the proper test of philosophy, then was not theirs the right and true philosophy with Christian regeneration for its most worthy end? That was the Art of Democritus commemorated by Lord Bacon in a passage before quoted, but which, for its value's sake, as well as on account of the notoriety, we take leave to recite—That if any skillful minister of nature shall apply force to matter, and by design torture and vex it in order to its annihilation, it, on the contrary, being brought under this necessity, changes and transforms itself into a strange variety of shapes and appearances; so that at length, running through the whole circle of transformations and completing its period, *it restores itself*, if the force be continued. And that method of binding, torturing, and detaining will prove the most effectual and expeditious which makes use of manacles and fetters; that is to say, lays hold of and works upon matter in the extremest degrees[44]. That is, in the last exigence of life; when it is about to be born again from out the oblivion of this worked and its defilements, by attraction of the recreative Light within.

Then she is Isis, the Divine I AM, by the Greeks called Myrionymous, or the goddess with a thousand names; hereby to denote the capacity with which such a Matter is endowed of understanding, and of being converted to all or any of the Forms or degrees of specific Law, which it may please the Supreme Reason to impress upon her. As respects herself, she is *Nothing*;—no one apostate particular,—neither animal nor vegetable nor mineral apart; but,—pre-existent to them all,—she is the mother of all; and her birth, according to the Adepts, is singular and not without a miracle. Her very complexion is miraculous and different from every other whatsoever, and that which she brings forth by the Fire of nature lawfully conceived, is is miraculous and different from every other whatsoever, and that which she brings forth by the Fire of nature lawfully conceived, is Orus, the Philosophic Sun. And hence, and from the whole above, we may have gathered some approximating idea of the multinominal goddess appearing as she was described by the initiated, who celebrated her Mysteries in the Eleusian fane, and further, as follows, by one of the no less intimately experienced fraternity of the Rosy Cross.

I am a Goddess for beauty and extraction, famous, born out of our *own proper sea*, which compasseth the whole earth, and is ever restless. Out of my breast I pour forth milk and blood; boil these two till they are turned into silver and gold. O, most excellent subject! Out of which all things in the world are generated. Though at the first sight thou art poison adorned with the name of the flying eagle; thou are the *First Matter*: the *Seed* of Divine benediction, in whose *body* there is *heat* and *rain*; which notwithstanding are hidden from the wicked, because of thy *habit* and *virgin vestures*, which are scattered over the whole world. Thy parents are the Sun and Moon (philosophical); in thee there is *water* and *wine*, and *gold* also, and *silver* upon the *earth*, that mortal man may rejoice. After this manner God sends us his blessing and wisdom with rain, and the beams of the *sun*, to the eternal glory of his name. But consider, O man, what things God bestows upon thee by these means. *Torture the* EAGLE *till she weeps; and the* LION *being weakened, bleeds to death.* The blood of this Lion incorporated with the *tears* of the *Eagle* is the treasure of the whole earth. These creatures used (in their circulatory course) to devour and kill one another; but notwithstanding this their love is mutual, and they put on the property and nature of a Salamander; which, if it remains in the fire without any detriment, cures all the diseases of men and metals. After that the ancient philosophers had perfectly understood this subject they diligently sought in this mystery, for the center of the middlemost tree in the *Terrestrial Paradise*, entering in by five *litigious gates*. The first gate was the *knowledge of the true matter*, and here arose the first, and that a most bitter conflict. The second was the *preparation* by which the matter was to be qualified, that they might obtain the embers of the *eagle* and the *blood* of the *lion*. At this gate there is a most *sharp fight*, for it produceth *water* and *blood*, and the *blood* of the *lion*. At this gate there is a most sharp fight, for it produceth *water* and *blood*, and a *spiritual bright body*. The third gate is the *fire* which conduceth to the *maturity* of the *medicine*. The fourth gate is that of *multiplication* and *augmentation* in which *proportions* and *weights* are necessary. The fifth and last gate is *projection*. But most glorious, full, rich, and highly elevated is he who attains but to the fourth gate; for his has got an universal medicine for all diseases. This is the great character of *the book of Nature*, out of which her whole *alphabet* doth arise. The fifth gate serves only for *metals*. This mystery, existing from the foundation of the world and the creation of *Adam*, is of all others the most ancient; a knowledge which God Almighty, by his Word, breathed into nature; a miraculous power, the blessed Fire of Life; the transparent carbuncle and red gold of the Wise men, and the divine benediction of this life. But this mystery, because of the malice and wickedness of men, is given only to few; notwithstanding it lives and moves every day in the *sight* of the whole world, as it appears also by the following parable:

I am a poisonous dragon, present everywhere, and to be had for *nothing*. My water and my fire dissolve and compound; out of my body thou shall draw the green and red lion; but if thou dost not *exactly* know me, thou wilt with my fire destroy thy *five senses*. A most pernicious quick-poison comes out of my nostrils, which hath been the destruction of many. *Separate*, therefore, the thick from the thin *artificially*, unless thou dost delight in extreme *poverty*. I give thee faculties both male and female, and the powers both of heaven and earth. The mysteries of my art are to be performed *magnanimously* and with great courage, if thou wouldst have me overcome the violence of the fire, in which attempt many have lost their labour and their substance. *I am the Egg of nature, known only to the Wise*, such as are pious and modest, who make of me a little world. Ordained was I, by the Almighty God, for men; but though many desire me, I am given only to a few, that they may relieve the poor with my treasures, and not set their mind on gold that perisheth. I am called of the philosophers Mercury: my husband is *Gold philosophical*. I am the Old Dragon that is present everywhere on the face of the earth. I am father and mother, youthful and antique, weak yet powerful, life and death, visible and invisible, hard and soft, descending to the earth and ascending to the heavens, most high and most low, light and heavy. In me the order of nature is *oftentimes inverted* in colour, number, weight and measure. I am, within, the Light of nature; I am dark and bright: I spring from the earth and I come out of heaven; I am well known and yet a mere nothing; all colours shine in me and all metals, by the beams of the Sun; I am the carbuncle of the Sun, a most noble clarified Earth, by which thou mayest turn copper, iron, tin, and lead into most pure gold[45].

Involve we then our thoughts, if we would intrinsically conceive the wonderful Nature that is set before us; and in however small a proportion the grain of faith be naturally allotted, if it be but real, let us believe in it, and nourish and educate, that it may increase with knowledge, and finally prove its own reward in practical experience: without faith, without the ideal conception, nothing is or can be proven; for is not this, in fact, the leader of all experimental inquiry? The faith we invite is no blind credulity, but such a liberty of thought, as, bearing its own evidence independently of common observation, can glance beyond this boundary into the integral probability of Life. Such a faith, however small or insufficient of itself, will lead on, by a proper pursuit, unto the thing hoped for, and bring to evidence the occult Causality of Nature: and be it for gold, then, or science, or health, or higher purity and wisdom, he is inquiring on this basis—we repeat it—the percipient right-believer will not be deceived.

The Matter of all things is One and proved simple in the experience; throughout all her various manifestations—as agent, patient, hot, cold, dry, moist; by whatever colour, quality or species designated—whether singular or plural in manifestation, Nature remains one and the same Unknown Identity through all; neither water, air, earth, nor gold is so compact, every tyro in chemistry concludes they are no elements; but Her, the true element, they have never found; for she eludes their tests and closest vessels; all except those of her own ethereally wise construction, in which she bears her Universal Offspring, hermetically sealed through the flood and wreck of this dissolute existence to a resurrection always glorious, and immortal at last.

> AELIA LAELIA CRISPIS.
> *Nec vir, nec mulier, nec androgyna,*
> *Nee puella, nec juvenis, nec anus,*
> *Nec casta, nec meretrix, nec pudica,*
> *Sed omnia !*
> *Sublata neque fame, neque ferro, neque*
> *Veneno, sed omnibus !*
> *Nec coelo, nec terris, nec aquis,*
> *Sed ubique jacet !*
>
> LUCIUS AGATHO PRISCUS. *Nec maritus, nec amator, nec*
>   *necessarius,*
> *Neque moerens, neque gaudens, neque flens,*
> *Hanc*
> *Neque molem, neque pyramidem, neque sepulcrum, Sed omnia!*
> *Scit et nescit cui posuerit,*
> *Hoc est sepulcrum certè, cadaver*
> *Non habens, sed cadaver idem,*
> *Est et sepulcrum !*
>
> AELIA LAELIA CRISPIS.
> *No male, nor female, nor hermaphrodite,*
> *Nor virgin, woman, young or old,*

Nor chaste, nor harlot, modest hight,
But all of them you're told —
Not killed by poison, famine, sword,
But each one had its share,
Not in heaven, earth, or water broad
It lies, but everywhere!

LUCIUS AGATHO PRISCUS.
No husband, lover, kinsman, friend,
Rejoicing, sorrowing at life's end.
Knows or knows not, for whom is placed
This—what?
This pyramid, so raised and graced
This grave, this sepulcher?
'Tis neither,
'Tis neither—but 'tis all and each together.
Without a body I aver,
This is in truth a sepulcher;
But notwithstanding, I proclaim
Both corpse and sepulcher the same!

All is identical—need we repeat it?—in the Universal Identity, and every possible assertion of it will be true, and the reverse in annihilation. All life, body, soul, and spirit—the three hypostatic relations—are born in it, one out of another: conjoin, die, and are mortified, one within the other; are fortified and increased, the one by the other; differing only, in respect either one of the other, as agent, patient, and that universal offspring which is the All in all, without foreign admixture: as it is written,—Thou hast disposed all things, in number, weight, and measure.— For these are the length, and breadth, and profundity of Nature, which the Spirit in her emanative Law displays; from the point proceeding into the line, from the root into the square superficies, and from the square by multiplication into that cubic form which is the supernatural foundation of the New physical Whole.

The battle's fought, the conquest won,
The Lyon dead revived;
The Eagle's dead which did him slay,
And both of sense deprived.

The showers cease, the dews, which fell
For six weeks, do not rise;
The ugly toad, that did so swell,
With swelling, bursts and dies.
The Argent field with Or is stained,
With violet intermixed;
The sable blacke is not disdained
Which shows the spirit's fixed;
The compound into atoms turned,
The seeds together blended,
The flying soul to th' earth returned,
The soaring bird descended.
The king and queen contumulate,
And joined as one together,
That which before was two by fate
Is tyed, which none can sever.
The king is brother to his wife,
And she to him is mother;
One father is to both, whose life
Depends upon each other.
The one when dead, the other dies,
And both are laid in grave;
The coffins one in which both lies,
Each doth the other save:
Yet each the other doth destroy,
And yet both are amended;
One without th' other hath no joy,
Both one, of one descended.
Twice forty days do come and go,
To which twice five are added;
These do produce a perfect crow,
Whose blackness cheers hearts sadded;
Twice fifteen more produce a dove,
Whose wings are bright and tender;
Twice ten more make the soul above
To need no fire defender;
For soul and body so combine,
The spirit interceding,
Tincture to give of silver fine,

MARY ANNE ATWOOD

> *The soul, the body, inleading.*
> *Also such fixity to add*
> *Against the flames prevailing,*
> *Which may the chymist make full glad,*
> *The sophister still failing,*
> *Who seeks in fancies for to find*
> *Our Art so much concealed,*
> *Not duly weighing in his mind*
> *That 't is a fountain sealed,*
> *Which one thing only can unlocke;*
> *This one things learn to know,*
> *Lest you the same event should mock,*
> *That these same lines do show*[46].

The same tradition of the manifold powers and preservation of the One Thing runs in symbol throughout the Gentile Mythology, and the Arkite Mysteries have reference to the physical secret of the regeneration throughout the Gentile Mythology, and the Arkite Mysteries have reference to the physical secret of the regeneration throughout. The god, dead and revived, is a principal character in all their ceremonial rites— Cadmillus amongst the Cabiri, Atys in Phrygia, Adonis in Lydia, Osiris amongst the Egyptians.

> *Once to by Thee, as sacred poets sing,*
> *The heart of Bacchus, swiftly slaughtered king,*
> *Was saved in Aether when, by fury fired,*
> *The Titans fell against his life conspired;*
> *And with relentless rage and thirst for gore*
> *Their hands his members into fragments tore.*
> *But ever watchful on thy Father's will,*
> *Thy power preserved him from succeeding ill,*
> *Till from the secret counsels of his Sire,*
> *And from the secret counsels of his Sire,*
> *And born from Semele thro' heavenly fire,*
> *Great Dionysius to the world at length*
> *Again appeared with renovated strength*
> *Once too thy warlike axe with matchless sway*
> *Lopped from their savage necks the heads away*
> *Of furious beasts, and thus the pests destroyed*

> Which long all-seeing Hecate annoyed,
> By thee benevolent, great Juno's might
> Was roused to furnish mortals with delight;
> And thro' life's wide and various range 'tis thine,
> Each part to beautify with arts divine.
> Invigorated hence, by thee we find
> A demiurgic impulse in the mind;
> Towers proudly raised and for protection strong,
> To thee dread guardian Deity belong,
> As proper symbols of th' exalted height,
> Thy series claims amidst the courts of Light[47].

All the heroes are reported to have passed though an ordeal of the same kind;—Cadmus, Deucalion, Osiris, Bacchus, Hercules, Orpheus, etc.,—and to have gained wonderful powers and advantages thereby. All their adventures, indeed, are so many records of the difficulties and dangers that the soul must endure overcoming her household enemies within the stronghold of life. Nor are they few, but many and fearful ones that have to be encountered; for those passions, desires, vices, which t or deadened conscience are trifling and palliable, when viewed within the senses' prison, by the revealed light of equilibrate justice, are monstrous; and, without a metaphor, in their imaged atmosphere appear terrific; and in the divine language of Poemander, do force the inwardly placed man to suffer sensibly. For they do not suddenly depart, or easily, even from him in whom the exemplary virtue is revealed; but, as we may remember in the early tradition of Mysteries, the material inflictors are roused to vengeance by the decrees of fate against the rebels of her laws; nor is it any trifling exertion which the will has to make to overcome the compact which it has made to sense; but herein consists the meritorious struggle of the powers, until, by artificial force of heat and exhalation, the Light, so long hidden and enshrined in the Archaeus, comes forth as a dry splendour, surviving through all. And this is that Tincture of the Sapphiric Mine before alluded to, and that Subtendent which is found seminally equal to the whole of the parts whence it is derived. *In hac aqua rosa latet hieme*; in this water, when destruction has done its worst with the elements of life, the principle of all is artificially preserved, as Noah in the Ark, who, surviving, was able to renew all things out of the remnant of creation that was saved therein; that elect remnant, worthy the sacrifice that was made even of the whole corruptible humanity, that has power to reproduce all and each with tenfold perfection and increase out of itself.

Thus Wisdom is the perpetual theme of early poetry, and though unknown to modern philosophy the ground of ancient science; of theology, the true End and proper subject of Divinity. For this Wisdom is the vehicle of the Catholic Reason in Identity, the bearer and measure of the Demiurgic Fire—that Fire which the sensual conception occultates, and so forcibly restricts, that man does not suspect it even; but in his willing thralldom, fancies himself at liberty, not knowing in truth what it is to be free when, the integral efficience of this Identity set in motion, effects follows the voluntary Axle in a necessitous full accord.—That was free Will, not the motiveless chimera which human fancy has been prone to coin, but the operative Almighty Magnet freed from Tartarean bondage and obscurity, and drawn upward to the glorious consciousness of the revolving Light above.

And the whole secret of this discovery, it would seem, consists in the sanquinary circulation of the Vital Spirit; in which there is a threefold Law, as before explained, which has to be revolutionized also in three period; called by the Alchemists, for certain accurate reason, Altitude, Latitude and Profundity; Altitude and Profundity, being united at their extreme poles, make Latitude; and so the wheel of Life is turned about: the Profundity is the subjective life, the water that is below; the Altitude is the objective Light, the steam that is above; and the conflux of these two is in a Calx, out of which, as from a rocky fountain, the physical Tetractys springs through the contrite experience into life, with attributes prolific and enduring fruits.

That was the Water so much magnified by the wise Adepts, the miraculous product of the spiritual poles of mind in sublime conjunction at their source; this was their *Stilla roris, Lac Virginis, Elixir, Aqua Vitae, Azoth, Prima Materia Lapis et Rebis*, regenerate in its once assumed body, visible, tangible, and sensible to every sense, local and finite, made manifest of itself regeneratively, by the obstetric hand of the physico-chemical art for benefits and uses almost infinite.

> *Fresher liquor there is none to taste,*
> *And it will never consume nor waste;*
> *Tho' it will never be less in store;*
> *Which Democrit named to his intent,*
> *Lux umbra caresn, Water most orient;*

> And Hermes said, no liquor so necessary,
> As was water of crude Mercury:
> And this shall stand, said that noble clerke,
> For the Water within our werke[48].

Another Tablet is here which Philosophy upon a time grateful, erected to the memory of her early friend.

> Blessed be thou, Experience!
> Full mighty is thy Influence,
> Thy wondrous works record full well,
> In world of worlds where thou dost dwell;
> In earth, in heave, and in hell,
> That thou art the very same,
> That didst from nothing all things frame;
> Wherefore, now blessed thy name!
> By whose pure and simple Light,
> All creaton sprung forth Bright,
> Flames and floods began to roar,
> And to present their hidden store
> Of spirits, that sing evermore,
> All glory and magnificence,
> All humble thanks and reverence,
> Be given to Experience!
> To that most Sapient,
> The High Omnipotent!
> That said, Be IT, and it was done,
> Our earth, our heaven, were begun;
> I am, quoth she, the most in might,
> In word, in life, and eke in light,
> In mercy and in judgment right.
> He depth is mine, and so is the Height,
> The Cold, the Hot, the Moist, the Dry,
> Where all in all is, there Am I.

What thing can tell when I began, or where I make an end, Wherewith I wrought, and what I might, or what I did intend To do, when I had done The work I had begun?

For when my Being was alone,
One Thing I made when there was none;
A mass confused and darkly clad,
That in itself, all Nature had To form and shape the good and bad;
And then, as time began to fall,
It pleased me the same to call,
The first Material Mother of all.
And from that lump divided I foure sundry elements,
When I commanded for toreigne in divers regiments;
In kind they did agree,
But not in qualitye.
Whose simple substance I did take,
My seat invisible to make;
And of the qualities compound,
I made the starry sky so round,
With living bodies on the ground,
And blessed them infinitely,
And bade them grow and multiply!
One tings was employed,
Which shall not be destroyed;
It compasseth the world so round,
A matter easy to be found,
And yet most hard to come by:
A secret of secrets pardye,
That is most vile and least set by,
But it's my love and darling,
Conceived with all living ting,
And travels to the world's ending
A childe begetting his own Father, and bearing hys Mother,
Killing himself to give life and light to all other,
Is that I meane,
Most milde and most extreme.
Did not the world that dwelt in me
Take form and walk forth visibly;
And did not I then dwell in It,
That dwelt in me for to unite,
Three Powers in one seat to sit[49].

And these are the Three continually noted in Alchemy, the Sulphur and Mercury and Slat, the active and the passive, and the resulting experience of life. The first, I the regeneration, is the Word of God independent without all human will, miraculously conceived and confessed Divine in the new birth: the second is of the Humanity, *i.e.*, of the selfhood, prepared and sanctified; and the result of these two in unison is the Bodily Substance of things thenceforth created. By a severance from real being, nonbeing, that is to say matte, s produced; and the sacrifice that is gratefully provided of the material nature in their reunion, as supplying body to the Divine, excites the Powers to participation, conceives them when they accede, and consciously unfolds them into visibility and act. And hence we may be enabled to conceive perhaps, in a measure at least, how the microcosmical tradition arose, how the human hypostatis becomes, through a self-perceivance, into universal intelligence, and of its own voluntary resignation, of the nothingness of self oblivion, to be the All, precedent to that wherein is all. For with the desire of rest and contact, there is a power of accessions, and with accession a sufficiency, operative and universal.

Come and see, says the Rabbi in Zohar, Thought is the Principle of all that is; but it is as first *Unknown* and shut up in itself. When the Thought begins to develop itself forth, it arrives at that degree when it becomes *Spirit*. Arrived at this estate, it takes the name of *Intelligence*, and is no longer as before it was shut up in itself. The Spirit, in its turn, develops itself in the bosom of the mystery with which it was shut up in itself. He Spirit, in its turn, develops itself in the *bosom of the mystery* with which it is surrounded; and there proceeds a voice which is the reunion of the celestial choirs, a voice which rolls forth in distinct utterance articulate, for It comes from the Mind[50].

THOUGHT IS THE PRINCIPLE OF ALL THAT IS. Magnificent, yet impervious assertion, shall we say? Or what conceptive height may struggle to confirm it? What imagination strong or hardy enough to glance into the full faith? To Be the Understanding of that Light, of which all Nature is the Efflux, to move One with the First Mover, and Be His Will, who is at once the Antecedent and Final Cause of all? We cannot, profanely as we live without the knowledge of ourselves, attain to the Divine Idea; either to entertain or think It self-actively is impossible. For the Thought which is of God creative is the inversion of our thought; and to know Him in It is self-annihilation in the life which is eternal.

Yet if thou wilt even break the Whole, instructs Poemander, and see those things that are without the world, thou mayest. Behold how great power and swiftness thou hast! Consider that which contains all things, andunderstand that nothing is more capricious than that which is incorporeal, nothing more swift, nothing more powerful; but it is most capacious, most swift, and most strong. And judge of this by thyself, assimilating, for the like is intelligible by the like. Increase thyself into an immeasurable greatness, leaping beyond every body, and transcending time, become Eternity, and thou shalt understand God. If thou art able to believe in thyself, that nothing is impossible, but perceivest thyself to be immortal, and that thou canst understand all things, every art, every science, and the manner and custom of every living thing; become higher than all height, lower than all depth, comprehend in thyself the qualities of all the creatures; of the fire, the water, the dry, and the moist, and conceive likewise that thou canst at once be everywhere, in the sea and in the earth; Thou shalt at once understand thyself, not yet begotten, in the womb, young, old, to be dead, the things after death and all these together, as also times, places, deeds, qualities, or else thou canst not yet understand God. But if thou has shut up thy soul in the body, to abuse it; and say, I understand nothing, I can do nothing, I am afraid of the sea, I cannot climb up into heaven, I know not who I am, I cannot tell what I shall be; what hast thou to do with God? For thou canst understand none of those fair and good things, and It is the greatest evil not to know God. But to be able to know, and to will, and to hope, is the straight way and the divine way proper to the Good; and it will meet thee everywhere thereafter and everywhere be seen of thee, plain and easy, even when thou dost no longer expect or look for it. It will meet the waking, sleeping, sailing, traveling by night and by day, when thou speakest and when thou keepest silence. For there is nothing which is not the Image of God[51].

But the exemplary Logos is hidden,—slain from the foundation in the exterminating fiat of our Identity; and the occultation of this does not take place therefore, but in two poles or principles diametrically reverse. We must pass the eternal wheel of the vicissitudes of things, from the manifest created individuality, back into the Initial germ; through all ages, all revolutions and the infinitude of soul experience, until life, as an ocean tide flowing to its extreme boundary, returns to refund its treasury again its First Source. Most mighty and surpassing magic of Reflection.—And thou august Mother of all things, Divine Experience.—Thought emanating Light, as by Intelligence excruciated, Life springs forth with motion, feeling itself to Be.—In the which affirmation, in the Divine I Am, is by the Cabal signified the Substant Unity of all that is; the fountain of Universal nature and her Exemplary Law, the source of so many miracles and magical accordances, as of every natural and supernatural increase—where Experience is present with Power, and Effect in substance to bear them witness—where WISDOM IS POURED FORTH LIKE WATER AND GLORY FAILETH NOT BEFORE HIM FOR EVER.

For visibles here are said verily to spring out of that which is invisible, as from the precedent nothingness Something is produced; and thus the recreation was seen to be a stupendous metaphysical birth out of the Infinite into Light, according to that notable saying of the Sybil in Boissard,

VERBUM INVISIBLE FIET PALPABILE ET GERMINABIT UT RADIX.

Ought we not therefore to take That which is impalpable and imperfectly conceived at first, and work faithfully, as the philosopher tells us, until it be the Divine pleasure to make it appear; to dissolve, coagulate, resolve, refine, and regulate, until reason BECOMING A BRIGHT Light in the periphery of her fiery essence remains immortal, and is the Mistress of Life?

HIC EST MERCURIUS NOSTER NOBILLISSIMUS, ET DEUS NUNQUAM CREAVIT REM NOBILIOREM SUB COELO PRAETER ANIMAM RATIONALEM.

And here the External and Internal Worlds were seen to blend together in confluent harmony, proving and establishing each other, and leaving reason nothing more to doubt of, or the senses to desire, but a fulfillment under the Universal Law.

---

1. Vaughan's Coelum Terrae, p. 93, etc.
2. Theatrum Chemicum, vol. iii., p. 763
3. Kuhnrath, Amph. Sap. Etern., Isag. in fig. cap. viii.
4. Mystère de la Croix, chap. xiii.
5. Orpheus Eucharisticus Emblema LVI.—Apodosis.
6. Pierce, the Black Monk, on the Elixir.
7. Mercury's Caducean Rod, sub init.
8. Proverbs of Solomon, iv, 8, 9.
9. Tract. Aur., cap. ii., and Ripley Revived.
10. Mystère de la Crois, chap. xiii.
11. Kuhnrath, Amph. Sap. Etern., chap. viii.
12. Ripley Revived, pp. 108, 198.
13. 1 Corinthians, xv.: 6,7.

14. Mehung in Vaughan's Coelum Terrae, p. 122.
15. And, therefore, Hermes says, that the sure quality of the golden m,atter and the nature thereof is not sweetness, etc., cap. vii.
16. Böhme's Turned Eye, Quest. 37.
17. 1 Corinthians xv.: 42, etc.
18. I Corinthians, xv.: 51, etc.
19. Rogeri Bachonis Radix Mundi, lib. iii.
20. Sendivogius, New Light, Treatise v; Kuhnrath, Amph. Sap., cap. viii.
21. Maieri Atalanta Fugiens, Emblema xxi.
22. Lucerna Salis, p. 39 : from the latin verse, Aurum Sapientum &c.
23. Jamblichus' Life of Pythagoras, chap. 28
24. Enigma Philosophicum, Ashmole's Theatrum, p. 423
25. Maier Atalanta Fugiens, Epigramma xxi.
26. Chap. xi., ver. 22
27. And this appearance of the Universal Idea in the mind is singularly corroborated in that spiritual analysis of ordinary bodies which Paracelsus and Van Helmont allude to, saying, that by separation of their parts the specific impress is to be perceived in the vessel containing the decomposed spirit, and that the whole creature may be also resuscitated from thence—these are the words of Marcus, in his Defensio Idearum Operaticium. *Quid quaesco dicerunt hi tanti philosophi, si plantam quasi momento nasci in vitreo case viderent, cum suis ad vivum coloribus, et rursum interire, et renasci, idque quoties, et quando luberet? Credo daemonum arte magica inclusum dicerent illudere sensibus humanis.* Such an impress, however, whether real or fictitiously represented, would be but as a secondary vestiment or witness of that which is in the Archetypal mind creatively efficient.
28. Hesiod, Epic Cycle, The Weeks and the Days.
29. Blackwell's Mythology, letter vii.
30. Ovidii Fastorum, lib. i.104
31. Ovid, Metam., lib. I.
32. Blackwell's Mythology, letter vii.
33. Ecclesiasticus i.:6, 7, 8, &c.
34. Wisdom of Solomon vii. 9
35. Kuhnrath, Amphitheatr. Sap. Etern., Isag. in fig.
36. The Divine Poemander of Hermes Trismegistus, book ii.
37. St John's Gospel, x.
38. 1 Corinth. iii.15, &c.
39. Zohar, part iii., fol. 152, verso; Frank, p. 165; Origen Homil. 7, in Levit.
40. 1 Cor. x. 1,2,3,4.
41. See Lumen de Lumine, p. 66. Norton's Ordinal, cap.iii.
42. Eireneus's Experiments, at the end of his Ripley Revived, p. 6, etc.. Norton, etc.
43. From Synesius' True Book concerning the Philosopher's Stopne, in fine.
44. Bacon's Wisdom of the Ancient, Fable of Proteus.
45. As given in the Coelum Terrae of Vaughan, from the Latin original of the Fraternity.
46. Eireneus's Ripley Revived, p. 188, &c.
47. Proclus' Hymn to Minerva, by Taylor, in his Sallust.
48. See Norton's Ordinal, chap. iv.
49. See Ashmole's Theat., p. 336; Experience and Philosophy.
50. Part i. 246 verso; Frank. Part ii. p. 101
51. Hermes' Divine Poemander, book x.

Chapter 4. Of the mental requisites and impediments incidental to individuals either as Masters or Students in the Hermetic Art

TO WHICH ARE ADDED VARIOUS PRACTICAL INSTRUCTIONS CONCERNING THE MEANS AND INSTRUMENTS THAT HAVE TO BE ARRANGED AND CALLED TOGETHER IN FURTHERANCE OF THIS UNDERTAKING, THE QUALIFICATIONS OF EXTERNAL CIRCUMSTANCES AND ACCORDANCES OF FITTING SEASONS AND PLACES FOR OPERATION.

> *Querunt Alchimiam falsi quoque recti,*
> *Falsi sine numero, sed hi sunt rejceti;*
> *Et cupiditatibus, heu! Tot sunt infecti,*
> *Quod inter mille, millia, vix sunt tres electi*
> *Istam ad scientiam.*
>
> — Norton's Ordinal, Proheme

To those whom inclination has led thus far, with a benevolent spirit, to the Inquiry, it may appear no trifling object that we are in pursuit of, or irrational, if we may help to recover the Ancient Experiment of nature into her Causal Light: nor, et us be assured, will a few short years of study or idle handling of the matter, be sufficient to admit a man to the arcane of Hermetic science. Neither does it follow (and which is more to be regretted), that because all men have the material and live by it, that every one s therefore fitted to handle the same, or able to improve, promote and profit by it in the manner here proposed. Few, we fear, judging by our own observation, and very few according to the testimony of more experienced observers, are endowed with a disposition naturally adapted towards this peculiar research; for that it is peculiar and distinct from every other branch of philosophy, may, without a more lengthening demonstration, have become apparent. To save fruitless labour, therefore, and deter the idle, it may be well to learn at once, before we enter on the routine of Practice, what the impediments are, and those mental endowments most insisted on, for securing success in the experimental pursuit.

Geber, who, in his *Sum of Perfection*, writes at length, and better than many, on this head, excludes several classes, which may serve as a foundation for developing the defects of each. Natural Impotency, he asserts, is manifold, and may proceed partly from the physical defects of the artist, and partly from his soul; for either the organ may be weak or wholly corrupted, or the soul in the organ having nothing of rectitude or reason in itself; or because it is fantastical, unduly susceptive of the contrary of forms, and suddenly extensive from one thing knowable to its opposite, without discrimination. If a man have his faculties therefore so incomplete, he cannot come to the completion of this work; no more either than if he were sick, or blind, or wanting in his limbs, because he is helped by those members, *by mediation of which likewise, as ministering to nature, this art is perfected.* And further on, respecting the Impediments of Mind, the Arabian continues, He that hath not a natural sagacity and soul, *searching subtly, and scrutinizing natural principles, the Fundamentals of Nature, and Artifices which can follow Nature* in the properties of her action, cannot find the *true Radix* of this most precious science. As there be many who have a *stiff neck*, void of ingenuity and every sort of perscrutation. Besides these, we find many who have a soul easily opinionating every *phantasy*; but that which they believe to be truth is all imagination, deviating from reason, full of error, and remote from natural Law; because there is replete with *fumosities*, it cannot receive the true *intention* of natural things. There be also, besides these, others who have a soul movable from opinion to opinion, and from will to will; as those who suddenly believe a thing and *will* the same, without any ground at all of *reason*; and a little after do believe another thing, and accordingly *will* another. And these, being so changeable, can ill *accomplish* the least of what they *intend:* but rather leave it *defective.* There be, moreover, others who cannot *discern any truth at all to look after* in natural things, no more than beasts; others again, who condemn this science and believe it not to be; whom, in like manner and together with the rest, this science contemns and repels from the accomplishment of this most pious work. And there are some besides who are slaves, loving money, who do affirm this to be indeed an admirable science, but are afraid to *interposit* the necessary *charges.* Therefore, although they *approve, and according to reason have* sought the same, yet to the experience of the work they attain not, through *covetousness* of money. Therefore our science comes not to them. For how can he who is ignorant or negligent in the pursuit of truth, otherwise attain it?[1]

Now, if some of these should appear forced, or rather fanciful obstacles to the pursuit of science, we pray the reader to consider their application more closely, and whether, by particularizing, we may be able to discover their real drift. And to begin with this first and last defect of Avarice; those mammon-worshippers appear indeed formerly to have believed but too much; nor that miserable division of them only who sought in ignorance, from inert matter, without a ray of light to guide their benighted hopes. These did but small harm comparatively, it is not they who are so greatly oblivious to philosophy; but may be rather compassionated for their folly, who found nothing but loss and disappointment in exchange for years of patient and expectant labour. There have been others, far more blameworthy, than these, and more fallacious, against whom the true adepts have unanimously declaimed; depraved minds, that having entered, as Geber implies, by the right way of *reason*, forsook her guidance nevertheless, and basely entangling the clue of life, climbed by it into forbidden regions of self-sufficiency, and in the open face of Truth, stole her young hopes, the first fruits of her divining growth, and slew her there.

> *Mammon led them on; mammon that least erected sprit that fell*
> *From heaven, for e'en in heaven his looks and thoughts*
> *Were always downward bent, admiring more*
> *The riches of heaven's pavement-trodden floor*
> *Than ought divine or holy else enjoyed*
> *In vision beatific*[2].

These are they who have been held in abhorance by the good in all ages; who, having succeeded in inducing an exalted energy, have willfully denied the Light its true fulfillment, and substituting their own hasty purpose instead of the Divine, defiled it; compelling the Spirit to their private ends. And what will not the subject soul suffer when pressed by so execrable an evil? For such is the constitution of things, that it must either be filled with a superior or inferior power; and as the former is the reward of piety and proximate to the Final Cause, the latter is the punishment of the impious who defile the divine part of their essence, insinuating an evil spirit in the place of the Divine.—They have discovered secrets, says the prophet, and they are those who have been *judged*: for they know every secret of the *angels*, every *oppressive* and secret power of *devils*, and every power of those who commit *sorcery*, as well as of those who make *molten images* in the whole earth. They know *how* silver is produced from the *dust* of the earth, and how, on *earth*, the *metallic drop* exists; for lead and tin are not produced from the earth as the *primary fountain* of their production. There is an angel standing upon it, and that angel struggles to prevail. They have discovered secrets, and these are they who are to be judged[3]; who have turned the discovery of nature to an ill account; and these are they to whom Geber alludes, *who do affirm this to be indeed an admirable science, and have sought it also according to reason, yet could not enter into the experience, being afraid in their own persons to interposit the necessary charges,* i.e., to abandon the life of selfhood, and return the product to a benevolent and truthful end. Just to the point, we have the story of an Arabian Magician, who must needs steal a little boy, to go with him to the *mountain*, in order to supply the material his own wickedness did not suffer him to approach.

No impure leaven (need we repeat it?) can enter into Wisdom; she scorns to promote folly in any guise, much less will she suffer defilement at man's finite hand. But if anything can be done against the right of nature, she forsakes the polluted tabernacle and is lost. Know, likewise, says the pious author of the *Aquarium*, that if by reason of that gift vouchsafed to thee by God, thou happen thereupon, even after thou hast it, to wax proud or be covetousness, under whatever cover of false pretense, and dost hereby tempt thyself to a turning away from God, by little and little; know, for speak the truth, that this *art will vanish from under thy hands,* insomuch that thou shalt not know even that thou hadst it. The which, verily, hath befallen more than one without their expectation[4]. Does any one at this day, really conversant with the Subject, ridicule such an assertion; or are our minds so far estranged from the sphere of final causes, as to be unable to conceive the accountability of moral evil under the Law? Is not destruction to the wicked? Says Job, and *a strange* punishment *to the workers of iniquity? Doth not He see my ways, and count all my steps? If I have walked with vanity, or if my foot hath hasted to deceit; let me be weighed in an even balance, that God may know mine integrity. If my step hath turned out of the way, and mine heart walked after mine eyes, and if any blot hath cleaved to mine hands:* then *let me sow, and let another eat;* yea, *let my offspring be rooted out.*—*If I have made gold my hope, or have said to the fine gold,* Thou art my *confidence; if I rejoiced because my wealth was great, and because mine hand had gotten much; if I beheld the sun when it shined, or the moon walking in brightness: and my heart hath been secretly enticed, or my mouth hath kissed my hand:* this also were an iniquity to be punished by the *Judge: for I should have denied the God that is above*[5].

That was the transgression of Eve, and of Adam, who sought to hide his iniquity in his bosom[6]; but so multifarious are the estrangements of sense, and so rapidly are effects carried along and remotely imaged in this world, that their source becomes less and less an object of general regard. The Laws of Nature indeed are examined into, and practically demonstrated to be just what they appear to be; the moral, the physical, and the organic are well reasoned, and shown apart; as in their constitutional consequences, all alienated from each other, fixed and independent. For nature at the circumference subsists in this way; animals, birds, insects, fishes, herbs, too, and minerals, having their parts so variously qualified, that not anything homogeneous is discovered to sight. Each creature nevertheless has its class; and a kingdom in common belongs to each specific variety. As a tree, with its flowers, leaves and branches, in plural manifestation, is at the root one; and as the flower may die and the leaves still survive, or the trunk without either live to endure the winter's blast, so with respect to the natural laws; and in such a respect are they seen, independent and apart from each other; neither more nor less, for in their root are they not also one? Let the virus but once reach this by either channel, the moral, the physical, or the organic vitally infringed, the whole structure sympathizing decays. It is true, a man may be unjust, cruel, avaricious; may indulge in many vices without suffering in health, provided the structural Laws be well conditioned and obeyed: contrariwise, also, the best men may suffer from physical defects and infringement of the organic law. In mechanical arts, too, and ordinary intellectual operations, we image out ideas by suitable subjects independently; so that, whether it be for the sake of gain, fame or object of whatever kind, whether the work be undertaken with a benevolent, malicious, or other uncertain intent, the thing resulting may be the same, and remain to image, not the motive instigatory, but the Idea. It is either well or ill done, beautiful or deformed, according to the pattern and skill that have been exercised, irrespective of the individual intention which gave it birth. The pictures, of Holbein are not less beautiful for all the covetous spirit that reigned with their conception; the deformity of the artist's soul was, as the Laws of Nature, apart, nor ever manifested in his produced work. The motive springs of humanity are very generally made occult, and like the armament within the Trojan Horse, are often admitted under other pretext, to develop their force securely, whether good or evil, in the world. And whilst yet they are borne along in outward consequence far from their originating source, the many are slow to perceive it, though they should retain all the while possibly, in the abiding purpose, the conscious regards of its own kind.

But in Alchemy, where the nature of things is altogether altered and ultimately reversed, Final Causes are of all things most manifestly revealed, and that in their immediate act and operation no less than in the effect. Here is no gathering of grapes from thorns, or figs from thistles, as in this life is attempted; but the intention is received back according to its kind most exactly; where the subject, object, and result, through every phase of life agree together, where the end is determinate from the beginning, as the beginning is by the end made manifest, without intervention or concealment in the ministering Spirit throughout. Springing directly from ourselves, this highly effective agent, even in the natural state, inclines, as the will directs, to image the conceived Idea; how much more, when promoted through a second to a third of concentration, does it become fortified; and further multiplying in the Conjunction, impose in sure consequences on him who wields it the inherent accountability? An eye for an eye, a tooth for a tooth; so does the Law of Justice exact retribution in those spheres: hence so much caution and secrecy, that the Power might only be discovered through the long labour of an experienced and upright mind. Hence so much continued warning off the profane; lest, deviating, they should either break or become broken necessitiously upon the Wheel of Life. Sons of science! For this reason are the philosophers said to be envious, declares Hermes, not that they grudged the truth to religious or just men, but to fools, ignorant and vicious, who are without self-control and beneficience, lest they should be made powerful and able to perpetuate sinful things, for of such the philosophers are made accountable to God, and evil men are not accounted worthy of this Wisdom[7].

> *Mais tryeful, merveylous, and Archimastyre*
> *Is the tincture of holi Alkimy;*
> *A wonderful science, and secret filosophy*
> *A singular grace and gift of the Almightye;*
> *Which never was found, as witness we can,*
> *Nor ths science was ever taught to man,*
> *But he were proved perfectly with space,*
> *Whether he were able to receive this grace.*
> *For his trewth, virtue and for his stable wit,*
> *Which, if he faill, he shall never have it.*
> *Also no man should this science teach,*
> *For it is so wonderful, and so selcouth,*
> *That it must needs be taught fro' mouth to mouth;*
> *Also he must (if he be never so loath),*
> *Receive it with a most sacred oath,*
> *That, as we refuse great dignity and fame,*
> *Soe he must needly refuse the same.*
> *And this science must ever secret be,*
> *The cause whereof is this, as ye may see,*
> *If one evil man had hereof all his will,*
> *All Christian peace he might easily spill;*
> *And with his pride he might pull downe,*
> *Rightful Kings and Princes of renowne;*
> *Wherefore the sentence of peril and jeopardy*
> *Upon the teacher resteth dreadfully.*
> *So that for doubt of such pride and wealth*
> *He must beware, that will this science teach,*
> *No man therefore may reach this great present,*
> *But he hath virtues excellent.*
> *Soe tho' men weene possessors not to aide*
> *To hallow this science, as before is saide,*
> *Neither seem not blessed effectually,*
> *Yet, in her order, this science is holy.*
> *And forasmuch as no man may her find*
> *But only by grace, she is holy in her kind.*
> *Also it is a work and cure divine,*

> *Foul copper to make gold and silver fine;*
> *No man may find such change by his thought,*
> *Of divers kinds which God's hands have wrought;*
> *For God's conjunctions man my not undoe,*
> *But if His grace fully consent thereto,*
> *By help of this science, which our Lord above,*
> *Has given to such men as He doth love,*
> *Wherefore old Fathers, conveniently,*
> *Called this science Holy Alkimy*[8].

None ever truly attained to the fruits of this philosophy, as the wise declare, without rectitude of intention and the blessing of God on a well tried experience: and it is the reiterated assertion of this grateful truth that has encouraged us, by a natural faith, to pursue the inquiry and recommend it to others who are desirous of instruction. To say that the pursuit is without danger to the ill-informed would be presuming too much on late acquaintanceship and contrary to the to the credible assertion of adepts. But there are many degrees of success in the legitimate path, and every step is progressive where the Rule of Reason is pursued. Avarice, or ambition, or a curious hope, may long to prove the golden promise of Alchemy; but neither will be found to be the true *Form of Gold;* Reason alone can enter into It; Mammon may draw the dead metal in heaps about its sordid circumference; but it cannot quicken the aurific seed in life; that Spirit is too gross to permeate the ethereal profundity; all he can draw from it is stolen; for he is the first to fly from Wisdom's fiery ordeal, not able to enter with his camel form, or daring to prove vaporous essence in Her pure Light.

But to proceed; next above the Covetous, Skeptics are condemned by Geber; but as these by their own choice remain in ignorance, they would merit less reproval were it not that they endeavor to hinder others as well as themselves from the pursuit of truth. And of all evil spirits that haunt this world and set up their bar to human advancement, infidelity perhaps is the most absurd: by infidelity, we mean that fashionable kind of faithlessness, which, without rational foundation, denounces everything that is new, or not seeming immediately to square with the received commonplace, and which in truth conceives nothing worthy to be believed, or held in veneration. The age of religious intolerance has passed gradually away, and great allowances are now made for most things, all kinds of folly and diversities of opinion; but so much higher does the folly of skepticism run than heretofore, over all boundary, test of reality and probability of truth, that we had as lieve the days of Galileo had been ours, as live so much later to see the recovered secret of ages dwindle and sink into obloquy for lack of faith and mind verily to bear it witness in manifestation.

It is the wisdom of modern skeptics to ape the thing which they stand most in need of, viz., sound reason; the deficiency too is doubled in their disguise, as, ignorant of their own ignorance, they push forward as so many stolid bolts before the gate of Truth. Yet, despite of all the rejectors and scoffers, Nature opens her hospitable door to the multitude in the highways and byways, seeking them out to alleviate their sufferings and offer a new guide to knowledge and felicity. We allude to Mesmerism: neither ashamed, but grateful to acknowledge the neglected Door-keeper that gave us first introduction to the vestibule of antique science. Do they not perceive how she has risen up, lifted by a few faithful hands out of their reach? Those scoffers? But her monarchy was established and triumphant even before they perceived her, or ever their wicked crusade against her was begun. They warred with they knew not what, or wished, would it avail without faith to stimulate in the pursuit. Nature, who is liberal of her common gifts and lavishes earthly blessings without personal respect, opens not this casket after the same rule; she must be moved to it subtly, conscientiously, courteously, and then she will surrender to none but a philosopher, one too that has been disciplined in her schools, tried and proven to ensure his ability to bear the sacred trust.

> Therefore no man shulde be too swifte,
> To cast away our Lord's precious gifte,
> Consideringe how the Almighty God,
> From great doctors hath this science forbod;
> And granted it to few men of is mercy,
> Such as be faithful, trew and lowly,
> And as there be but planets seven
> Among the multitude of stars in heaven,
> Soe among millions of millions of mankind
> Scarcely seven men maie this science finde.
> Wherefore laymen ye may hear and see
> How many doctors of great authority,
> With many searchers have this science sought,
> Yet all their labours have turned to nought.

And if they did cost, yet found none availe,
But in their purpose often tyme did faile,
Then in despair, they reason and departe.
And then they say how there is noe such arte;
But faimed fables, they name it they goe,
A fals fond thing, they say it is alsoe.
Such men presume too much upon their minde,
They weene theire wits sufficient this arte to finde;
But of their slander and wordes of outrage,
We take thereof trewly little charge:
For such be not invited to our feast,
Which weeneth themselves wise, and doe leaste.
Albeit such men list not longer to pursue,
Yet is this science of Alkimy full trew;
And albeit such men list not longer to pursue,
Yet is this science of Alkimy full trew;
And albeit some proud clerks say nay,
Yet every wise clerke well consider may,
How he which hereof lawful witness be;
For it were a wondrous thing and quiente
A man that never had sight to peinte.
How should a born blinde man be sure
To write or make good portraiture?
To build Poule's steeple might be greate doubte
For such proud clerks to bring aboute;
Such might be apt to break their crowne,
Ere they could wisely take it downe.
Wherefore all such are full far behinde,
To fetch out the secretest pointe of kinde;
Therefore all men, take their fortune and chance,
Remit such clerks to their ignorance[9].

Rational skepticism has quite another object and never exhibits itself in the refractory form of its mock ally. It is the province of reason to inquire and endeavor, by perscrutination, to prove all things, that, finally rejecting the false, it may holdfast that which is true. Such skepticism, more properly perhaps called discrimination, is as much required by the Hermetic Student as the other is obnoxious. For this kind of analytic exercise helps to corroborate the mind, and cultivate that distinctive supremacy of truth in the understanding which is so essential to success in the practical research; but which is very rarely to be met with in uneducated minds. And, being without it, need we wonder that so many are now, as in Geber's and Norton's time, opinionative, unstable in purpose, willful and dissimulating; or that they who have never entertained the true ideal should fail to recognize the image when represented before their eyes? The searcher of nature ought to be, as she herself is, faithful, simple, patient, constant, giving his mind to the discovery of truth alone, hopeful and benevolent. It behooves him, also, who would be introduced into this hidden Wisdom, says the hermetic Master, to free himself from the usurpation of vice, and to be good, just, and of sound reason, ready at hand to help mankind, of a serene countenance, diligent to save, and be himself a patient guardian of the arcane secrets of philosophy[10]. And if to these qualifications a convenient leisure be added, all may be hoped for progressively passing by a living experience into the Light. But neither will a busy head nor a faithless heart, by impure hands, be able; nor does a vagabond inclination enter in by the narrow way of life.

With respect to the impediments of body mentioned by Geber, these are less numerous and more commonly supplied: Hands and eyes are to be had in abundance, and where these are conjoined with the foregoing conditions, other hindrances with respect to the artist, for the occasion, be passed by. Then for the student; he should, as a matter of course, be possessed, or learn, at least, to cultivate the incipient qualifications he intends afterwards to bring to practice. The same patient hope and free perspicuity of thought and imagination also will be called for, in acquiring the Hermetic doctrine, by perusal, as is afterwards needed for the experimental proof. Reading was not formerly adapted to the million, as it now is, in thought, language, and reference—familiarized and made easy to the understanding of all. No such alluring baits to idleness are to be found on the title pages of the middle age school of philosophy;—no such simplifications of science, as we now hear of, are belonging to Alchemy. It is true, there are Revelations, Open Entrances, New Lights and True Lights, Sunshine and Moonshine, and other Auroras, and pictured Dawns; Manuals, Introductory Lexicons of obscure terms, with meanings no less obscured; Triumphal Chariots also, Vans, Gates, Keys, and Guides too without number, all directing on the same Royal Road when this is found; but useless to most wayfarers; nothing that we observe at all suited to the means or taste of the millinary class of readers whose understanding, like that of pampered children, has grown flaccid; and, by excess of object-teaching, has forgotten how to think.

Very few there will be found to relish the enigmas of the old Alchemists; no thoughtless experimentalist, persisting in his mere senses —no hopeful receipt-monger, sectarian fanatic, or fact idolator—no idling curiosity seeker, or dilettanti imaginist, will find even his leisure well occupied in this pursuit: we warn them all, the subject is too abstruse, and too intricately dealt with, for the natural understanding to apprehend at first view. But it is true as the adepts indeed foretold, their records have proved like a curious two-edged instrument—to some it has cut out dainties, and to others it has only served to cut their fingers; yet are they not altogether to be blamed. It is not for the ignorant to blame the power of that which they do not known how to handle; or would it not be a ridiculous tings, if some child or arrogant rustic were to denounce the language of Astronomy, or say that Chemistry was a vain science, and merely because the terms are not comprehensible without instruction? In almost all the records of Alchemy, the inner sense is held aloof from the literal; and if, by hazard or benevolent design, the truth has escaped in plain discourse, it has been either slighted over or disbelieved. Thus Sendivogius relates it had frequently happened to him, that having intimated the Art to some friends, word by word explaining it, they could by no means understand him, not believing, as he quaintly expresses it, *that there was any water in our sea;* and yet, says he, they would be accounted philosophers. Other instances of the same kind are given, amongst whom, Eireneus, in the run of his allegory relates—There were a multitude of men, who, seeing my Light in my hand, which they could not discern well, they being in that darkness which would not be enlightened; but, as through a thick cloud beholding my candle, judged it ominous, and left their stations. For their eyes with darkness and smoke were made so tender, that my candle overpowered them, and they could not bear its luster; therefore they, crying out, ran away. I mused much at this, continues the philosopher how they could be in such Cimmerian darkness; and as I wondered, I bethought me, that they had with them another light, as it were, Fox-fire or Rotten wood, or Glow-worm's tails; and with this they sat in consultation, reading Geber, Rhasis, and such whom I heard them name, and commenting on them, not without much pleasantness. Then I considered that the light which I had brought with me did not enlighten that place, but stood separated, as it were, from the darkness; and withal I remembered that there was once a Light in the

World, and the Darkness comprehended it not: and that darkness I now perceived had a false fore of its own, with which it seemed to its inhabitants to be wonderfully well enlightened[11].

This humorous interlude of Eireneus, in the outward application, bears not unaptly to our conclusion, that the abstruse light of Alchemy is not fir for the understanding of all, neither is perceptible to the gross intelligence of the mass of mankind. But this singular fate of incredulity has seemed always to attend, lest folly or willfulness, precipitously passing into practice, should either perish or break the divine legislation in inharmonious effects. And thus the Art will probably continue concealed though many ages still; nor, except by a very few, be more accredited, though all early Christendom should rise up in attesting array to give it evidence. For what is truth to triflers, or light to the indifferent worldling, who cares not to be undeceived? How enlist him in a search so arduous, so uninteresting to his affection, and inimical to his self-love? No! Wise in his generation, rather let him sleep on; for what would it profit him to learn to believe without the power of realizing any good? Without a stable theory, and the desire of truth absolutely leading, all is mere vanity and a vexation of the spirit.

> *It were much better for such to cease,*
> *Than for this art to put them in presse;*
> *Let such-like butterflies wonder and pass,*
> *Or learne this lesson both now and lasse,*
> *Following the sentence of this holi letter,*
> *Attingens a fine usque ad finem fortiter,*
> *Disponens omnia suaviter;*
> *That is proceede mightily to th' End*
> *From the beginning maugre the Fiend.*
> *All things disposing, in the meane space,*
> *With great suavity that cometh of grace,*
> *All short-witted men and mutable*
> *Such must needes be variable;*
> *And some do every man believe,*
> *Such credence doth their coffers grieve;*
> *To every new tale of them told,*
> *They give credence and leave the old.*
> *But some Lords be of stable wit,*
> *Such only be apt to finish it*[12].

Adepts all therefore advise discretion, and are circumspect in their revealments, lest That, which in the hands of a philosopher becomes most precious, should be otherwise made worthless, or worse than all. He that understands, says the royal artist, let him understand and advance; but let him that cannot, be ignorant still. For this treasure is not to be bought with money; and as it cannot be bought, so neither can it be sold[13]. Ye sons of Avarice and Ignorance, cries Geber, and ye of evil manners, avaunt and fly from this science, for it is inimical to you, and will bring you to poverty. For this great gift of God is, by his judgment, hidden from you for ever; and therefore we treat of it in such words as to the wise shall, by pursuit become intelligible: but to such as we have described, mean of mean capacity, will be most profound; and fools shall be absolutely debarred entrance therein[14].

Common language is suited to express common ideas, and to convey them to the vulgar conception; but the Alchemists, for various sufficient reasons, have not thought fit to deliver their Wisdom in this way, as if it could be syllabled out like a romance or a common ballad, for the amusement of the first runner by, who would deign look with his mere eyes and read. They better knew the value of their instructions, and so studiously veiled it, that he only who was really desirous, and made fit by long study to pursue the work, should be able to understand them.—The words of the wise are as goads, says the preacher, and as nails fastened by the master of assemblies which are given by one shepherd.—One spirit indeed reigns throughout, and one intention; but she is so hedged in with cabalisms, metaphors, types, emblems, and sophistications there is but One Leader, who should undertake the deliverance; one only, we repeat; he that is allied—the same that, in practice strengthening, afterwards is enabled to raise the allegoric siege of life; and by the fire of his divine wrath enkindled, to overcome the stronghold of evil therein allied.

And let the sapient artificer, concludes the prince, studiously peruse our books, collecting our dispersed intention, which we have described in divers places that we might not expose it to malignant, ignorant men; and let him prove his collection even into the knowledge, studying and experimenting with the instance of sagacious labour, till he come to an entire understanding of the whole. Let the student exercise himself, in order to find out this our proposed way of investigation, so as to acquire a plenary knowledge of the verity of perfecting and corrupting Matter and Form[15]. And again,—I beg of thee, my son, says the adept Richardus, to examine the writings of the philosophers; for if thou art slothful at thy books, *thy* mind cannot be prepared for the work; nor will he be able advantageously to bring his Hand to the practice whose Mind is sluggish in studying the theory. But he with more security shall advance to the work who has stored his mind with resources: ignorance is wiped off by study, which restores the human intellect to true science and knowledge, and by these enigmas the Dagon is overthrown[16]. Zachary likewise, in his *Opusculum*—This I tell thee, he says, that thou ought first to read with unwearied patience and perseverance the writings of the philosophers before thou extendest thy Hand to the Philosophic Work, and pray to God for his grace and wisdom to help thee therein; for no one ever acquired this art by chance, but by prayer rather than by other means. Mediums nevertheless are to be employed[17]. Pray, says Sendivogius, pray; but work. God indeed gives understanding; but thou must know how and when to use it[18]. Arnold, in his *Rosary*, mentions three requisites, viz., subtlety of mind, manual skill, and a free will for the operation[19]; to which Lully, likewise adds a sufficiency of the Divine Favour, and books to open the understanding and give it zest for truth[20]. The author of the *Lucerna Salis*, moreover, agrees that in order to acquire this science study is required in the beginning, and meditation, that a good foundation may be laid; for that without this God does not reveal His grace nor unless He be prompted thereto by the fervent prayers of him who desires so signal a favour. He does not either grant it immediately to any person, but always *by mediate dispositions*, to wit, by instructions and the labour of the hands; to which He gives a thorough blessing it He be invoked thereto with a sincere heart: whereas, when recourse is not duly had to Him by prayer, He stops the effect thereof, either by interposing obstacles to things already begun, or else suffering them to conclude with an evil event[21].

These several preliminary requirements will not appear astonishing to those who have obtained an insight into the nature of this science, nor will it be deemed by any, we hope, a canting pretense or affectation for philosophers to talk of praying for Divine assistance in a research which is so much wrapped in and about the Desire as to be ultimately made manifest through its means. Besides, are we not accustomed to seek for benefits where we think they are to be found?, if we go to the musician to learn music, the chemist to procure instruction in his art, to the astronomers, builder, or other mechanist to learn their several acquirements, how much more ought we not to apply to the Causal Fountain for Wisdom, which is His alone and voluntarily to bestow? And as the learned of this world must be won by some means to impart their knowledge, shall we not by the same parallel endeavor to move the Divine Nature by prayers, who has promised all things to those humbly and early seeking Him? For to desire and covet after wisdom is to seek to be a partaker of that Divinity to which we aspire, and no otherwise can we be made partakers, it is taught, but by a voluntary assimilation.—My son, instructs the wise Hermes, I admonish thee to love God, in whom is the strength of thy undertaking and the bond of whatsoever thou meditatest to unloose, and this science I have obtained by the sole gift of the living God inspiring me[22]. Man may conditionate:—ought, by patient labour disciplining, to prepare the way of the Greater in the Lesser Good; but he cannot compel, much less impart, the Divine blessing on his handiwork, neither cement the spiritual union or give it increase. There is a period too, when in conjunction, the Spirit transcends all earthly control, and passing under the Divine Hand, recreates by His sovereign will alone. But it is vain to look for a blessing from Nature without His cooperation who is her Will; for without controversy, as the Scripture alludes, the Lesser is blessed by the Greater.—Every good gift and every perfect gift comes from the Father of Lights in whom there is no variableness or shadow of turning.—And again, Paul may plant and Apollos may water, but God alone giveth the increase.—And God withholds not this increase alone, but deprives the talent likewise, where it is wasted or hoarded without interest or promotion. To them that have and use is given more abundantly, but from him that improves not there is taken away even that which he has. For the Almighty will not permit his gifts to remain idle, much less may they suffer abuse, being immortal; and he therefore must be a good steward who would overlook the rich treasury of life.

> *Our gold and silver ben no common plate,*
> *But a sperme owte of a body I take,*
> *In the which is alle, Sol, Lune, Life and Light,*
> *Water and Earth, Fyre and Fryght:*
> *And alle cometh of one Image,*
> *But the Water of the Wood, maketh the marriage.*
> *Therefore there ys no other waye*
> *But to take thee to thy beades and pray:*
> *For covetous men yt findeth never*
> *Though they seek yt once and ever:*
> *Set not your hearts in thys thing*
> *But only to God and good lyvinge*

And he that will come thereby
Must be meeke and full of mercy:
Both in spyrit and in countenance,
Full of charitie and good governance,
And ever more full of alms deede.
Symple and pewerly hys lyf to leade:
With prayers, penances and piety,
And ever to God a lover be,
And all the riches, that he ys sped,
To do God worshippe with almes ded.
All you that have sought manie a day,
Leave worke, take your beades and pray[23].

With the nature and effects of prayer, in ordinary life, all men are familiar in one degree or other; for every desire of the mind is in its kind a prayer and preparative for the acquirement of its object; and if prayer effected nothing else, it certainly collects the mind, and corroborates the faculties in their pursuit; for when the thoughts are concentered, means and adjuncts suggest themselves, which do not occur when they are indifferently shown; and thus by a prayerful communion we often obtain and divine things which otherwise we should not. But the esoteric ground brings us acquainted with prayer in a far deeper sense, and adepts are eloquent in their imputations of its efficacy with prayer in a far deeper sense, and adepts are eloquent in their imputations of its efficacy in Spagyric Works, when the mind is lifted up;—even in the midst of the operations of Vital Chemistry, full of labour and toil, they prayed, says Kirchringius, and every man knows, that hath entirely devoted himself to this business, how effectual prayer is, and how often those things which he long sought and could not find, have been imparted to him in a moment, as it were, infused from above, or dictated by some good genius. That also is of use in solving riddles and enigmatical writings; for if you burn with a great desire of knowing them, that is *prayer*: and when you incline your mind to this or that, variously discussing and meditating many things, this is *cooperation*: that your prayer may not be, for want of exertion a tempting of God; yet all endeavor is vain until you find the *solution*. Nevertheless, if you despair not, but instantly persist in desire, and cease not from labour, at length, in a moment, the solution will fall in; this is a *revelation*, which you cannot receive unless you pray with great desire and labour, using your utmost endeavor; and yet you cannot perceive how from all those things, of which you thought, which were not the solution of the Enigma, the solution itself arose. This unfolding of the Riddle opens to you the mystery of all things, and shows how available prayer is for the obtainment of things spiritual and eternal, as well as corporeal and perishing goods: *and when prayer is made with a heart not feigned, but sincere, you will see that there is nothing more fit for the acquiring of what you desire.* Thus piety is available for all things, as the oracles declare, and prayer especially, which is its principle exercise, is profitable for great undertakings[24].

But lest, with all this, it should appear to any superstitious or otherwise unrighteous to invoke the Divine aid to this particular undertaking, as if God were mutable, we take leave to add a few further considerations in defense, and the different kinds of invocation which were employed by the ancients in their celebration of Theurgic rites.

Prayer, according to Jamblicus, was divided into three classes, The first of which, as pertaining to the early initiations, was called *Collective*, having for its object to gather the mental powers into accord with their leader, seeking a clue whereby it may enter the intelligible profundity of the Enigma. The second *effects the bonds of concordant spirits;* calling forth, prior to intellectual alliance. The third is the *final authoritative seal of union;* when the desire, leading from faith, becomes into its true end. The first, recapitulates our author, pertains to Illumination; the second, to a Communion of Operation; but through the energy of the third, we receive a perfect plenitude of Divine Fire. And supplication, indeed precedes, like a precursor, preparing the way before the *sacrifice appears;* but sometimes it intercedes as a *mediator*[25]; and sometimes *accomplishes the end of sacrificing. No operation, however, in sacred concerns, can succeed without the intervention of prayer.* Lastly, the continual exercise of prayer nourishes the vigour of our intellect, and renders, the *receptacles* of the soul far more *capacious* (by enlarging the desire) for the communications of the gods. *It likewise is the Divine Key which opens to men the penetralia of Wisdom;* accustoms us to the splendid rivers of supernal light; and by these, in a short time, perfects the inmost recesses and disposes them for the ineffable knowledge and contact of Divinity; nor does the adoration desist till it has raised the sublimated soul up to the summit of all. For it gradually and silently draws upwards the manners of the soul, by divesting her of every thing foreign to a Divine nature, and clothes her with the perfections of the god. Besides this, it produces an indissoluble communion and friendship with Divinity, nourishes a Divine love, and inflames the Divine part of the soul. Whatever is of an opposive and contrary nature it helps to expiate and purify, expels whatever is prone to generation, and retains nothing of the dregs of mortality in its ethereal and splendid spirit; perfects a good hope and faith, concerning the reception of Divine Light, and in one word, renders those by whom it is employed the familiars and domestics of the gods[26].

Such then being the advantages of prayer, and such the connection of adoration with sacrifice, and the end of Theurgic sacrifice is a conjunction with the Demiurgic Intellect; hence does it not follow, that the benefit of prayer, if we concur at all in opinion concerning these things, is of the same extent with the good which is conferred by such an alliance? And these three terms of adoration, in which, according to the authorities, all the Divine measures are contained, not only conciliate the warring elements of life, but extend to man three supernal benefits; as, translated from one form of perfection to another, Life progresses bringing forth an offspring to be sacrificed on the alternating confines of each; as it were three Hesperian Apples of Gold.

And thus the end of all adoration is attained, and there the rational inquiry rests as in its proper object, and there the true attraction of love is to be found, and there the true attraction of love is to be found, which in this life never can be put by an ablation of it. For the attractions which are here supplied to the sensible perception, and for which so many pray, are transitory, and the desire of them is nothing more than the desire of images which lose ultimately the magnetic virtue imparted to them by the idea, because without it, when in the possession, they are found to be neither truly desirable, nor sufficient, nor good.

But if, in the indifferent concerns of life, men pray and for a general prosperity in public worship, hoping to be heard, how much more should not the desire be conceived effectual when addressed within the Living Temple to the Divine Light within; when, in the congress of allied mind, the Spirit wakes to consciousness; and in their universal harmony conspiring, dissolves the total life to love.

I called upon the Lord, exclaims the Psalmist, and He heard me out of His holy temple, and my cry came before Him, even unto his ears. I prayed, and understanding was given to me; I called upon God, and the Spirit of Wisdom came to me.—And hence it may more readily be conceived, how prayer and self-sacrifice conspiring, mutually corroborate and confer on each other a perfect efficacy in Divine works; since, even Matter itself is said to be extended to the desirable, *i.e.*, to the Good;

and though this desire is filled as many goods as it is able to participate. And when things have run up so far as to this Sufficiency they become tranquil in it, and are liberated from the parturitions, and the desire which they naturally possess. Neither will it therefore be proper to omit any part of this concord, or deny any faculty of the mind its due exercise in the *Preparation*, since these diversified parts of the Spirit are in the renascent harmony made one; thence again to be evolved in catholic procession to complete the equilibriated circle of their Law. And this much may suffice concerning the nature of prayer, and the corroborative efficacy of the Human Will, acting in concert with its Final Cause to fulfill It.

The next difficulty presenting itself to the mind of the student, after he has obtained a general knowledge of the Hermetic ground, with a hopeful desire to commence operations, has been to find suitable assistance in the undertaking; many have halted there a long while unprofitably, for it is evident that without a Subject to work with and reciprocate the design it remains abortive, as a statue in the conception without the marble to give it utterance.

The ascent to Unity is arduous, and the descent is not undertaken in safety alone; neither is there any increase of the Spirit, as we have already shown, without a medium and a bond.—Behold, two are better than one, says the Preacher, because they have a good reward for their labour, and mutually assist each other by the way; but for one alone, there is no end of his labour; and for whom do I labour, saith he, and bereave my soul of food? This is vanity, yea, it is a sore travail[27].

But so much has been written, and with such a deal of sophistication, about the Philosophic Vessel and its multiform distillatory apparatus, of nerves, veins, and alembics, that we should be in doubt where to choose a guide in this respect sufficiently intelligible, and who is at the same time trustworthy and of equal fame; one hint, however, in the sum of Norton's *Ordinal*, may help to extricate us from the difficulty of explaining many more:

> Which are full derke,
> To ordeyne instruments according to the weke.
> As every Chapter hath divers intents,
> So hath it divers instruments,
> Both in matter, also in shape,
> In concord that nothing may mishap;

*As workers of division and separation
Have small vessels for their operation;
But vessels broad forhumectation,
And some deale broad for circulation;
But long vessels for precipitation;
But short and long serve sublimation;
Narrow vessels and four inches high
Serve correction most properly.
Of vessels some be made of leade,
And some of clay both quick and dead;
Dead clay is called such a thing,
As hath suffered great roasting;
Such meddled in powder with good raw clay
Will fier abide and not go away;
But many clays will leap in fier,
Such for vessels doe not desire.
Other vessels be made of stone,
For fier sufficient, but few or none;
Among workemen, as yet is founde
In any county of Englishe grounde,
Which of water nothing drinke shall
And yet abide drie fier withal;
Such Stones, large for our intente,
Were a precious instrument;
But other vessels be made of glasse,
That spiritual matters should not outpasse;
Of ashes, of ierne in this londe everi each one
Be made, but elsewhere be of stone:
Of our glasses, the better kinde,
The morning stuffe ye shall it finde,
Which was ahses the night before,
Standing in heate, all nighte and more,
The harder stuffe is called Freton,
Of clipping of other glasses it come;
Tincture with annealing of glasiers
Will not perse him as they reherse.
By this doctrine chuse or refuse,
Take that which you woll unto your use,
For in figures of vessels kinde,*

> *Every man followeth his own minde;*
> *The best fashion is ye maie be sure,*
> *She that concordeth with vessel of nature;*
> *And figure that best concordeth with quantity,*
> *And with all circumstances, to matter best is she,*
> *And this sheweth best Albertus Magnus,*
> *In his Boke De Mineralibus.*
> *Hereof a secreate disclosed was,*
> *By my good Master, to more or lesse,*
> *Saying, Si Deus non dedisset nobis vas Nihil dedisset, and that is glasse*[28].

The Spirit finally constructs its own vessel and vitrifies it; and since the artist is at liberty to make choice according to convenience of his instruments in the beginning, and each one would be likely to vary in his preference, we avoid a superfluity of description; besides, of the many that may be called together, at first, few, it will be understood, are chosen to proceed beyond the exigencies of the preliminary Gross Work. And them, will they not speak for themselves? Those philosophic vessels, like the planks of Argo, on occasion, are still oracular; being felled fro the selfsame ground too, in the same classic grove, made vocal by Apollo.

> *And methinks few potters within this Realm,*
> *Have made at ony tyme such cunning ware,*
> *As we, for our science, doe fashion and prepare.*
> *Few ever formed such, nor the like of them,*
> *Yet they are plain without wrinkle or hem;*
> *One within another, it is a pretty feate,*
> *The Third without them to guide up the heate.*
> *First then with the potter thou must begin,*
> *Which cannot make what he hath never seen.*
> *In order that thy vessels be made to thy mind*
> *Stand by while he worketh more surety to finde*
> *And shew him what to do by some sign or similitude,*
> *And if his wits be not too dull and rude,*
> *He will understand what thou dost meane*[586].

A humorous story is related in continuation, by this author, of the difficulties he met with in the practice from indifferent assistance; and how, after so much vexation and loss of time, he was obliged to take the whole of the Manual labour upon himself.

> *For servants doe not passe, how our worke to frame,*
> *But have more delighte to play and to game.*
> *A good servant, saith Solomon, let him be unto thee,*
> *As thine own hearte, in each degree:*
> *For it is precious a faithful servant to finde,*
> *Not wreckless, but sober, wise and quiet,*
> *Such a one were even for my dyet[29].*

The value of such assistance may be better appreciated when we come to speak of the Preparatory Practice which Norton, naively, and without much envy, describes, enumerating also the needful qualification and numbers of individuals employed about the Gross Work, as follows: —

> *The Second Concord with this Arte is,*
> *When ye can finde apt Ministers*
> *Noe Minister is apt to this intent*
> *But he is sober, wise, and diligent;*
> *Trewe, and watchful, and also timerous,*
> *Close of tongue, of body not vicious,*
> *Clenly of hands, in tuching curious,*
> *Not disobedient, neither presumptuous;*
> *Such servants may your workes of charge*
> *Minister, and save from all outrage:*
> *But trust me that two such servants or three*
> *Maie not sufficient for your worke be;*
> *If your matter be of quantity reasonable,*
> *Then eight such servants be convenable;*
> *But upon little quantitye, find ye shall*
> *Four men able to perform alle:*
> *Then one half of them must werke*
> *While the other half sleepeth or goeth to kerke:*
> *For of this Arte ye shall not have praye*
> *But it be ministered as well by night as daye;*
> *Continually, except the holi Sunday alone;*
> *From Evensong begin till Evensong be done.*
> *And while they worke they must needs eschew*

> *All ribaldry, else they shall finde this trewe,*
> *That such mishap shall them befall*
> *They shall destroy part of their weks or all;*
> *Therfore all the ministers must be men,*
> *Or els thei must all be women;*
> *Set them not occupied with another,*
> *Though some to you be sister or brother;*
> *Yet their must have some good disporte,*
> *Their greate labors to recomforte:*
> *Then nothing shall better avaunce*
> *Your worke than shall this Concordaunce.*
> *Yet Instruments useful there be more,*
> *As be Furnaces ordeyned therefore;*
> *Oldmen imagined for this Arte*
> *A special furnace for every parte*
> *Every each devising after his owne thoughte*
> *But many furnaces of them be noughte;*
> *Some were too broad, some too long,*
> *Many of them did nature wrong.*
> *Therefore some furnaces may well be used*
> *But many of them must be refused*[30].

The true furnace has been described as *a little simple shell*; thou mayst easily carry it, says Vaughan, in one of thy Hands; the glass is one, and no more; but philosophers have sued two, and so mayest thou. As for the work itself, it is no way troublesome; a lady may read the *Arcadia*, and at the same time attend this philosophy without disturbing her fancy. For my part, continues the philosopher, I think women are fitter for it than men, for in such things they are more neat and patient. And again, in the *Lumen de Lumine*—the excitation of the Fire is a very trivial, slight, almost a ridiculous thing; nevertheless, all the secrets of corruption and generation are therein contained[31]. Geber calls this furnace Athanor; and from his example, others have described the same with a misleading subtlety, little commendable or instructive to any.

> *But who knoweth the power, the working, and kinde*
> *Of every furnace, hemaye well treuth finde;*
> *But he which thereof dwelleth in ignorance,*
> *All his worke falleth upon chance.*

> *Noe man is sure to have his Intent*
> *Without full concord of arte with hys instrument.*
> *Mani more instruments occupied ye shall see*
> *Than in this chapter now rehearsed be,*
> *Which ye must ordayne by good or sad advice,*
> *And prove them before hand, if ye be wise*[32].

After showing that indeterminate instruments must be employed in the beginning, until the determinate shall declare themselves as by the Spirit they are proved fit, Norton proceeds in due order to point out the best local and other outward circumstances for carrying on the different Hermetic operations, as follows: —

> *The Fourth Concord is full notable*
> *Between this arte and places convenable.*
> *Someplaces must needs be ever more drie,*
> *Close from aier and no waies windy;*
> *Some must be darke and dim of sight,*
> *In which Sun-beams none may light;*
> *But for some place, the trewth so is,*
> *Thei cannot have too much brightness:*
> *Some places must needes be moist and cold,*
> *For some workes as Auctors toulde;*
> *But in our workes in verie place,*
> *Wind will hurt in everie case:*
> *Therefore for every worke in season*
> *Ye must ordaine places by reason.*
> *Philosophers said, by their engine,*
> *How it should be wrought within locks nyne.*
> *Astrologers said it was a grace*
> *To finde a fitting wirking place:*
> *For manie things will wondrous doe*
> *In some places and elsewhere no soe;*
> *But contrarie wonders be of one thinge,*
> *In contrarie countries wrought without leasing;*
> *Whereof none to her cause maye appear,*
> *But only contrarye places of the spheare:*
> *Whereto places contrairye of the grounde,*
> *To them concordant and obedient be founde;*

Hereof great evidence and wittnes full cleare,
In the Magnet's stone openly doth appeare,
Whose northe pointe draweth towards his countrye,
Which under the South Star driveth needles away.
Found some places concordant, some places not[33].

Secrecy having been a principal object with those practicing this Art, difficulty was found often to secure this, and at the same time supply the other conditions, which vary with the constitution and instinct of the spiritual guide. Just such a locality as Virgil appointed for his Bees, has been mentioned as desirable with all his appropriate allegorical exceptions of corrupt and evil associates. Strong currents of air are well known to disturb communion; and the entranced Subject is more or less susceptible of all imaginative impresses, which, even after their act has passed away, hang and pollute the ether of their pertinacious abode, as adepts well testify, and Cornelius Agrippa, in his Occult Philosophy, diffusely expounds, showing that truly,

It is a grace
To finde a fitting working-place.

The following lessons of an English Adept, neither antique nor envious, may not be in conclusion of the rest.—If thy desire leads thee on to the practice (that is of the ultimate Philosophic Work), says Vaughan, consider well with thyself what manner of man thou art, and what it is that thou wouldst do: For it is no small matter. Thou hast resolved with thyself to be a co-operator with the living God, and to minister to Him in his work of generation. Have a care, therefore, that thou dost not hinder his work; for if thy heat exceeds the natural proportion, thou hast stirred up the wrath of the moist natures, and they will stand up against the central fire, and the central fire against them, and there will be a terrible division in the Chaos; but the sweet spirit of Peace, the true eternal Quintessence, will depart from the elements, leaving both of them and thee to confusion; neither will he apply himself to that Matter as long as it is in thy violent destructive Hands. We should always remember that doctrine of Zeno, that Nature gave us one tongue and two ears, that we might hear much and speak little. Let not any man therefore be ready to vomit forth his own shame and ignorance; let him first examine his knowledge, and especially his practice, lest upon the experience of a few violent knocks he presume to judge of Nature in her very sobrieties. But if thou knowest the principal First Matter, know also for certain thou hast discovered the Sanctuary of Nature. There is nothing between thee and her treasures but the Door: that indeed must be opened. Have therefore a charitable seraphic mind, charitable and not destructive to thyself. There is in every true Christian a spice, I will not say a grain, of faith, for then we could work miracles. But know that as God is the Father, so Charity is the nurse of Faith. For there springs from charitable works (from the effects of spiritual beneficience), a hope of heaven; and who is he that will not gladly believe what he hopes to obtain? On the contrary, these springs no hope at all from the works of darkness, and by consequence of no faith, but that faith of devils to believe and tremble.—*Settle not in the lees and puddles of the world. Have thy heart in heaven and thy hands upon earth. Ascend in piety and descend in charity.* For this is the Nature of Light and the way of the children of it. You must live, as says Agrippa, according to God and the angels, rejecting all things that are dissimilar *to the heaven;* otherwise thou canst have no communion with superiors. Lastly, *Unus esto non solus.* Avoid the multitude, as well of passions as of persons. And, in conclusion, I would have thee understand that every day is a contracted year, and that each year is an extended day. Anticipate the year in the day, and lose not a day in the year. Make use of indeterminate agents till thou canst find a determinate one: the many wish well, but one only loves. Circumferences spread, but centers contract; so superiors dissolve and inferiors coagulate; stand not long in the *sun* nor long in the *shade,* where extremes meet, there look for complexions. Learn from thy errors to be infallible, and from they misfortunes to be constant. There is nothing stronger than *Perseverance*, for it ends in miracles[34].

Abundant evidence might here be brought to bear; but sufficient has been said for suggestive purposes, and addition would be as little likely to stimulate inquiry without practical information as to satisfy the incredulous. Nothing is more generally insisted on, next to benevolence and rectitude of intention, than perseverance for this experiment; and if to the foregoing instructions we add in sum, that effects rationally investigated lead into their causes, and that as the plant of is seed is reared, and according to its proper species germinates in a congenial soil, so in this philosophy the end is implied in the beginning, and the purpose is by the product made manifest—the motive, through the resulting action, by the metaphysical cause, into physical effect;

Mary Anne Atwood

Qui capit, Ille sapit.

And with this advice we conclude our introduction, as it may be called, to the Sphinx's lair.—The first link in the chain of vital causes moves, as we apply the Master Key.

Portus
Explicit, at Praxis manuAlis caetera pandet.

---

1. Summa Perfect., lib. i. cap. iii.
2. Paradise Lost, Book I.
3. Book of Enoch, cap. lxiv., sect. ii.
4. Aquarium Sapientum, Appendix.
5. Job xxxi. 3-24
6. Idem, 33
7. Tract. Aur., cap. i.
8. Norton's Ordinal, chap. I. in Ashmole's Theatrum.
9. Norton's Ordinal, chap. I.
10. Tract. Aur., cap. ii.
11. Ripley Revived, First Gate, p. 121.
12. Norton's Ordinal, chap. vi.
13. Calid in Salmon, p. 30.
14. Summa Perfect. In fine.
15. Epilogue to the Invest. of Perfection.
16. See Lucerna Salis, many passages to the same effect. Richardi Ang. libel. cap. iii.
17. Zachary Opuscule, p. 69.
18. New Light, p. 122.
19. Arnoldi Rosarium, lib. ii. cap. v.
20. Lullii Theor. Test. C. 31.; Et ideirco fili tibi dico, quod tria requiruntur, scilicet, iugenium subtile naturale non sophisticam, manuum operatio, et liberum arbitrum, et hoc requirit sapientiam, divitias, et libros. Sapientiam, ad sciendum facere : divitias, ad habendum potestatem faciendi : libros ad intellectum aperiendum diversum qui est in multis gentibus. And Richardus — Studium secundum doctores amovet ignorantiam et reducit humanum intellectum ad veram scientiam ct cognitionem cujuslibet rei. Ergo in primis necesse est per studium hujus suavis operis scientiam acquirere et per philosophica dicta ingeminn acuere, cum in ipsis sit cognita via veritatis si ergo laborantes laborem non despexerint fructum inde provenientem dulciter gustabunt, &c. — Theat. Chem. vol. ii. p. 419. Richardi Anglici Libellus, cap. ii.

    Mental Requisites and Impediments. 411

    prayer, He stops the effect thereof, either by inter- posing obstacles to things already begun, or else suf- fering them to conclude with an evil event . 1

    Theatr. Chem., vol. 2, p.419. Ricardi Anglici Libellus, cap. ii.
21. Digby's Translation of the Lucerna Salis, p. 320, Recapitulation.
22. Tract. Aur., cap. i. and ii.
23. Pierce, the Black Monk, on the Elixir, in Ashmole's Theatr.
24. See the Annotations of Kirchringius on Basil Valentine, sub init., p. 5.
25. See St. Paul's Epistle to the Romans, viii. 26, 27.
26. See Jamblicus, De Mysteriis, cap. xxxvi.

27. Eccels. iv. 8,9.
28. Norton's Ordinal, chap. vi. p. 94.
29. Idem, chap. iii.
30. Norton's Ordinal, chap. vi.
31. See Vaughan's Lumen de Lumine, etc.; Coelum Terrae, p. 118, &c.; and Sendivogius' New Light; and Eireneus' Introitus Apertus, chap. viii and xxiv.
32. Norton's Ordinal, chap. vi.
33. Norton's Ordinal, chap. vi.
34. Anima Magia Abscondita, p. 51, etc.; Coelum Terrae, p. 137.

Part Four
The Hermetic Practice

Chapter 1. Of the Vital Purification, commonly called The Gross Work

which developes the actual mode of operation practised by the Ancients, and mechanic means employed to dissolve the vital compound and eradicate the inbred evil of life — the mode of rational investigation likewise by which the Spirit is induced to yield up her light and hidden virtue to increase it.

Dii sudoribus vendunt Artes

— Arcanum Ignis Aquae Resp. 6

Next the preliminary aids already noted, and a sufficient theory to being with, follows the Preparation of the Philosophic Subject, which is performed, says the Monk Basil, by operation of the Hands, that some real effect may be produced. From preparation arises knowledge, even such as opens all the fundamentals of Alchemy and Medicine. Operation of the hands, continues he, requires a *diligent application* of itself, but the praise of the science consists in experience; but the praise of the science consists in experience; hence that notable maxim—*Physician, heal thyself.* But the difference of these, anatomy (that which is spiritual) distinguisheth: *operation* shows thee how all things may be brought to light and exposed to sight visibly; but *knowledge, i.e.,* experience *reveals the practice and shows further how to proceed, and that whence the true practitioner is,* and is no other than a confirmation of the previous work: because the operation of the hands manifests something that is good, and draws the latent and hidden nature outwards, and brings it to light for good. And thus, as in Divine things the way of the Lord is to be prepared, so also, in these (spiritual) things, *the way has to be opened and prepared, that no error be made from the right path*: but that progress may be made without deviation in the direct way to health. —*Manual operation* is chiefly required, therefore; without which, indeed, every other operation, like a ship without ballast, floats and is uncertain. But it is difficult to express this with a pen; *for more is learned by once seeing the work done, than can be taught by the writing of many pages*[1].

Although the Alchemists have written diffusely on the manual Practice, and delivered many Keys, whereby, as they say, we may enter into the sanctuary of philosophy and open her interior recesses; yet the first way of approach and shut entrance to these has not been unfolded, nor would it be possible, we think, for any one to discover the Practice from their books alone. For although it is called a play of children, and represented as a very trivial, slight, almost a ridiculous thing, one linear decoction throughout and dissolution by line, yet neither instinct nor reason would probably suggest, without instruction, the tractive artifice now made publicly easy of entrancing the senses in their own medial light.

But recent observation has proved various means of effecting this, and determining the natural life to an interaction of its beams, by the hand or eye of another mesmerizing, or by a passive fixed gaze; the virtues of ether and chloroform too are familiar, and in these days ignorantly preferred to the former expedients, since their effects are considered analogous and more easily supplied; which however are very different, as proved by the contrariety of their cause. For, whereas the one, overcoming in light, oxygenates, purifies, and sublimes the arterial blood, and in proportion the intellectual powers; the other contrariwise, by influxion of darkness, drowns the oxygenating spirit, prostrates and confounds the mental powers, and, further overwhelming, often produces syncope and death. But we have no space to dwell here on errors that daily experience promises to remove. The ancients appear to have been acquainted with other analogous means and media of curative repute; other revolutionary arts, too, by which the human spirit may be involuted and converted to its proper spheres. But to effect this was, as we have repeatedly shown, a beginning only of the Hermetic art; the medium in its natural state is volatile, immanifest, phantastic, irrational, and important, compared with what it subsequently is become. The Alchemists, we repeat therefore, did not remain satisfied with a few passes of the hand, or any first phenomena whatever, but they proceeded at once scientifically to purify, depriving the ether of its wild affections and impressions by a dissolution of the circulating body in its own blood. For this is that Brazen Wall celebrated by Antiquity, which surrounds our Heaven and must be scaled, and passed through before any one can hope to discern the equilibriate felicity of Being within.—Take the occult Nature, which is our Brass, says Albertus, and wash it that it may be pure and clean; dissolve, distill, sublime, increate, calcine, and fix it; the whole of which is nothing else than a successive dissolution and coagulation to make the fixed volatile, and volatile fixed. The beginning of the whole work is a perfect solution[2].

Now, although there are many ways of including the sensible medium and of unfolding the interior light temporarily, yet for the Purification we read but of one way, called by the Adepts *Manual, and their Linear way*, which supersedes all other from beginning to end of the Dissolution. And, according to their general testimony, and for other explicable reasons, we judge that the Hand was the instrument employed, not only to impart the Spirit as a natural gift, but by a continual mechanic trituration, as it were, to dissolve and ultimately obliterate its innate defects. The Mercury of the philosophers, says Lully, comes not but by help of ingenuity, and the Manual operations of man. And Vaughan says, nature is not moved by theory alone, but by sagacious Handicraft and human assistance.—Nature cannot of herself enter into the dissolution, says the author of the *Filum Ariadne*, because she has no hands.—The Hand, says Van Helmont, is the instrument of instruments, which the soul likewise useth, as a means by which it bears its image into operation[3]. We could bring together a multitude of passages showing the literal application of these, but have a doubt about the utility, since they would prove nothing to unbelievers; and those who are disposed to inquire for themselves, looking to context and probability, may be readily convinced. We are less than ever anxious at this late stage of inquiry to persuade others, or induce trial of the practice where theoretic power is deficient; but leave the incredulous therefore to their incredulity, until faith has independently established the fact over their heads. For neither will the preclude of Hermetic practice be attractive to the idle, but continual labor is exacted throughout the performance—patience, toil, skill, unremitting attention, in the execution, and a free will to the discovery of error, without discordant slurring or disguise.

He that neglects the knowledge, being disheartened by the difficulties thereof, shall never find where the disease lieth, says Crollius, for these

Chemical Secrets will never be fingered by those slothful or sottish despisers of them, by reason of their indisposition and unaptness for Manual operation. As also of the profane, lewd, and unworthy, there will be little danger of their apprehending and discerning Divine Mysteries; because they want the spirit of Wisdom, and are not quick of understanding in these things[4].—Some indeed, amongst the ignorant and pseudo-chemists, says Eireneus, imagine that our work is a mere recreation and amusement from beginning to end, holding indeed the labor of this artifice in light account. In the work which they account so easy, however, we observe they reap an empty harvest for their idling pains; we know next the Divine blessing and a *good principle* to begin with, that it is by *assiduity and industry* that we accomplish the *First Work*. Nor is the work so easy that it should be considered as a mental recreation either (since a concentrated attention is necessary), but *according to the labor* we do likewise reckon the reward; as Hermes says—I spared no labor either of mind or body; which also verifies that proverb of Solomon—The desire of the idle shall cause him to perish. Neither is it wonderful that so many chemical students were in former times reduced to poverty, since they spared labor, but no expense. But, continues the same author, we, who know the truth, *have worked*, and we know beyond doubt that there is no work more tedious than our First Operation, concerning which Morien gravely warns King Calid, saying that many philosophers have been overcome with the fatigue of this work. Neither would I have these things understood figuratively, continues he; I am not speaking here indeed of the commencement of the Supernatural Work, but of things as we *first* find them: and to *well dispose the matter*, this truly is a labor and a work[5].

The work of philosophers, says Arnold, is to dissolve the Stone in its own mercury, that it may be reduced into its first Matter.—*Opus namque philosophorum, est dissolvere Lapidem in suum Mercurium, ut in priman reducatur materiam*[6]. This Labor has, by the author of the *Hermetic Secret*, Urbigeranus, and some others, been styled a labor of Hercules. For there is such a mass of heterogeneous superfluities adhering to our subject, that nothing short of dissolution can give it rest; and, which Adepts say, it will be entirely impossible to accomplish without the Theory of their Arcanum, in which they show the medium by which the Royal Diadem may be extracted from our Sordid Subject. And even when this is known, continual labor is required in the application, lest remaining in any part, of left alone, before the total solution of her enigma, the Sphinx should retrieve her dominion unawares and frustrate the work begun—*Tere, coque, et reitera, et non te taedeat*—Grind, coct, says the wise author of the *Rosarium*, and reiterate your labor and be not weary[7]. Work not today and be sorry tomorrow; but lay sorrow aside and continue your labor steadfast unto the end, lest peradventure God hoodwink and make open the Light, says the Spirit to Dr Dee; the labor is equal to the work, and to fight against the Powers of Darkness requires great force[8]. And let him who would learn, says Van Helmont, buy coals and fire, and discover those things which watching successive nights, and expenses, have afforded to philosophers[9]. Kings and powerful princes have not been ashamed to set their hand to work in order to seek out, by their sweat and labors, the secret of Nature, which they have faithfully bequeathed[10].

> *Ardua prima via est; et qua vix mane recentes*
> *Enitantur equi*[11].

Fresh horses there are verily needed to this Celestial Ploughshare and laborious assistance for a toil that is incessant, to clear the wasted field of human life, and harrow it for a more congenial growth: nor once nor twice; but many times the labor must be repeated, as each dying is renewed into a better life. This the wise poet, in his *Georgics*, teaches; and this recalls to mind the advice of Norton and his brother Adepts about the choice of servants, their capacities and qualifications, which moreover are tried in a double, single manifold, and triply complicated sense. All the operators, says Zachary, supply themselves with three or four, sometimes ten, furnaces or more—as for solution, sublimation, calcinations—and the *matter* passes through vessels innumerable; but not all would avail without a Method in their distribution; one would not advance in effect beyond another, unless the operation were altered; there is indeed but one way of working, in one matter, *one linear way throughout*, one vessel uniform throughout, *except removal. Unicus operandi modu in unico vase, in unica fornacula, praeter amotionem, donec decoctio compleatur*[12].

The Preparing Spirit dissolves the *body* of Light, and cleanses it from the corrupting causes, and extracts a Second Spirit subsisting and tinging in the body, and reduces the bodies by dissolution into itself; and these, says the Adept, are the advantages of the Spirit preparing its body and extracting from it the tinging spirit: for this Argent vive was at first gross, unclean, fugitive, being mingled with extraneous Sulfurs; but by the operation of Art it was cleansed and renewed, and coagulated by its own internal sulfur, red and white, and is double; not viscous, but acidulated, subtle, and very penetrative, resolving the bodies mineral.

But our evidence runs in advance; as we remark by the way that this Argent vive, which is decocted *lineally*, is generated *pontically*, as it were by a reciprocal alternation, distributing its advanced virtue by hand to hand.—And know, say Eireneus, that the exact preparation of the philosophic Eagles may be considered the first degree of perfection in this Art, in the knowledge of which there is required also some sagacity of mind, For do not suppose that this science has become known to any of us by chance, or by a happy guess of the imagination; but we have worked and sweated daily, and passed many sleepless nights, much labor and *sweating* truly we have undergone in the pursuit of truth. You, therefore, that are but beginning, as a tyro, in this study, be assured that nothing can be achieved in the First Operation without sweating and much labor. In the Second, however, Nature alone operates, and without any imposition of hands, by the sole assistance of a *well-regulated external fire*[13].

> *Avicen, in Porta, wrote, if ye remember,*
> *How ye shoulde proceede perfection the engender,*
> *Trewly teaching as the pure truth was,*
> *Comedas ut bibas, et bibas ut comeda;*
> *Eat as it drinketh and drink as it doth eate,*
> *And in the meane season, take it a perfect sweate.*
> *Rasis set the dietary and spake some deale far,*
> *Non tamen comedat res festinanter,*
> *Let not your matters eate over hastily.*
> *But wisely consume their foode leisurlie.*
> *Hereof the prophet made wondrous mention,*
> *If ye apply it to this intention*
> Visitasti terram et inebriasti eam,
> Multiplicasti locupletare eam,
> Terram fructiferam in salsuginem
> Et terram sine aqua in exitus aquaram.
> *If I have plenty of meate and drinke.*
> Men must wake when they desire to winke;
> For it is labor of watch and paines greate,
> Also the foode is full costly meate.
> Therefore all poore men beware, says Arnolde,
> For this Art 'longeth to greate men of the worlde.

> *Trust to his words, ye poore men all,*
> *For I am witness, the soe ye finde shall.*
> *Esto longanimus et suavis, said he,*
> *For hasty men th' end shall never see.*
> *The length of clensing matters infected*
> *Deceiveth much people for that is unsuspected.*
> *Excess of one half quarter of an hour*
> *May destroy all; therefore chief succour,*
> *In primo pro quo et ultimum pro quo non*
> *To know the simperings of our Stone,*
> *Till it may no more simper do, nor cease,*
> *And yet long continuance may not cause increase.*
> *Remember that water will bubble and boyle,*
> *But butter must simper and also oyle;*
> *And so with long leisure it will waste*
> *And not with bubbling made in haste*[14].

Frequent advises are given against haste in the preparation, lest the centers should be stirred up before the circumferences are ready to conceive them; and we may observe that Oedipus, he who of yore overcame the Sphinx, was lame and impotent in his feet, signifying by this (amongst other abstruse allusions) that we should not make too much haste to the solution of her riddle, lest she should expound herself without a proper understanding unawares—Alciatus, painting a dolphin wreathed about an anchor, for an emblem, wrote these words—*Festina Lente*—Make not too much haste —which admonition applies not only well to the common affairs of life, but especially to the trituration of the Philosophic Subject, which ought to be slow, gentle, and continuous.

> Gutta cavat lapidem non vi sed saepe cadendo.

And therefore the Adepts, again and again, admonish and caution, lest by too great excitation the internal agent awakening should cause a disseveration in the Chaos, and the two Principles stand up one against the other, before the intended mastery is secure.—Cause, therefore, wings to be prepared for the Matter by *Juno, Bacchus*, and *Vulcan*; but as you love your life, says he, permit it not to fly suddenly, rather deliver it to Mercury, to be instructed by him gradually to accustom itself to flying; yea, bind it with a *cord*, lest (as a bird got out of its cage and past your reach) it through ignorance approach too near the *Sun*, and like Icarus, having its unproved feathers burnt, fall headlong into the sea; but after you have detained it for its *due time*, loose its *bonds* that it may fly and come to those fortunate Islands towards which all sons of Art *direct their sight*, and whereunto all Adeptists aim to arrive as to their *long-desired* and sought for harbor[15]. Take the flying bird, says Hermes, and drown it flying; and divide and separate it from its redness, which holds it in death; draw it forth and repel it from itself, that it may live and answer thee not by flying away indeed to the region above, but truly by forbearing to fly. For if thou shalt deliver it out of its prison, after this thou shalt govern it according to Reason and according to the days specified; then it will become at companion to thee, and by it thou shalt become an honoured Lord. Extract from the ray its shadow and its obscurity, by which the clouds hang over it and corrupt, and keep away the light; by means of its constriction also and fiery redness it is burned. Take, my son, this watery corrupted redness, which is, as a live coal holding the fire, which if thou shalt withdraw so often until the redness is made pure, then it will *associate* with thee, by who it was cherished and in who it rests[16].

> *He that would seek tincture most specious,*
> *Must needly avoid all things wild and vicious;*
> *Of manifold means each hath his property*
> *To do his office after his degree,*
> *With them hid things be outset*
> *Some that will help, and some that would let.*
> *Who would have trew worke may no labor spare,*
> *Neither yet his purse, though he make it full bare;*
> *And in the Gross Worke he is furthest behind,*
> *That dayly desireth the end thereof to find.*
> *If the Grosse worke with all his circumstance*
> *Were done in three years it were a blessed chance*[17].

This is meant chiefly in reference to the Second Operation, and the periods are often to be understood metaphorically with respect to the discovery of the philosophic Salt. Some have met the Light sooner, some later, and the natural periods are protracted by faulty conditions from the commencement, by the indisposition of patients, as by the ignorance of agents, which things are more or less implied. Years have been employed by some in the Preparation, the perplexity of the records have added to the natural difficulty, and to others it has never been vouchsafed. Eireneus, mentioning his case as remarkably favored, says that in the course of two years and a half the whole Arcanum was revealed to him.—I made, says he, not five wrong experiments in it before I found the true way, although in some particular turnings of the Encheiresis I erred often; yet, so that in my error I knew myself a master, and in no less than two full years and a half, of a vulgar ignoramus I became a true Adept, and have the secret through the goodness of God[18].

It is to be imagined that the better foundation there is laid in theory from the commencement, other things being equal, the surer, easier, and more rapid would be the result; but from books, general principles only can be gathered, and instruction from particular experience. The working theory, as we long ago suggested, can be obtained through the practice only; for the way develops itself I the practice by rational inquisition of the Light within. And this may be a matter of gratulation to students, that whilst adepts are so very abstruse and envious in their disguises, to learn that the Hermetic Art is not so much the offspring of natural intelligence as of involved thought. *Ab actionibus procedit speculatio* is a famous maxim of Aristotle's and eminently applies to this philosophy, where each discovery opens into a new field of inquiry, and the fruit of contemplation is ever more sown in order to bring about the solution of its proper dilemma in the explanatory growth of truth.

> *Not all by reading, nor by long sitting still;*
> *Nor fond conceit, nor working all by will;*
> *But, as I said, by grace it is obtained:*
> *Seek grace therefore, let fools be refrained*[19].

See k grace; and, by importunity of reason, seek for the clue of Truth within the Spirit's life; if haply she may find it, or we be able to discover whether she have it or not—*That* which analyzes even must be analyzed; that, returning analytically, it may resolve the separable Selfhood and reiterate the same by alternation until it arrives at the inseparable Unit of Truth.—*Liber librum explicit*—And this is the way of rational permeation, by the Understanding of Nature, into her Causal Light.

> *So shalt thou instant reach the realms assign'd*
> *In wondrous ships self-moved, instinct with mind;*
> *No helm secures their course, no pilotguides;*

> *Like man intelligent they plough the tides,*
> *Conscious of every coast and evey bay,*
> *That lies beneath the Sun's all-seeing ray;*
> *And, veiled in clouds impervious to the eye,*
> *Fearless and rapid through the deep they fly*[20].

And that court of King Alcinous, to which Ulysses became admitted, is the dominion of Intellect, which, in the description of these Phoeacian ships, also, is admirably signified; the hyperbole, in fact, would be absurd without other reference, and the well-illumined Taylor has shown, in his *Dissertation*, that the whole of the Odyssey is an allegory pregnant with latent meaning and the recondite Wisdom of antiquity.

Here again, then, we observe that it is not from a moderate study or a few spontaneous revelations of the Spirit's virtue, or natural instinct, that we should presume to judge of the Hermetic Mystery; since brazen walls and adamantine are between, and all the breadth of that vast sea to be passed over before we can hope to set foot upon the royal coast; a sea —

> *Huge, horrid, vast—where scarce in safety sails*
> *The best built ship, tho' Jove inspires the gales*[21].

Even with these advantages, and after the first floodgates and barriers are overpast, greater obstacles await him, and Herculean labors, who dares, approaching to the Nether confines, to make choice of Light. No one may hope, without toil and perseverance, to obtain it. Wisdom is the reward of voluntary and arduous research. Perseus passed through dangerous encounters, struggling with monstrous Chimera's; and Theseus before Ariadne vouchsafed her love and assistance; Bacchus, Ulysses, Hercules, and the rest; Jason, also, passing through many hopes and fears, and performing dangerous feats and supernatural labors, before Medea led him to the Field of Mars.

> *For the Gross Worke is foule in her kinde,*
> *And full of perils as ye shall finde,*
> *No man's wit can hi so avile*
> *But that sometimes he shall make a faile:*
> *As wellthe layman, so shall the clerke,*
> *And all that labor in the gross worke.*
> *Wherefore Anaxagoras said trewly thus —*

Nemo prima fronte reperitur discretus[22].

They all set forth expectant heroes only in the beginning, content also with the company of their rude deserts, and it is satisfactory to learn with all this prospective discouragment, that —

> *He shall end it once for certaine*
> *Shall never have neede to begin againe.*
> *Much I might write of the Nature of Mynes*
> *Which in the gross worke be but engines;*
> *For in this worke find ye nothing shall,*
> *But handie crafte, called Art mechanical,*
> *Wherein a hundred ways and moe,*
> *Ye may commit a fault as ye therein goe*
> *Wherefore believe what old Auctors tell;*
> *Without experience ye may not do well.*
> *Consider all circumstances, and set your deligte*
> *To keep Uniformity of all things requisite;*
> *Use one manner of vessel in matter and in shape,*
> *Beware of Commixtion that nothing miscape.*
> *And hundredth foultes in speciall*
> *Ye may make under this warning generall.*
> *Netheless this doctrine woll suffice*
> *To him that can in practice be wise.*
> *If your ministers be witty and trew,*
> *Such shall not need your workes to renew*[23].

And here we may bethink ourselves how Flammel learned discretion from his Second Book, and how Eireneus promises a guide, and describes him too in his *Ripley Revived*. And, in Vulcan's labors, says Kuhnrath, I have worked indefatigably with no small expense, but, thanks to God, my own alone; now in companionship, and now not; both happily sometimes, sometimes without success. But how should he do well who never has done amiss? What was wrong taught me what was right, from day to day *one book throwing light upon another*, I was enabled to interpret them. *I observed what nature taught me by the ministry of art*. O thou edifying Cabal of much profit! How hath she not advance me! Meanwhile, carefully keeping note of conversations, experiments, and conceptions *of my own as well as others*: when ye, my contemporaries, were idly dozing, I was watching and at work. Meditating earnestly day and night on what I had seen and learnt—sitting, standing, recumbent, by sunshine and moonshine, by banks, in meadows, streams, woods, and mountains[24]. And thus we read, in the *Hermetical Triumph*, how the Stone of Philosophers, which is a pure petrification of the Spirit, is prepared by those who trace nature with the assistance of the Lunar Vulcan, as we long ago suggested, is meant the first prepared Subject, which is also called Diana, and the secret natural interior Fire of Adepts, and because this same Lunar Caustic is brought into act by an exterior excitation.—*Sol est Fons totius caloris, Luna autem Domina Humiditatis*. The ethereal humidity nourishes the Solary Light and educates it; and this is that Nemean Lion said to be born of her foam.

With respect to the rule of Investigation, however, having opened thus much, we would add a few remarks, for neither is it said to be expedient to inquire about Ends so much as about things pertaining to ends, the Artist holding his right intention from the beginning. This principle Aristotle, in his *Ethics*, astutely argues. For neither, he observes, does a physician consult whether he shall heal the sick, nor a rhetorician whether he shall persuade, nor the politician whether he shall persuade, nor the politician whether he shall establish an equitable legislation, nor does any one of the remaining characters consult about the End. But, proposing a certain end, they consider how and by what Medium it may be obtained. If also it appears that this end is to obtained through many media, they consider through which of them it may be obtained in the easiest and best manner. But if through one medium they consider how it may be accomplished, and through what likewise this may be obtained until they arrive at the first Cause which is discovered in the last place. For he who consults, continues the artful moralist, appears to investigate and analyze in the above-mentioned manner, as if her were investigating and analyzing a diagram[25].

Even so, in the Hermetic Inquiry, he who consults, the end being proposed which is not immediately in his power, investigates the Medium by which he hopes to obtain it; and if this Medium be not entirely enlightened, he explores another, and further till he discovers the first Medium which is immediately in his power, in the discovery of which inquiry terminates, and the work, beginning from thence, passes into accomplishment. That Medium, therefore, which is last in the analysis is first in generation being proved able to the accomplishment, and of the many called to the consultation of means few are chosen to proceed with the Philosophic Work. For philosophers were not wont to investigate trifles, but they inquired about such things as tend to purification and the method of perfecting life. And when things, thus truly eligible, are the objects of inquiry, the Divine Will being conciliated, Wisdom runs lovingly by her own rule to fulfill it; and hence our deeds and discourses extend their Hands, as it were, to assist us in our assent, and Will is the greatest power of purgation. And then That which from the first is efficacious returns into its proper Efficient, how much more will not those strokes, reverberating, be effectual to overcome?

> *Ille pius CHEIRON justissimus omnes*
> *Inter Nubigenas et Magni Doctor Achillis.*

This is he who, in his double capacity of Power and Motive in alliance, corrects and educates the Heroic Fire, tames and directs its illimitable virtue, and rectifies the Armed Magnet by an infallible rule. And that Intellect rides through the abyss of sensual monarchy, secure in its Ether; and, as a ship upon the stormy seas is directed by the beacon-light, it follows until integrally related, when, center meeting center, the consciousness transcends in revolutionary Light.

We know that, in common life, the hands perform innumerable offices and image mind about, by material subjects, in a variety of ways. And as the mind more easily retains that which the hand before has noted by its exterior sense; so, in Hermetic works, the hand is found best able to express and impart what the mind has well premeditated; and thence, from its replenished members, thought carries itself by voluntary motion into effect. Such were those *Dactyli Idaei*, literally the Fingers of Mount Ida, so renowned in fable for their medicinal and magic skill, who worked, it is said, at the foot of the Parnassian Mountain to exhibit by their incessant fiery artifice the metallic veins therein imbedded[26]. So Pallas is fabled, by the help of Vulcan, to have been brought forth from Jove; for, without the instrumentality of Motion, which the lame god personates, the Fabricate Intellect is not born. But if thereafter it should happen, says the wise Adept, that Pluto's Palace should be exposed to any one together with Minerva's Artifice, or if Vulcan stands together with her at the Altar there, the Association is ominous.

> *Coexistunt namque naturalia opera splendore,*
> *Vitifer Ignis,*

Cnetro incitans seipsum lumine resonante.
Fontanum alium, qui Empyreum mudum ducit,
Centrum quo omnes, usque quo forte equales fuerint[27].

To instruct the ignorant is no part of the present object; but to stimulate the inquiry of such as are already enlightened, and to advance the faithful in the pursuit of truth, we conclude with such instruction as may be finally needful concerning this said hyper-physical Gross Work.

The Second part of the Gross Work is described by Vaughan as one of the greatest subtleties of the Art; Cornelius Agrippa, he observes, knew the First Preparation, and has clearly discovered it; but the difficulty of the Second made him almost an enemy to his own profession. By the Second Work we are to understand, therefore, the Solution of the Philosophic Salt (*i.e.*, the voluntary bond); which is a secret which Agrippa did not rightly know, as it appears by his practice at Malines, and as he confesses in the first book, of *Occult Philosophy*, that he could not increase the transmutative virtue, nor would Natalius teach him teach him for all his frequent and serious entreaties. This was it, adds his disciple, that made his necessities so vigorous and his purse so weak, that I can seldom find him at full fortune. But in this he is not alone: Raymond Lully received not this mystery wither from Arnold, but, in his first practices, he followed the common tedious process which after all is scarcely profitable. Here he met with a drudgery almost invincible. Ripley also labored for new inventions to putrefy this Red Salt which he enviously calls his Gold; and his Art was to expose it to alternate fits of *heat and cold*, but in this he is *singular*; Faber is so wise that he will not understand him. Let us return then to Raymond Lully, who became so great a master that he performed the Solution in nine days, and this secret he had from God himself since this is his profession.—*Nos*, says he, *de primâ illâ nigedine a paucis cognitâ bnigmum Spiritum extrahere affectantes, pugnam ignis vincentum, et nos victum, licet sensibus corporis multotiespalpavimus, et oculis propriis illum vidimus; Extractionis tamen ipsius notitiam nos habuimus quacumque scientiarum vel arte : ideoque sentiebamus nos adhuc aliqua rusticitate excaecatos, quia nullo modo eam comprehendere valuimus, donce alius Spiritus prophetiae, spirans a Patre Luminum descendit, tanquam suos nullatenus deserens, aut a se postulantibus deficiens, Qui in somniis tantam claritatem mentis nostrae oculis infulsit ut Illam intus et extra, remota omni figura, gratis revelare dignatus est insatiabili bonitate nos reficiendo demonstrans, ut ad eam implendam disponeremus corpus ad unam naturalem decoctionem secretam, quâ penitus ordine retrogrado cum pungenti lancea tota ejus natura in meram nigredinam visibiliter dissolveretur* [28].

In the first act of the physico-chemical works, explains Kuhnrath, by diverse instruments and labors and the various artifice of the Hands and of Fire, from Adrop (which in its proper tongue is called Saturn, *i.e.*, the lead of the Wise), our heart of Saturn, the bonds of coagulation being dexterously relaxed, the Green Duenech and the Vitriol of Venus, which are the true matters of the Blessed Stone will appear. The Green Lion, lurking and concealed, is drawn forth from the Cavern of his Saturnine Hill by attractions and allurements suitable to his nature. All the blood copiously flowing from his wounds, by the acute lance transfixed, is diligently collected *ule* and *lili*; the mud earth, wet, humid, stagnant, impure, partaking of Adam, the First Matter of the creation of the Greater World of our very selves and of our potent Stone, is made manifest—the Wine which the Wise have called the Blood of the Earth, which likewise is the Red of Lully, so name on account of its tincture which is the color of its virtue, thick, dense, and black, blacker than black, will then be at hand; the bond by which the soul is tied to the body and united together with it into one substance is relaxed and dissolved. The Spirit and the Soul by degrees depart from the body and are separated step by step; whilst this takes place the fixed is made volatile, and the impure body (of the Spirit) from day to day is consumed, is destroyed, dies, blackens, and goes to Ashes. These Ashes, my Son, deem not of little worth; they are the diadem of thy body; in them lies our pigmy, conquering and subduing giants. In the *Second Operation*, which takes place in one circular crystalline vessel justly proportioned to the quality of its contents, also in one theosophic cabalistically sealed furnace of Athanor, and by one fire, the body, spirit and soul, externally washed and cleansed and purged with the most accurate diligence and Herculean labors, and again compounded, commingle, rot of themselves and without manual cooperation, by the sole labors of nature, are dissolved, conjoined, and reunited; and thus the fixed the fixed becomes volatile wholly; these three principles also are of themselves coagulated, diversifiedly colored, calcined, and fixed; and hence the World arises renovated and new[29].

Here then liest the Gordian Knot of the Hermetic Mystery—and who is he that is bale to untie it, enquires the philosopher?—He who knows the Salt and its solution, knows the secret of the Ancient Sages. And if it be again asked who? We have already named him, and openly; but this

Light shining everywhere in Darkness, how hardly should it be comprehensible without Itself?

> *Janua clausa est, vah quae lamentabilis haec vox;*
> *Orcina sedfrustra pulsabitis ostia pugnis;*
> *Vestrae namque Manus nequeunt diffingere ferru.*

What then ought we to be doing, since hands and intellect are here alike incapable, and the truth of this discovery was never yet put to paper, and for this sufficient reason, that it is proper alone, as Lully says, to God to reveal it; since it is His alone prerogative, and no mortal can communicate it to another unless the Divine Will be with him.—Not every messenger, says Van helmont, approacheth to the mine of Sontes; but he alone, who, being loosed from his bonds, has known the wars, being fitted forhis journey, a friend to the places and who has virtue. They err, therefore, who ascribe this single combat only to Corrosives; to wit, they too much trusting to Second qualities, as being ill secure, do sleep thereupon, and through a neglecting of specifical qualities, also appropriated ones (which are only extended on their proper object), being slighted, they have gone into Obscurity. For the Ostrich does not digest iron or little birds flints, through an emulous quality of corrosion; but there is a virtue of loosing the bars and bolts of Tartar. It is convenient to meditate about this virtue, continues the physician, and of what I have spoken; blessed be that God of Wonders, who hath sometimes converted the Water into Rocks, and at other times the Rocks into pools of Water[30]. Who then shall ascend into the Mountain of the Lord, or who shall stand in His Holy Place? He that hath clean hands and a pure heart, who hath not given up his soul unto vanity nor sworn deceitfully. He shall receive the blessing from the Lord, and righteousness from the God of his salvation.

We do not quote casually, or because the Scriptural phrase is popular; but because it is apt, as seen and proved on the Divine Ground; where man indeed may experiment, plough, plant, and irrigate, but cannot of himself (or in alliance, unless he dare a deadly sin), compel the Divine Blessing without its free accord.—Wisdom was with thee, says the Hermetic Master; it was not gotten by thy care, or, if it be freed from redness, by thy study[31]. So neither, it is written, is he that planteth anything, neither he that watereth, but God, that giveth the increase[32]. He therefore must be propitiated, not by prayer and supplication alone, but by faithful and charitable works preparing the way before Him; nor would it be thought astonishing, perhaps, if Antimony should cause a sudden transpiration, or that an Iron Key should help to unlock a treasury of fine Gold. Desire leads into its object by faith immediately; but mediately, by just works, that hope is engendered which, kindling into faith immediately; by ecstacy, penetrates to its First Source.—Our *Antimony*, says Basil Valentine, which is fixed, searcheth out fixed diseases and eradicates them; which purgers, not fixed, cannot do; but they do only carry away some spoil from diseases; or they may be compared to water which, driven by force through a street, penetrates not the earth itself. Fixed remedies purge not by the inferior parts, because that is not the true way of expelling fixed venoms; and that way they would not touch the kernel, as it may be called, or center of the disease; but by expelling sweat, and otherwise, they strike at the very inmost root of the disease, not contented with a certain superficial expulsion of filths. Therefore we admonish all and every one, that all venomous impurity is totally to be taken away from *Antimony*, before it can either be called a medicine truly or administered with safety—in other words, that all arrogant self-will, sensuality, folly, avarice, and variability of purpose, all but the one voluntary faith to rectify and perfect, be removed from the mind of him who is to enter into the radical dissolution of Life. For the weapons of this warfare are not carnal, as the Apostle teaches, but mighty through God to the pulling down of strongholds; casting down imaginations, and every high thing that exalteth itself against the Knowledge of God, and bringing into captivity every thought to the obedience of Christ[33]. And for this cause, continues the monk, the good must be separated from the evil, the fixed from the unfixed, the medicine from the venom, with accurate diligence, if we hope by the use of *Antimony* to obtain true honor and true utility; but Fire only can effect that, and Vulcan is the sole and only master of all these. Whatsoever the Vulcan in the Greater Orb leaves crude and perfects not, that in the Lesser World must be amended by a certain other Vulcan, ripening the immature, and cocting the crude by heat, and separating the pure from the impure. That this is possible, no man will doubt; for daily experience teaches the same, and it very apparent in the corporeal aspect of colors which proceed from the Fire. For by separation and Fire, which perfects its fixation, venomosity is taken from the Medicine, and of good and evil; which however is a thing that none of the physicians either dares or can truly and fundamentally own or demonstrate, unless he who hath firmly contracted friendship with Vulcan, and instituted the Fiery bath of Love[34].

There is one operation of heat, says Vaughan, whose method is vital and far more mysterious than all other, and there be but few of that Spirit that can comprehend it: But because I will not leave thee without some satisfaction, I advise thee to take the Moon of the *Firmament*, which is a *middle Nature*, and place her so that every part of her may be in two elements at one and the same time; *these elements also must equally attend her body*; not one further off, nor one nearer than the other. In the regulation of these there is a twofold geometry to be observed, natural and artificial. Flammel also, speaking of the Solar and Lunar Mercury, and the plantation of the one in the other, gives this instruction, Take them, he says, and cherish them over a fire in thy Alembic; but it must not be a fire of coals, nor of any wood, but a bright shining fire like the Sun itself, whose heat must neither be excessive, but always of one and the same degree[35]. Our operation, concludes Morien, is nothing else but extracting water from the earth and returning it again, so long and so often until the earth is completely putrefied; for by elevation of the moisture the body is heated and dried, and by returning it again it is cooled and moistened; by the continuation of which successive operations it is brought to corrupt and to lose its Form, and for a season to remain dead[36]. This then is the true intention and manner of working to supply the right condition for attracting the Divine Seed, by action and reaction raising successively actives by passives, and, vice versa, passives by actives, until the spiritual ability is complete.

> *For what one doth concoct t'other will drive away;*
> *But if thou canst each work perform apart,*
> *And knowest them afterwards to reconcile,*
> *Then thou art master of a princely Art*
> *The very success will thy hopes beguile;*
> *Thou hast all Nature's works ranked on a file,*
> *And all her treasures at command dost keep;*
> *On thee the Fates will never dare but smile.*
> *No mystery is now for thee too deep:*
> *Th' art Nature's darling whether dost wake or sleep.*
> *Pardon my plainness, of the Art, thou knowest*
> *It was the fruit of my untamed desire*
> *To profit any; and, without a boast,*
> *No man above my candor shall aspire*
> *My zeal was kindled by Minerva's Fire*[37].

But for an explanation of the whole difficulty, adds the same author, in his *Open Entrance*, attend to these instructions—Take four parts of our Fiery Dragon, which bears in his belly the Magic Steel, and conjoin to nine parts of our Lodestone, that by a violent concussion they may be reduced in to a mineral water; reject the superfluous scum which swims upon it; leave the Shell and take the Kernel; and *purge thrice with Salt and with Fire*: which will be easy to do, if Saturn have chanced to regard his beauty in the glass of Mars.—Hence comes the Chamelion which is our Chaos, in which all the Arcana are contained; not in act as yet, but in virtue[38].—*Non igitur externus solis coelestis calor est qui profundum terrae calefacit sed potius solis terrestris innatus calor; duplex denim est calor, unus reverberationis qui externus est, alter influxionis et penetrationis, qui internus est, de quo jam loquor, cujus nature est vivificare augmentare conservare per sustentaculum radicalis humoris in hoc ignite contenti*[39].

Which Vulcanic action, to destroy life and to maintain it, Democritus before all, and as it were pyrographically, portrays, as—Drawing the fixed Brass out bodily, instructs this Abderite, thou shalt compose a certain oblong tongue, and placing it again upon the coals, stir Vulcan into it; now irradiating with the Fossil Slat, now with the incessant Attic Ochre, adorning now the shoulder and the breast of Paphia till she shall appear more manifestly beautiful, and, throwing the glaucus veil aside, shall appear entirely Golden. Perchance it was when Paris gazed on such a Venus, he did prefer her both to Juno and Minerva[40].

This evidence may suffice for the present occasion, which is to promote inquiry rather than pursue it. For when the inquirer has learned how he ought to begin with, having increased also his natural store of inclination and faith by practice in equal companionship and reciprocal benefaction, he will not despair; and even though the riddle should appear ever so intricate at first, it will solve itself at every stage, opening into new prospects within the veil of life. Labor to know causes, advises the philosopher; he that seeks *rationally* finds the true end, not otherwise; for such a conduct conciliates Minerva, and at her behest Jove prospers the undertaking. Everything depends upon the Motive, which is the true spiritual ferment; and according to the virtue of the fermenting principle is the result obtained.

Sie finis ab origine pendet.

The end depends from the beginning; and as the vine draws its sap from the foeculent impure earth, and yields a fluid fruit, which by the fermentive art is turned into wine, spiritualized, and advanced into a more permanent form of being; so in the Hermetic art, the philosophic matter, drawn in part from the heterogeneous air and defiled breath of vitality, is purified by successive interchanging of ferments, fretted, dissolved, and rectified into a consummate and immortal Form of Light. Bit Nature halts many times before this final rest, at each stage offering the fruits of her conceptive imagination to allure; if the artist be ambitious, however, and a true philosopher, he will accept of none of these, but will proceed, sacrificing all the intermediate benefits, again and again torturing her, and, with relentless hands, slaying the firstborn offspring until the Divine Perfection is attained.—For other foundation can no man lay, as says the apostle, than that which is laid, which is Jesus Christ. Now if any man build upon this foundation gold, silver, precious stones, wood, hay, stubble; every man's work shall be made manifest: for the Day shall declare it, because it shall be revealed by Fire; and the Fire shall *try* every man's work of what sort it is. If any man's work *abide* which he hath built *thereupon*, he shall receive a reward. If any ma's work shall be burned, he shall suffer loss: but he himself shall be save; yet so as by Fire. Know ye not that ye are the Temple of God, and that the Spirit of God dwelleth in you? If any man defile the Temple of God, him shall God destroy; for the Temple of God is holy, which Temple ye are[41].

It is vain to look in expectation, or believe ourselves in the hereditary possession, of a treasure, without so much as opening or suspecting even the casket in which it is shut up. The common elements of Nature obscure their Divine Original, and Chemistry and all our experimental physics drive it forcibly without the means of Identification. Yet as the experienced Chemist knows how, by a skillful application of his art, to analyze the common elements, and distill them to a high virtue and strength of refinement, so the Alchemists long since have taught by amore subtle apparatus and artifice, and tests more cogent than all, to rectify the Universal Element, and compress its invisible vapor into a tangible Form. By applying the proper voluntary corrosive they teach to obliterate its defilements; by gentleness to mollify its Durity; by beneficence to sweeten its acerbity; by justice to moderate its intensity, and to irradiate it with hope, truth, beauty, and universal intellection; supplanting the sensual dominion, and rectifying, until finally, by an actual subversion of the selfhood, they made their Sublimate sublime.

Thus he who, like Oedipus, is able to solve the Enigma of the Sphinx;

in other words, to penetrate rationally the darkened essence of his natural understanding, will, by conversion illuminating its obscurity, cause it to become lucid throughout, and to be no longer what it was before.—For Mind is the Key of this Hermetic Enigma, and no sooner does it attain to Self Knowledge, by proper inquiry within, than the Efficient proceeds out wards to image its motive in operation, so that which before lay in speculation only is carried out in Life. But it is not until the right Motive is discovered, and until the mundification of the Spirit is completed in both kinds, and all things are reduced to a crystalline diaphaneity, that the Philosophic Work has been said truly to being. For, as was before observed, if any permanent confection is made or suffered to take place beforehand, the immature offspring does not abide.

> *He that would seek Tincture most specious*
> *Must needly avoid all things wild and vicious.*
> *The philosopher's worke doe not begin*
> *Till all things be pure without and within*[42].

---

1. B. Valentine, Triumphal Chariot of Antimony; Kirchringius in Basil, idem.
2. Secret. Tact. Alberti Mag. In fine; Ars Auriferae, p. 130 and another.
3. R. Lully, Theoria et Pratica; Vaughan, Coelum Terrae; Le Filet d'Ariadne; Norton, Ordinal, c. iv.; Helmont, Oreatrike, Introd. and cap. c.
4. Crollius, Phil., p.10.
5. Introit. Apert., cap. viii.; Morieni de Tans. Metal.
6. Arnoldi, Rosar., cap. ix., lib. i.
7. Rosar., cap.iii.
8. Dee's Conversat., sub init.
9. Oreatrike, fol. p. 710.
10. Digby's Lucerna Salis, Dialog.
11. Ovidii, Metam., lib. i. 64.
12. Zacharius, Opusc. Lucerna Salis.
13. Introitis Apertus, cap. vii.
14. Ordinal, chap. iv.
15. Kirchringius in Basilio, Latin, 12 mo., p. 160 ; Eng. 74.
16. Tract. Aur., cap. ii.
17. Norton's Ordinal, cap. iv.
18. Ripley Revived, p. 87.
19. See Kelly's Verses in Ashmole's Theatrum.
20. Pope's Homer's Odyssey, lib. viii. 55, &c.
21. Idem.
22. Ordinal, cap. iv.
23. Idem.
24. Amph. Sap. Etern., in medio.
25. Nichomachean Ethics, book iii. cap. iii.
26. See Bell's Pantheon, p. 209.

27. Oracula Chaldeor Mundus, Anima, Natura.
28. See the passage quoted in Vaughan's Preface to the Fame and Confession of the R.C.
29. Kuhnrath, Ampitheat. Sap. Isag.in fig. c;
30. Oreatrike, cap. vi. p. 710.
31. Tract. Aur., cap. iv.
32. 1 Corinth., cap. iii. v.7.
33. 2 Corinth. x. 4, 5.
34. Triumph. Char. of Antim.; Kirchringius, Eng. ed. p.58.
35. Coelum Terrae; Flamelli Summula.
36. De Trans. Metal.
37. Eireneus, Ripley Revived, verses in fine.
38. Introitus Apertus, cap. vii.
39. Nuysement, Sal Lumen, the Latin of Combachius.
40. In Flamelli Summula, Quae ex Democrito colleguntur.
41. 1 Corinth. iii. 11-17.
42. Norton's ordinal, cap. iv.

Chapter 2. Of The Philosophic or Subtle Work

which affords by a theoretic conduct suggestions amply leading to a practical understanding of the most abstruse secret of the Hermetic philosophy, showing the Trinitarian method of operation which Reason follows recreatively for the verification of her light to discover, magnify, and know the Causal Nature transitively in being and in imaged manifestation.

Omnia in omnibus primum, omni Tertio traditit (ex omni primo secundo) omnia in omnibus primum secundum, ut inde omnia in omnibus, et omnia, catholice, agnosceret, cognosceret ac possideret.

— Enigma Kuhnrath, Amph. Sap.

As there are three reigns or grand distinctive distributions of the kingdoms of Nature, so we are informed that in the Philosophic Work, preceding her, there is a threefold order of legitimate operation and a relation of Causal sequences which merits especial note. For these three operations, which are in fact so many degrees through which the Spirit passes from conception to manifestation, are perplexed by the Adepts in their records, and reserved strictly under the Master Key of their Dilemma, in order that the mysteries of this most venerable science might not be discovered to the profane. And shall we, who have hitherto presumed so far on their indifference as to break the preliminary signets and unloose so may covertures of occult learning, more audacious still, approach those final cerements unannealed, and with a full discovering hand expose before all indiscriminately the Art of simple Nature, which the ancients kept so holily, and which the Wisest in modern times have deemed it unprofitable to reveal? The unworthy alone would have it so; the intelligent lovers of truth would bewail nothing more than a desecration of it in incapable hands; nor will they be offended or grudge the additional pains which a conscientious reserve may occasion them to discover, by a theoretic conduct, the ultimate Art of Life.

The tradition of the preliminary practice, as it has been delivered by each one following his own guide independently, may be regarded as it were a track in the sands easily changeable, and where we ought to conduct ourselves rather by the polar star-light than by any footsteps which are seen implanted there. Besides the confusion of the tracks which the many wayfarers have left is so great, and one finds so many different paths and willful deviations, that it is almost impossible not to be led astray from the right road, which the Star alone points out for all and each one by his proper sight beholding it. The willful confusion of the Hermetic doctrine has doubtless checked many aspirants; some in the beginning, others in the middle of their philosophic career, have been disappointed; many even with a perfect knowledge of the preliminary work, and having the true Matter in Hand also and means of purification, are said to have faltered in defect of the ultimate theory whereon to proceed; some, even when they understood this, having already approached through much labour and contemplation towards the end of their journey, having the Final Purpose also in mind, which their predecessors had dug in the midway between them and the fulfillment of their destined course. I vow sincerely to you, says Eudoxus, in that introduction of his to the *Six Keys*, that the practice of our Art is the most difficult thing in the world, not in regard to its operation, but in respect of the difficulties which are in it, to learn it distinctly fro the books of the philosophers. For if, on the one side, it is called with reason a recreation and play of children; on the other hand, it requires in those who search for the *Truth* a profound knowledge of the principles and of the operations of Nature in the Three Kinds: Thus Norton says —

> *Greate neede hath he to be a clerke*
> *That would discerne this Subtill Werke:*
> *He must know hys first filosophie,*

Mary Anne Atwood

If he trust to come by Lakimie.

It is a great point to find out the True Matter and proper Subject of this work; even for this we must pierce through a thousand obscure veils wherewith it has been overspread: we must distinguish it by its proper idea and name, among a million of pseudonyms and abstruse appellations, whereby the Adepts have chosen to express it: we must learn to understand the properties of it, in order to judge of the possibility of the miracles alleged; and before we can into the abstruse Original of Nature, we must reflect profoundly and patiently, in order to discriminate the secret Fire of the Wise, which is the only agent granted by Art to purify and dispose Nature to a sacrifice of her last life. This, we must know, and the Divine Law that succeeds to animate her by a revolutionary course. We must learn further how to convert and congeal the new-born Quintessence or mercurial water into an incombustible fixed unguent, and, by the entire revolution of its body, to awaken the occult Light to Life.

And to effect this, moreover, adds our author of *The Triumph*, you must make the conversion of the Elements, the separation and the reunion of the Three Principles; you must learn how to make thereof a white Mercury and a citrine Mercury, and you must fix this Mercury and nourish it with its own blood, to the end that it may be converted into the fixed Sulphur, which is the Stone of Philosophers.

These are the fixed principles of the hermetic Art, in which there is no variableness but in their discovery, which, having already discussed, we proceed to redeem our promise of a more subtle application to practice; and this, without incurring too great a responsibility on ourselves, may we trust be intelligibly conceived from such succeeding evidence as it is expedient only to afford.

We read, in the Egyptian Fable of Isis and Osiris, that they were sister and brother, and being conjoined in marriage likewise, that their kingdom was cruelly divulsed and usurped by their brother Typhon, who in a malignant and envious spirit killed Osiris, cut his body into pieces and scattered his members to the four winds. Isis however, recollecting these, preserved them in a chest which floated on the Nilotic waters in safety until the period arrived for a restitution; when the king was thenceforth resuscitated, and came forth invulnerable from his ashes, and far more powerful than he was before, to the enjoyment of his dominions and rightful throne.

Now in this fable, already explained in part, Plutarch, with the Adepts also being witnesses, is profoundly couched not only the principiating action of Intellect but the methodical art of the same subtle Antecedent to bring itself, by begetting a supernatural offspring, into natural effect.

And since it is requisite, according to the ancient Metaphysics, to consider the doctrine of Causes from its Principle, and causes are said to subsist in a fourfold respect, one of which they assert to be essence, and that the subsisting as a certain particular thing, and *cause and principle* form the *First Why;* but the *second cause* is matter and that which subsists as a *subject; A Third* is that whence the *beginning of motion* is derived; and The *Fourth* is a *cause opposite* to this, viz., That for the *sake* of which the inquiry subsists, and the Good which is the end of regeneration[1].

Hence, referring this Peripathetic scheme of investigation to the art of Wisdom for realization, we may conceive the whole intellectual relationship; and how the speculative Motive of the first Cause is finally produced in reversionary order from the Third, in whom it becomes efficient, by the Second into the Fourth; as it were a triplicate being of Thought, Will, and Understanding, which, resting in the sole vision of its only begotten perfection, desires not to surpass itself; but, perceiving itself indeed to be the Final Object of its own First Cause, is *good*, according to the words of the Stagyrite, and the end of spiritual generation.

These, then, are the universal principles which it has sometimes been deemed expedient in practice to represent, and these are their several relations:

> *Primus dicatur in quo sensus dominatur.*
> *Sensibus awquato gaudet natura Secundo.*
> *Tertius excedit, cujus tolerantia laedit.*
> *Destructor sensus nescit procedere Quarto.*

And, as respects the operation of the these, viz., of the natural, unnatural, and the supernatural Fires, they should be quickly lighted, says the Adept[2], lest one should put out the other, or that this should stifle that: over all which the Fourth, partaking of the aerial fiery element, supervenes for the accomplishment o the work. And, as respects the Vessels, the First indeed may be considered to be opaque, the Second less so, and the Third still less so. This last containing truly Him who is to be born; as the embryo in the mother is protected with a triple covering and sustained within until mature, even so is the metaphysical offspring said to be involved: which, by the birth of Horus in the Egyptian fable, is accurately represented, when, Typhon being vanquished, the lawful empire is resumed.—*Triuna universalis essentia, quae Jehovah appellatur et ex Uno, divina essentia, dein ex Dubus, Deo et homine. Ex Tribus, personis et una Divina Essentia, quem-admonum etiam ex Quinque tribus personis, et duabus Essentiis nimirum, divinus et simul humanus est*[3].

Hence the Divine Monarchy consists, and is established; the primary principles whereof, as here announced, are in their representation familiar; but of the form of the Fourth in that Burning Fiery Furnace, we may conceive only from what is written.—Behold I will send you Elijah, the prophet, before the coming of the Great and terrible Day of the Lord, and he shall turn the hearts of the Fathers unto the Children, and the hearts of the Children to their Fathers, lest I come and strike the earth with a curse[4]. But, say the Adepts, *Natus est jam Elias Artista*[5]; Elias, the artist, is born already; and this is he that was appointed a forerunner, baptizing with the water unto repentance3, who has foreshown all things in his apparition to the wise, whose birth is miraculous in the hypostatic transfiguration, and prior to the Divine Light.

> *Whom to seeke it availeth right nought,*
> *Till the white medicine be fully wrought.*
> *Alsoe both medicines in their beginninge*
> *Have one manner of vessel and workinge,*
> *As well for the White as for the Red,*
> *Till all quick things be made dead;*
> *When vessels and forme of operation*
> *Shall chaunge in matter, figure, and graduation.*
> *But my herte quaketh, my hand in tremblinge,*
> *When I write of this most selcouth thinge.*
> *Hermes brought forth a true sentence and blounte,*
> *When he said, Ignis et Azoth tibi sufficient*[6].

It will be unnecessary now to remind the attentive reader of what has been before explained. Nature, indeed, provides us with the foundations of Wisdom, and materials wherewith to construct her immortal Edifice of Light; but it is the work only of a Master mason, of Grand Architects, as the Lodge has it, to erect structures in the air. The task is too onerous for inferior craftsmen[7]. It is the part of Mind alone to represent herself in this way by her own reflective energy, to embody the ethereal Image, and chisel it out in Light.—O blessed watery Form! That dissolveth the Elements! Now it behooves us with this watery soul to possess ourselves of a sulphurous Form, and to mingle the same with our Acetum. For when by the power of the Water the composition is dissolved, it is the Key of the Restoration. And when thou shalt pour forth thy Fire upon the Foliated Sulphur, continues the Master, the boundary of hearts (*i.e.*, the Final Cause) does enter in above it, and is washed in the same, and the mortal matter thereof is extracted. *Then is he transformed in his Tincture.* Our Son the King takes his Tincture from the fire and death even, and darkness and the waters flee away. The Dragon shuns the sunbeams which dart through the crevices, our dead Son lives. The King comes forth from the Fire, and rejoices with his spouse, and the occult treasury is laid open. The Son, already vivified, is become a warrior in the Fire, of tincture super-excellent. For this Son is the treasury, bearing even (in his hand) the Philosophic Matter[8].—Now then bring ye the gifts of salutation to the *Rain*; that, not being *withholden*, it may descend upon you; and to the *dew*, if it has received from you gold and silver. Open your eyes, and lift up your horns, ye that are capable to comprehend the *Elect One*; before whose *feet* all his *antecedents* fall away, and are *consumed*. Those *mountains* which thou hast seen, the mountain of *copper*, the mountain of *silver*, the mountain of *gold*, the mountain of *fluid metal*, and the mountain of *lead*, all these in the presence of the Elect One shall be like a honeycomb before the Fore; and like water descending from above upon the mountains, and shall become debilitated before his feet. All these things shall be *rejected* when the Elect One shall appear in the presence of the Lord of Spirits[9].— Behold, I will send my *Messenger* and he shall *prepare* the way before me: And the Lord, whom *ye seek*, shall suddenly come to his *Temple*, even the *messenger* of the *covenant*, whom ye delight in: behold who shall abide the day of his coming? And who shall abide the day of his coming? And who shall *stand* when he *appeareth*? For he is like a *Refiner's Fire*, and like *fuller's* soap; and he shall sit as a refiner and purifier of silver: and he shall purify the sons of Levi, and purge them as gold and *silver*, that they may offer unto the Lord an *offering* in righteousness[10].

This was He whom the Patriarchs and Hebrew prophets looked for, and the Ethnic philosophers, in anticipation, adored; who in the sacred humanity of Jesus Christ was at last made manifest; whom of Jesus Christ was at last made manifest; whom the Apostles and early Christian

Fathers, Saints, and martyrs testify of, and with understanding worshipped; even—That which was from the Beginning, which they had heard, and seen with their eyes, which they had heard, and seen with their eyes, which they had looked upon, and their hands had handled, of the Word of Life; for the Life was made manifest, and they had seen it, and bear witness, and shew unto us that Eternal Life was made manifest, and they had seen it, and bear witness, and shew unto us that Eternal Life, which was with the Father, and was manifested unto them[11]. And *now* also the *axe* is laid unto the root of the trees: therefore every tree which bringeth not forth good fruit is hewn down, and cast into the fire. I indeed baptize you with Water unto repentance: But He that cometh after me is mightier than I, whose shoes I am not worthy to bear: He shall baptize you with the Holy Ghost and with Fire: Whose fan is in his Hand, and he will thoroughly purge his floor, and gather his wheat into the garner; but the chaff he will burn up with unquenchable fire[12].

O mysteries truly sacred! Exclaims the Bishop of Alexandria in holy transport, O pure Light; at the Light of Torches, the veil that covers God and Heaven falls off. I am holy now that I am initiated. *It is the Lord himself who is the Hierophonta. He sets his seal upon the Adepts, whom he illuminates with his beams: and whom he illuminates with his beams:* and whom, as a recompense for faith, he will recommend to the eternal love of the Father. These are the orgies of my mysteries, come ye and be received[13].

Thus the Mysteries of Antiquity changed their form only to appear more resplendent when Christianity came to be the prevailing religion; when baptismal regeneration was an effectual rite, and the Eucharist a true initiation; when Faith, by humiliation under the exemplary cross of Christ, brought Him forth anew in each regenerate life, identically perfect in all things, immortal, and transcending every precedent revelation of the Light; as St Paul, in his Epistle to the Hebrew, also bears witness:— God, who at sundry times and in divers manners spake in times past unto the Fathers by the prophets, hath in these last days spoken unto whose Son, whom he hath appointed heir of all things, by whom also he made the worlds; who bring the brightness of his glory and the express image of his person, and upholding all things by the Word of his power, when he had by himself purged our sins, sat down in the right hand of the Majesty on High[14].

Meditate, therefore, says the Theosophist, and study theosophically to reduce the Ternary by the Quaternary, through the rejection of the Binary, to the simplicity of the Monad; that thy body, soul, and spirit be gathered to rest in the name of Jesus[15]. Learn to unite the Principles of our Chaos to a new Life, and they will be regenerated by Water and the Spirit. These two are in all things, and each has in himself, as Trismegistus says, the seed of his own regeneration[16]. Proceed then *patiently* but not *manually*. The work is performed by an *invisible Artist;* for there is a secret incubation of the Spirit of God upon nature; you must only see that the outward heat fails not, but with the subject itself you have no more to do than the mother with child that is in her womb. The two former principles perform all. The Spirit makes use of the water to purge and wash his body, and he will bring it at last to a celestial immortal constitution. Does any one think this impossible? Further inquires the Adept.—Remember, that in the incarnation of Jesus Christ, the Quaternarius, or four elements, as some call them, were united to their eternal Unity and Ternarius. Three and Four make seven. This Sepentary is the true Sabaoth, the rest of God, into which the creature shall enter. This is the best and plainest manuduction that I can give you; in a word, Salvation is nothing else but a Transmutation[17]—of the component principles of life in the circulation. And this is the true metempsychosis which has been the source of many errors in the common acceptancy; but which, in the Ancient Schools of Divinity, signified neither more nor less than a transmigrating of the human Identity out of this animal terrene existence through the ethereal elements of its original formation. Which elements are the universal fundamentals of nature; but in the Human form alone are found to attain to that supremacy of Reason which re-enters to its First Cause; when, by a Triplicate growth of Light in the Understanding, becoming consciously allied, It emanates a Fourth Form, truthful, godlike, being the express image of its motive magically portrayed.

- I. IN THE BEGININNG WAS THE WORD,
- II. AND THE WORD WAS WITH GOD,
- III. AND THE WORD WAS GOD.

All things were made by Him, and without Him was not any thing made that was made. In Him was Life, and the life was the Light of Men. And the Light shineth in Darkness; and the Darkness comprehendeth it not

- IV. THERE WAS A MAN SENT FROM GOD WHOSE NAME WAS JOHN.

The same came for a Witness, to bear witness of the Light that all men through *him* might *believe*. He *was not that Light*, but was sent to bear *Witness* of that Light. That was the *True Light*, which lighteth every man that cometh into the world[18];— which in the Saviour was perfected; one ray of which, intrinsically permeating, is able to cleanse this leprous life of ours, and convert it to the virtue and perfect potency of its Whole.

And whosoever in any other Light or Form of Light should look for the First Cause, or for any other Final Cause in this, except the First, would seek contrary to reason, against the divine ordinance, and against himself; for nothing else is worth seeking, or can terminate in good, but will be the fruit of the Fall only, which Adam took upon himself; the mortal consequences of which are hourly expiated by our race, and which no one, unless he were insane, haply would labour to increase. The rule of Wisdom, in the verification of her Light, is absolute, and though intermediates apply themselves naturally for the generation, they are rejected in the accomplishment; as it is explained—*Non fit ad monadis simplicitatem reductio, nisi rejiciaturprius binarius, non enim cum Jehovah unto nisi prius a teipso devitatio et tui abnegatio.*—For as the absolute Identification in theory is not conceived but by self-ablation and avoidance, so, practically, neither is Nature reduced to the Monadic simplicity of her Element but by rejection of her Binary conception. For if in the Duad the divine Idea were suffered immediately to bring forth, an imperfect offspring would result, and discordant by predominance of either generating extreme, as in this life is manifest; but by carrying the circulation upward through a Third principle for reprobation, it is rectified, overcome in its proper volition, and dying (if the divine rule be thenceforth followed), is raised again by reversion, and through a diligent analysis passing, as it were, from heaven to earth and from earth to heaven, it receives the strength of superiors and of inferiors, to make manifest the Flower of Intellect retrospectively to its Archetypal Source, according to the Hermetic Riddle:

OMNIA IN OMNIBUS PRIMUM, OMNI TERTIO TRADIDIT, EX OMNI PRIMO SEGUNDO, OMNIA IN OMNIBUS PRIMUM SECUNDUM, UT INDE OMNIA IN OMNIBUS, ET OMNIA CATHOLICE AGNOSCERET, CONOSCERET AC POSSIDERET.

THE FIRST ALL THINGS IN ALL GAVE THE FIRST SECOND ALL THINGS IN ALL, FROM THE ALL IN THE FIRST SECOND TO THE THIRD ALL; THAT HE MIGHT DISCOVER, KNOW, AND POSSESS ALL THINGS UNIVERSALLY.

And this, it would seem, is the Catholic Art of Reason investigating her First Source, which the Chaldaic oracle no less orderly pursues.

> *Where the Paternal Monad is?*
> *The Monad is enlarged which generates Two,*
> *For the Duad sits beside him and glitters with intellectual sections,*
> *And to govern all things and to order everything not ordered.*
> *For in the whole world shineth the Triad over which the Monad rules.*
> *This order is the beginning of all sections:*
> *For the mind of the Father said that all things be cut into Three—*
> *Whose will assented; and then all things were divided.*
> *And there appeared in it (the triad) Virtue, Wisdom, and multscient Verity;*
> *This way floweth the form of the Triad, being pre-existent, not the First (Essence) but where they are measured.*
> *For thou must conceive that all things serve these three Principles.*
> *Their First Course is sacred, but in the middle another, and the third Aerial which cherisheth the Earth in Fire;*
> *And Fountain of all Fountains,*
> *The Matrix containing all things, hence abundantly springs forth The generation of multi-various matter;*
> *Whence is extracted a Prester the Flower of glowing Fire,*
> *Flashing into the cavities of the world, for all things from thence begin to extend downwards their admirable beams*[19].

Such is the recreant progress of mind, ascending and descending throughout life, for the investigation of its manifold resources and powers; where there is an exact machinery to be observed, a method which, though simple, is difficult for common sense to conceive aright—a mainspring exquisitely tempered, an enduring pivot, wheel within wheel revolving vitally, Mercury, Sulphur, and an immortal Salt. And as steel draws the loadstone and the loadstone in like manner turns toward steel, so is it with the separated principles of Will and Understanding in their freed state. It is true, moreover, that our loadstone contains in its inmost center an abundance of that marvelous Salt, which is that menstruum in the sphere of Saturn mentioned by Eireneus, which can calcine gold. This center turns naturally towards the Pole where the virtue of the steel is gradually strengthened. In this Pole is the heart of the mercury, which is a true Fire, in which its Lord rests; and passing through this great sea, guided by the Light of that Polar Star which our Magnet exhibits, it arrives at its original destination.—The Wise will rejoice, adds the Adept, but fools and the ignorant will hold it for a small things, nor yet learn Wisdom, though they should see the Central Pole extravasated and bearing the notable Sign of Omnipotence. But let the Son of Philosophy hearken to the Words of the Wise, who unanimously declare that their work may be likened to the creation of the world.—In the *Beginning* God made *Heaven and Earth*. And the *Earth* was without *Form* and *void;* and *Darkness* was upon the *Face* of the *Deep*. And the *Spirit of God* moved upon the *Face* of the *Waters*. And *God* said, Let there be *Light:* and there was *Light*.—and these words may suffice, continues the philosopher; for the Heaven and Earth philosophical, even as agent and patient, must be united upon the throne of friendship and love, where they will thereafter reign together in everlasting honour[20].

> *Maria sonat breviter quod tralia tonat,*
> *Gummis cum binis fugitivum figit in imis,*
> *Horis in trinis vinclat fortia finis.*
> *Maria lux roris ligam ligat in tribus horis,*
> *Filia Plutonis consortia jungit amoris Gaudet in assata per Tria sociata*[21].

Thus exalted by a rotary circulation, as it were, from the lowest to the most perfect form of vitality —from its beginning in voluntary indigence, through each succeeding sphere of resolute conception, the Spirit goes on to increase and multiply its hidden light outwardly, until its substance, being replenished, it is brought forth to sight. The First has it and refuses it; the Second fives it and regards it not—And the Fourth, as the artist, applies it to the work in the furtherance, thus proving himself from first to last to be essential, and the greatest Handicraft of all;—when the Stone, so singularly raised up by the builders each in turn rejecting each it, becomes the Head Stone of the Corner.—This is the Lord's doing, and it is marvelous in our Eyes.

And as the Stone of the Wise is completed in three successive circulations, so likewise was the Temple of mighty Solomon built up by the joint assistance of Hiram and Queen Sheba, and wonderfully adorned with gold, and silver, and constelled beams; as in the book of *Jezirah* we also read—that, with the Fiery Letters of the Law, also read—that, with the

Fiery Letters of the Law, He engraved the empty, and the void, and the obscure mind, and made, as it were, a heap of grain and a straight statue, and intersected it with joined beams[22]. Which brings to mind those lines in the nineteenth book of the *Odyssey*, when Ulysses and Telemachus, removing the weapons out of the armory, Minerva preceded them, having a golden Lamp, with which she produced a very beautiful Light, on perceiving which, Telemachus thus immediately addresses his Father: O Father! This is certainly a most admirable thing which presents itself to my eyes. For the walls of the House, the beautiful spaces between the rafters, the fir beams, and the columns appear to rise in radiance as if on fire. Certainly some one of the gods is present who inhabit the extended heaven. But the wise Ulysses thus answered him: —Be silent, repress your intellect, and do not speak. For this is the custom of the gods in Olympus[23]. Homer, therefore, in common with the philosophers of his age, indicates that for the proper reception of divinity, quietude and a cessation of mental energy are becoming and necessary to the consummating knowledge of the First Cause.—And the knowledge of it, says Trismegistus, is a most Divine Silence, and a rest of all the senses; for neither can he that understands *That* understand anything else, nor he that sees *That* see anything else, in sum move the body. For, shining steadfastly up and around the whole mind, it enlighteneth all the soul, and loosing it from the bodily senses and motions, it draweth it from the body, and changeth it wholly into the Essence of God.

We awaken from the Intellectual Intuition, says Schelling, as from a *state of death*—and we awaken, by reflection, into that created personality wherein it is impossible any longer to know Him.—The vision graven in hallowed memory is all that remains to us; for the object of human reason is the limit of its power, and the pure zero of all relative conception waits before the throne of God.—But to our work.

> *The last concord is well known to Clerkes*
> *Between the sphere of Heaven and our Subtil Werkes*
> *Nothing in erth hath more simplicitie,*
> *Than th' elements of our Stone woll be,*
> *Wherefore their, being in worke if generation,*
> *Have most obedience to constellation:*
> *Whereof concord most kindly convenient*
> *Is a direct and Fiery ascendant,*
> *Being sign common for this operation,*

For the multitude of their iteration:
Fortune your ascendant with his Lord alsoe,
Keeping th' aspect of shrews them fro';
And of they must let, or needly infect,
Cause them look with a triune aspect,
For the white Worke make fortunate the Moone,
For the Lord of the Fourth House likewise be it done;
For that is Thesaurum absconditum of old clerkes;
Soe of the sixth house for servants of the Werkes;
Save all them well from great impediments,
As it is in picture, or like the same intents,
Unless that your nativity pretend infection,
In contrariety of this Election,
The virtue of the over of the orbe is formall,
The virtue of the eight sphere is here intrumentall,
With her signs and figures and parts aspectual,
The planet's virtue is proper and speciall,
The virtue of the elements is here materiall,
The virtue infused resulteth of them all;
The First is like to a workman's mind,
The Second like to his hand ye shall finde;
The Third is like a good instrument,
The remnant like a thing wrought to your
Intent Make all the premises with other well accord,
Then shall your merits make you a greate Lord.
In this wise Elixir, of whom ye make mencion,
Is engendered a thing of Second Intention[24].

I could tell thee, says Vaughan, of a first and second sublimation, of a double nativity, visible and invisible, without which the Matter is not alterable as to our final purpose. I could tell thee also of sulphurs simple and compounded, of three Argent vives and as many Salts, and all this would be bad news (as the schoolmen phrase it), even to the best learned in England. But I hope not by this discourse to demolish any man's castles; for why should they despair when I contribute to their building[25]?

Our magistery is Three, Two, and One —
The Animal, Vegetable, and Mineral Stone.
First, I say, in the name of the Holy Trinity,

> *Look that thou join in one persons Three —*
> *The Fixt, the Variable, and the Fugitive —*
> *Till they together taste death and live.*
> *The first one is the Dragon fell,*
> *That shall the other twaine both slay and quell;*
> *The Sun and Moon shall lose their light,*
> *And in mourning sable, they shall seem dight,*
> *Three score days long, or neere thereabouts;*
> *Then shall Phoebus appear first out,*
> *With strange colours in all the Firmament,*
> *Then our joy is coming and at Hand present,*
> *Then Orient Phoebus in his hemisphere*
> *To us full gloriously shall appear:*
> *Thus he who can work wisely,*
> *Shall attain unto our Maistery*[26].

Which magistery is a fiery form of Light inspisate, made manifest by a triplicate introversion and multiplication of the hypostatic unit by the circulatory medium throughout life.

> *Already see the laurel branches wave!*
> *Hark! Sounds tumultuous shake the trembling cave.*
> *Far, ye profane, far off with beauteous feet,*
> *Bright Phoebus comes and thunders at the gate.*
> *See! The glad sign the Delian Palm hath given,*
> *Sudden it bends; and hovering in the heaven,*
> *Soft sings the Swan with melody divine.*
> *B*URST OPE YE BARS! YE GATES, YOUR HEADS EXPAND.
> *H*E COMES! THE GOD OF LIGHT, THE GOD'S AT HAND.
> *Begin the song, and tread the sacred ground*
> *In mystic dance symphonious to the sound.*
> *Begin, young men! Apollo's eyes endure*
> *None but the good, the perfect, and the pure.*
> *Who view the god are great, but abject they*
> *For whom he turns his favouring eyes away.*
> *All-seeing God! In every place confessed,*
> *We will prepare, behold thee, and be blessed.*
> *He comes, young men! Nor silent should ye stand,*
> *With harp or feet, when Phoebus is at hand*[27].

Fit thy roof to thy God in all thou canst, continues the philosopher, and in what thou canst not he will help thee; thou must prepare thyself till thou art conformable to Him whom thou wouldest entertain, and that in every way of similitude. Thou hast three that are to receive, and there be here accordingly that give. And when thou hast set thy house in order, think not that thy guest will come without invitation.

> *Perpetual knockings at his doore,*
> *Teares sullying his transparent rooms,*
> *Sighs upon sighs, weepmore and more,*
> *He comes.*

This is the way that thoumust walk, in which, if thou dost, thou shalt perceive a sudden illumination —- *Eritque in te cum Lumine Ignis; cum Igne Ventus; cum Ventus Potestas; cum Potestas, Scientia; cum Scientia, sanae mentis integritas*[28].—And then it is requisite to believe that we have seen Him, says Plotinus, when the Soul receives a sudden Light. For the Light is with Power, and is God. —And then it is proper to think that He is present, when, like another Divinity entering the house of some one who invokes him, he fills it with splendour. For, unless he entered, he would not illuminate it, and then the soul would be without Light, and without the possession of God[29]. But when illuminated, it has That which is sought for; and the Thought and understanding are in the experience One.

NEC SENTIRE DEUM NISI QUI PARS IPSE DEI SIT.

That was the sum of the Hermetic Mystery, and the ultimate object of the Alchemical Art to accomplish; and by such a subtle analysis and pure synthesis of vital agencies and effects, the Word of Life would seem to have been sought after by our ancestors, and experimentally found: what their neglected Scriptures everywhere testify of, and the Smaragdine Tablet yet lives summarily instructing us to reprove.

TRUE WITHOUT ERROR, CERTAIN AND MOST TRUE; THAT WHICH IS ABOVE IS AS THAT WHICH IS BELOW, AND THAT WHICH IS BELOW IS AS THAT WHICH IS ABOVE, FOR PERFORMING THE MIRACLES OF THE ONE THING. AND AS ALL THINGS WERE FROM ONE, BY THE MEDIATION OF ONE, SO ALL THINGS PROCEEDED FROM THIS ONE THING BY ADAPTATION. THE FATHER OF IT IS THE SUN, THE MOTHER OF IT IS THE MOON, THE WIND CARRIED IT IN ITS BELLY; THE NURSE THEREOF IS THE EARTH. THIS IS THE FATHER OF ALL

PERFECTION AND CONSUMMATION OF THE WHOLE WORLD. THE POWER OF IT IS INTEGRAL, IF IT BE TURNED INTO EARTH. THOU SHALT SEPARATE THE EARTH FROM THE FIRE, THE SUBTLE FROM THE GROSS, GENTLY, WITH MUCH SAGACITY. IT ASCENDS FROM EARTH TO HEAVEN, AND AGAIN DESCENDS TO EARTH; AND RECEIVES THE STRENGTH OF THE SUPERIORS AND OF THE INFERIORS. SO THOU HAST THE GLORY OF THE WHOLE WORLD: THEREFORE LET ALL OBSCURITY FLEE BEFORE THEE. THIS IS THE STRONG FORTITUDE OF ALL FORTITUDES, OVERCOMING EVERY SUBTLE AND PENETRATING EVERY SOLID THING. SO THE WORLD WAS CREATED. HENCE WERE WONDERFUL ADAPTATIONS, OF WHICH THIS IS THE MANNER. THEREFORE AM I CALLED THRICE GREAT HERMES, HAVING THE THREE PARTS OF THE PHILOSOPHY OF THE WHOLE WORLD. THAT WHICH I HAVE SPOKEN IS CONSUMMATED CONCERNING THE OPERATION OF THE SUN.

The six following "Keys", delivered into the safe hand of the intelligent inquirer (since they will be useful to none else), may be acceptable; that, without involving more responsibility on ourselves, he may apply their explanatory words as he thinks fit. But we would deter all from hasty trial and avow our willful reservation of an important link in the application of these principles to practice, lest any attempting to realize without a full investigation of the methods, should fail utterly in the pursuit.

---

1. See Aristotle's Metaphysics, book I.
2. Maieri Symbola Aureae Mensae, p. 256.
3. Aquarium Sapientum in Mus. Herm., p. 112.
4. Malachi iv. 5,6.
5. Introit. Apertus, cap. xiii.
6. Norton's Ordinal, cap. v.
7. See Carlile's Manuel of Free Masonry, part iii. p.17.
8. Tractatus Aureus, cap. ii.
9. Book of Enoch, xcix.
10. Malachi iii. 1-4.
11. First Epistle Gen. St. John, St Paul to the Hebrews.
12. St Matthew iii. 10, etc
13. Clemens Alexandrinus, See De Septchenes, Relig. of the Greeks, chap. ii.
14. St Paul to the Hebrews, i. 1, &c.
15. Kuhnrath Amp. Sap. Etern. in medio.
16. See the Divine Poemander, Sermon on the Mont of Regeneration.
17. Lumen de Lumine, p. 92.
18. St John's Gospel i.
19. Chaldaic Oracles, i.
20. See Introitus Apertus, chap. iv.; Genesis, chap. i.
21. Maria Practica, &c.; Ars Aurifera, vol. ii. p. 208.
22. Cap. i.
23. Odyssey, book xix.

24. Norton's Ordinal, chap.vi.
25. See Vaughan's Lumen de Lumine.
26. Theatrum Chemicum Brit; Conclusion of Bloomfield's Camp of Philosophy.
27. Callimachus' Hymn to Apollo, by Dodd.
28. Anima Magia Abscond., p. '7, &c.
29. Plotinus' Select Works, Taylor, p. 453.

Chapter 3. The Six Keys of Eudoxus, opening into the Most Secret Philosophy

leading into the most secret Philosophy of the Multiplication and Projection, Rewards and Potencies, Nature, Properties, Analogies, and Appliances of the Philosopher's Stone.

THE FIRST KEY

The First Key is that which opens the dark prisons in which the Sulphur is shut up: this is it which knows how to extract the seed out of the body, and which forms the Stone of the philosophers by the conjunction of the spirit with the body — of sulphur with mercury. Hermes has manifestly demonstrated the operation of this First Key by these words: *In the caverns of the metals there is hidden the Stone, which is venerable, bright in colour, a mind sublime, and an open sea.* This Stone has a bright glittering: it contains a Spirit of a sublime original; it is the Sea of the Wise, in which they angle for their mysterious Fish. But the operations of the three works have a great deal of analogy one to another, and the philosophers do designedly speak in equivocal terms, to the end that those who have not the Lynx's eyes may pursue wrong, and be lost in this labyrinth, from whence it is very hard to get out. In effect, when one imagines that they speak of one work, they often treat of another. Take heed, therefore, not to be deceived here; for it is a truth, that in each work the Wise Artist ought to dissolve the body with the spirit; he must cut off the Raven's head, whiten the Black, and vivify the White; yet it is properly in the First operation that the Wise Artist cuts off the head of the Black Dragon and of the Raven. Hence, Hermes says, *What is born of the Crow is the beginning of this Art.* Consider that it is by separation of the black, foul, and stinking fume of the Blackest Black that our astral, white, and resplendent Stone is formed, which contains in its veins the blood of the Pelican. It is at this First Purification of the Stone, and at this shining whiteness, that the work of the First Key is ended.

THE SECOND KEY

The Second Key dissolves the compound of the Stone, and begins the separation of the Elements in a philosophical manner: this separation of the elements is not made but by raising up the subtle and pure parts above the thick and terrestrial parts. He who knows how to sublime the Stone philosophically, justly deserves the name of a philosopher, since he knows the *Fire of the Wise*, which is the only instrument which can work this sublimation. No philosopher has ever openly revealed this Secret Fire, and this powerful agent, which works all the wonders of the Art: he who shall not understand it, and not know how to distinguish it by the characters whereby it is described, ought to make a stand here, and pray to God to make it clear to him; for the knowledge of this great Secret is rather a gift of Heaven, than a Light acquired by the natural force of reasoning; let him, nevertheless, read the writings of the philosophers; let him meditate; and, above all, let him pray: there is no difficulty which may not in the end be made clear by Work, Meditation, and Prayer. Without the sublimation of the Stone, the conversion of the Elements and the extraction of the Principles is impossible; and this conversion, which makes Water of Earth, Air of Water, and Fire of Air, is the only way whereby our Mercury can be prepared. Apply yourself then to know this Secret Fire, which dissolves the Stone naturally and without violence, and makes it dissolve into Water in the great sea of the Wise, *by the distillation which is made by the rays of the Sun and Moon*. It is in this manner that the Stone, which, according to Hermes, is the vine of the Wise, becomes their Wine, which, by the operations of Art, produces their rectified Water of Life, and their most sharp Vinegar. The Elements of the Stone cannot be dissolved but by this Nature wholly Divine; nor can a perfect dissolution be made of it, but after a proportioned digestion and putrefaction, at which the operation of the Second Key of the First Work is ended.

THE THIRD KEY

The Third Key comprehends of itself alone a longer train of operations than all the rest together. The philosophers have spoken very little of it, seeing the Perfection of our *Mercury* depends thereon; the sincerest even, as Artefius, Trevisan, Flammel, have passed in silence the Preparation of our Mercury, and there is hardly one found who has not feigned, instead of showing the longest and the most important of the operations of our Practice. With a design to lend you a hand in this part of the way, which you have to go, and where for want of Light it is impossible to know the true road, I will enlarge myself more than others have done on this Third Key; or at least I will follow in an order, that which they have treated so confusedly, that without the inspiration of Heaven, or without the help of a faithful friend, one remains undoubtedly in this labyrinth, without being able to find a happy deliverance from thence. I am sure, that you who are the true Sons of Science will receive a very great satisfaction in the explaining of these hidden Mysteries, which regard the separation and the purification of the *Principles of our Mercury*, which is made by a perfect dissolution and glorification of the body, whence it had its nativity, and by the intimate union of the soul with its body, of whom the Spirit is the only tie which works this conjunction. This is the Intention, and the essential point of the Operations of this Key, which terminate at the generation of a new substance infinitely nobler than the First.

After the Wise Artist has made a spring of living water come out of the stone, and has pressed out the vine of the philosophers, and has made their wine, he ought to take notice that in this homogeneous substance, which appears under the form of Water, there are three different substances, and three natural principles of bodies—Salt, Sulphur and Mercury—which are the spirit, the soul, and the body; and though they appear pure and perfectly united together, there still wants much of their being so; *for when by distillation we draw the Water, which is the soul and the spirit, the Body remains in the bottom of the vessel*, like a dead, black, and dredgy earth, which, nevertheless, is not to be despised; for in our subject there is nothing which is not good. The philosopher, John Pontanus, protests that the very superfluities of the Stone are converted into a true essence, and that he who pretends to separate anything from our subject knows nothing of philosophy; for that all which is therein superfluous, unclean, dredgy—in fine, the whole compound, is made perfect by the action of our Fire. This advice opens the eyes of those, who, to make an exact purification of the Elements and of the Principles, persuade themselves that they must only take the subtile and cast away the heavy. But Hermes says that power of it is not integral until it be turned into earth; neither ought the sons of science to be ignorant that the Fire and the Sulphur are hidden in the centre of the *Earth*, and that they must wash it exactly with its spirit, to extract out of it the *Fixed Salt*, which is the Blood of our Stone. This is the essential Mystery of the operation, which is not accomplished till after a convenient digestion and a slow distillation. You know that nothing is more contrary than fire and water; but yet the Wise Artist must make peace between the enemies, who radically love each other vehemently. Cosmopolite told the manner thereof in a few words: *All things must therefore being purged make Fire and Water to be Friends, which they will easily do in their earth, which had ascended with them.* Be then attentive on this point; moisten oftentimes the earth with its water, and you will obtain what you seek. Must not the body be dissolved by the water, and the Earth be penetrated with its Humidity, to be made proper for generation? According to philosophers, the Spirit is Eve, the Body is Adam; they ought to be joined together for the propagation of their species. Hermes says the same in other terms: *For Water is the strongest Nature which surmounts and excites the fixed Nature in the Body, that is, rejoices in it.* In effect, these two substances, which are of the same nature but of different genders, ascend insensibly together, leaving but a little facces in the bottom of their vessel; so that the soul, spirit, and body, after an exact purification, appear at last inseparably united under a more noble and more perfect Form than it was before, and as different from its first liquid Form as the alcohol of Wine exactly rectified and actuated with its salt is different from the substance of the wine from whence it has been drawn; this comparison is not only very fitting, but it furthermore gives the sons of science a precise knowledge of the operations of the Third Key.

Our Water is a living Spring which comes out of the Stone by a natural miracle of our philosophy. The first of all is the water which issueth out of this Stone. It is Hermes who has pronounced this great Truth. He acknowledges, further, that this water is the foundation of our Art. The philosophers give it many names; for sometimes they call it wine, sometimes water of life, sometimes vinegar, sometimes oil, according to the different degrees of Preparation, or according to the diverse effects which it is capable of producing. Yet I let you know that it is properly called the Vinegar of the Wise, and that in the distillation of this Divine Liquor there happens the same thing as in that of common vinegar; you may hence draw instruction: the water and the phlegm ascend first; the oily substance, in which the efficacy of the water consists, comes the last, etc. It is therefore necessary to dissolve the body entirely to extract all its humidity which contains the precious ferment, the sulphur, that balm of Nature, and wonderful unguent, without which you ought not to hope ever to see in your vessel this blackness so desired by all the philosophers. Reduce then the whole compound into water, and make a perfect union of the volatile with the fixed; it is a precept of Senior's, which deserves attention, that *the highest fume should be reduced to the lowest; for the divine water is the thing descending from heaven, the reducer of the soul to its body, which it at length revives.* The Balm of Life is hid in these unclean faeces; you ought to wash them with this celestial water until you have removed away the blackness from them, and *then your Water shall be animated with this Fiery Essence, which works all the wonders of our Art.*

But, further, that you may not be deceived with the terms of the Compound, I will tell you that the philosophers have two sorts of compounds. The first is the compound of Nature, whereof I have spoken in the First Key; for it is Nature which makes it in a manner incomprehensible to the Artist, who does nothing but lend a hand to Nature by the adhibition of external things, by the means of which she brings forth and produces this admirable compound. The second is the compound of Art; it is the Wise man who makes it by the secret union of the fixed with the volatile, perfectly conjoined with all prudence, which cannot be acquired but by the lights of a profound philosophy. The compound of Art is not altogether the same in the Second as in the Third Work; yet it is always the Artist who makes it. Geber defines it, a mixture of Argent vive and Sulphur, that is to say, of the volatile and the fixed; which, acting on one another, are volatilized and fixed reciprocally into a perfect Fixity. Consider the example of Nature; you see that the earth will never produce fruit if it be not penetrated with its humidity, and that the humidity would always remain barren if it were not retained and fixed by the dryness of the earth. So, in the Art, you can have no success if you do not in the first work purify the Serpent, born of the Slime of the earth; it you do not whiten these foul and black faeces, to separate from thence the white sulphur, which is the Sal Amoniac of the Wise, and their Chaste Diana, who washes herself in the bath; and all this mystery is but the extraction of the *fixed salt* of our compound, in which the whole *energy* of our Mercury consists. The water which ascends by distillation carries up with it a part of this fiery salt, so that the affusion of the water on the body, reiterated many times, impregnates, fattens, and fertilizes our Mercury, and makes it fit to be fixed, which is the end of the second Work. One cannot better explain this Truth than by Hermes, in these words: *When I saw that the water by degrees did become thicker and harder I did rejoice, for I certainly knew that I should find what I sought for.* It is not without reason that the philosophers give this viscous Liquor the name of Pontick Water. Its exuberant ponticity is indeed the true character of its virtue, and the more you shall rectify it, and the more you shall work upon it, the more virtue will it acquire. It has been called the Water of Life, because it gives life to the metals; but it is properly called the great Lunaria, because of its brightness wherewith it shines....

Since I speak only to you, ye true scholars of Hermes, I will reveal to you one secret which you will not find entirely in the books of the philosophers. Some of them say, that of the liquor they make two Mercuries—the one White and the other Red; Flammel has said more particularly, that one must make use of the citrine Mercury to make the Imbibition of the Red; giving notice to the Sons of Art not to be deceived on this point, as he himself had been, unless the Jew had informed him of the truth. Others have taught that the White Mercury is the bath of the Moon, and that the Red Mercury is the bath of the Sun. But there are none who have been willing to show distinctly to the Sons of Science by what means they may get these two mercuries. If you apprehend me well, you have the point already cleared up to you. The Lunaria is the White Mercury, the most sharp Vinegar is the Red Mercury; but the better to determine these two mercuries, feed them with flesh of their own species — the blood of innocents whose throats are cut; that is to say, the spirits of the bodies are the Bath where the Sun and Moon go to wash themselves. I have unfolded to you a great mystery, if you reflect well on it; the philosophers who have spoken thereof have passed over this important point very slightly. Cosmopolite has very wittily mentioned it by an ingenious allegory, speaking of the purification of the Mercury: *This will be done, says he, if you shall give our old man gold and silver to swallow, that he may consume them, and at length he also dying may be burnt.* He makes an end of describing the whole magistery in these terms: *Let his ashes be strewed in the water; boil it until it is enough, and you have a medicine to cure the leprosy.* You must not be ignorant that *Our Old Man is our Mercury*; this name indeed agrees with him because He is the *first matter* of all metals. He is their water, as the same author goes on to say, and to which he gives also the name of steel and of the lodestone; adding for a greater confirmation of what I am about to discover to you, that if *gold couples with it eleven times it sends forth its seed, and is debilitated almost unto death; but the Chalybes conceives and begets a son more glorious than the Father*. Behold a great Mystery which I reveal to you without an enigma; this is the secret of the two mercuries which contain the two tinctures. Keep them separately, and do not confound their species, for fear they should beget a monstrous Lineage.

I not only speak to you more intelligibly than any philosopher before has done, but I also reveal to you the most essential point in the Practice; if you meditate thereon, and apply yourself to understand it well; but above all, if you work according to those lights which I give you, you may obtain what you seek for. And if you come not to these knowledges by the way which I have pointed out to you, I am very well assured that you will hardly arrive at your design by only reading the philosophers.

Therefore despair of nothing—search the source of the Liquor of the Sages, which contains all that is necessary for the work; it is hidden under the Stone—strike upon it with the Red of Magic Fire, and a clear fountain will issue out; then do as I have shown you, prepare the bath of the King with the blood of the Innocents, and you will have the animated Mercury of the wise, which never loses its virtue, if you keep it in a vessel well closed, Hermes says, that there is so much sympathy between the purified bodies and the spirits, that they never quit one another when they are united together: because this union resembles that of the soul with the glorified body; after which Faith tells us, there shall be no more separation or death; because the spirits desire to be in the cleansed bodies, and having them, they enliven and dwell in them. By this you may observe the merit of this precious liquor, to which the philosophers have given more than a thousand different names, which is in sum the great Alcahest, which radically dissolves the metals — a true permanent water which, after having radically dissolved them, is inseparably united to them, increasing their weight and tincture.

THE FOURTH KEY

The Fourth Key of the Art is the entrance to the Second Work (and a reiteration in part and development of the foregoing): it is this which reduces our Water into Earth; there is but this only Water in the world, which by a bare boiling can be converted into Earth, because the Mercury of the Wise carries in its centre its own Sulphur, which coagulates it. The terrification of the Spirit is the only operation of this work. Boil them with patience; if you have proceeded well, you will not be a long time without perceiving the marks of this coagulation; and if they appear not in their time, they will never appear; because it is an undoubted sign that you have failed in some essential thing in the former operations; for to corporify the Spirit, which is our Mercury, you must have well dissolved the body in which the Sulphur which coagulates the Mercury is enclosed. But Hermes assumes that our mercurial water shall obtain all the virtues which the philosophers attribute to it if it be turned into earth. An earth admirable is it for fertility — the Land of Promise of the Wise, who, knowing how to make the dew of Heaven fall upon it, cause it to produce fruits of an inestimable price. Cultivate then diligently this precious earth, moisten it often with its own humidity, dry it as often, and you will no less augment its virtue than its weight and its fertility.

THE FIFTH KEY

The Fifth Key includes the Fermentation of the Stone with the perfect body, to make thereof the medicine of the Third order. I will say nothing in particular of the operation of the Third work; except that the Perfect Body is a necessary leaven of Our Paste. And that the Spirit ought to make the union of the paste with the leaven in the same manner as water moistens meal, and dissolves the leaven to compose a fermented paste fit to make bread. This comparison is very proper; Hermes first made it, saying, *that as a paste cannot be fermented without a ferment; so when you shall have sublimed, cleansed and separated the foulness from the Faeces, and would make the conjunction, put a ferment to them and make the water earth, that the paste may be made a ferment*; which repeats the instruction of the whole work, and shows, that just so as the whole lump of the paste becomes leaven, by the action of the ferment which has been added, so all the philosophic confection becomes, by this operation, a leaven proper to ferment a new matter, and to multiply it to infinity. If you observe well how bread is made, you will find the *proportions* also, which you ought to keep among the matters which compose our philosophical paste. Do not the bakers put more meal than leaven, and more water than the leaven and the meal? The laws of Nature are the rules you ought to follow in the practice of our magistery. I have given you, upon the principal point, all the instructions which are necessary for you, so that it would be superfluous to tell you more of it; particularly concerning the last operations, about which the Adepts have been less reserved than at the First, which are the foundations of the Art.

THE SIXTH KEY

The Sixth Key teaches the Multiplication of the Stone, by the reiteration of the same operation, which consists but in opening and shutting, dissolving and coagulating, imbibing and drying; whereby the virtues of the Stone are infinitely augmentable. As my design has been not to describe entirely the application of the three medicines, but only to instruct you in the more important operations concerning the preparation of Mercury, which the philosophers commonly pass over in silence, to hide the mysteries from the profane which are only intended for the wise, I will tarry no longer on this point, and will tell you nothing more of what relates to the Projection of the Medicine, because the success you expect depends not thereon. I have not given you very full instructions except on the Third Key, because it contains a long train of operations which, though simple and natural, require a great understanding of the Laws of Nature, and of the qualities of Our Matter, as well as a perfect knowledge of chemistry and of the different degrees of heat which are fitting for these operations. I have conducted you by the straight way without any winding; and if you have well minded the road which I have pointed out to you, I am sure that you will go straight to the end without straying. Take this in good part from me, in the design which I had of sparing you a thousand labours and a thousand troubles, which I myself have undergone in this painful journey for want of an assistance such as this is, which I give you from a sincere heart and a tender affection for all the true sons of science. I should much bewail, if, like me, after having known the true matter, you should spend fifteen years entirely in the work, in study and in meditation, without being able to extract out of the Stone the precious juice which it encloses in its bosom, for want of knowing the secret fire of the wise, which makes to run out of this plant (dry and withered in appearance) a water which wets not the hands, and which by a magical union of the dry water of the sea of the wise, is dissolved into a viscous water — into a mercurial liquor, which is the beginning, the foundation, and the Key of our Art: Convert, separate, and purify the elements, as I have taught you, and you will possess the true

Mercury of the philosophers, which will give you the fixed Sulphur and the Universal Medicine. But I give you notice, moreover, that even after you shall be arrived at the knowledge of the Secret Fire of the Wise, yet still you shall not attain your point at your first career. I have erred many years in the way which remains to be gone, to arrive at the mysterious fountain where the King bathes himself, is made young again, and retakes a new life exempt from all sorts of infirmities. Besides this you must know how to purify, to heal, and to animate the royal bath; it is to lend you a hand in this secret way that I have expatiated under the Third Key, where all those operations are described. I wish with all my heart that the instructions which I have given you may enable you to go directly to the End. But remember, ye sons of philosophy, that the knowledge of our Magistery comes rather by the Inspiration of Heaven than from the Lights which we can get by ourselves. This truth is acknowledged by all artists; it is for good reason that it is not enough to work; pray daily, read good books, and meditate night and day on the operations of Nature, and on what she may be able to do when she is assisted by the help of our Art; and by these means you will succeed without doubt in your undertaking. This is all I have now to say to you. I was not willing to make you such a long discourse as the matter seemed to demand; neither have I told you anything but what is essential to our Art; so that if you know the Stone which is the only matter of Our Stone, and if you have the Understanding of Our Fire, which is both secret and natural, you have the Keys of the Art, and you can calcine Our Stone; not by the common calcination which is made by the violence of fire, but by a philosophic calcination which is purely natural. Yet observe this, with the most enlightened philosophers, that there is this difference between the common calcination which is made by the force of Fire and the natural calcination; that the first destroys the body and consumes the greatest part of its radical humidity; but the second does not only preserve the humidity of the body in calcining it, but still considerably augments it. Experience will give you knowledge in the Practice of this great truth, for you will in effect find that this philosophical calcination, which sublimes and distills the Stone in calcining it, much augments its humidity; the reason is that the igneous spirit of the natural fire is corporified in the substances which are analogous to it. Our stone is an Astral Fire which sympathizes with the Natural Fire, and which, as a true Salamander receives it nativity, is nourished and grows in the Elementary Fire, which is geometrically proportioned to it.

The Keys of Eudoxus open no more; and as these last ones, entering to the Multiplication and Projection, are avowedly defective, and the information may be interesting to the studious, we propose to supply it briefly from another and not less credible source.

It remains only for the work of Multiplication, says the Author of the *Open Entrance*, to take one part of the Perfect Matter and to join it with three or four parts at most of the Mercury of the First Work, and to place both in a vessel well luted and sealed; and, by the help of a gentle and well-regulated fire, you will see with satisfaction all the operations before named pass through rapidly in seven days, and the virtue is augmented a thousand times in this revelation above what it was before. Then repeat thereupon the same operation, and all will be run through before your eyes in three days, and the matter will have again attained by this a *redoubled virtue*. After this, if you desire to repeat the same work, one natural day will complete the whole, and every regiment of the colors will in that brief space be passed through; which, if the same process be again repeated, an hour will suffice, increasing likewise in multiplicable proportion, thousands by thousands; so that at length, if you multiply it a fifth time, you will no longer be able to calculate the strength of the medicine. Render thanks to God, then, who hath put into thy possession the universal treasury of nature. —

And for the final Projection, as the metalline perfectibility of the matter is sometimes called, we have this concluding advice: —Take one part of your Perfect Stone, whether white or red; then cause to be melted in a crucible four parts of one of the fixed metals, *i.e.*, silver of it be for the white, or gold if it be for the red; join to this one part of the Stone, according to the kind that you desire to produce; throw the whole into a horn, and there will result to you a pulverizable mass. Take then ten parts of mercury purged and purified, place it on the fire, and when it begins to crackle and to smoke throw in one part of your powder, which will, in the twinkling of an eye as it were, penetrate the mercury; melt this with an augmented fire; and you will have the medicine, though of an inferior order. Take one part of this last matter and project it on any metal so that it be only purified and set in fusion; project only as much of the Stone as you desire to tinge of the metal, and you will have gold or silver more pure than that which nature ever yields. However it is always best to make projection by degrees until the Stone yields no more tincture; because in projecting a small quantity of powder on a large quantity of imperfect (except indeed out *Mercury* alone), the Stone sustains great loss on account of the impurities with which they abound. Therefore, the more the metal is *purified* before projection, the more successful will be transmutation[1].

But, be it remembered, there is a twofold fermentation—a spiritual and a bodily. The spiritual fermentation is performed by multiplying the tinctures, which is not done with common gold to silver; for they are not tinctures, but gross compacted bodies.—Be thou well advised, says Sendivogius in his *Praxis*, that thou takest not common gold or silver, for these are dead; take Ours which are living; then put them into Our Fire and let there be made of them a dry liquor: first of all the earth will be resolved into Water which is called the Mercury of philosophers, and that water shall resolve those bodies of gold and silver, and shall consume them so that there shall remain but the tenth part with one part; and this shall be the radical moisture of the metals. Then take water and salt-nitre, which comes from Our Earth in which there is a river of living water, if thou digest the pit knee deep, therefore take the water out of that; but take that which is *clear*; upon this put that radical moisture; and set it over the fire of putrefaction and generation, not on such a one as thou didst in the first operation: govern all things with a great deal of discretion, until colors appear like a peacock's tail; govern it by digesting it, and be not weary, until these colors be ended, and there appear throughout the whole one green color, and so of the rest; and when thou shalt see in the bottom ashes of a fiery color and the water almost red, open the vessel, dip in a pen, and smear some Iron with it; if it tinge, have in readiness that water which has been spoken of, and put in so much of that water as the cold air was which went in, boil it again with the former fire, until it tinge again. So far reached my experience:—I can do no more, says the wary Artist, I found out no more.—Now that water must be the menstruum of the world, out of the sphere of the Moon so often rectified until it can calcine gold[2].

And when thou hast made the Stone and magic medicine, says Vaughan, and it is become a liquid fiery spiritual substance, shining like the sun, in this complexion, if you would project it, you would hardly find the just proportion: the virtue of the medicine is so intensive and powerful. The philosophers therefore take one part of their Stone and cast it upon ten parts of pure molten gold—this single grain brings all the gold to a bloody powder; and, on the contrary, the gross body of the gold abates the spiritual strength of the projected grain. This descent or incorporation, some wise authors have called a bodily fermentation; but the philosophers did not use common gold to make their Stone (though so many deceptively write about it), they used it only to qualify the utensive power of it when it was made, that they might the more easily find what quantity of base metal they should project upon. By this means they reduced their medicine to a dust, and this dust is the Arabian Elixir. This Elixir the philosophers could carry about them; but the medicine itself not so, for it is such a subtle moist fire that there is nothing bit (its proper) glass that will hold it[3].

> *And it sufficeth in one glasse to put*
> *So much of composition as may cost*
> *The price of half an ounce of fold, which shut*
> *With Hermes' seal, no fear it should be lost;*
> *Except some error be committed, which*
> *How to avoid I faithfully shall teach*[4].

And because our intention is to the changing of metals into gold, says the Author of Lucerna Salis, it is requisite that they should first be fermented with very good and most pure gold; for otherwise the imperfect metals would not be able to support its too great and supreme subtlety; but there would rather ensue loss and damage in the projection. The imperfect and impure metals (let not the allusion here be misapprehended) must also be purified, if one will draw any profit therefrom; one drachm of gold is sufficient for the fermentation in the red, and one drachm of silver for the fermentation in the white. And the artist need not be at the trouble of buying gold or silver for this fermentation, because, with one single very small part, the tincture may afterwards be augmented more and more in such a manner that whole ships might be loaded with the precious metal that would accrue from this confection. For if this medicine be multiplied, and be again dissolved and coagulated by the virtue of its mercury, white or red, of which it was prepared, then the tinging virtue will be augmented each time by ten degrees in perfection, which may be reiterated as often as one pleases[5].

> *Like the sun's atoms 'tis a powder fine,*
> *White for the white, and red for red projection.*
> *The metals, by it teined, exceed the mine*
> *In purity; and such is its perfection*
> *That he who hath it in an hour's space*
> *And less than, may command in any place.*

Mary Anne Atwood

At first it is of virtue very small,
Compared with the might it doth attain
By oft reiteration; who so shall
It oft dissolve, and then congeal again,
Shall find a medicine that will translate
Innumerable parts to Sol's estate.

'Tis ponderous and yet in grains divided,
That powder all appears as soft as silk,
On metal it, like wax, in flux is guided
To enter to the centre, just like milk
Is penetrated by the Rennet sour,
And curdled in the minute of an hour.

This medicine is best thus to project:
First on a portion of the metal pure,
Which of the powder is to be effect
As red on gold, on silver eke be sure,
The white to throw, one part of this, your
Stone On four of metal, or else five to one.

Then brittle like to glasse that masse will be,
Of colour bright and shining very clear,
Yet not transparent, also thou shalt see
Its virtue lessened, which will appear
To view most glittering, like a ruby fair,
Then upon Argent vive cast this with care.

On ten parts one so long project until
The tincture to decrease thou shalt perceive
Which being done, also thou shalt see
Most perfect Sol and Lune from fire receive;
Thus guide thy operation and be sure,
The effect will prove both gold and silver pure.

And if thou list thy essence to augment
In goodness or in weight, thou so maist work,
That never shall thy stock with use be spent,

So great a power in this Stone doth lurk,
That it, like fire, is apt to multiply
Itself in weight as eke in dignity.

A portion once I saw, and found by proof,
That which a man's belief might far exceed
Of the Red medicine, which for behoof
Of such how to this science may proceed,
I shall declare, by which may well appear
That useless it is not, as many fear......

I saw then, as I said, a powder so
Increast in virtue, scarce to be believed
That so small quantity, as scarce would show
In bulk a grain, nor weighed much more indeed,
Which yet to gold so great a quantity
Could well transmute as may be deemed a lye.

No man by art its number could attain,
So great it was, yet it was the tincture sound,
For on an ounce projected was that grain,
In which perfection did so abound,
That all was essence made, of which one grain
Was cast upon ten times as much again.

That is one ounce in ten, and these likewise
On ten times more, which yet was medicine made,
Ten more to one of these would not suffice
To metal it to bring; nor was't allay'd,
So with these oft projection made before,
But one at last ting'd ninety thousand more[6].

And the Author of the Rosary declares that he who shall have accomplished this Art, even though he were to live thousands of year, and every say maintain thousands of men, of curing all yet he would never know scarcity; having attained this blessed abundance, also, not by the oppression of others or by unlawful means, but by industry, patience, and the labor of his own hand. And not only, continues Eireneus, could he transmute baser metals into gold and silver, but make precious stones also more beautiful and perfect than those of nature; and would possess a universal medicine, moreover, capable of curing all diseases; even one Adept, were he permitted, might impart health to the whole world[7].

But lest this kind of testimony should grow egregious, and our book, by ill hazard falling into the hand of some credulous dunce or adventurous gold-seeker, should detain either for a moment to deliberate about looking at home for that which their instinct and proper destiny would otherwise direct them to find abroad, we desist therefore, and implore these, should there be any, as they value their own lives and peace of mind and fortune, to regard nothing of all that has been written. For would it not, even supposing the whole of the assertions to be true (and which literally taken they are not) would it not, we ask, be a delirious speculation for any one to undertake to make the precious metal which is to be had in plentiful abundance, all ready elaborated by nature, ripe, and easy to his hand; to be had for the mere gathering, and if not without some natural, yet without laborious study or other mystical alloy?—Let not one then be allured by the ultimate promises of Alchemy; which are the rewards only of a long-suffering and laborious life; of unwearying thought, patience under afflictions, conquest over unruly passions, hunger, thirst, stripes merited and unmerited, persecutions, indigence, self-denial—all which philosophers have undergone, even encountering the terrors of death and hell itself in pursuit of their object; which was not gold however, or silver, but the substance of these things, which, after all, when it was gotten by them, was despised and swallowed up in the vision of a yet more alluring prospect of the Light.

To sum up then, lest we should never come to an end of this fugitive pursuit—In the last operation the union of the Philosophic Stone is said to be finally cemented, in its component parts agreeing and having relation to the external world; which union or consummation of its transmutative virtue is called Fermentation. Mark the harmonious mystery—that which in the Cabal is denominated the union of man, reduced to the simplicity of the Monad, with God, that in physico-chemistry is called Fermentation. The most pious and experienced amongst the Adepts do not demur either to compare the phenomena of their work to the Gospel tradition of the Life of Christ and our human redemption; Kuhnrath, Böhme, Freher, Grasseus, and various others amongst the more modern, agree with the early Adepts; pointing out too how, in every minute respect, their magistery not only corresponds, but is in every deed a type, and promise, and foundation of our Christian Creed. Not, be it understood, that they identify or in the least confound the metalline perfection, which belongs to the primary evolution of life only, with the ultimate Divine association; but they show that their Stone exhibits, alike in its origin, development and artificial preparation throughout, the Universal Law of Light in Nature. And as man, united with God, becomes divinely empowered, and therefore can do what he wills, since he wills what God Himself does in consonance with reason; so does the Philosopher's Stone in the greater world. Fermented in its parts by reason of the fermentation, transform itself into which it wills, and works for the diverse natures of all things, coequals itself to all, to every and each, and to universals.

It is the universal medium of restoration and preservation, says Kuhnrath, which by its own equilibrate virtue expels suffering and every disease whether of mind or body; in either Kingdom of nature rectifying, according to the capability of each. Metals it is said to benefit by transference of their radical moisture, depriving its terrestreity and foreign oxides; vegetables, by an increase of their efflorescent spirit; and animals, according to the natural exigence of their being. Azoth of our Stone, continues he, reduces bodies to their First Matter and reanimates them with the Universal Form, crystals it advances to gems, and many pearls artificially it concretes into one. Metals, also, as I myself have seen, crystals, gems, as well as gold, it makes fluid and potable; it frees animals from disease, and preserves them in the strength of its virtue; I refreshes vegetables; tough nearly dead it will revive them; fermented with the specific essence of simples, and methodically applied in a fitting lamp, its enduring water, lighted by art, burns perpetually, for ever. It expels and drives away evil spirits from the possessed—wherefore not? There are particular potencies in nature which malignant powers give way to—why not to the universal? The author of confusion could not endure symmetry.—It exalts and ennobles natural ability in the healing art, and it *draws down sublime memory and prudence*. It wonderfully excites perpetual joy, and an honest boldness and fortitude of mind exhilarating all life. And, that I may include many things in a few words, it is miraculously efficient in all the production of nature, also the sublunary spirits, for every and all of these, by an inherent necessity, obey this Stone[8].

For this powerful vivific Ens is of the same origin as that which it assimilates—viz., the Universal Spirit, which has been so often fermented, rectified, and recalcined, until the central force, wholly drawn out, acts forcibly at the circumference, and is able to draw, by a supernatural magnetism, the Homogeneal Nature everywhere into itself, according to the Rational Form inbred. And hence we may conceive why the Hermetic philosophers have given it the name of *Azoth, which adheres to bodies*; which if thou dost *rightly conceive,* says Kuhnrath, thou art he of whom it may be truly said, He who has begun aright, has done half of the whole. The Stone is fermented with its metal existing in the highest purity, with pure silver for the White, and with Red for fine Gold. And this is the work of three days[9].

The Stone is here said accurately to be fermented with its own metal: for is not Light the true Aurific Seed; not common Light, but that which in the first rotary wheel of life becomes efficient, which is potentially included everywhere in either kingdom of nature, though laid asleep? Or what else should possibly transmute or multiply by its own assimilative virtue? What else but Light can multiply, or does multiply, anyhow or anywhere; and if everywhere else, why not in the mineral kingdom, when set free to attract its proper fuel indeficiently, without heterogeneous hindrance or alloy?

And if in the mineral kingdom it can overcome no great inertness, and renews the vegetable spirit, imparting health and increase to decaying nature, how much greater benefits will it not bestow on man who nourished it? Nor in the outward ministration of the medicament only, but above all, and most permanently, in the vital rectification. Thus Julian, in his *Oration to the Extra-Mundane Mother,* for example, tells us that when the soul gives herself to Divinity, and wholly delivers herself to the guidance of a better nature, divine institutions, through purification, taking the lead, the Divine Light will immediately shine on her; and, in consequence of being thus deified, she transfuses a certain vigorous strength into her connate spirit, which when included, and as it were possessing dominion, becomes, through this spirit the cause of safety to the whole body. For, continues the Emperor, diseases, or at least the greater part, happen from the mutative and erroneous motion of the spirit—which physicians likewise allow; or, at all events, that those most difficult to be cured originate from thence. For health is a certain symmetry or equilibrium of nature, which it is the pre-eminent power of the Telestic art to impart, ordering all things by the unity within. And, indeed, the oracles testify the truth of these assertions, when they declare that through purifying ceremonies bodies become worthy of receiving divine assistance and health, and that the mortal vestment of bitter matter will be by these means be preserved.

> *Harmonia resonat namque, sub qua est corpus mortale.*
> *Extendens, igneam mentem, as opus pietatis, etfluxile corpus servabit[10].*

And that which a man has received, will he not be able to impart again, and bestow of this exuberant felicity for the benefaction of others? Or at it is so related of Hippocrates, that he cured extraordinary maladies because he was endowed with a divine nature, and had carried up medicine from a low estate unto great achievements. For he was the descent of *many generations*, and a *divine man*, as the tradition says, by direct descent from *AEsculapius* on the father's side, and by his mother *Praxithea* of the race of the *Heraclides*. Wherefore from *both seeds* he had his origin from the *gods*. For he was initiated as a young beginner in medicinal affairs by his *great-grandfather*, so far as he *knew*. But himself did also teach himself —*having made use of a divine nature*—the whole art. And, in the industry of his mind, he as far excelled his *progenitors* as he also exceeded them in the excellency of Art. For he takes away (continues the narrator) not only the kind of bestial, but also of brutishly fierce and wild diseases, through a great part of the land and sea; dispersing the succours of AEsculapius, even as Triptolemus the seed of Ceres; balmy health and healing virtues,

> *Such as sage Chiron, sire of pharmacy,*
> *First taught Achilles, and Achilles thee[11].*

Therefore he hath most justly obtained divine honors in many places of the earth; and is made worthy by the Athenians of the same gifts with Hercules and AEsculapius. And this man is the father and preserver of health, the curer of all griefs. In sum, this man is the prince of divine knowledge, concludes the Persian, Petris, in his epistle addressing Artaxerxes—send thou for Him[12].

Honor the physician with the honor due unto him, says Solomon; for the Lord created him—as if he specially were above all men created by God, who is able to heal the sick and restore life to the distressed, which all physicians, however, are notable—But a physician chosen by God, continues Helmont, His own signs shall follow, and wonders for the schools; for he shall prepare to the honor of God his free gifts, to the comfort of his neighbor; compassion shall be his leader. For he shall *possess* truth in his heart, and knowledge in his understanding; charity and the mercy of the Lord shall enlighten his way; and he shall *bestow* favor of the Lord, and the hope of gain shall not be in his thoughts. For the Lord is rich and liberal, and will give him one hundred fold in an heaped-up measure: He will fructify his work, and anoint his Hands with Blessing. He will fill his mouth with consolation and with the trumpet of His Word, from which diseases shall flee. He will fill his *life* with length of days, his *house* with riches, and his children with the fear of the Lord. His footsteps shall bring felicity, and diseases shall be in his *sight* as snow in the noon-day of summer in an open valley. Curse and punishment shall flee away, and health shall follow him. These are the promises of the Lord unto physicians whom He hath chosen. These are the blessings of those who walk in the path of mercy. Because the Lord loveth those that work mercy; and therefore he will enlighten them with his Spirit, the Comforter. For who is liberal as the Lord, who giveth many things freely, and, for some *small matter*, bestoweth al things? Blessed is the Lord who saves the merciful, and who saves him that is to be saved freely. And consolation shall meet the merciful man in the way of hope, because he has chosen a faithful master.—But, continues the same estimable narrator, arrogance and sloth, which long since extinguished Charity, but a few ages ago sequestered a chirurgeon also from a physician; wherefore afterwards servants handled the manual instruments and operations; as if the unbeseemed a Christian to help his neighbor with his hands. In the mean time some noble matrons healed defects with their own hands that were despaired of by physicians. And truly after that the study of ambition and gain were practiced, *charity grew cold, mercy was extinguished, art perished*, and the Giver of Lights withdrew his Gifts; the number of our calamities increased, and physicians were made the fable of the vulgar. *Truth remained buried in the grave of science*; and instead thereof a confused kind of brawling arose, being discursive, which was accounted for doctrine. And those false doctors described and drew of themselves a whole army of diseases, almost grieving, too, that the catalogue of them was yet so small. For they, being allured with the facility of the art of Galen, promised to measure all diseases by the geometrical demonstrations of degrees of heat and cold, and to heal them all thereby. Chirurgeons also, as well the modern as the ancient, from an imitation and emulation of these, largely and widely treated promiscuously all diseases, snatching the cures of them all under themselves, in the sight and despite of their former masters. Because at first, and from the root of medicinal ordination, all things belonged to be cured only and alone by physicians; but unto chirurgeons afterwards only by permission and from favor. Both of them have failed, however, under a confused strife and become inefficient[13].

So the origin, decline, and fall of the Healing Art has been pictured by one of its brightest ornaments; and truly is it not deplorable to think that knowledge once so perfectly attained and demonstrated in its efficacy, should, by a degenerate usage, have been lost to mankind? The accounts given by Van Helmont of the cures which he himself alone effected of some 10,000 individuals yearly, without any diminution of his medicine, would now be unaccredited, except by those few, perhaps, who, with a fragment of the same virtue, have, by a benevolent application, learnt to conceive something of the illimitable powers and artificial increase of vitalization. These will vindicate the Light, if any, who observing its first dawn, shall suffer it again to fall into disuse through negligence, or by obloquy be tempted to an uncharitable ambuscade.

And then have we no other defects than those of body to distress us? Are not our minds, too, ailing, and is there no balm ready? Is there no physician there? In Greece there were many temples to many gods—to Ceres, Minerva, Apollo, Bacchus, and the rest, all ministering to the defects of mind, educating and disciplining the understanding for the conception of Wisdom and a better life within. Aesculapius was a demigod only amongst them, who is of modern Mesmerism the only just pride.—Honor the physician with the honor due unto him for the use you may have of him, for the Lord created him. There is a time when in his hands there is a good success; then let him not go from thee, for hast need of him[14].—But to whom hath the root of Wisdom been revealed; or who hath known her wise councils? Unto whom hath the knowledge of Wisdom been made manifest? Or who hath understood her great Experience? She is with all men, replies the prophet, according to his gift; but Her secret is with the Faithful[15].

Now such a faith as the Scriptures inculcate as bestowing Wisdom on the possessor is unknown at this day; nor does man any longer seek after the Truth that is in himself, rarely imagines it even, so far do we live without the true knowledge of ourselves. We pray the liberal reader to reflect, therefore, and link his imagination to the probabilities of reason, and ponder on the testimony of experience, and believe that Mesmerism, as it is mechanically practiced in the present day, is a first step indeed, and this only before the entrance of that glorious temple of Divine Wisdom which a more scientific Handicraft enabled the ancients experimentally to enter, and from its foundation build up, as it were, a crystalline edifice of Light and Truth. The materials are yet present with us; the foundations easily laid; the will only is wanting to discover the way, and faith to resuscitate the Corner Stone, which ignorance has rejected from immemorial time, but science only can refute.

For if man does not enter in to understand himself, and the evil under which he lies enchanted in this life, he cannot understand the ancient doctrine concerning the fall or regeneration, or presume to deliver matter from the original curse, or be instrumental in the restoration.—While Adam stood in Paradisiacal innocency, explains the theosophist, The Eternal Word was his leader, and had dominion in him: his life, which was a clear flame, burned in and was nourished by that pure spirit of the divine substantiality, which, together with the water of eternal life, generated in the angelical world, gave forth a glorious and bright shining Light. Immediately after the fall of man, God said to the *Serpent*, I will put enmity between thee and the woman, and between thy seed and her seed; her seed shall bruise thy head, and thou shalt bruise his heel. Herein the Philosophers' Stone or tincture lyeth. For though this concerneth man, in the first place, yet secondly it concerneth the whole creation. The bruising of the serpent's head is done spiritually and corporally, both in nature and in the soul, and though in different degrees, yet by a parallel process in each. The serpent's sting is the wrath fire, and the woman's seed the light and love fire: these two are in every thing; the former predominated in outward nature, by the fall, and therefore the latter must be raised up, and by its shining through the wrath, must subdue and keep it under; taking away from it its predominant power, so that it may exercise its true natural office as a servant to the light; that these two may no more stand in opposition to each other, but be one thing reharmonized by light and love, and re-introduced into Paradise; when the dark poisoning Mercury is thus tinctured, his anguishing death is turned into triumphing life, and his former dark desire into the desire of light, which is able to make a pure love and light substantially, viz., a heavenly body out of an earthly. The whole work therefore consists summarily herein—That Two Natures be reduced to One, as they were at the beginning. A heavenly and an earthly matter are to be mutually united and brought to a heavenly consistency. Earth must be turned in, and Heaven out. The Mercury which is therein doth all this itself: the Artist is not to attempt it —he cannot do it—he is to prepare the way, the matter as is requisite, and leave the work to be done by the workman which is in it already; nevertheless, understanding and faith are required of him. His design being no less than to redeem matter from the curse, and to raise it from the dead, which never can be done by one who is dead himself in his understanding and internal life[16].

Who then is competent, who qualified to minister in so great a matter? Who but he that the Spirit has already prepared, and endowed with prudence for the undertaking; he that is holy, he that is true, he that hath the Key of David, he that openeth, and no man shutteth; and shutteth, and no man openeth[17]. Or what man is he, asks Solomon, that can know the counsel of God? Or who can think what the Will of the Lord is? For the thoughts of mortal men are miserable, and our devices are but uncertain. For the corruptible body presseth down the soul, and the earthly tabernacle weigheth down that mind that museth upon many things. And hardly do we guess outright at things which are upon earth, and with labor do we find the things that are before us; but the things that are in heaven who hath searched out? And thy counsel who hath known, *except thou give Wisdom and send thy Holy Spirit from above?* For so the ways of them which lived on the arth were reformed, and men were taught the things that are pleasing unto thee, and were saved through Wisdom. She preserved the first formed Father of the World that was created alone, and brought him out of his fall, and gave him power to rule all things. But when the righteous went away from her in his anger, he perished also in the fury wherewith he murdered his brother. For whose cause, the earth being drowned with the Flood, *Wisdom again preserved it, and directed the course of the righteous in a piece of wood of small value.* Moreover, the *nations* in their *wicked conspiring* being confounded, she found out the righteous and preserved him blameless unto God, and kept him strong against his tender compassion toward his *Son*. When the ungodly perished, she delivered the *righteous man* who fled from *Fire*, which fell upon *five cities*, of whose wickedness, even *to this day*, the waste land that smoketh is a testimony, and plants bearing fruit that never come to ripeness, and a *standing pillar of Salt is a monument to an unbelieving soul*. But Wisdom delivered from pain those that attended upon her. When the *righteous* fled from his *brother's* wrath, she guarded him in right paths, *showed him the kingdom of God*, and gave him *knowledge* of holy things; made him *rich* in his travels, and *multiplied the fruit of his labors*. In the covetousness of such as oppressed him, she stood by him and made him rich; she defended him from his enemies, and kept him safe from *those* that lay in wait, and, in a *sore conflict*, she gave him *the victory: that he might know that godliness is stronger than all.* She entered into the soul of the servant of the Lord, and withstood dreadful *kings* in wonders and signs. She rendered to the *righteous* a reward of their labors, guided them in a *marvelous way*, and was unto them for a cover by day and a light of Stars in the night season; brought them through the RED SEA, and led them through *much water*. But she drowned their enemies, and cast them up out of the bottom of the *Deep*. Therefore the righteous spoiled the ungodly, and praised thy Holy Name, O Lord, and magnified, with one accord, thy Hand that fought for them. For Wisdom opened the mouth of the *dumb*, and made the tongues of *them* that cannot speak eloquent. She prospered their works in the Hand of the Holy Prophet[18].

When once the Divine Light is loosened in life, everything is prospered as long as her Rule is observed; for the understanding then bears its motive energy into effect.—And the Word of the Lord is unto them *Line upon line, Precept upon precept*, (purifying and perfecting) *here a little and there a little*[19]. The whole individual is occupied; every look and action is by rule and with power; as it is not likewise written, *The Hands of the Wise are very heavy. The right hand of the Lord bringeth mighty things to pass.*—And His brightness was as the light, says Habbakuk, and he had horns coming out of his hand, and there was the hiding of his power[20]. Is it not promised, moreover, that the horn of the righteous shall be exalted, and his seed made triumphant over many nations? Be thou faithful into death, and I will give thee a crown of life[21]. And again of Wisdom,—Length of days is in her right hand, and in her left riches and honor. Exalt her and she shall promote thee, she shall bring thee honor when thou dost embrace her, she shall give to thy head an Ornament of Grace, a Crown of Glory shall she deliver unto thee[22].

Nor are these the only passages in Scripture where with Wisdom a promise is given of more material fruits: —He that hath an ear to hear, let him hear what the Spirit saith unto the Churches:

To him that overcometh will I give to eat of the Tree of Life, which is in the midst of the Paradise of God.

And he that overcometh and keepeth my works unto the end, to him will I give power over the nations; and he shall rule them with a rod of iron; as the vessels of a potter shall they be broken in shivers as I received from my Father. And I will give him the Morning Star.

He that overcometh the same shall be clothed in White Raiment. And I will not blot out his name out of the Book of Life. Behold I come quickly: hold fast that which thou hast that no man take thy Crown.

Him that overcometh will I make a pillar in the Temple of my God, and he shall no more go out: and I will write upon him the name of my God which is New Jerusalem, which cometh down out of heaven from my God: and I will write upon him my New Name.

Behold I stand at the door and knock, and if any man hear my voice and open the door I will come in with him, and sup with him, and he with me.

And to him that overcometh will I grant to sit with me in my throne, even as I also overcame, and am set down with my father in his throne.

He that hath an ear to hear let him hear what the Spirit saith unto the Churches.[23]

But as Agrippa says, *Clausum est Armarium*—the Scripture is obscure and mystical throughout; even in the simplest details most profound, but significant in the promises even of material blessings and gifts. For when we begin to love the Spirit, adds the disciple, then he sends us these things as tokens and pledges of his love, to whom all hearts are open, all desires known, and from whom no secrets are hid; whose prolific virtue is the source of all things, and in the conscious alliance becoming known, potentializes the whole in each individual universally without reserve.

That was the ground of ancient doctrine, the foundation of those creeds in the shadowy tradition of which mankind now live. They are all plain to him that hath understanding, as Solomon says, and right to them that find knowledge. Behold instruction is better than silver, and knowledge than choice gold. Wisdom is better than rubies, and all the things that may be desired are not to be compared to Her. I, Wisdom, dwell with prudence, and find out knowledge of witty inventions. Counsel is mine and sound Wisdom; I am Understanding; I have strength. Riches and honor are with me, yea, durable riches and righteousness. My fruit is better than gold; and my revenue than choice silver. I love them that love me, and those that seek me early shall find me[24].

They, the, who have been fortunate enough to perfect this work, having received s much grace from the Father of Lights as to obtain this inestimable gift of Divine Wisdom, what more one earth should they desire, but that it may be always applied aright in obedience to the Divine Will, for the benefaction of mankind and vindication of true virtue? For not only were they exempt from human ills, having the means of abundant wealth, power, and health at their command, but, moreover, they had a manifest token of divine favor, and sure promise of immortality in a life to come. Nor is to to be wondered, therefore, why philosophers, when they have obtained this medicine, have not cared to lengthen their days, or make a vain parade of their riches to the world which they despised, with every temporal power and advantage, in comparison of that which, in the acquirement of these things, was by their art foreshown. Or who now having human perfectibility, and a prospect of a happy immortality set before them in plain physical type and experience, would rest in a mere metalline good, like Midas, who, preferring an earth-born harmony to the music of the spheres, was dishonored by the god, and bore evidence of his misfortune in sight of the whole world?

Many prophecies there are of times to come, and those days are even said to be at hand, when the Fourth Monarchy, which is the Intellectual reign of Truth and Peace, shall predominate, when the Mother of sciences will come forth, and greater things be discovered than have been hitherto in the past monarchies of the world. But we do not tarry about these matters; the revelation of all things is always at hand for him who knows how to investigate, and the rest will always be far behind. If truly there be minds prepared, or if the great era approaches more rapidly than is given us yet even in faith to foresee (for notwithstanding so many signs that are appearing, and signal rumors of a coming change, yet they are fewer and far between and more rare yearly which indicate the progression of Truth); but if, we say, a better age is approaching, which at some period of time must come, when abundance of all things by an equitable distribution of all, shall help break down the competitive barrier of society, and introduce a cooperative alliance amongst mankind, then this incentive to enquiry may not be inopportunely offered, to advance the foremost intellect, and fix its dominion in the self-discovery of truth.

At the present time, when all are more or less eagerly engaged in the pursuance of eternal advantages, and under penalty of being cast into the fiery furnace of the world's scorn, do fall down and worship that earth-born goddess of temporal Utility, which opinion has set up, it would be vain enthusiasm to attempt to divert attention, but for a moment, from so favored an idol, were it not that in the minds of all, even its most degraded votaries, there exists a most real and bitter sense of its insufficiency and latent deformity; everywhere without, the evil is apparent, and presses closer as time speeds on, fatally accelerating as if it neared some attracting focus. Yet hope still lingers in expectation; and, with that abiding patience which is the test of faith in a good cause, may we continue to seek on, not vaguely around us for passing excitements, but with steady perseverance looking within, until Conscience reveal to us those higher objects of pursuit, and truer attractions, which will not suffer the mind aspiring to them to fall into dishonor; but purifying and corroborating as they draw, will, when at length they are worthily won, untie with and transmute their worshipper into that Harmony and Beauty, which, in the dim beholding, he venerated and loved.

> *Begin today, nor end till evil sink*
> *In its due grave; and if at once we may not*
> *Declare the greatness of the work we plan,*
> *Be sure at least that ever in our mind*
> *It stand complete before us, as a dome*
> *Of light beyond this gloom, a house of stars*
> *Encompassing these dusky tents; a thing*
> *Absolute, close to all, though seldom seen,*
> *Near as our Hearts and perfect as the Heavens.*
> *Be this our aim and model, and our*
> *Hands Shall not wax faint until the work is done.*

The Idea of the Good, the Pure, and the True is the alluring object which we all innerly worship—the progeny of Divine Intellect, immortal and strong—even Moral beauty which, though obscurely now, as through the mists of sense and selfishness, ever shines attractively—our Polar Star.

> *When from the lips of Truth one mighty breath*
> *Shall kike a whirlwind, scatter in its breeze*
> *The whole dark pile of human mockeries,*
> *Then shall the reign of Mind commence on earth,*
> *And starting fresh, as from a second birth,*
> *Man, in the sunshine of the World's new Spring,*
> *Shall walk transparent like some holy thing.*

Having discussed thus much of the Hermetic Mystery, and suggested certain particulars concerning the Practice at this latter end, which may be unfamiliar to the reader, we would repeat our warning to beware of hasty interpretation and trials of skill, without a proper foundation laid by study of the Hermetic records and scientific Laws of Art. Many things have no doubt escaped us inadvertently; others we have designedly reserved, lest falling into incapable hands, the highest trust of Nature should be betrayed, and the way of truth become perplexed by duplicity in the pursuit. In vain the ignorant, in vain the avaricious, the selfish, faithless, or frivolous, will in vain seek to percolate this Mystery. The right-minded and studious alone benevolently, conscientiously, and rationally persisting to the end, will unravel it: and in this case each must labor singularly for himself. The success of the experiment, as we have repeatedly shown, depends on the discovery of the true Intention. And this being more or less involved in every mind, is not clearly distinguishable in all; nor are they many, therefore, but few only, who have been found to enter in by the narrow way of life. The talent is granted only to a few, and for them conditions are needful to draw it forth to increase; for them we have written, and to persuade those only who may be able amidst so many heterogeneous elements of Nature, to discern the rational possibility by the infallible touchstone of her Original Light.

> *Tunc mentis divinae oracular caeca,*
> *Volventes animo ancipiti vix tempore longo,*
> *Experti multa, et non parvis sumtibus illam*
> *Invenere artem, qua non ars dignior ulla est,*
> *Fingendi Lepidem Aetherium, quem scire profanes*
> *Haud quaquam licet, et frustra plebs improba quaerit.*
> *Quem qui habet, ille potest, ubi vult habitare decenter:*
> *Nec fortunae iram metuit, nec brachia furum,*
> *Sed tanto paucos dignantur munere divi*[25].

Injunctions likewise are frequent respecting the sacred nature of the ministration, and of the responsibility incurred by those even who are favored in the undertaking, lest desiring too little or presuming too far in self-sufficient pride, it should fall, and Satan establish a monarchy upon the most holy of works. Does any smile at the surmise? It is of small account, so he be ignorant; those warnings do not apply, nor were ever meant to scare his complacency, who, without the Light of Reason, would be least of all able to precipitate its downfall. But lest the desire of such a one should lead him to practice, which by good fortune it may not, we advise him of our knowledge, and of the vindicative Spirit of Wisdom for the justification of her Rule—*Ne tu augeas fatum*—Enlarge not thy destiny —O! Neither break a superficies, as the Pythagoric precept runs—lest the sin of the agent be multiplied in the patient, it should survive in the unhappy offspring unto the third or fourth generation. The Spirit of Wisdom runs lovingly by her own Rule to fulfill it; but leaves him to hopeless confusion who abandons the Divine purpose for the accomplishment of private ends.

So the Israelites, that so wonderfully stiff-necked race, suffered for their rebellion and selfish lusts; falling into a multitude of snares and misfortunes—by fire, famine, and sword, and no less miserable captivity, by the Divine command. And that those errors might be guarded against, and that no presumption might thereafter arise, the Lawgiver, in his book of *Deuteronomy*, instructs them to be grateful, and mindful, throughout the passage, of past benefits received, nor ever to murmur at the decrees of God.

—But thou shalt consider in thy heart, he says, that as a man chasteneth his son, so the Lord thy God chasteneth thee. Therefore thou shalt keep the commandments of the Lord thy God, to walk in his ways, and to fear him. For the Lord thy God bringeth thee into a Good land; a land of brooks of water, of fountains, and depths that spring out of valleys and hills; and of wheat, and barley, and vines, and fig-trees, and pomegranates; a land of oil-olive, and honey; a land wherein thou shalt eat bread without scarceness, thou shalt not lack anything in it; a land whose stones are iron, and out of whose hills thou mayest dig brass. And when thou hast eaten and art full, then thou shalt bless the Lord thy God for the good land which he hath given thee. Beware that thou forget not the Lord thy God, in not keeping his commandments, and judgments, and statutes: lest, when thou hast eaten and art full, and hast built godly houses and dwelt therein; and when thy herds and thy flocks multiply, and thy silver and thy gold is multiplied, and all that thou hast is multiplied: then thy heart be lifted, and thou forget the Lord thy God, which brought thee forth out of the Land of Egypt, from the house of bondage: who led thee through that great and terrible wilderness, wherein were fiery serpents, and scorpions, and drought, where there was no water; who brought thee forth water out of the rock of flint. Who fed thee in the wilderness with manna, which thy fathers knew not; that He might humble thee, and that He might prove thee, to do thee good at thy latter end: and lest thou say in thine heart my power the might of mine hand hath gotten me this wealth. But thou shalt remember the Lord thy God; for it is He that giveth thee power to get wealth, that he may establish his covenant which He sware unto thy fathers, as it is this day. And it shall be, if thou do at all forget the Lord thy God and walk after other gods, and serve them and worship them, I testify against you this day that ye shall surely perish[26].

For immortality is only to be consummated in union, and in the abandonment of the dual selfhood and its volition to the Divine Will. Wherefore I abhor myself, cries Jacob (when all else being deprived, he renounced himself), and repent in dust and ashes.—Look on every one that is proud and abase him, and tread down the wicked in their place. Hide them in the dust together, and bind their faces in secret.—THEN WILL I ALSO CONFESS UNTO THEE THAT THINE OWN RIGHT HAND CAN SAVE THEE[27].

That was the path and promise to blameless souls which the wise men and prophets constantly pursued, passing through every ordained discipline, ordeal rite, and humiliation, in order that they might become conformable to the Divine Perfection they desired to approach. Once delivered from the exterior bondages of sense and heterogeneous desire, from the passions and false affections of this transitory life, the final step is declared comparatively easy; as transcending by the energy of faith, from the separable selfhood, the Identity passes into universal accord.— To go forth and to return; therefore was the agreement cut off—so says the Cabal—Close thy eyes and meditate: and if thy heart fail thee, return again; since therefore it is written,

EGREDERE ET REGREDERE, ET PROPTEREA PACTUM PRAECISUM EST[28].

This is the work—this is the Hermetic method and its end: The line returns to form a circle into its' beginning, and they join not in time, for their union is Eternity. This, reader, is the true Christian Philosopher's Stone, which, if it be a chimera, than is the universe itself not stable, of which it has been proven to be the most exact epitome, having passed the test of experimental reason not only, but, analyzed to the last extremity of contrite consciousness, is confirmed in operation, visibility, and luminous increase, when rising in rational supremacy over sense and finite reflection, the Ethereal Hypostasis revolves in its First Cause.

---

1. From the Introitus Apertus of Eireneus Philalethes, cap. xxxiv.
2. Sendivogius' New Light of Alchemy, treatise xi.
3. Vaughan's Lumen de Lumine, p. 95. ; Norton's Ordinal, chap. ii.
4. Marrow of Alchemy, Book iii. p. 77.
5. See Digby's Lucerna Salis, cap. viii.
6. Eireneus' Marrow of Alchemy, Book iii., v. 45, &c.
7. Introitus Apertus, cap. xxxv. De Multiplici hujus Artis.
8. Kuhnrath, Amph. cap. ix., etc., in fine.
9. Amph. Sap. Etern., cap.viii. p. 211.

10. Oracula Chadaica; Anima, Corpus, Homo; Julian's Orations ii., in fine.
11. Iliad, b. xi.
12. Helmont, Tumulus Pestis.
13. Tumulus Pestis, chap. i.
14. Ecclesiasticus, viii.
15. Idem., i.
16. See D. A. Freher, Of the Analogy in the Process of the Phil. Work with the Redemption of Man through Jesus Christ.
17. Revel., Chap. iii. v. 7.
18. Wisdom of Solomon, xxi.
19. Isaiah xxxviii. 13.
20. Habbakuk, iii. 4.
21. Revelations ii. 10.
22. Proverbs viii.
23. Revelation St. John, ii. iii.
24. Proverbs, chap. viii.
25. Palingenius, Zodiacus Vitae, Theat. Chem. ii.
26. Deuteronomy viii, from ver. 10.
27. Job xl, 12, &C. xlii.
28. Sephir Jezirah, cap. i.

Chapter 4. The Conclusion
in summary of the whole, comparing this Philosophy, its method, relations, and ultimate promise, with those of more modern acceptation and repute.

It has been our endeavor, as clearly as the limits prescribed by evidence and our understanding would enable us, to discuss the ground and practical pretensions in general of the Hermetic Mystery. To explain all would require an extensive range and a closer opportunity of experience than has hitherto been granted us. Nor with these auxiliaries, perhaps, should we become more intelligible, since caution very usually increases with observation, and the truth has been so intricately, arbitrarily, and in many folds enveloped, and the cloud of witnesses is such that it might puzzle Apollo himself to explicate the whole Enigma intelligibly to the world. To induce research, therefore, we pretend only to have signalized the Light, that any one fortunately perceiving, might be led along by its attracting presence to the discovery of Truth. Evidence has constantly preceded, neither have we ventured many assertions of our own; but the reputable witness of individuals of various ages and nations, whose names are renowned in philosophy, have been gathered together in aid of this Inquiry, and in support of the dignity of the Hermetic Science; which they have not only judged to be true, but many add their personal experience in conformation, attesting the reality of the Philosopher's Stone.

The confection of this miraculous substance, moreover, they have helped us to trace in theory from its foundation in the free Ether, through an artificial process of elaboration, into manifest effect. And the principle of Transmutation, they have shown to be relating not to Species but to their Universal Subject, whose concentrated virtue the Stone likewise itself is.

And Man was the proper laboratory of the whole Art; not only the most perfect chemical apparatus, devised by Nature for the distillation of her Spirit, but having besides the whole fermentative virtue, motive, and principle of vital melioration and every requisite complete within himself, for the rectification and furtherance of her prescribed Law; mind and manual efficacy, as it is narrated, by the Divine Will, to effect all things, though concealed in this life by the external attraction and obstructive energies of cause.

This hidden capacity it has been shown to be the purpose of the hermetic artifice to explore; and that adepts well-skilled, as they profess, in the vital analysis of bodies, by such means discovered the life of man therein circulating to be a pure fire incorporated in a certain incombustible ethereal vapour; also, that the Universal Efficient was in this fire, and the diverse kingdoms of nature, as it were, bound together in the threefold enchantment of his natural Identity; one of which only, the animal life, being developed to consciousness, the other two, viz., the vegetable and mineral, are known only to those who have entered experimentally within to prove the hypostatic action and passion of the working essences in life.

Partly, also, on the authority of the Ancients, coupled with certain other arguments, not altogether speculative, we have been thence led to regard the Mysteries celebrated at Eleusis and the rest, in a more important light than heretofore; not as mere external ceremonials, pictured scenes of suffering and beatitudes, but as real inductions of the Understanding Spirit to its Source.

And with the development of these Mysteries we have been enabled to connect Alchemy; and with these both, in their preliminary practice, the modern art, called Mesmerism, strikingly accords; which we have proposed suggestively, therefore, as a first key opening to the vestibule of this Experiment, where sits the Sphinx with her eternal enigma, still to perplex intruders, and open to philosophers only the inner halls of Light.

Bearing these things in mind, by the assistance of the Greek Ontologists, we have ventured, intimately pursuing their course, to follow mysterious Nature through many intricate windings and circumstantial difficulties, into her Initial Source; and there observed her, after operating voluntarily about her own annihilation, to survive and establish a stable monarchy upon her redeemed Light.

Particulars, also, of the metaphysical experience we have attempted to delineate, and to show the catholicity and casual reference of the Hermetic Work throughout.

From impediments likewise described, and rare intellectual conditions, it has been shown why the Divine Experiment has been so seldom attempted and more rarely brought to a legitimate conclusion on this earth. And why philosophers, in all ages, considering the unfitness of the multitude, and fearful consequences that might ensue from individual abuse, have concealed their knowledge, communicating almost by word of mouth only the practical device.

If we have been freer in our expositions, the spirit was not the more reckless, but because the thresholds of ignorance are already overpast, and experiment is in need rather of a motive to dignify it than practical machinery. What if the darkness should contend with and prevail awhile, yet there in the center the light will kindle and increase, and gain strength to radiate upwards through the whole circumference, despite every effort of ignorant selfishness and folly to prevent. So reason instructs that we should have faith in humanity as in the ultimate realization and prevalence of good. But they are all now incredulous who were formerly dreaded in their belief; and under that safe guardianship we leave them, happily supine in the conviction that our conduct will neither be attractive or intelligible, much less practically useful to the profane multitude of mankind. For although this Art of Alchemy is eminently experimental and practical in its consequences, yet it is wholly unsuited to minds commonly so styled practical, who are impatient of every proposition that is not immediately applicable to the affairs of life. For these the hermetic Art is no more suited than they for it; it needs a philosopher, one of the antique mould, a true lover of Wisdom, who, for her sake, will devote everything else, studious, simple, ardent, and withal suscipient of appearing truth.

They who in a kindred spirit have pursued this Inquiry, may have divined many things which will be hidden from the indifferent and thoughtless reader; for we have spoken of principles with reference to practice, and in an order indirectly indicative of the genealogical method of ascent; even that artistic fabrication of the Fire which Prometheus received from Vulcan, and Minerva disseminated providentially for the sake of her luminous radix, lest it should be smother in our irrational alliance, and perish ungratefully without return.

In the course of this vital experiment the ancients discovered the whole of the philosophy they teach, the quintessence of Universal nature and her fruitful springs: by this pyrotechnical induction, powers were revealed to conscience, the whole regenerative original and those temptations which Reason also, purified and singled out by Art for the encounter, is able entirely to withstand.

And that ray of motive Light, pure, vital, and efficient, we have shown to be the true Form of Gold, the alone universal principle of increase and perfection, the same which in the circulatory system, becoming dominant, is made concrete in life; and is the transmutative ferment—even the Philosophic Stone.

And this is the grand Hermetic secret, that there is a Universal Subject in nature, and that Subject is susceptible of nourishment in Man; and this is the greatest mystery, of all mysteries the most wonderful, that man should be able not only to find the Divine Nature, not only, but to effect It.

The philosophers sought after Wisdom for her own sake; for her beauty and bright divinity they wooed her, and gained with her an ample dowry, gold, silver, and the glittering treasures of her creative light in abundance. And some have dwelt gratefully on these intermediate benefits, recording them, but were, above all, careful to celebrate the primary attraction which led them in for the discovery of life. And we have omitted many things, to which, to the many, might be more attractive, even than gold or silver, or a more remote prospect of immortality; for every desire is, in the magic region, made prolific, embodying itself, by the ethereal conception, as a principle to enact its voluntary accord. But to allure by particular promises, however rich or real, which might restrict to individual interests a virtue which is infinite, forms no part of our design; man is sufficiently bounded already in all—how many ways is he not fettered, by the poverty of his imagination and the littleness of his love?

Having then run cursorily through the circuit of the Hermetic Tradition, without attempting, however, to include the whole length, which would embrace a far wider field of philosophical inquiry than is commonly imagined, it may be proper, in conclusion, to consider the several bearings of the same with respect to other sciences, and their comparative value to mankind at large.

Between the physical and Moral sciences, commonly so called, though there are links found indicative of a radical relationship, yet each are throughout their departments divergent, and the class of mind usually occupied by either is distinct. The former, based externally, having the senses for chief evidence, makes practical utility its end and only value; whilst the latter, having its evidence and object alike within mind, attaches less consequence to worldly benefits, misprising the lights of sense also as inferior and comparatively insecure. And thus Philosophy stands divulsed at this day, the Spiritual unable to prove itself absolutely, or the Material to disprove the other practically; they accordingly maintain on either side a negative, though relatively assured, ground. But the Hermetic Science, supposing this indeed to be well founded, would include both in the ample compass of its experiment, as passing from whither extreme of Mind and matter, to prove them, it arrives at the Catholic Effect of Life. And here the external and internal worlds are said to blend together in confluence harmony, establishing each other, and leaving reason nothing more to doubt or the senses to desire, but a fulfillment under the Law.

If then, in contrariety to every popular prejudice, and on the only evidence of defunct philosophers, we can yet imagine this Art of Alchemy to be real, and an experimental foundation of science, notwithstanding all the learned cavils and clamours of disappointed chemists that have been raised against it;—if it be true that there is a Subtle Nature pervading the universe, which is the All in every thing and susceptible of artificial alteration through all; and if man by his especial prerogative of Reason and rectitude of purpose is able, by a development of these, to advance and bear the life within him through dissolution into a new birth, superior to nature and beyond the reach of elementary discord to destroy; and if all this has been accomplished, passed through in the conscious experience, and proved demonstratively in facts, visible deeds, and effects; them these things supposed, and experience being the admitted test of philosophy, will it not follow that theirs was the right and true philosophy, which at the vertex of a double ignorance has been forgotten and despised?

For the experienced of intellect would, under the supposition, be esteemed pre-eminently above that of sense, inasmuch as the one revelation is naturally superior and acknowledged, even in this life, before the other; and that kind of evidence would be necessarily preferred by all which is universally inclusive and leading out from the Causal Fountain into natural effect. But by no reason that comes from sense will such an evidence be obtained, nor shall we ever learn, without Identic co-operation, how Nature works, or by what occult virtue the grain of wheat is even instigated, so that it grows and bears its abundant increase upon earth. All our knowledge without the experience is empirical, the result only of observation of remote effects. And therefore Alchemy has been declared to be the only true glass of the mind, which shows how to enter, and to touch, and to discover the Truth in her own simplicity and univocal demonstration. Neither does it therefore brig so many arguments, as might be, to prove itself, since the evidence is self-sufficient, and without itself cannot, however truly imaginable, be known. Such a demonstration would stand above all common sense conclusions, above imagination, above opinion, and all logical proof, which is barren without self-knowledge, and isolated and erring upon the plane of Truth.

Yet this is the only guide we now can boast of, which, if stable in its own criterion, yet being dependent on externals for matter and practical pursuit, fluctuates, and hence many evils arise and those diversities of opinion which distract mankind. The world, so imperfectly ruled, has instituted a sort of free-will standard of its own; men will believe as they like, see or not see, assume as suits their convenience, or reject their own criterion at pleasure, even the testimony of their own highly esteemed sober senses, when these do not tally with their pre-conceived prejudices, interests, or hopes. But it is evident, irrespective of all particular objections that true science does not consist in the exhibition of phenomena, neither can anything short of the Causal Discovery fulfill the Idea of Truth. The doubt would not rest therefore about the superiority of Causal science, if it were possible, but whether it be truly possible or not. If the philosophy of the Ancients is without a true foundation, if there is not any other essence of things besides that which is apparent and has a sensible subsistence, then the Physical will indisputably be the first and only science; but if otherwise there is proved to be a certain immutable Being of all, pre-existent to sensibles, which can be proven in intellect and confirmed in sensible phenomena, as the Alchemists and Greek physicians assert, then this will be prior, surer, and the best philosophy.

To those in whom the spirit of observation has been wholly drawn to externals, it may have seemed a ridiculous thing to speak of life and intellect independently, as apart from their manifest operations; still more so to enter on specific idioms and modes of spiritual subsistence, seeing we have no tangible proof calculated by any means to satisfy the searchers of exact science; that as life is nowhere seen apart from organization, or moral consciousness from either, they are phenomena little likely to be discovered apart or practically understood—Against such an opinion we have no present demonstration to offer; our own assertion would have nothing to the authorities already cited; inquiry is the only antidote of rational skepticism. For this we have laboured to supply means; and the natural subsistence of Universals in the human mind may afford a ground of probability whence to proceed into their proof. That we are deprived of the power of apprehending the ancient doctrine of internal Wisdom is not proof that it is untrue; there is a strongly enchanted fortress about it, whose forces yield not either to impertinent curiosity or the peremptory demands of sense. Nor can all the negative evidence of sensual certainty in array disprove, or for an instant nullify, assertions which belong to another Experience and another probability of Art and Nature.

But, it will be objected, that which has never been in our thought, things so far above us, are nothing to us? Truly, if beyond our possible attainment, they would be indifferent; but benefits are not the less real because unexpected, or promises to be cast away because the means of fulfillment are not immediately discernable. The evils of this life are manifold, and a prospect of escape, or melioration even, will not be obnoxious to those who are fortunately able to perceive it. Neither let it be supposed, that because the Wisdom of the ancients transcends, that it by any means contradicts human reason, but quite otherwise; that was, in truth, the basis of their philosophy, which is with us the boundary and summit of our knowledge. That Faith alone, indeed of all else, remains to us in common—in that we are, we have a witness which believes and infers, a reality beyond present experience; and hence it is in vain that metaphysicians, inductively arguing, have sometimes endeavored to reduce the Idea of Cause to mere antecedence or juxtaposition in time. The instinct of human nature is constantly opposed to them, and believes, heedless of all doubt and difficult discussion. For Power is latent everywhere, and we feel it in the shadow, and recognize its presence spontaneously in every action of life. Striking upon this Faith therefore, in default of its true object, and taking to witness some of the closer records of transcendental experience, we have hoped to awaken the imaginative centers to such an accord as might stir Reason from her long lethargy to seek for genuine reminiscence in her root of Light.

> *Though from our birth the faculty divine*
> *Is chained and tortured, cabin'd, cribb'd, confin'd.*

And bred in darkness, lest the light should shine
Too brightly on the uninstructed mind,
The beams pour in, and truth and skill may couch the blind.

Were t not that the ancients acknowledge and uniformly insist on the use of means for removing the barriers by which the Divine Light is here held in thralldom, we might more consistently despair of their Wisdom; but it was avowedly a thing acquired, the reward only of peculiar and arduous discipline; not such as mere school logic or the mathematics now afford, but as different and far above as was the promise and ultimate aim. No modern institutions, either secular or religious, furnish anything analogous, no effectual means of moral elevation, no rites of purifying or awakening efficacy to the mind. We plant and increase knowledge, and give precepts and devise examples, and draw forth the observing faculties to their superficial contentment; but all our circumstantial labours do not rectify the mind, or turn the inbred inclination out of life. Circumstances indeed do modify, and, according as they are well or ill devised, improve or deteriorate the habitual character of mankind; but they do not recreate; no power that is not vital can touch the evil that is inbred, or even discover it truly without introspective proof. That which generation binds dissolution only can unloose—the evil must be met by its proper antidote, overcoming darkness by Light in the hypostatical alliance; every accessory means of melioration will be preparative to this which restores the human mind to integrity and universal science.

Man has never been observed to advance himself individually through adventitious acquirements; but, on the contrary, the increase of luxury, to which thought is now applied, enervates the moral character, fosters selfishness by competition, fraud, and emulous hate. Institutions, framed by the same defective pattern, multiply the evil, as every advance we make in externals leads us further off from the First Source. And until Wisdom shall have effected that individual reformation, which above all things we now need, it is vain to look in externals for a perfection and felicity which have not been imaged there. We may alter, and improve, and educate, and prepare the way with advantage; but the notion will be variable, and every plan defective without the Exemplary Light.

But some one will consider the discovery impossible, or, if possible, yet that this Wisdom is too difficult perhaps in the pursuit? To the former objection, supposing it to be inveterate, we oppose nothing, having nowhere undertaken to convince, but only to promote investigation.

Incredulity is the strongest barrier of possibilities over the world, no doubt wisely provided to prevent a too rapid movement of mind into practice, before it is well prepared and disposed to the pursuit of truth. With respect to the difficulties of the pursuit, we have nowhere denied them, or that they are insuperable to the common herd of mankind. Without an earnest desire of discovery, the liveliest faith will be frustrated, and labour will be vain unless reason give direction to the persuasion of faith. But how hardly can these wither subsist without the other? Since faith is the very attracting loadstone which hope pursues, and desire and reason, and the whole willing armament of Mind, to which, in her allied forces, nothing is impossible; or what apparition of difficulties would deter conviction steeled to the purpose of her Motive Light?

Or does any one, persisting to calumniate this Philosophy, say it threatens to sacrifice important temporal interests for the sake of visionary and remote gains? Such objections however will not be rational, but spring out of the baser affections of humanity and short-sighted sense. The eye is not satisfied with seeing, nor is the ear filled with hearing, nor does any transitory good suffice to human desire; above all, there is no selfish object worthy the pursuit of Intellect; nor is any worldly recompense found corresponding to its need. But the proper object of the rational faculty is in its Source, which lies profoundly buried in this life of sense. And this it is the province of Hermetic Artifice to resuscitate and bring through self-knowledge into the experience of life. For this same Root of Reason is Wisdom, and that saving Salt which philosophers were wont anciently to excavate and by so many circulating media to exalt. The diadem of Wisdom is even beset with this Stone, which, as a halo or crown of light, the regenerate soul puts on as a new body, wherein it can rule over the elementary world and pass through it, overcoming evil and falsehood, and ignorance and death.

To the faculty of Reason, therefore, nothing is more attractive than this philosophy, which immortalizes it; yet, will it be argued, there are other faculties of the human mind equally real, if not as important, and which ought not to be despised? Neither, we reply, is any faculty of the soul repudiated in that supernal alliance; but all are present together in that supernal alliance; but all are present together in obedience to their rightful rule and habitude; or if any one is refractory during the passage, it is the occasion of suffering to the better natures, which are all engaged voluntarily in the restitution of their King. But if they all must be sacrificed for the sake of him who is their source, would not this be expedient, rather than that he should continue in an illegitimate thralldom under all? Such is not the ultimate necessity of the case however; for the *brethren* all are renewed together with him, and every dignified sentiment is set in accord, to testify and maintain the triumphant Monarchy of Light.

And what more alluring to a cultivated Imagination than this pursuit, which abounds in ideality and the beautiful symbolism of universal truth, which discovers the occult springs of Classic inspiration, tradition, mythology, fable, and every graceful remain?

And will not Veneration, too, be intimately invited by the prospect of its own antique worshipful Idea— there where, in the presence of Divinity, true awe is felt, and man discovers and knows the perfect goodness, which profanely without the temple's veil he cannot, or unless the understanding is absolutely conjoined?

And are not Hope and Benevolence interested in this research, and Justice longing for an equilibrium, and Self-respect and Piety, and every honourable motive herein allied? And to know the First Truth of things really and experimentally, and to revolve the Causal Light in permanence of intellection, is not this the highest privilege that man may propose to himself? And when we are told that all things are added to that felicity, that the springs of Universal Nature, with her growth and fruits, are at our delegate disposal, if we can believe, what else is worthy our whole desire? And what kind of science, supposing it real, would be so conclusive as this, which exhibits all things in their constructive Causes, such as no other science does. Or other conviction can do, but that only which, Identically penetrating, enters into the Whole of Existence?

Let no one therefore conceive that this philosophy is unattractive, which has occupied the best faculties of the best minds, and at the topmost summit of their capacity. Nor are the rewards so remote, either as indolence and adverse inclination may cause them to appear. But if inferior interests should yet complain, as in danger of their present dominion, and pride or avarice, or ambition or ignorance, accustomed to rule in this life, should disdain the subaltern station which the Divine Law assigns to them, let not one enlist or be drawn by promises, however alluring, lest they be deceived and swallowed up in the gulph of their own overwhelming delusion. As who would wish it should otherwise, unless it were to generate evil by the viperous progeny of self-love?

Should it be considered, on the other hand, that the research of Causes is altogether impious, and above the destined capacity of man, and vain, since, as Job says, *no one by searching can find out the Almighty to perfection—*

we would observe, with respect to this last assertion, that it is easily explicable; for though it is eminently true that man, searching in his own will alone, is incompetent to the Divine Discovery, yet, by conditionating, in obedience to the Divine Will, he comes into the integral alliance and power—*Knock and it shall be opened unto you, ask and ye shall receive, that your joy may be full.*

With respect to the charge of impiety, should this persist, the evil is inherent in the preposterous idea; nor can we be at the pains just now to vindicate the most sacred science from such an aspersion; but recommend those who really think in this way, with the rest already warned off, to desist from inquiry, nor give heed to the subject as long as the fatal suggestion lurks; lest it should become manifested forth in some practical form of pusillanimity, or faithless attempt to interrogate the profundity it fears. These is nothing impure, or of itself impious, much less the Art of Wisdom, long distinguished as holy. But to him that esteems a thing unclean, as St Paul says, *it is unclean, for the thought will defile it. Hone soit qui mal y pense. Let not this good then be evil spoken of. All things are indeed pure; but it is evil for that man who eateth the bread of life with offense.*

The Art of Alchemy is of all Arts therefore distinguished as holt, since it has been piously occupied, and aided the most devout minds, in times past, to the attainment of their common end. Not that we would insinuate that human salvation is dependent on a mere art—far otherwise; the Divine Will operates its fulfillment alone; but the Art is said to be a remedy of imperfect souls, and offers the means of assimilation; whether a knowledge of these means is absolutely necessary, we dare not take on ourselves to determine—the power of God is infinite; but Adepts declare that He has always revealed them to his elected children.

If doubt yet further should arise about this Wisdom; seeing she did not reveal herself in common arts and the discoveries of human invention; it may be plainly observed that such particulars are foreign to the Divine purpose, they are foolishness to her; she teaches an Art which supersedes all these and comprehends every liberal science in sublime freedom of intellection and every subordinate discovery in her revealed accord. Yet who will now believe?

It is by the searching and proving of His own Identity, not otherwise, that man can arrive at the assurance of this Wisdom, which is above science, art, and every other kind of faith; which includes all knowledges, arts, and every particular which the inquiring Spirit seeks within itself. This is that Well of Heraclitus in which the Truth yet lies profoundly hidden; whence also those philosophic tears. This is that Nothing which Socrates knew, on account of which the oracle pronounced him to be the wisest of mankind; which Democritus, beholding, laughed at other things: it was this which warned Friar Bacon from the error of his ways, and convicted Agrippa of the vanity and confusion of his youth, when at length in his manhood he came to know that to know Nothing was the most happy life. For he who in such wise knows Nothing—no one apostate particular—has the All, and, being composed of the whole, he is able to discern, to make, and to effect the whole; but falling off from this, in becoming dividual, he ceases to be the Universe: returning again, however, into the Universal and abandoning the selfhood, he raises himself on high, and governs the world.

And when we consider the highly elevated philosophy of the Platonic successors; the profound yet simple metaphysics of the Hebrew Cabal, as it has been partially transmitted, with a persuasion of reality unequaled in modern language; the soul-stirring syllables of the Hermetic and Chaldaic Fragments; the refined enthusiasm of the Middle Age Adeptists; and all these and many more separately agreeing in the same divine tradition; and added to these all, the Christian doctrine of fulfillment in the Gospel; we cannot but feel regret, mingling with the satisfaction these things might otherwise afford, that so early and great a promise of the human mind should have been blighted, not only, but forgotten almost in the world. Or can we recall such lights without reflection, and incuriously believe that knowledge was once granted to man by revelation, but has since, we cannot tell why, passed away for ever? Are we the children of a second fall, or what spell holds us that we no longer aspire even to understand the language of our Fathers, or desire to pass into the life of those elder times, when Man, not yet always the poor servant and interpreter f Nature, moved under his God, her Lord and Master? Are we not all born of one generation, in the same surrounding world; the identical sun now enlightening us as formerly shone upon the bards and hallowed sages of Asia Minor? Yet, whilst they so many centuries ago bear testimony to a knowledge of their Creator and his intimate works, we continue still in uncertainty, blind and baffled everywhere about the beguilements of sense. No longer careful for ourselves, life is wasted on externals, which, always ungrateful, yield new burdens and perplexities in proportion as they increase. Theoretic science is everywhere condemned; but there is no such thing at this day; since, with all her extolled artifice, array of disciplines and powers, the Wisdom of Antiquity has disappeared from amongst men.

And to what are we arrived without her? Even at the proudest pinnacle of external science, the whole physical nature explored, and facts of all generations accumulated together before our eyes, what would we be wiser without the Causal knowledge of these things? What single advantage have we gained by misprising the ancients? Those low, literal, spiritless interpretations of poetic fable and philosophy—what satisfaction have they afforded? Or of what use will they ever be but to memorialize our ignorance to future generations? It is true, they have flattered our self-complacency for a while into a belief that former Wisdom was foolishness, and that men never lived in reality who were more knowing, religious, and virtuous than ourselves. But then the evil far outlives the temporary gratulation of those conceits —conceits which have stripped the Ideal Standard of all excellency, and shorn the imagination of its brightest hopes of beauty, goodness, and immortal truth. All has been swept away with a remorseless hand; all veneration and faith in ideality, whilst sense has been the acknowledged beacon light, and practical utility the highest good.

Is it not full time to return, when things are arrived at the precipice of self-oblivion, when experimental philosophy labours for selfish aggrandizement, and self is least of all served in the attempt; when thought wastes its eternal substance in the pursuit of time; and the idea of Truth is mangled in the reckless machinery of Error? Has not Lord bacon himself, the leader of this exterminating chase, whilst endeavoring to supersede the bare exercise of logic, and clear the field of Learning in his *Inauguration*, recommended the pursuit of Causes above every other, and taught, by his own energetic example, to inquire of the ancients, and to experiment after their hidden Wisdom, though he knew it not, but only burned about the lights which they had bequeathed? What more, then, should we add to exhort, extol, or explicate, having studied to revive these and relics of the Sacred Art long buried in oblivion? If their witness is disbelieved, addition would be useless; if otherwise, we await the result.—It would be as impossible in an exposition of this kind to conciliate all tastes, as to draw divergent prejudices into accord. There is one pleasure of a horse, another of a dog; a goat differs from either in his natural choice; and in man every various inclination is to be found, and a multifarious understanding in the affairs of life; so that those arguments which to some would be convincing, by others are not discerned, or needed by many more who are endowed with an instinctive faith and appreciation. Truths which are grateful to certain persons are odious to hers, according as they may be constituted or habitually trained. In this Inquiry, therefore, we have sought to attract those chiefly to whom such a pursuit would be naturally pleasing, and such as have been customarily esteemed worthy of the reward.

With respect to the practical benefits, our hopes, though not enlarged, are vigorous and of the most grateful kind; for those to whom it is addressed the Light will attract, and to them will not be moderately useful, if they advance by it to the true end.

That the subject is worthy of inquiry from the highest order of minds, we repeat our persuasion, and at the same time entertain a belief that the period is not far distant when this will be obtained, and the truth, by these means, be so manifestly presented before the eyes of all, that contrary prejudices, and doubts, and false interests, will be merged in the revelation of power and irresistible fact.

The catholic torch, miraculously kindled, kindles the Light of Universal Nature, and either externally or internally, morally or physically, or in all these ways, according to the application, works from thence through every part, diffusing energy, life and joy, in either if the three kingdoms, as we have shown, by its voluntary assimilation, increasing and promoting things to their utmost boundary of strength. But, above all, it rejoices in the Mind of Man, when, in conscious rectitude of thought and action, he bears it in comprehensive superiority elect over the rest—when, including all in the catholic perceivance of this Reason, he submits his own omnipotence to the omniscience of its Rule—when Nature opening up to him the vast resources of her essence and the mystery of the most wonderful creation, with every temptation of self-idolatry laid open to view, oblivious of all else in admiration and love of so much Wisdom and integral perfection, he co-operates with the First Cause.

Some may consider we have opened too much, others too little of a mystery irrelevant to the common understanding of mankind, and no doubt our conduct is blameworthy in other respects; yet those for whom we have laboured will not prove ungrateful if they attain to the end of our proposed discovery. For the discovery of the Causal Nature is doubtless of all parts of knowledge the worthiest to be sought after, if it be possible to be found; and, as to the possibility, they are computed for ill discoverers that think there is no land because they discern nothing but sea.—

Believe it, then, beyond the turbulent sea of sense, there is a haven and signal marks to direct where the Promised Land is to be found. And Life is the nucleus of the whole Hermetic Mystery, and the Key thereof is Intellect; the golden ore of which, likewise, we have lavishly shown. If, however, the Key is wanting, how may we presume to enter; or, without it, explain the intricate intelligence of those mirific wards which were constructed by it, and for it to pass through, and for it alone? They, we repeat, who can understand the language of the philosophers, will understand their Art; for this we have opened the way only, which if any one will consent to travel in, we assure him of success, but not otherwise; for neither was this research undertaken indiscriminately, nor can it be prosecuted without a congenial Light. But he who desires to enter, let him search for the Root of Reason rationally, and hold by it, and conspire with It, if he would have Truth at last. He who knows the first entrance, and how to render the fixed tincture of life volatile, and to return it, being free, is already admitted to the temple of Divine Science, and joins in with the whole conclave; because, through all the interior recesses, the method is allied. Let him search into the enigmas, peruse the fables, and consider the parables and maxims of the wise Adepts. They all tend to one discovery, and declare the same, and even in their inconsistencies will be instructive to him who has the Key. And he who sets himself in this wise to the comprehension of the whole philosophy, will be a competent judge of our labours, how much assistance we have added towards the recovery of lost Wisdom, and with what sincerity we have opened the way permeating into those antiquated abodes of Light.

THE END

Copyright © 2022 by Alicia Editions.
Credits: www.canva.com
File:Hermes Mercurius Trismegistus.jpg By Sdelodder - Own work, Public Domain, https://commons.wikimedia.org/w/index.php?curid=4942761
All rights reserved.
No part of this book may be reproduced in any form or by any electronic or mechanical means, including information storage and retrieval systems, without written permission from the author, except for the use of brief quotations in a book review.

www.ingramcontent.com/pod-product-compliance
Lightning Source LLC
LaVergne TN
LVHW032003070526
838202LV00058B/6276